Spaces of Neoliberalism

Urban Restructuring in North America and Western Europe

Edited by

Neil Brenner and Nik Theodore

Blackwell
Publishing

Contents

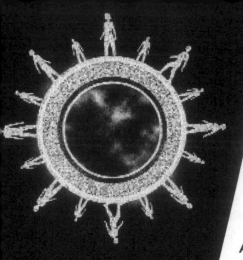

THE **Antipode**
BOOK SERIES

Series Editors:
Noel Castree, Jamie Peck
and Jane Wills

Antipode: A Radical Journal of Geography remains
the only journal to offer a radical-Marxist/ socialist/
anarchist/ feminist/ sexual liberationist-analysis of
geographical issues and whose intent is to contribute to
the praxis of a new and better society.

As it enters its fourth decade, *Antipode* is a strong,
vigorous and respected journal with a distinctive place in
geography. Part of this distinctiveness lies in combining
Antipode's long-held core objectives in progressive political
change with initiatives designed to stretch the journal's
boundaries and keep it abreast of new developments in radical
geographical scholarship. This is not simply a question of
identifying innovative or novel radical research and ensuring that
Antipode becomes its natural home. More than this, the journal's
strong reputation and the current vibrancy of Left scholarship in
human geography means that it is an opportune moment to extend
the reach and remit of *Antipode* with a book series. With a unique
identity in the field of geography publishing, *the Antipode book series*
will extend boundaries and visions of radical scholarship within geography

For more information please contact
Dr Noel Castree, Coordinating Editor, School of Geography,
University of Manchester, Manchester, M13 9PL, UK,
email **noel.castree@man.ac.uk**

www.blackwellpublishing.com

Preface: From the "New Localism" to the Spaces of Neoliberalism

Neil Brenner and Nik Theodore

In recent decades, the notion of a "revival of the local" has attracted widespread attention from academics and policy-makers. In contrast to the pervasive naturalization of national states, national economies, and national societies that prevailed during much of the Fordist-Keynesian period, localities and places are now back on the agenda across the political spectrum and within numerous strands of social-scientific analysis. In a geoeconomic context defined by massive upheavals of entrenched interscalar relations, local (and regional) spaces are now increasingly being viewed as key institutional arenas for a wide range of policy experiments and political strategies. These include new entrepreneurial approaches to local economic development as well as diverse programs of institutional restructuring intended to enhance labor market flexibility, territorial competitiveness, and place-specific locational assets.

Paradoxically, much of the contemporary political appeal to the "local" actually rests upon arguments regarding allegedly uncontrollable *supra*local transformations, such as globalization, the financialization of capital, the erosion of the national state, and the intensification of interspatial competition. Under these conditions, in the absence of a sustainable regulatory fix at global, supranational, or national scales, localities are increasingly being viewed as the only remaining institutional arenas in which a negotiated form of capitalist regulation might be forged. From this perspective, as Eisenschitz and Gough (1993:11) explain, localities are frequently represented as sites in which "the apparent opposites of enterprise and community, of efficiency and welfare, of economic means and local ends" might be reconciled. A variety of policy experiments have subsequently been advocated in order to unleash the latent innovative capacities of local economies, to foster a local entrepreneurial culture, and to enhance the flexibility of local governance systems. In short, the new localism has become a forceful call to arms through which local (and, in some cases, national) political-economic elites are aggressively attempting to promote economic rejuvenation from below.

Crucially, this new localism and its associated politics of place contain a number of deep ambiguities. Does the local really serve as a site of empowerment in the new global age, or do contemporary discourses of globalization/localization in fact conceal a harsher reality of institutional deregulation, regulatory downgrading, and intensifying zero-sum interspatial competition? Have localities and cities really acquired new institutional capacities to shape their own developmental pathways, or are their fates now being determined—or at least significantly constrained—by political-economic forces that lie beyond their control? Are local regulatory experiments actually improving local social conditions, or are they rendering local and regional economies still more vulnerable to global financial fluctuations, state retrenchment, and the capricious investment decisions of transnational corporations? These ambiguities arguably lie at the very heart of the new forms of policy experimentation and place-production that have proliferated in urban and regional economies throughout the older industrialized world during the last two decades. They present significant intellectual puzzles for analysts of place-making processes under contemporary capitalism; and they also pose profound strategic dilemmas for activists concerned with reshaping places towards more progressive, democratic, and socially just ends.

This collection builds upon these debates regarding the new localism, the transition to urban entrepreneurialism, the rescaling of political-economic space, and the dynamics of place-making within contemporary "glocalized" capitalism. However, we confront these matters through a very specific but relatively neglected analytical lens: that of *neoliberalism* and its evolving political-economic geographies.

Since the crisis of the Fordist-Keynesian accumulation regime and the breakdown of the Bretton Woods monetary system in the early 1970s, the global capitalist system has become increasingly neoliberalized. This multifaceted, multiscalar dynamic of neoliberalization has entailed the loosening or dismantling of the various institutional constraints upon marketization, commodification, the hyperexploitation of workers, and the discretionary power of private capital that had been established through popular struggles prior to and during the postwar period (see Bourdieu 1998; Lipietz 1994; McMichael 1996; Moody 1997). Particularly since the early 1980s, processes of deregulation, liberalization, and state retrenchment—the linchpins of the neoliberal policy repertoire—have been imposed at a range of spatial scales, from the global and the continental to the national and the local, albeit always in context-, territory-, and/or place-specific forms. The crystallization of this worldwide regime of "disciplinary neoliberalism" (Gill 1995) has been examined at some length in the literatures on international political economy, both with reference to the consolidation of the supranational modes of governance embodied in the World Bank, the International Monetary Fund, the World Trade Organization, the North American Free Trade Agreement, the European Union, and the like, and—just as importantly—with reference to the increasing neoliberalization of national regulatory systems in the older industrialized world, in developing countries and, after 1989, in erstwhile state-socialist regimes (for overviews see Agnew and Corbridge 1995; Overbeek 1993).

Surprisingly, however, the politics, institutional dynamics, and socio-spatial effects of neoliberalism have rarely been theorized explicitly at the *urban* scale in the older industrialized world. More generally, even though discussions of the rise, consolidation, and diffusion of neoliberalism generally contain any number of implicit geographical assumptions, the complex spatialities of these developments have yet to be examined and theorized systematically, whether with reference to cities, regions, national territories, or supranational spaces.

Against this background, the present collection on *Spaces of Neoliberalism* confronts two closely related analytical tasks. First, the contributions to this volume examine the role of neoliberal political projects since the late 1970s in shaping the dynamics of urban change in North America and Western Europe. Second, by exploring the role of neoliberal politics in molding urban spaces and, more generally, in reproducing and intensifying uneven spatial development within and between cities, this collection seeks to illuminate some of the broader geographical contours, dynamics, and trajectories of neoliberalism itself as a multiscalar geoeconomic and geopolitical project. Both of these tasks are, we submit, extraordinarily urgent, both intellectually and politically. As the contributors to this volume demonstrate in a variety of ways, neoliberalism represents a strategy of political-economic restructuring that—to borrow a phrase used by Henri Lefebvre (1978:262) in a different context—uses space as its "privileged instrument." In sum, by examining the role of neoliberal political-economic agendas in the contemporary remaking of urban space, we seek to advance recent debates on the contested politics of urban restructuring while, at the same time, opening up a wider research agenda through which the contradictory and continually evolving geographies of neoliberalism within post-1970s capitalism might be explored.

Neoliberal programs have, of course, had profound ramifications for urban development in cities and city-regions throughout the world economy. A comprehensive inquiry into the issues sketched above would therefore need to examine the particular ways in which neoliberalism has shaped trajectories of urban development in each zone of the world economy during the last two decades. Yet, as a number of contributors to this collection emphasize, the effects of neoliberalism must necessarily be understood in contextually specific ways: they hinge upon the path-dependent interaction of neoliberal programs with inherited institutional and social landscapes. Our focus on the impact of neoliberalism within older industrialized countries—in which neoliberal policies were mobilized within regulatory landscapes that had been molded in the preceding decades by Fordist-Keynesian regulatory arrangements—is consistent with this methodological emphasis on contextual specificity and, more generally, on the path-dependency of regulatory/spatial change. Due to limitations of space, time, and expertise, a broader inquiry into the dynamics of neoliberalization in cities located beyond the North Atlantic zone could not be undertaken in this collection. Nonetheless, it is our hope that the methodological strategies developed and deployed in this volume might also prove useful for scholars concerned with elucidating the urban dimensions of neoliberalism in other regions of the world economy—from sub-Saharan Africa and Eastern Europe to Latin America and East/Southeast Asia—where neoliberal programs have been imposed upon very different regulatory landscapes inherited from the legacies of imperialism, import-substitution growth strategies, and, most recently, programs of export-led industrialization.

Structure of the Volume

The contributions to this volume were initially presented at a small conference on Neoliberalism and the City, sponsored by the Center for Urban Economic Development (CUED) at the University of Illinois at Chicago (UIC) in early September 2001. The papers were prepared prior to the events of September 11. The urgent question of how the political–economic geographies of neoliberalism have been rearticulated at various spatial scales in the post-9/11 world therefore lies beyond the scope of this book (but see Smith 2002 for a useful starting point). During the course of the conference, the participants articulated a number of common themes, concerns, and claims. While a broad range of methodological approaches and empirical reference points is represented in this volume, the following papers confront the urban geographies of neoliberalism in at least three ways—(1) by developing theoretical frameworks through which to explore the intersection between neoliberalism and urban development; (2) by analyzing the logics, dynamics, and contradictions of state intervention in neoliberalizing urban spaces; and (3) by examining the divisive sociospatial effects of neoliberal urban policies. The volume is there-fore divided into three parts that reflect the contributors' efforts to grapple with these closely intertwined conceptual and empirical issues.

Part 1 explores various ways of conceptualizing the neoliberaliza-tion of urban life during the last two decades. On the one hand, these essays address the vexing question of how to theorize the urban geog-raphies of neoliberalism under conditions of intensifying geoeconomic instability. On this basis, the essays examine various ways of analyzing the path-dependent and deeply contradictory dynamics of neoliberal urban policies. Just as importantly, this part of the collection suggests that, since the early 1990s, the reproduction of neoliberalism has become increasingly contingent upon specifically urban strategies of various kinds. In other words, the point is not only that neoliberalism affects cities, but also that cities have become key institutional arenas in and through which neoliberalism is itself evolving.

Part 2 explores the new geographies of state regulation that have emerged in conjunction with the neoliberalization of urban space during the last two decades. These analyses demonstrate that the implementation of neoliberal strategies in cities has entailed, *not* the rolling back of state intervention, but rather its political, institutional, and geographical reorganization. One important contribution of these essays is to map out some of the divergent forms in which neoliberal projects of state intervention have been articulated and some of the diverse institutional pathways through which those projects have evolved. In addition, these essays underscore the deeply dysfunctional yet extraordinarily malleable character of neoliberal statecraft. Despite the serial failure of neoliberal policies to establish a sustainable basis for socioeconomic regeneration, neoliberal orthodoxy retains its hold over municipal policy-making throughout much of the developed capitalist world. However, as these contributions demonstrate, neoliberal urban policies—and the state institutions through which they are deployed—have evolved considerably since the early 1980s, as political-economic elites have attempted to confront their profoundly disruptive socioeconomic consequences without calling into question the basic neoliberal premise of market-driven growth.

Finally, Part 3 examines the new forms of social exclusion, injustice, and disempowerment that have been inscribed upon the urban landscape during the last few decades of neoliberalization. The authors in this section explore a variety of ways in which neoliberal projects of political-economic restructuring collide with pre-existing sociospatial cleavages and, in turn, create new forms of inequality, political disenfranchisement, and economic immiseration. Moreover, as these contributors indicate, cities have become a key arena in which the everyday violence of neoliberalism has been unleashed.

By way of conclusion, it is worth emphasizing that much theoretical, empirical, and political work remains to be done in order to critically decode—and ultimately dismantle—the "utopia of unlimited exploitation" (Bourdieu 1998) that has underpinned the neoliberalization of urban life during the last two decades. One particularly urgent issue, which this collection only begins to address, is the strategic role of cities as sites of resistance and oppositional mobilization against neoliberalism. For, even if cities have been subsumed within neoliberal agendas of various kinds in recent decades, they also remain vibrant sociopolitical arenas in which alternative practices of everyday life, a whole range of institutional experiments, and various traditions of political utopianism continue to flourish. Even in an age of neoliberal dominance, cities remain crucially important arenas for struggles in the name of social justice, radical democracy, popular empowerment, and the politics of difference. The demand for an urban life based upon grassroots democratic participation and the satisfaction of social needs rather than the imperatives of private profit—to which Lefebvre ([1968] 1996) famously referred as the "right to the city"—continues to percolate in many cities despite the neoliberal assaults of the last few decades. This demand is powerfully evidenced, for instance, in living-wage campaigns, projects to deepen and extend civil rights and civil liberties, environmental justice movements, antiworkfare activism, new forms of community-labor organizing, and ongoing social struggles regarding the right to decent, affordable housing. By providing an initial analysis of the complex political-economic geographies within which such struggles are embedded, we hope that this volume may also contribute, in some way, to the project of imagining and constructing alternatives to the neoliberal city.

Acknowledgments

We thank Jamie Peck, Jane Wills, and the *Antipode* editorial board for providing us with a medium in which to pursue this project. Special thanks are due to Ros Whitehead of *Antipode* for her expert editorial assistance at every stage of this project. Without her extraordinary diligence and guidance, this project could never have been completed, and without her cheerfulness and encouragement, it would never have been such an enjoyable task. We are grateful to David Perry and Joy Pamintuan of the UIC Great Cities Institute and Esteleta Cameron, Yibing Li, and Bill Lester of CUED for their assistance in organizing the conference. Thanks are also due to the many referees who reviewed the papers with remarkable expertise, engagement and enthusiasm even under the pressure of extremely tight deadlines. Finally, a toast goes to Chicago's now-defunct House of Tiki lounge on 53rd Street, where the idea for this project first emerged.

References

Agnew J and Corbridge S (1995) *Mastering Space*. New York: Routledge
Bourdieu P (1998) *Acts of Resistance: Against the Tyranny of the Market*. New York: New Press
Eisenschitz A and Gough J (1993) *The Politics of Local Economic Policy: The Problems and Possibilities of Local Initiative*. Basingstoke: Macmillian
Gill S (1995) Globalisation, market civilisation and disciplinary neoliberalism. *Millennium* 24:399–423

Lefebvre H (1978) *De l'État: Les contradictions de l'État moderne*. Vol 4. Paris: Union Générale d'Éditions

Lefebvre H ([1968] 1996) "The right to the city." In Eleonore Kofman and Elizabeth Lebas (eds) *Lefebvre: Writings on Cities* (pp 63–184). Cambridge, MA: Blackwell

Lipietz A (1994) The national and the regional: Their autonomy vis-à-vis the capitalist world crisis. In R Palan and B Gills (eds) *Transcending the State-Global Divide* (pp 23–44). Boulder: Lynne Rienner

McMichael P (1996) *Development and Social Change*. Thousand Oaks, CA: Sage

Moody K (1997) *Workers in a Lean World*. New York: Verso

Overbeek H (ed) (1993) *Restructuring Hegemony in the Global Political Economy: The Rise of Transnational Neoliberalism in the 1980s*. New York: Routledge

Smith N (2002) Scales of terror: the manufacturing of nationalism and the war for U.S. globalism. In M Sorkin and S Zukin (eds) *After the World Trade Center: Rethinking New York City* (pp 97–108). New York and London: Routeledge

Part 1 The Urbanization of Neoliberalism: Theoretical Debates

Chapter 1
Cities and the Geographies of "Actually Existing Neoliberalism"

Neil Brenner and Nik Theodore

This essay elaborates a critical geographical perspective on neoliberalism that emphasizes (a) the path-dependent character of neoliberal reform projects and (b) the strategic role of cities in the contemporary remaking of political-economic space. We begin by presenting the methodological foundations for an approach to the geographies of what we term "actually existing neoliberalism." In contrast to neoliberal ideology, in which market forces are assumed to operate according to immutable laws no matter where they are "unleashed," we emphasize the contextual *embeddedness* of neoliberal restructuring projects insofar as they have been produced within national, regional, and local contexts defined by the legacies of inherited institutional frameworks, policy regimes, regulatory practices, and political struggles. An adequate understanding of actually existing neoliberalism must therefore explore the path-dependent, contextually specific interactions between inherited regulatory landscapes and emergent neoliberal, market-oriented restructuring projects at a broad range of geographical scales. These considerations lead to a conceptualization of contemporary neoliberalization processes as catalysts and expressions of an ongoing creative destruction of political-economic space at multiple geographical scales. While the neoliberal restructuring projects of the last two decades have not established a coherent basis for sustainable capitalist growth, it can be argued that they have nonetheless profoundly reworked the institutional infrastructures upon which Fordist-Keynesian capitalism was grounded. The concept of creative destruction is presented as a useful means for describing the geographically uneven, socially regressive, and politically volatile trajectories of institutional/spatial change that have been crystallizing under these conditions. The essay concludes by discussing the role of urban spaces within the contradictory and chronically unstable geographies of actually existing neoliberalism. Throughout the advanced capitalist world, we suggest, cities have become strategically crucial geographical arenas in which a variety of neoliberal initiatives—along with closely intertwined strategies of crisis displacement and crisis management—have been articulated.

Introduction

The linchpin of neoliberal ideology is the belief that open, competitive, and unregulated markets, liberated from all forms of state interference, represent the optimal mechanism for economic development. Although the intellectual roots of this "utopia of unlimited exploitation" (Bourdieu 1998) can be traced to the postwar writings of Friedrich Hayek and Milton Friedman, neoliberalism first gained widespread prominence during the late 1970s and early 1980s as a strategic political response to the sustained global recession of the preceding decade. Faced with the declining profitability of traditional mass-production industries and the crisis of Keynesian welfare policies, national and local states throughout the older industrialized world began, if hesitantly at first, to dismantle the basic institutional components of the postwar settlement and to mobilize a range of policies intended to extend market discipline, competition, and commodification throughout all sectors of society. In this context, neoliberal doctrines were deployed to justify, among other projects, the deregulation of state control over major industries, assaults on organized labor, the reduction of corporate taxes, the shrinking and/or privatization of public services, the dismantling of welfare programs, the enhancement of international capital mobility, the intensification of interlocality competition, and the criminalization of the urban poor.

If Thatcherism and Reaganism represented particularly aggressive programs of neoliberal restructuring during the 1980s, more moderate forms of a neoliberal politics were also mobilized during this same period in traditionally social democratic or social christian democratic states such as Canada, New Zealand, Germany, the Netherlands, France, Italy, and even Sweden. Following the debt crisis of the early 1980s, neoliberal programs of restructuring were extended globally through the efforts of the USA and other G–7 states to subject peripheral and semiperipheral states to the discipline of capital markets. Bretton Woods institutions such as the General Agreement on Tariffs and Trade (GATT)-World Trade Organization (WTO), the World Bank, and the International Monetary Fund (IMF) were subsequently transformed into the agents of a transnational neoliberalism and were mobilized to institutionalize this extension of market forces and commodification in the Third World through various structural-adjustment and fiscal austerity programs. By the mid-1980s, in the wake of this dramatic U-turn of policy agendas throughout the world, neoliberalism had become the dominant political and ideological form of capitalist globalization.

The global imposition of neoliberalism has, of course, been highly uneven, both socially and geographically, and its institutional forms and sociopolitical consequences have varied significantly across spatial scales and among each of the major supraregional zones of the world economy. While recognizing the polycentric and multiscalar character of neoliberalism as a geopolitical and geoeconomic project, the goal of this collection is to explore the role of neoliberalism in ongoing processes of *urban* restructuring. The supranational and national parameters of neoliberalism have been widely recognized in the literatures on geopolitical economy. However, the contention that neoliberalism has also generated powerful impacts at subnational scales—within cities and city-regions—deserves to be elaborated more systematically.

This introductory essay provides a "first cut" towards theorizing and exploring the complex institutional, geographical, and social inter-faces between neoliberalism and urban restructuring. We begin by presenting the methodological foundations for an approach to the geographies of what we term "actually existing neoliberalism." In contrast to neoliberal ideology, in which market forces are assumed to operate according to immutable laws no matter where they are "unleashed," we emphasize the contextual *embeddedness* of neoliberal restructuring projects insofar as they have been produced within national, regional, and local contexts defined by the legacies of inherited institutional frameworks, policy regimes, regulatory practices, and political struggles. An understanding of actually existing neoliberalism must therefore explore the path-dependent, contextually specific interactions between inherited regulatory landscapes and emergent neoliberal, market-oriented restructuring projects at a broad range of geographical scales. These considerations lead to a conceptualization of contemporary neoliberalization processes as catalysts and expres-sions of an ongoing creative destruction of political-economic space at multiple geographical scales. While the neoliberal restructuring pro-jects of the last two decades have failed to establish a coherent basis for sustainable capitalist growth, they have nonetheless profoundly reworked the institutional infrastructures upon which Fordist-Keynesian capitalism was grounded. The concept of creative destruction is presented to describe the geographically uneven, socially regressive, and politically volatile trajectories of institutional/spatial change that have been crystallizing under these conditions. The essay concludes by discussing the role of urban spaces within the contradictory and chronically unstable geographies of actually existing neoliberalism. Throughout the advanced capitalist world, we suggest, cities have become strategically crucial geographical arenas in which a variety of neoliberal initiatives—along with closely intertwined strategies of crisis displacement and crisis management—have been articulated.

Towards a Political Economy of Actually Existing Neoliberalism

The 1990s was a decade in which the term "neoliberalism" became a major rallying point for a wide range of anticapitalist popular struggles, from the Zapatista rebellion in Chiapas, the subsequent series of Gatherings for Humanity and Against Neoliberalism, and the December 1995 mass strikes in France to the mass protests against the WTO, the IMF, the World Bank, and the World Economic Forum in locations such as Davos, Genoa, London, Melbourne, Mumbai, Nice, Prague, Seattle, Sydney, Washington DC, and Zürich, among many others. As such struggles continue to proliferate in the new millennium, anticapitalist forces throughout the world have come to identify neoliberalism as a major target for oppositional mobilization.

Among activists and radical academics alike, there is considerable agreement regarding the basic elements of neoliberalism as an ideological project. For instance, Moody (1997:119–120) has described neoliberalism concisely as "… a mixture of neoclassical economic fundamentalism, market regulation in place of state guidance, economic redistribution in favor of capital (known as supply-side economics), moral authoritarianism with an idealized family at its center, international free trade principles (sometimes inconsistently applied), and a thorough intolerance of trade unionism." However, as Moody and others have emphasized, there is also a rather blatant disjuncture between the ideology of neoliberalism and its everyday political operations and societal effects. On the one hand, while neoliberalism aspires to create a "utopia" of free markets liberated from all forms of state interference, it has in practice entailed a dramatic intensification of coercive, disciplinary forms of state intervention in order to impose market rule upon all aspects of social life (see Keil this volume; MacLeod this volume). On the other hand, whereas neoliberal ideology implies that self-regulating markets will generate an optimal allocation of investments and resources, neoliberal political practice has generated pervasive market failures, new forms of social polarization, and a dramatic intensification of uneven development at all spatial scales. In short, as Gill (1995:407) explains, "the neoliberal shift in government policies has tended to subject the majority of the population to the power of market forces whilst preserving social protection for the strong." During the last two decades, the dysfunctional effects of neoliberal approaches to capitalist restructuring have been manifested in diverse institutional arenas and at a range of spatial scales (see Amin 1997; Bourdieu 1998; Gill 1995; Isin 1998; Jessop and Stones 1992; Peck and Tickell 1994). As such studies have indicated, the disjuncture between the ideology of self-regulating markets and the everyday reality of persistent economic stagnation— intensifying inequality, destructive interplace competition, and generalized social insecurity—has been particularly blatant in precisely those political-economic contexts in which neoliberal doctrines have been imposed most extensively.

Crucially, the manifold disjunctures that have accompanied the worldwide imposition of neoliberalism—between ideology and practice; doctrine and reality; vision and consequence—are not merely accidental side effects of this disciplinary project of imposing a new "market civilization" (Gill 1995). Rather, they are among its most essential features. For this reason, we would argue, a purely definitional approach to the political economy of neoliberal restructuring contains significant analytical limitations. For, as Peck and Tickell suggest in their contribution to this collection, we are dealing here less with a coherently bounded "ism" or "end-state" than with a process, as they term it, of *neoliberalization*. Hence, in the present context, the somewhat elusive phenomenon that needs definition must be construed as a historically specific, ongoing, and internally contradictory process of market-driven sociospatial transformation, rather than as a fully actualized policy regime, ideological form, or regulatory framework. From this perspective, an adequate understanding of contemporary neoliberalization processes requires not only a grasp of their politico-ideological foundations but also, just as importantly, a systematic inquiry into their multifarious institutional forms, their developmental tendencies, their diverse sociopolitical effects, and their multiple contradictions.

For purposes of this essay, we shall describe these ongoing neoliberalization processes through the concept of actually existing neoliberalism. This concept is intended not only to underscore the contradictory, destructive character of neoliberal policies, but also to highlight the ways in which neoliberal ideology systematically misrepresents the real effects of such policies upon the macroinstitutional structures and evolutionary trajectories of capitalism. In this context, two issues deserve particular attention. First, neoliberal doctrine represents states and markets as if they were diametrically opposed principles of social organization, rather than recognizing the politically constructed character of all economic relations. Second, neoliberal doctrine is premised upon a "one size fits all" model of policy implementation that assumes that identical results will follow the imposition of market-oriented reforms, rather than recognizing the extraordinary variations that arise as neoliberal reform initiatives are imposed within contextually specific institutional landscapes and policy environments.[1]

Our approach to the political economy of actually existing neoliberalism is grounded upon five core premises, which, taken together, provide a methodological basis on which to circumvent the aforementioned ideological pitfalls. These premises are summarized briefly as follows:

1. *The problem of capitalist regulation.* The social relations of capitalism are permeated by tensions, antagonisms, and conflicts that continually destabilize the accumulation process. Capitalist regulation occurs as systems of rules, habits, norms, and compromises are established within particular institutions, thereby embedding these conflictual social relations within relatively stabilized, routinized, and sustainable spatiotemporal frameworks (Lipietz 1996). In turn, the latter endow the

capitalist system with a marked, if constantly evolving, institutional coherence. Since the industrialization and urbanization of capital on a large scale during the course of the 19th century, the survival of capitalism within each national territory has been secured through the production of historically specific institutional landscapes composed of at least five basic dimensions (see Lipietz 1996; Petit 1999; Swyngedouw 1997): (1) *the wage relation*—the structure of capital/labor relations in the spheres of production and reproduction; (2) *the form of intercapitalist competition*—the framework within which capitalists jostle for market share and technological advantages; (3) *forms of monetary and financial regulation*—the organizational structure of capital circulation; (4) *the state and other forms of governance*—the ensemble of institutionalized political compromises through which the basic contradictions of capitalist society are negotiated; and (5) *the international configuration*—the mechanisms through which national and subnational economic relations are articulated with worldwide processes of capital accumulation.

2. *The unstable historical geographies of capitalism.* The process of capital accumulation and its associated regulatory problems are always articulated in territory-, place-, and scale-specific forms (Harvey 1989; Massey 1985; Smith 1984). Capitalist development therefore necessarily unfolds through the production of historically specific patterns of sociospatial organization in which particular territories, places, and scales are mobilized as productive forces—whether in the form of agglomeration economies, regional production systems, infrastructural configurations, transportation and communications networks, or spatial divisions of labor (Swyngedouw 1992a; Storper and Walker 1989). It is in this sense that the long-term survival of capitalism is premised upon the "production of space" (Lefebvre [1974] 1991).

Yet, due to its inherent dynamism, capital continually renders obsolete the very geographical landscapes it creates and upon which its own reproduction and expansion hinges. Particularly during periods of systemic crisis, inherited frameworks of capitalist territorial organization may be destabilized as capital seeks to transcend sociospatial infrastructures and systems of class relations that no longer provide a secure basis for sustained accumulation. As the effects of devaluation ripple through the space-economy, processes of creative destruction ensue in which the capitalist landscape is thoroughly transformed: the configurations of territorial organization that underpinned the previous round of capitalist expansion are junked and reworked in order to establish a new locational grid for the accumulation process.

It should be noted, however, that the creative destruction of capitalist territorial organization is always unpredictable and deeply contested. Even within industrial landscapes that have been systematically devalued by capital, social attachments to place persist as people struggle to defend the everyday practices and institutional compromises from which capital has sought to extricate itself (Hudson 2001). At the same time, capital's relentless quest to open up fresh spaces for accumulation is inherently speculative, in that the establishment of a new "spatial fix" is never guaranteed; it can occur only through "chance discoveries" and provisional compromises in the wake of intense sociopolitical struggles (Harvey 1989; Lipietz 1996).

3. *Uneven geographical development.* Each round of capitalist development is associated with a distinctive, historically specific geographical landscape in which some places, territories, and scales are systematically privileged over and against others as sites for capital accumulation. The resultant patterns of core–periphery polarization and sociospatial inequality exist at all spatial scales; their contours are never inscribed permanently upon the geographical landscape but are continually reworked through capital's dynamic of uneven spatial development (Harvey 1982; Massey 1985). Uneven development is endemic to capitalism as an historical-geographical system: it is a key expression of capital's relentless drive to mobilize particular territories and places as forces of production; it is a basic geographical medium through which intercapitalist competition and class struggle are fought out; and it is an evolving spatial-institutional scaffolding within which processes of devalorization and revalorization unfold (Smith 1984).

4. *The regulation of uneven geographical development.* Each historical pattern of uneven development is in turn associated with a series of basic regulatory dilemmas: for the uneven development of capital serves not only as a *basis* for the accumulation process but may also, under certain circumstances, operate as a *barrier* to the latter. For this reason, uneven development is associated not only with new opportunities for capital but also with any number of potentially destabilizing effects that may undermine the "structured coherence" upon which sustainable capital accumulation depends. In response to these persistent dilemmas, capitalist states have mobilized a variety of spatial policies intended to regulate the uneven development of capital. Strategies of territorial development and place-promotion may be introduced in order to channel

economic capacities into particular locations and scales. Alternatively, strategies of territorial redistribution and other compensatory regional policies may be introduced in order to equalize the distribution of industry and population across a particular territory, and thus to alleviate the more pernicious, polarizing effects of uneven development.

5. *The evolving geographies of state regulation.* State strategies to regulate uneven development evolve continually in conjunction with contextually specific political-economic circumstances and sociopolitical struggles (Duncan and Goodwin 1987). Nonetheless, during successive phases of capitalist development, particular forms of state spatial policy have been institutionalized, albeit in divergent (national) forms, and have come to provide a key regulatory infrastructure for industrial growth. In this sense, the geographies of state institutions and policies are closely intertwined with evolving processes of uneven development: states provide a relatively stable regulatory landscape within which capital's locational dynamics are articulated; at the same time, states provide a key institutional arena in and through which new approaches to the regulation of uneven development may be introduced. Particularly during periods of systemic capitalist crisis, when uneven development threatens to undermine normalized patterns of accumulation and social reproduction, pressures to junk and rework extant institutional frameworks and regulatory strategies become particularly intense. Under these circumstances, a period of institutional searching and regulatory experimentation ensues in which diverse actors, organizations, and alliances promote competing hegemonic visions, restructuring strategies, and developmental models. The resultant "search for a new institutional fix" (Peck and Tickell 1994) generally entails the partial dismantling or reworking of inherited institutional landscapes in order to "open up a space" for the deployment and institutionalization of new regulatory strategies. Regulatory landscapes are continually made and remade through this intense, politically contested interaction between *inherited* institutional forms and policy frameworks and *emergent* strategies of state spatial regulation (see Brenner 2001; MacKinnon 2001; Peck 1998).

In our view, these methodological premises provide a useful starting point from which to analyze the turbulent geographies of actually existing neoliberalism during the post-1970s period. First and foremost, the preceding considerations suggest that an analysis of actually existing neoliberalism must begin by exploring the entrenched landscapes of capitalist regulation, derived from the Fordist-Keynesian period of capitalist development, within which neoliberal programs were first mobilized following the geoeconomic crises of the early 1970s. From this perspective, the impacts of neoliberal restructuring strategies cannot be understood adequately through abstract or decontextualized debates regarding the relative merits of market-based reform initiatives or the purported limits of particular forms of state policy. Instead, an understanding of actually existing neoliberalism requires an exploration of: (a) the historically specific regulatory landscapes and political settlements that prevailed within particular (national) territories during the Fordist-Keynesian period of capitalist development; (b) the historically specific patterns of crisis formation, uneven development, and sociopolitical contestation that emerged within those territories following the systemic crisis of the Fordist-Keynesian developmental model in the early 1970s; (c) the subsequent interaction of market-oriented neoliberal initiatives with inherited regulatory frameworks, patterns of territorial development, and sociopolitical alliances; and (d) the concomitant evolution of neoliberal policy agendas and restructuring strategies through their conflictual interaction with contextually specific political-economic conditions, regulatory arrangements and power geometries.

The contributions to this volume provide diverse case studies of the nationally and locally specific pathways of political-economic restructuring that underpin the geographies of actually existing neoliberalism. In the remainder of this essay, we analyze the spatialities (and, by implication, the temporalities) of contemporary neoliberalization processes in three closely related steps: first, by emphasizing the path-dependent character of neoliberal reform initiatives; second, by examining the destructive and creative "moments" of neoliberal policies and institutional changes; and third, by considering the ways in which cities have become strategically crucial arenas for neoliberal forms of policy experimentation and institutional restructuring.

Spaces of Neoliberalization (1): Path-Dependency

As numerous scholars in the regulationist tradition have indicated, the Fordist-Keynesian configuration of capitalist development was grounded upon a historically specific set of regulatory arrangements and political compromises that provisionally stabilized the conflicts and contradictions that are endemic to capitalism (see Aglietta 1979; Boyer and Saillard 1995). Although the sources of this unprecedented "golden age" of capitalist expansion remain a matter of considerable academic dispute, numerous scholars have emphasized the key role of the *national* scale as the pre-eminent geographical basis for accumulation and for the regulation of political-economic life during this period (Jessop 1999; Swyngedouw 1997). Of course, the exact configuration of regulatory arrangements and political compromises varied considerably according to the specific model of capitalism that was adopted in each national context. Nonetheless, a number of broad generalizations can be articulated regarding the basic regulatory-institutional architecture that underpinned North Atlantic Fordism (see Altvater 1992; Jessop 1992, 1999; Lipietz 1987; Peck and Tickell 1994; Swyngedouw 1997).

- *Wage relation*. Collective bargaining occurred at the national scale, often through corporatist accommodations between capital, labor, and the state; wage labor was extended and standardized with the spread of mass-production systems throughout national social formations; and wages were tied to productivity growth and tendentially increased in order to underwrite mass consumption.
- *Form of intercapitalist competition*. Monopolistic forms of regulation enabled corporate concentration and centralization within major national industrial sectors; competition between large firms was mediated through strategies to rationalize mass-production technologies; and national states mobilized various forms of industrial policy in order to bolster the world-market positions of their largest firms as national champions.
- *Monetary and financial regulation*. The money supply was regulated at a national scale through the US-dominated Bretton Woods system of fixed exchange rates; national central banks oversaw the distribution of credit to corporations and consumers; and long-term investment decisions by capital were enabled by a stabilized pattern of macroeconomic growth.
- *The state and other forms of governance*. National states became extensively engaged in managing aggregate demand, containing swings in the business cycle, generalizing mass consumption, redistributing the social product through welfare programs, and mediating social unrest.
- *International configuration*. The world economy was parcelized among relatively autocentric national economies and policed by the US global hegemon. Meanwhile, as the Fordist accumulation regime matured, global interdependencies among national economic spaces intensified due to enhanced competition among transnational corporations, the expansion of trade relations, and the ascendancy of the US dollar as world currency.
- *The regulation of uneven spatial development*. National states introduced a range of compensatory regional policies and spatial planning initiatives intended to alleviate intranational

sociospatial polarization by spreading industry and population across the surface of the national territory. Entrenched world-scale patterns of uneven development were nonetheless maintained under the rubric of US global hegemony and Cold War geopolitics.

During the early 1970s, however, the key link between (national) mass production and (national) mass consumption was shattered due to a range of interconnected trends and developments, including: the declining profitability of Fordist sectors; the intensification of international competition; the spread of deindustrialization and mass unemployment; and the abandonment of the Bretton Woods system of national currencies. Subsequently, the Fordist system was subjected to a variety of pressures and crisis-tendencies, leading to a profound shaking-up and reworking of the forms of territorial organization that had underpinned the "golden age" of postwar economic prosperity (Swyngedouw 1992b). The global political-economic transformations of the post-1970s period radically destabilized the Fordist accumulation regime, decentered the entrenched role of the national scale as the predominant locus for state regulation, and undermined the coherence of the national economy as a target of state policies. This "reshuffling of the hierarchy of spaces" (Lipietz 1994:36) has arguably been the most far-reaching geographical consequence of the crisis of North Atlantic Fordism in the early 1970s (Jessop 1999, 2000; Swyngedouw 1992b, 1997).

In a seminal discussion that spatializes some of Gramsci's key concepts, Lipietz (1994:35) has underscored the ways in which processes of capitalist restructuring are articulated in the form of struggles between "defenders of the 'old space'" (to which he refers as the "conservative bloc") and proponents of a "new space" or a "new model of development" (to which he refers as "the modernist bloc"). For Lipietz, the production of new spaces occurs through the conflictual interaction of conservative/preservationist and modernizing or restructuring-oriented political forces at diverse scales, generally leading to a new territorial formation that eclectically combines elements of the old geographical order with aspects of the "projected spaces" sought by the advocates of (neoliberal and/or progressive) modernization.

This conceptualization provides a useful basis for examining the political, institutional, and geographical transformations that unfolded following the crisis of Fordism. Throughout the subsequent decade, intense conflicts between preservationist and restructuring-oriented political blocs proliferated at a range of spatial scales, with highly uneven impacts upon the nationalized frameworks for accumulation and regulation that had been established during the postwar period (see Lipietz 1988). On the one hand, at the national scale, conservative/preservationist blocs initially mobilized diverse strategies of crisis management in order to defend the institutional infrastructures of the Fordist-Keynesian order. From the first oil shock of 1973 until around 1979, traditional recipes of national demand-management prevailed throughout the Organization for Economic Cooperation and Development (OECD) zone, as central governments desperately tried to recreate the conditions for a Fordist virtuous circle of growth. However, as Jessop (1989:269) remarks of the British case, such countercyclical tactics ultimately amounted to no more than an "eleventh hour, state-sponsored Fordist modernisation," for they were incapable of solving, simultaneously, the dual problems of escalating inflation and mass unemployment.

On the other hand, particularly following the "monetarist shock" of the early 1980s, a variety of modernizing, restructuring-oriented political alliances emerged within advanced capitalist countries that sought at once to dismantle existing regulatory frameworks and to establish a new institutional infrastructure for economic rejuvenation (Jessop 1994; Lipietz 1994). Since this period, such modernizing blocs have promoted a variety of regulatory experiments in their ongoing search for a new institutional fix; however, their strategies to revamp the regulatory infrastructure of capitalism should be understood as an open-ended, trial-and-error process of institutional searching rather than as the basis for a post-Fordist mode of social regulation (Peck and Tickell 1994). These modernizing projects have been associated with a variety of political ideologies and restructuring strategies, including: (a) neocorporatist programs that attempt to modernize industry while renegotiating social compromises; (b) neostatist programs that attempt to revitalize the economy through dirigiste, state-led projects to guide industrial transformation; and (c) neoliberal programs that attempt to impose new forms of market discipline upon all aspects of social, political, and economic life (Jessop 1994). In practice, however, these modernizing strategies rarely appear in such pure forms. Instead, real-world projects of capitalist restructuring are usually articulated as complex politico-ideological hybrids derived from contextually specific adaptations, negotiations, and struggles within particular political-economic conjunctures (see Gough this volume).

Even though only a relatively small number of advanced capitalist national states have explicitly adopted an orthodox program of neoliberal restructuring, it is crucial to recognize that neoliberal political projects have exercised tremendous influence upon the trajectory of capitalist restructuring in a range of supranational, national, and subnational institutional arenas during the last two decades. This influence can be attributed, on the one hand, to the increasingly hegemonic role of supranational institutions such as the IMF, the World Bank, the GATT, the OECD, and the European Commission, which are oriented explicitly and aggressively towards neoliberal goals such as deregulation, enhanced capital mobility, trade liberalization, and expanded commodification. On the other hand, core neoliberal priorities such as "lean" bureaucracies, fiscal austerity, enhanced labor market flexibility, territorial competitiveness, and the free flow of investment and capital have been integrated quite extensively into mainstream political programs, often through references to supposedly ineluctable trends such as "globalization" or through purportedly apolitical reform initiatives such as the New Public Management (see Jessop this volume; Leitner and Sheppard this volume; Peck and Tickell this volume).

For this reason, neoliberalism cannot be understood merely as one among many possible models of state/economy relations that national governments may choose to promote within their territories. While it would be problematic to subsume neocorporatist and neostatist approaches to capitalist restructuring under the encompassing rubric of neoliberalism, it would be equally misleading to treat those strategies as being analogous to neoliberalism in terms of their political influence, ideological reach, or institutional shape. At the present time, neoliberalism represents an actually existing framework of disciplinary political authority that enforces market rule over an ever wider range of social relations throughout the world economy (Peck and Tickell this volume). Accordingly, the notion of actually existing neoliberalism is intended not only to encompass the immediate impact of neoliberal political programs upon social, political, and economic relations, but also to characterize their more "subversive" role in transforming the broad geoeconomic and geopolitical fields within which struggles over the future shape of capitalist social relations are currently being fought at a range of spatial scales (Rhodes 1995).

Most crucially here, the notion of actually existing neoliberalism is intended to illuminate the complex, contested ways in which neoliberal restructuring strategies interact with pre-existing uses of space, institutional configurations, and constellations of sociopolitical power. As indicated, neoliberal programs of capitalist restructuring are rarely, if ever, imposed in a pure form, for they are always introduced within politico-institutional contexts that have been molded significantly by earlier regulatory arrangements, institutionalized practices, and political compromises. In this sense, the evolution of any politico-institutional configuration following the imposition of neoliberal policy reforms is likely to demonstrate strong properties of path-dependency, in which established institutional arrangements significantly constrain the scope and trajectory of reform.

Finally, it is worth noting the degree to which neoliberal policy agendas have themselves been transformed through their interaction with inherited institutional landscapes and power configurations during the last three decades. As Peck and Tickell indicate in their contribution to this volume, neoliberalism has evolved considerably during the last three decades, from a relatively abstract economic doctrine (1970s) and a means of dismantling or "rolling back" established Keynesian welfarist arrangements (1980s) into, most recently, a reconstituted form of market-guided regulation intended not only to release short-term bursts of economic growth but also to manage some of the deep sociopolitical contradictions induced by earlier forms of neoliberal policy intervention (1990s). In the present context, the key point is that these politico-ideological shifts have emerged, in significant measure, along a strongly path-dependent evolutionary trajectory: while first deployed as a strategic response to the crisis of an earlier political-economic framework (Fordist-Keynesian capitalism), neoliberal policies were subsequently modified qualitatively to confront any number of governance failures, crisis tendencies, and contradictions that were internal to neoliberalism itself as a politico-regulatory project (see Jones and Ward this volume; Peck and Tickell this volume). The transition from the orthodox, radically antistatist neoliberalisms of Reagan and Thatcher in the 1980s to the more socially moderate neoliberalisms of Blair, Clinton, and Schröder during the 1990s may therefore be understood as a path-dependent adjustment and reconstitution of neoliberal strategies in response to their own disruptive, dysfunctional sociopolitical effects.

Spaces of Neoliberalization (2): Creative Destruction

In order to grasp more effectively the path-dependent interactions between existing institutional forms and emergent neoliberal projects, we propose to analyze actually existing neoliberalism with reference to two dialectically intertwined but analytically distinct moments: the (partial) *destruction* of extant institutional arrangements and political compromises through market-oriented reform initiatives; and the (tendential) *creation* of a new infrastructure for market-oriented economic growth, commodification, and the rule of capital. Two important caveats must be immediately added to clarify this conceptualization of actually existing neoliberalism as a process of institutional creative destruction.

First, while our emphasis on the tendentially creative capacities of neoliberalism is at odds with earlier studies that underscored its overridingly destructive character (eg Peck and Tickell 1994), we would argue that this double-pronged, dialectical conceptualization can help illuminate the complex, often highly contradictory trajectories of institutional change that have been generated through the deployment of neoliberal political programs at various spatial scales. The point of this emphasis, however, is not to suggest that neoliberalism could somehow provide a basis for stabilized, reproducible capitalist growth, but rather to explore its wide-ranging, transformative impacts upon the inherited politico-institutional and geographical infrastructures of advanced capitalist states and economies. We would argue that this latter issue must be explored independently of the traditional regulationist question of whether or not a given institutional form promotes or undermines sustainable capitalist growth. Even when neoliberal policy reforms fail to generate short- or medium-term bursts of capitalist growth, they may nonetheless impose much more lasting evolutionary ruptures within the institutional frameworks, policy environments, and geographies of capitalist regulation.

Second, and relatedly, it should be recognized that the destructive and creative moments of institutional change within actually existing neoliberalism are intimately, inextricably interconnected in practice. Our use of the term "moments" to describe these interconnections is therefore intended in the Hegelian-Marxian sense of conflictual yet mutually related elements within a dynamic, dialectical process, rather than as a description of distinct temporal units within a linear transition.

Building upon the conceptualization of capitalist regulation developed above, Table 1 summarizes the basic elements within each of these moments of neoliberal institutional restructuring. As the table illustrates, neoliberalism represents a complex, multifaceted project of sociospatial transformation—it contains not only a utopian vision of a fully commodified form of social life, but also a concrete program of institutional modifications through which the unfettered rule of capital is to be promoted. Indeed, a sustained critique of the institutional forms, regulatory arrangements, and political compromises associated with the Fordist-Keynesian order—and a concerted program to dismantle the latter—lie at the very heart of neoliberalism as a project of politico-institutional transformation. Most crucially, the table indicates the ways in which both the destructive and the creative moments of actually existing neoliberalism have been mobilized through distinctively *geographical* strategies within each of the major institutional arenas in which capitalist regulation occurs. In the most general sense, the table illuminates the ways in which the geographies of actually existing neoliberalism are characterized by a dynamic transformation of capitalist territorial organization from the nationally configured frameworks that prevailed during the Fordist-Keynesian period to an increasingly "glocalized" configuration of global-national-local interactions in which no single scale serves as the primary pivot for accumulation, regulation, or sociopolitical struggle (Jessop 2000; Swyngedouw 1997).

Table 1 provides no more than a schematic starting point through which the dynamics of creative destruction associated with contemporary neoliberalization processes might be analyzed. For purposes

Table 1: Destructive and Creative Moments of Actually Existing Neoliberalism

Site of Regulation	Moment of Destruction	Moment of Creation
Wage relation	• Assaults on organized labor and national collective bargaining agreements • Dismantling of the family wage and the spread of generalized economic insecurity • Downgrading of national regulations ensuring equal employment opportunity, occupational safety, and workers' rights	• Competitive deregulation: atomized renegotiation of wage levels and working conditions combined with expanded managerial discretion • New forms of the social wage and new gender divisions of labor • Promotion of new forms of labor "flexibility"
Form of intercapitalist competition	• Selective withdrawal of state support for leading national industries • Dismantling of national protectionist policies • Dismantling of national barriers to foreign direct investment	• New forms of state support for "sunrise" industries • Extension of global commodities markets through trade liberalization policies codified in the WTO, the IMF, the European Union (EU), the North American Free Trade Agreement (NAFTA), and other supranational bodies • Establishment of global capital markets through GATT negotiations
Form of financial and monetary regulation	• Dismantling of Bretton Woods global monetary system and deregulation of money markets • Erosion of national states' capacity to control exchange rates • Dismantling of the regulatory constraints impeding monetary and financial speculation in global markets • Separation of financial and credit flows from productive sources of investment	• Creation of speculation-driven currency markets and "stateless monies" outside national regulatory control • Expanded role of global regulatory bodies (such as the Bank for International Settlements) in the monitoring of global financial transactions • Creation of offshore financial centers, international banking facilities, and tax havens

Table 1: Continued

Site of Regulation	Moment of Destruction	Moment of Creation
The state and other forms of governance	• Abandonment of Keynesian forms of demand-management • Dismantling of traditional national relays of welfare service provision • "Hollowing out" of national state capacities to regulate money, trade, and investment flows • De-centering of traditional hierarchical-bureaucratic forms of governmental control • Dismantling of traditional relays of democratic control at national and subnational levels • Strategies to "hollow out" the autocentric national economy as a target of state intervention • Erosion of traditional managerial-redistributive functions of national and subnational administrative agencies • Imposition of fiscal austerity measures aimed at reducing public expenditures • Shrinking of public sector employment	• "Rolling forward" of supply-side and monetarist programs of state intervention • Devolution of social welfare functions to lower levels of government, the social economy, and households • Mobilization of strategies to promote territorial competitiveness, technological innovation, and internationalization • Establishment of public–private partnerships and "networked" forms of governance • Creation of "new authoritarian" state apparatuses and "quangos" that are insulated from public accountability and popular-democratic control • Rescaling of state economic intervention to privilege strategic supranational and subnational spaces of accumulation • Underwriting the costs of private investment through state subsidies • Transfer of erstwhile forms of public employment to the private sector through privatization
International configuration	• De-centering of the national scale of accumulation, regulation, and sociopolitical struggle • Undercutting of regulatory standards across localities, regions, national states, and supranational economic zones	• "Relativization of scales" as relations among subnational, national, and supranational institutional forms are systematically rearranged • Introduction of policies to promote market-mediated, competitive relations among subnational (regional and local) levels of state power

Table 1: Continued

Site of Regulation	Moment of Destruction	Moment of Creation
Uneven spatial development	• Selective withdrawal of state support for declining regions and cities • Destruction of traditional relays of compensatory, redistributive regional policy (spatial Keynesianism)	• Mobilization of new forms of state policy to promote capital mobility within supranational trade blocs and to encourage capital (re)investment within strategic city-regions and industrial districts • Establishment of new forms of sociospatial inequality, polarization, and territorial competition at global, national, and subnational scales

of simplification, the destructive tendencies sketched in the table refer to those vestiges of the Fordist-Keynesian settlement that have been threatened or undermined through the neoliberal offensive. Concomitantly, the creative tendencies depicted in the table refer to various institutional realignments and political adjustments that have imposed new forms of market discipline upon global, national, and local social relations. As indicated, however, we conceive this dynamic of creative destruction not as a unilinear transition from one coherently bounded regulatory system to another, but rather as an uneven, multiscalar, multidirectional, and open-ended restructuring process that generates pervasive governance failures, crisis tendencies, and contradictions of its own. For, as Lipietz (1992) likewise emphasizes, the dynamic of creative destruction never occurs on a blank slate in which the "old order" is abruptly obliterated and the "new order" is unfurled as a fully formed totality. Rather, it takes place on an aggressively contested institutional landscape in which newly emergent "projected spaces" interact conflictually with inherited regulatory arrangements, leading in turn to new, unforeseen, and often highly unstable layerings of political-economic space (see also Lipietz 1994). These newly combined amalgamations of inherited and emergent institutional arrangements may then provide a political arena in and through which subsequent struggles over the regulation of accumulation, and its associated contradictions, can be articulated and fought out.

Throughout this discussion, we have underscored the thoroughly multiscalar character of contemporary neoliberalization tendencies. Clearly, the processes of creative destruction outlined above have been unfolding at a range of geographical scales and in a variety of institutional sites since the geoeconomic crises of the early 1970s. We would argue, however, that cities have become strategically crucial arenas in which neoliberal forms of creative destruction have been unfolding during the last three decades. The other contributions to this volume examine this ongoing urbanization of neoliberalism incisively through a variety of theoretical, methodological, political, and empirical lenses. Therefore, our goal in the penultimate section of this essay is to outline, in general terms, why cities may be viewed as key politico-institutional arenas within the broader geographies of actually existing neoliberalism.

Spaces of Neoliberalization (3): Cities

The preceding discussion underscored the ways in which the world-wide ascendancy of neoliberalism during the early 1980s was closely intertwined with a pervasive rescaling of capital-labor relations, intercapitalist competition, financial and monetary regulation, state power, the international configuration, and uneven development throughout the world economy. As the taken-for-granted primacy of the national scale has been undermined in each of these arenas, inherited formations of urban governance have likewise been reconfigured quite systematically throughout the older industrialized world. While the processes of institutional creative destruction associated with actually existing neoliberalism are clearly transpiring at all spatial scales, it can be argued that they are occurring with particular intensity at the urban scale, within major cities and city-regions.

On the one hand, cities today are embedded within a highly uncertain geoeconomic environment characterized by monetary chaos, speculative movements of financial capital, global location strategies by major transnational corporations, and rapidly intensifying interlocality competition (Swyngedouw 1992b). In the context of this deepening "global-local disorder" (Peck and Tickell 1994), most local governments have been constrained—to some degree, independently of their political orientation and national context—to adjust to heightened levels of economic uncertainty by engaging in short-termist forms of interspatial competition, place-marketing, and regulatory undercutting in order to attract investments and jobs (Leitner and Sheppard 1998). Meanwhile, the retrenchment of national welfare state regimes and national intergovernmental systems has likewise imposed powerful new fiscal constraints upon cities, leading to major budgetary cuts during a period in which local social problems and conflicts have intensified in conjunction with rapid economic restructuring.

On the other hand, in many cases, neoliberal programs have also been directly "interiorized" into urban policy regimes, as newly formed territorial alliances attempt to rejuvenate local economies through a shock treatment of deregulation, privatization, liberalization, and enhanced fiscal austerity. In this context, cities—including their sub-urban peripheries—have become increasingly important geographical targets and institutional laboratories for a variety of neoliberal policy experiments, from place-marketing, enterprise and empowerment zones, local tax abatements, urban development corporations, public–private partnerships, and new forms of local boosterism to workfare policies, property-redevelopment schemes, business-incubator projects, new strategies of social control, policing, and surveillance, and a host of other institutional modifications within the local and regional state apparatus. As the contributions to this volume indicate in detail, the overarching goal of such neoliberal urban policy experiments is to mobilize city space as an arena both for market-oriented economic growth and for elite consumption practices. Table 2 schematically illustrates some of the many politico-institutional mechanisms through which neoliberal projects have been localized within North American and western European cities during the past two decades, distinguishing in turn their constituent (partially) destructive and (tendentially) creative moments.

Table 2 is intended to provide a broad overview of the manifold ways in which contemporary processes of neoliberalization have affected the institutional geographies of cities throughout North America and Western Europe. For present purposes, two additional aspects of the processes of creative destruction depicted in the table deserve explication.

First, it is important to underscore that the processes of neoliberal localization outlined in the table necessarily unfold in place-specific forms and combinations within particular local and national contexts. Indeed, building upon the conceptualization of actually existing neo-liberalism developed above, we would argue that patterns of neo-liberal localization in any national or local context can be understood adequately only through an exploration of their complex, contested interactions with inherited national and local regulatory landscapes. The contributions to this volume provide abundant evidence for this proposition with reference to diverse pathways of neoliberal local-ization. Moreover, as these essays demonstrate, the different pathways of neoliberal urban restructuring that have crystallized throughout the older industrialized world reflect not only the diversity of neoliberal political projects but also the contextually specific *interactions* of such projects with inherited frameworks of urban political-economic regulation. An examination of the diverse pathways through which neoliberal political agendas have been imposed upon and reproduced within cities is therefore central to any comprehensive inquiry into the geographies of actually existing neoliberalism.

A second, equally important issue concerns the evolution and/or reconstitution of neoliberal forms of urban policy since their initial

Table 2: Destructive and Creative Moments of Neoliberal Localization

Mechanisms of Neoliberal Localization	Moment of Destruction	Moment of Creation
Recalibration of intergovernmental relations	• Dismantling of earlier systems of central government support for municipal activities	• Devolution of new tasks, burdens, and responsibilities to municipalities; creation of new incentive structures to reward local entrepreneurialism and to catalyze "endogenous growth"
Retrenchment of public finance	• Imposition of fiscal austerity measures upon municipal governments	• Creation of new revenue-collection districts and increased reliance of municipalities upon local sources of revenue, user fees, and other instruments of private finance
Restructuring the welfare state	• Local relays of national welfare service-provision are retrenched; assault on managerial-welfarist local state apparatuses	• Expansion of community-based sectors and private approaches to social service provision • Imposition of mandatory work requirements on urban welfare recipients; new (local) forms of workfare experimentation
Reconfiguring the institutional infrastructure of the local state	• Dismantling of bureaucratized, hierarchical forms of local public administration • Devolution of erstwhile state tasks to voluntary community networks • Assault on traditional relays of local democratic accountability	• "Rolling forward" of new networked forms of local governance based upon public–private partnerships, "quangos," and the "new public management" • Establishment of new institutional relays through which elite business interests can directly influence major local development decisions

Table 2: Continued

Mechanisms of Neoliberal Localization	Moment of Destruction	Moment of Creation
Privatization of the municipal public sector and collective infrastructures	• Elimination of public monopolies for the provision of standardized municipal services (utilities, sanitation, public safety, mass transit, etc)	• Privatization and competitive contracting of municipal services • Creation of new markets for service delivery and infrastructure maintenance • Creation of privatized, customized, and networked urban infrastructures intended to (re)position cities within supranational capital flows
Restructuring urban housing markets	• Razing public housing and other forms of low-rent accommodation • Elimination of rent controls and project-based construction subsidies	• Creation of new opportunities for speculative investment in central-city real estate markets • Emergency shelters become "warehouses" for the homeless • Introduction of market rents and tenant-based vouchers in low-rent niches of urban housing markets
Reworking labor market regulation	• Dismantling of traditional, publicly funded education, skills training, and apprenticeship programs for youth, displaced workers, and the unemployed	• Creation of a new regulatory environment in which temporary staffing agencies, unregulated "labor corners," and other forms of contingent work can proliferate • Implementation of work-readiness programs aimed at the conscription of workers into low-wage jobs • Expansion of informal economies

Table 2: Continued

Mechanisms of Neoliberal Localization	Moment of Destruction	Moment of Creation
Restructuring strategies of territorial development	• Dismantling of autocentric national models of capitalist growth • Destruction of traditional compensatory regional policies • Increasing exposure of local and regional economies to global competitive forces • Fragmentation of national space-economies into discrete urban and regional industrial systems	• Creation of free trade zones, enterprise zones, and other deregulated spaces within major urban regions • Creation of new development areas, technopoles, and other new industrial spaces at subnational scales • Mobilization of new "glocal" strategies intended to rechannel economic capacities and infrastructure investments into "globally connected" local/regional agglomerations
Transformations of the built environment and urban form	• Elimination and/or intensified surveillance of urban public spaces • Destruction of traditional working-class neighborhoods in order to make way for speculative redevelopment • Retreat from community-oriented planning initiatives	• Creation of new privatized spaces of elite/corporate consumption • Construction of large-scale megaprojects intended to attract corporate investment and reconfigure local land-use patterns • Creation of gated communities, urban enclaves, and other "purified" spaces of social reproduction • "Rolling forward" of the gentrification frontier and the intensification of sociospatial polarization • Adoption of the principle of "highest and best use" as the basis for major land-use planning decisions

Table 2: Continued

Mechanisms of Neoliberal Localization	Moment of Destruction	Moment of Creation
Interlocal policy transfer	• Erosion of contextually sensitive approaches to local policymaking • Marginalization of "home-grown" solutions to localized market failures and governance failures	• Diffusion of generic, prototypical approaches to "modernizing" reform among policymakers in search of quick fixes for local social problems (eg welfare-to-work programs, place-marketing strategies, zero-tolerance crime policies, etc) • Imposition of decontextualized "best practice" models upon local policy environments
Re-regulation of urban civil society	• Destruction of the "liberal city" in which all inhabitants are entitled to basic civil liberties, social services. and political rights	• Mobilization of zero-tolerance crime policies and "broken windows" policing • Introduction of new discriminatory forms of surveillance and social control • Introduction of new policies to combat social exclusion by reinserting individuals into the labor market
Re-representing the city	• Postwar image of the industrial, working-class city is recast through a (re-)emphasis on urban disorder, "dangerous classes," and economic decline	• Mobilization of entrepreneurial discourses and representations focused on the need for revitalization, reinvestment, and rejuvenation within major metropolitan areas

deployment in North American and western European cities during the late 1970s and early 1980s. Drawing upon the periodization introduced by Peck and Tickell in this volume (see pp 40–43), we have already alluded above to the various mutations that neoliberalization processes have undergone since the late 1970s. The essential point at this juncture of our discussion is that these mutations of neoliberalism have unfolded in particularly pronounced forms within major cities and city-regions. Indeed, we would argue that each of the broader phases of neoliberalization outlined by Peck and Tickell has been anchored and fought out within strategic urban spaces.

- During the initial phase of "proto-neoliberalism," cities became flashpoints both for major economic dislocations and for various forms of sociopolitical struggle, particularly in the sphere of social reproduction. Indeed, the problematic of collective consumption acquired such political prominence during this period that Castells (1972) interpreted it as the sociological essence of the urban phenomenon itself under capitalism. In this context, cities became battlegrounds in which preservationist and modernizing alliances struggled to influence the form and trajectory of economic restructuring during a period in which the postwar growth regime was being systematically undermined throughout the older industrialized world. Consequently, local economic initiatives were adopted in many older industrial cities in order to promote renewed growth from below while maintaining established sociopolitical settlements and redistributive arrangements.
- During the era of "roll-back" neoliberalism in the 1980s, the dominant form of neoliberal urban policy shifted significantly. In this era of lean government, municipalities were increasingly constrained to introduce various kinds of cost-cutting measures —including tax abatements, land grants, cutbacks in public services, the privatization of infrastructural facilities, and so forth—in order to lower the costs of state administration, capitalist production, and social reproduction within their jurisdictions, and thereby to accelerate inward investment. Traditional Fordist-Keynesian forms of localized collective consumption were retrenched, in this context, as fiscal austerity measures were imposed upon local governments by neoliberalizing national state apparatuses. Under these conditions, enhanced administrative efficiency and direct and indirect state subsidies to large corporations and an increasing privatization of social reproduction functions were widely viewed as the "best practices" for promoting a good business climate within major cities. The contradictions of this zero-sum, cost-cutting form of urban entrepreneurialism are now evident throughout North America and Western Europe. In addition to its highly polarizing consequences for major segments of local, regional, and national populations (see Keil this volume; MacLeod this volume), the effectiveness of such strategies for promoting economic rejuvenation has been shown to decline quite precipitously as they are diffused throughout urban systems (Cheshire and Gordon 1996; Leitner and Sheppard 1998).

- The subsequent consolidation of "roll-out" neoliberalism in the early 1990s may be viewed as an evolutionary reconstitution of the neoliberal project in response to its own immanent contradictions and crisis tendencies. Throughout this decade, a marked reconstitution of neoliberal strategies occurred at the urban scale as well. On the one hand, the basic neoliberal imperative of mobilizing economic space—in this case, city space—as a purified arena for capitalist growth, commodification, and market discipline remained the dominant political project for municipal governments throughout the world economy. Indeed, as Weber's contribution to this volume indicates, state institutions during this period became even more directly involved in the creative destruction of urban built environments (see also Hackworth and Smith 2001). On the other hand, the conditions for promoting and maintaining economic competitiveness were reconceptualized by many urban political and economic elites to include diverse administrative, social, and ecological criteria (Jessop this volume; see also Harloe 2001). The institutionally destructive neoliberalisms of the 1980s were thus apparently superseded by qualitatively new forms of neoliberal localization that actively addressed the problem of establishing nonmarket forms of coordination and cooperation through which to sustain the accumulation process (Gough this volume; Peck and Tickell this volume).

Under these circumstances, the neoliberal project of institutional creation is no longer oriented simply towards the promotion of market-driven capitalist growth; it is also oriented towards the establishment of new flanking mechanisms and modes of crisis displacement through which to insulate powerful economic actors from the manifold failures of the market, the state, and governance that are persistently generated within a neoliberal political framework (Jones and Ward this volume). Just as crucially, these mutations have also entailed a number of significant institutional realignments at the urban scale, including: (a) the establishment of cooperative business-led networks in local politics; (b) the mobilization of new forms of local economic development policy that foster interfirm cooperation and industrial clustering; (c) the deployment of community-based programs to alleviate social exclusion; (d) the promotion of new forms of coordination and inter-organizational networking among previously distinct spheres of local state intervention; and (e) the creation of new regional institutions to promote metropolitan-wide place-marketing and intergovernmental coordination (see Gough this volume;

Jessop this volume; Jones and Ward this volume; Leitner and Sheppard this volume).

Clearly, then, as this schematic discussion indicates, the creative destruction of institutional space at the urban scale does not entail a linear transition from a generic model of the "welfare city" towards a new model of the "neoliberal city." Rather, these multifaceted processes of local institutional change involve a contested, trial-and-error searching process in which neoliberal strategies are being mobilized in place-specific forms and combinations in order to confront some of the many regulatory problems that have afflicted advanced capitalist cities during the post-1970s period. However, as several contributors to this volume aptly demonstrate, even in the contemporary "roll-out" phase, neoliberal strategies of localization severely exacerbate many of the regulatory problems they ostensibly aspire to resolve—such as economic stagnation, unemployment, sociospatial polarization, and uneven development—leading in turn to unpredictable mutations of those very strategies and the institutional spaces in which they are deployed (see Jones and Ward this volume; Keil this volume; MacLeod this volume). Consequently, the manifold forms and pathways of neoliberal localization discussed in this volume must be viewed, not as coherent, sustainable solutions to the regulatory problems of post-1970s capitalism, but rather as deeply contradictory restructuring strategies that are significantly destabilizing inherited landscapes of urban governance and socioeconomic regulation throughout the older industrialized world.

Conclusion: From Neoliberalized Cities to the Urbanization of Neoliberalism?

It would appear, then, that cities are not merely localized arenas in which broader global or national projects of neoliberal restructuring unfold. On the contrary, as all of the contributions to this volume indicate, cities have become increasingly central to the reproduction, mutation, and continual reconstitution of neoliberalism itself during the last two decades. Indeed, it might be argued that a marked urbanization of neoliberalism has been occurring during this period, as cities have become strategic targets for an increasingly broad range of neoliberal policy experiments, institutional innovations, and politico-ideological projects. Under these conditions, cities have become the incubators for many of the major political and ideological strategies through which the dominance of neoliberalism is being maintained (see Smith this volume).

The causes, trajectories, and ramifications of this urbanization of neoliberalism remain a matter of intense discussion and debate among critical geographers and other radical scholars. The contributions to this volume may therefore be interpreted on at least two different levels: first, as attempts to document the manifold ways in which cities have figured in the reproduction and transformation of neoliberalism; and second, as attempts to analyze the complex, confusing, and often highly contradictory implications of this ongoing neoliberalization of urban political-economic space. While the contributions represent a range of theoretical, thematic, and political perspectives, they share a common concern: to decode the leaner and meaner urban geographies that have emerged throughout the older industrialized world during the last three decades. It is hoped that such critical decodings may also, in some modest way, help open up new perspectives for imagining and ultimately implementing strategies for pushing back the current neoliberal offensive, both at the urban scale and beyond.

At the present time, it remains to be seen whether the powerful contradictions inherent within the current urbanized formation of roll-out neoliberalism will provide openings for more progressive, radical democratic reappropriations of city space, or whether, by contrast, neoliberal agendas will be entrenched still further within the underlying institutional structures of urban governance. Should this latter outcome occur, we have every reason to anticipate the crystallization of still leaner and meaner urban geographies in which cities engage aggressively in mutually destructive place-marketing policies, in which transnational capital is permitted to opt out from supporting local social reproduction, and in which the power of urban citizens to influence the basic conditions of their everyday lives is increasingly undermined. As we contemplate this rather grim scenario of a neoliberalized urban authoritarianism, Harvey's (1989:16) suggestion from over a decade ago remains as urgently relevant as ever to contemporary struggles to work towards alternative urban futures, grounded upon the priorities of radical democracy, social justice, and grassroots empowerment:

> The problem is to devise a geopolitical strategy of interurban linkage that mitigates interurban competition and shifts political horizons away from the locality and into a more generalisable challenge to capitalist uneven development ... [A] critical perspective on urban entrepreneurialism indicates not only its negative impacts but its potentiality for transformation into a progressive urban corporatism, armed with a keen geopolitical sense of how to build alliances and linkages across space in such a way as to mitigate if not challenge the hegemonic dynamic of capitalist accumulation to dominate the historical geography of social life.

Acknowledgments

In writing this essay, we have benefited from discussions with a number of friends and colleagues, including Jamie Gough, Bob Jessop,

Martin Jones, Gordon MacLeod, Jamie Peck, and Kevin Ward. We would also like to express our gratitude to all of the participants in the Chicago Conference on Neoliberalism and the City for their critical engagement with these ideas. For helpful comments on earlier drafts of this essay, we are grateful to Margit Mayer and Loïc Wacquant. Needless to say, we assume full responsibility for all remaining errors of fact and interpretation.

Endnotes

[1] The utopian visions of competitive, self-regulating markets that are propagated within neoliberal ideology are situated, quite literally, "no place": the law of the market is presumed to operate in the same way, and with essentially the same effects, no matter where it is unleashed, leading in turn to economic stability, convergence, and equilibrium. In stark contrast, as we argue in more detail below, actually existing neoliberalisms are always embedded within inherited frameworks of institutional organization, political-economic regulation, and sociopolitical struggle that decisively shape the forms of restructuring that are subsequently induced.

References

Aglietta M (1979) *A Theory of Capitalist Regulation: The US Experience*. New York: Verso

Altvater E (1992) Fordist and post-Fordist international division of labor and monetary regimes. In M Storper and A J Scott (eds) *Pathways to Industrialization and Regional Development* (pp 21–45). New York: Routledge

Amin S (1997) *Capitalism in the Age of Globalization*. London: Zed

Bourdieu P (1998) *Acts of Resistance: Against the Tyranny of the Market*. New York: Free Press

Boyer R and Saillard Y (eds) (1995) *Théorie de la régulation: l'état des savoirs*. Paris: La Decouverte

Brenner N (2001) *Entrepreneurial Cities, "Glocalizing" States and the New Politics of Scale: Rethinking the Political Geographies of Urban Governance in Western Europe*. Working Paper 76a/76b. Cambridge, MA: Center for European Studies, Harvard University

Castells M (1972) *La question urbaine*. Paris: Maspero

Cheshire P and Gordon I (1996) Territorial competition and the predictability of collective (in)action. *International Journal of Urban and Regional Research* 20(3):383–399

Duncan S and Goodwin M (1987) *The Local State and Uneven Development*. London: Polity Press

Eisenschitz A and Gough J (1993) *The Politics of Local Economic Policy: The Problems and Possibilities of Local Initiative*. Basingstoke: Macmillian

Gill S (1992) Economic globalization and the internationalization of authority: Limits and contradictions. *Geoforum* 23(3):269–283

Gill S (1995) Globalisation, market civilisation and disciplinary neoliberalism. *Millennium* 24:399–423

Hackworth J and Smith N (2001) The changing state of gentrification. *Tijdschrift voor Economische en Sociale Geografie* 92(4):464–477

Harloe M (2001) Social justice and the city: The new "liberal formulation." *International Journal of Urban and Regional Research* 25(4):889–897

Harvey D (1982) *The Limits to Capital*. Chicago: University of Chicago Press

Harvey D (1989) From managerialism to entrepreneurialism: The transformation in urban governance in late capitalism. *Geografiska Annaler* 71B:3–17

Hudson R (2001) *Producing Places*. New York: Guilford Press

Isin E (1998) Governing Toronto without government: Liberalism and neoliberalism. *Studies in Political Economy* 56:169–191

Jessop B (1989) Conservative regimes and the transition to post-Fordism: The cases of Great Britain and West Germany. In M Gottdiener and N Komninos (eds) *Capitalist Development and Crisis Theory* (pp 261–299). New York: St. Martin's Press

Jessop B (1992) Fordism and post-Fordism: A critical reformulation. In M Storper and A J Scott (eds) *Pathways to Industrialization and Regional Development* (pp 46–69). New York: Routledge

Jessop B (1994) Post-Fordism and the state. In A Amin (ed) *Post-Fordism: A Reader* (pp 251–279). Oxford: Blackwell

Jessop B (1999) Narrating the future of the national economy and the national state: Remarks on remapping regulation and reinventing governance. In G Steinmetz (ed) *State/Culture: State Formation after the Cultural Turn* (pp 378–405). Ithaca, NY: Cornell University Press

Jessop B (2000) The crisis of the national spatiotemporal fix and the ecological dominance of globalizing capitalism. *International Journal of Urban and Regional Research* 24:323–360

Jessop B and Stones R (1992) Old city and new times: Economic and political aspects of deregulation. In L Budd and S Whimster (eds) *Global Finance and Urban Living* (pp 171–192). Routledge: London

Lefebvre H [1974] (1991) *The Production of Space*. London: Blackwell

Leitner H and Sheppard E. (1998) Economic uncertainty, interurban competition and the efficacy of entrepreneurialism. In T Hall and P Hubbard (eds) *The Entrepreneurial City* (pp 285–308). Chichester: Wiley

Lipietz A (1987) *Mirages and Miracles: The Crisis of Global Fordism*. London: Verso

Lipietz A (1988) Reflections on a tale: The Marxist foundations of the concepts of regulation and accumulation. *Studies in Political Economy* 26:7–36

Lipietz A (1992) A regulationist approach to the future of urban ecology. *Capitalism, Nature, Socialism* 3(3):101–110

Lipietz A (1994) The national and the regional: Their autonomy vis-à-vis the capitalist world crisis. In R Palan and B Gills (eds) *Transcending the State-Global Divide* (pp 23–44). Boulder: Lynne Rienner Publishers

Lipietz A (1996) Warp, woof, and regulation: A tool for social science. In G Benko and U Strohmayer (eds) *Space and Social Theory* (pp 250–283). Cambridge, MA: Blackwell

MacKinnon D (2001) Regulating regional spaces: State agencies and the production of governance in the Scottish highlands. *Environment and Planning A* 33(5): 823–844

Massey D (1985) *Spatial Divisions of Labour*. London: Macmillan

Moody K (1997) *Workers in a Lean World*. New York: Verso

Peck J (1998) Geographies of governance: TECs and the neo-liberalisation of "local interests." *Space & Polity* 2(1):5–31

Peck J and Tickell A (1994) Searching for a new institutional fix: The after-Fordist crisis and global-local disorder. In A Amin (ed) *Post-Fordism: A Reader* (pp 280–315). Oxford: Blackwell

Peck J and Tickell A (1995) The social regulation of uneven development: "Regulatory deficit," England's South East and the collapse of Thatcherism. *Environment and Planning A* 27(1):15–40

Petit P (1999) Structural forms and growth regimes of the post-Fordist era. *Review of Social Economy* LVII(2): 220–243

Rhodes M (1995) "Subversive liberalism": market integration, globalization and the European welfare state. *Journal of European Public Policy* 2(3):384–406
Smith N (1984) *Uneven Development*. Oxford: Blackwell
Storper M and Walker R (1989) *The Capitalist Imperative: Territory, Technology and Industrial Growth*. London: Blackwell
Swyngedouw E (1992a) Territorial organization and the space/technology nexus. *Transactions, Institute of British Geographers* 17:417–433
Swyngedouw E (1992b) The Mammon quest: "Glocalisation," interspatial competition and the monetary order: The construction of new scales. In M Dunford and G Kafkalas (eds) *Cities and Regions in the New Europe* (pp 39–62). London: Belhaven Press
Swyngedouw E (1997) Neither global nor local: "Glocalization" and the politics of scale. In K Cox (ed) *Spaces of Globalization* (pp 137–166). New York: Guilford

Neil Brenner is an Assistant Professor of Sociology and Metropolitan Studies at New York University. He is currently writing a monograph entitled *New State Spaces: Urban Restructuring and State Rescaling in Western Europe*. His research and teaching focus on critical urban studies, state theory and sociospatial theory.

Nik Theodore is an Assistant Professor in the Urban Planning and Policy Program and is Director of the Center for Urban Economic Development at the University of Illinois at Chicago. His research focuses on labor-market restructuring, urban inequality, contingent work, and employment policy.

Chapter 2
Neoliberalizing Space

Jamie Peck and Adam Tickell

This paper revisits the question of the political and theoretical status of neoliberalism, making the case for a process-based analysis of "neoliberalization." Drawing on the experience of the heartlands of neoliberal discursive production, North America and Western Europe, it is argued that the transformative and adaptive capacity of this far-reaching political-economic project has been repeatedly underestimated. Amongst other things, this calls for a close reading of the historical and geographical (re)constitution of the process of neoliberalization and of the variable ways in which different "local neoliberalisms" are embedded within wider networks and structures of neoliberalism. The paper's contribution to this project is to establish a stylized distinction between the destructive and creative moments of the process of neoliberalism—which are characterized in terms of "roll-back" and "roll-out" neoliberalism, respectively—and then to explore some of the ways in which neoliberalism, in its changing forms, is playing a part in the reconstruction of extralocal relations, pressures, and disciplines.

Neoliberalism seems to be everywhere. This mode of free-market economic theory, manufactured in Chicago and vigorously marketed through principal sales offices in Washington DC, New York, and London, has become the dominant ideological rationalization for globalization and contemporary state "reform." What began as a starkly utopian intellectual movement was aggressively politicized by Reagan and Thatcher in the 1980s before acquiring a more technocratic form in the self-styled "Washington consensus" of the 1990s. Neoliberalism has provided a kind of operating framework or "ideological software" for competitive globalization, inspiring and imposing far-reaching programs of state restructuring and rescaling across a wide range of national and local contexts. Crucially, its premises also established the ground rules for global lending agencies operating in the crisis-torn economies of Asia, Africa, Latin America, and the former Soviet Union, where new forms of "free-market" *dirigisme* have been constructed. Indeed, proselytizing the virtues of free trade, flexible labor, and active individualism has become so commonplace in contemporary politics—from Washington to Moscow—that they hardly even warrant a comment in many quarters.

The new religion of neoliberalism combines a commitment to the extension of markets and logics of competitiveness with a profound antipathy to all kinds of Keynesian and/or collectivist strategies. The constitution and extension of competitive forces is married with aggressive forms of state downsizing, austerity financing, and public-service "reform." And while rhetorically antistatist, neoliberals have proved adept at the (mis)use of state power in the pursuit of these goals. For its longstanding advocates in the Anglo-American world, neoliberalism represents a kind of self-imposed disciplinary code, calling for no less than monastic restraint. For its converts in the global south, neoliberalism assumes the status of the Latinate church in medieval Europe, externally imposing unbending rule regimes enforced by global institutions and policed by local functionaries. Meanwhile, if not subject to violent repression, nonbelievers are typically dismissed as apostate defenders of outmoded institutions and suspiciously collectivist social rights.

Although Margaret Thatcher was never right to claim that "there is no alternative" to the neoliberal vision of a free economy and a minimalist state, two decades later the global hegemony of this mode of political rationality means that the burden of proof has shifted: neoliberalism is no longer a dream of Chicago economists or a night-mare in the imaginations of leftist conspiracy theorists; it has become a commonsense of the times. Hence Bourdieu and Wacquant's (2001:2) portrayal of neoliberalism as a "new planetary vulgate" and Beck's (2000:122) characterization of the same nebulous phenomena as an ideological "thought virus." It is revealing, perhaps, that such resorts to metaphor are not unusual in attempts to develop proximate conceptualizations of neoliberalism, the power of which would seem to have become as compelling as it is intangible. Confronted with an apparently extant neoliberal hegemony, the new challenges are simultaneously theoretical and political. They concern the ways that neoliberalism is conceived and characterized, how it is imposed and reproduced, and the identification of its command centers and its flanks of vulnerability.

Attempts to conceive neoliberalism in specifically geographical terms also call for a careful mapping of the neoliberal offensive—both in its heartlands and in its zones of extension—together with a dis-cussion of how "local" institutional forms of neoliberalism relate to its more general (ideological) character. This means walking a line of sorts between producing, on the one hand, overgeneralized accounts of a monolithic and omnipresent neoliberalism, which tend to be insufficiently sensitive to its local variability and complex internal constitution, and on the other hand, excessively concrete and contin-gent analyses of (local) neoliberal strategies, which are inadequately attentive to the substantial connections and necessary characteristics of neoliberalism as an extralocal project (see Larner 2000). It is our contention here that critical discussions of neoliberalism have tended to lean in the latter direction of closely specified, institutionally contingent accounts, typically focused on more concrete forms of neoliberalism, such as particular Thatcherite restructuring strategies. While conscious of the risks of overreaching, we seek here a preliminary way to push out from this useful starting point to explore some of the more generic and abstract features of the neoliberalization process. Our explicit focus is on the neoliberal heartlands of North America and Western Europe, which have been at the same time its principal centers of discursive production and sites of intensive institutional reconstruction. Paradoxically, perhaps, critical analyses of the extralocal characteristics of neoliberalism have been somewhat underdeveloped in these its "home" spaces, in contrast to the compelling work that has been carried out on the extension of neoliberalism into the second and third world (see Bond 2000; DeMartino 2000; Peet with Hartwick 1999; Veltmeyer, Petras and Vieux 1997; Weiss 1998).

Like the globalization rhetorics with which they are elided, discourses of neoliberalism have proved to be so compelling because, in representing the world of market rules as a state of nature, their prescriptions have a self-actualizing quality. Even as they misdescribe the social world, discourses of globalization and neoliberalism seek to remake it in their own image (Bourdieu 1998; Piven 1995). Discourses of neoliberalism are "strong discourses" in part by virtue of this self-actualizing nature and in part because of their self-evident alignment with the primary contours of contemporary political-economic power.

> [T]his initially desocialized and dehistoricized "theory" has, now more than ever, the means of *making itself true* ... For neoliberal discourse is not like others. Like psychiatric discourse in the asylum ... it is a "strong discourse" which is so strong and so hard to fight because it has behind it all the powers of a world of power relations which it helps to make as it is, in particular by orienting the economic choices of those who dominate economic relations and so adding its own—specifically symbolic—force to those power relations. (Bourdieu 1998:95; emphasis in original)

There are, in fact, many parallels between analytical treatments of globalism and those of neoliberalism. Both have been associated with a mode of exogenized thinking in which globalism/neoliberalism is presented as a naturalized, external "force." Both ascribe quasiclimatic, extraterrestrial qualities to apparently disembodied, "out there" forces, which are themselves typically linked to alleged tendencies towards homogenization, leveling out, and convergence. And both have attributed to them immense and unambiguous causal efficacy: while conservative commentators emphasize the (ostensibly ubiquitous) benign effects of globalization, critics focus instead on the (just as pervasive) malign effects of neoliberalism. Yet their common flaw is that they have tended to naturalize and exogenize their object of study—be this in the form of an all-powerful globalization process or the all-encompassing politics of neoliberalism. Certainly, critical analyses do have the virtue of underscoring the inescapably *political* character of the globalization project and the hegemonic position of neoliberalism in global agencies and discourses. However, there is more to be done, both theoretically and empirically, on the specification and exploration of different processes of neoliberalization. This would need to take account of the ways in which ideologies of neoliberalism are themselves produced and reproduced through institutional forms and political action, since "actually existing" neoliberalisms are always (in some way or another) hybrid or composite structures (see Larner 2000). On the other hand, though, analyses of neoliberalism in general cannot afford to reduce this multifaceted process to its concrete manifestations.

With the benefits of hindsight, and particularly in light of neo-liberalism's "long boom" of the 1990s, our objective here is to explore the (subtly transformed) process of neoliberal*ization* in the context of recent history, and in doing so to refine, develop, and modestly revise the received conception of neoliberal*ism*. Taking certain cues from the globalization debate, we propose a processual conception of neo-liberalization as both an "out there" and an "in here" phenomenon whose effects are necessarily variegated and uneven, but the incidence and diffusion of which may present clues to a pervasive "metalogic" (Amin 1997; Dicken, Peck and Tickell 1997). Like globalization, neoliberalization should be understood as a process, not an end-state. By the same token, it is also contradictory, it tends to provoke counter-tendencies, and it exists in historically and geographically contingent forms. Analyses of this process should therefore focus especially sharply on *change*—on shifts in systems and logics, dominant patterns of restructuring, and so forth—rather than on binary and/or static comparisons between a past state and its erstwhile successor. It also follows that analyses of neoliberalization must be sensitive to its con-tingent nature—hence the nontrivial differences, both theoretically and politically, between the actually existing neoliberalisms of, say, Blair's Britain, Fox's Mexico, or Bush's America. While processes of neoliberalization are clearly at work in all these diverse situations, we should not expect this to lead to a simple convergence of outcomes, a neoliberalized end of history and geography.

The process of neoliberalization, then, is neither monolithic in form nor universal in effect. However, in the course of the last quarter-century there have been significant *internal* shifts in its institutional form, its political rationality, and its economic and social consequences. Focusing on the changing situation in the neoliberal "heartlands," we wish to outline—and simultaneously problematize—the complex evolution that has taken place, from the experimental proto-neoliberalisms of the 1970s through the constitution of neoliberalism as an explicit political-economic project during the 1980s to the "deep neoliberalisms" of the past decade. Perhaps the most controversial aspect of this process of complex evolution concerns the status of neo-liberalism as a *regulatory* "project" or "regime," given the (contested and uneven) shift that has taken place from the Thatcher/Reagan era of assault and retrenchment to the more recent experience of normalized neoliberalism which has been associated with, inter alia, the technocratic embedding of routines of neoliberal governance, the aggressive extension of neoliberal institutions and their seeming robust-ness even in the face of repeated crises, and the continuing erosion of pockets of political and institutional resistance to neoliberal hegemony, including the "soft neoliberalisms" most clearly epitomized by the Third Way.

In short, in this North Atlantic zone at least, there seems to have been a shift from the pattern of deregulation and dismantlement so dominant during the 1980s, which might be characterized as "roll-back neoliberalism," to an emergent phase of active state-building and regulatory reform—an ascendant moment of "roll-out neoliberalism." In the course of this shift, the agenda has gradually moved from one preoccupied with the active *destruction and discreditation* of Keynesian-welfarist and social-collectivist institutions (broadly defined) to one focused on the purposeful *construction and consolidation* of neoliberalized state forms, modes of governance, and regulatory relations. It is this more recent pattern of institutional and regulatory restructuring, which we characterize here as a radical, emergent com-bination of neoliberalized economic management and authoritarian state forms, that demands both analytical and political attention. This may represent a critical conjuncture, since it reflects *both* the contradictions/limitations of earlier forms of neoliberalization *and* the attainment of a more aggressive/proactive form of contemporary neo-liberalization. In the process, forms of "shallow" neoliberalization—during the Thatcher/Reagan years—that were understood by many at the time as a moment of destructive and reactionary "antiregulation" (see Peck and Tickell 1994a) might now need to be confronted as a more formidable and robust pattern of proactive statecraft and per-vasive "metaregulation." Granted, it may still be (politically) inappro-priate to regard the contemporary manifestation of neoliberalization as a form of regulatory "settlement," but its multifaceted normaliza-tion during the 1990s and beyond surely calls for more sharply focused analyses both of actually existing neoliberalisms and of the disciplinary force-fields in which they are embedded. In its diffuse, dispersed, technocratic, and institutionalized form, neoliberalism has spawned a free-market in social regression, but simultaneously it is becoming vulnerable—from the inside as well as the outside—in wholly new ways.

From Jungle Laws to Market Rules

In an earlier attempt to understand neoliberalism, we presented it as the political essence of the (after-Fordist) crisis, a form of "jungle law" that broke out in the context of the exhaustion of the postwar social contract (Peck and Tickell 1994a; Tickell and Peck 1996). Shaped by the experiences of the "Thatcher decade" (Jessop et al 1988; Overbeek 1990), many of the ramifications of which were genuinely international in scope, this conception of neoliberalism was antagonistic to those analyses that presented the deregulation and retrenchment of the 1980s as the precursor to some kind of "post-Fordist" mode of social regulation (see Jessop 1989), contending that the politics of neoliberalism were—by definition—disorderly and destructive. Under such conditions, social relations were being reconstituted in the image of a brutal reading of competitive-market imperatives, while their geographical corollary—interlocal relations— were also being remade in competitive, commodified, and monetized terms, with far-reaching consequences for local political conditions and regulatory settlements (whether neoliberal or not).

Thus, in contrast to the Fordist-Keynesian golden age, when the national-state became the principal anchoring point for institutions of (gendered and racialized) social integration and (limited) macro-economic management, neoliberalization was inducing localities to compete by cutting social and environmental regulatory standards and eroding the political and institutional collectivities upon which more progressive settlements had been constructed in the past (and might again be in future). In this context, our earlier analysis portrayed the 1980s and early 1990s as a period of institutional searching and experimentation within restrictive (and ultimately destructive) neoliberal parameters. Extralocal rule regimes at this time seemed critically to undermine the potential of non-neoliberal projects at the local scale, while engendering a lemming-like rush towards urban entrepreneurialism, which itself would only serve to facilitate, encourage, and even publicly subsidize the accelerated mobility of circulating capital and resources (see Harvey 1989). As if to add insult to injury, regimes of public investment and finance, too, would increasingly come to mimic these marketized conditions (see Cochrane, Peck and Tickell 1996; Jessop, Peck and Tickell 1999).

For all the implied pessimism of this analysis, however, a decade ago it appeared to us that neoliberalism was unsustainable. In both its American and British heartlands, the early 1990s witnessed significant economic retrenchment, as the irrationalities and externalities of fundamentalist neoliberalism began to take their toll. Well documented at the time were the tendencies, for example, to exacerbate and deepen the macroeconomic cycle, to license short-termist, plundering strategies on the part of competing capitals, to widen social, economic, and spatial inequalities, to undermine the production of public goods and collective services, to degrade social and environmental resources, to constrain and weaken socially progressive alternatives to (or even conservative ameliorations of) market liberalism, and so forth. The transatlantic recessions of the early 1990s, while certainly also having "local" causes, seemed at the time to be vivid precursors of these inherent and substantially "internal" crisis tendencies (Peck and Tickell 1995). The politics of the crisis, it seemed, were working their natural course.

The flexible recessions of the early 1990s and the mounting popular unease with the process of state withdrawal—which were to fatally undermine the Thatcher/Major and Reagan/Bush I projects—appeared, then, to be highlighting at least two key essences of neoliberalism. First, the reactive politics of the after-Fordist downswing seemed to lack the capacity for sustainable reproduction in the medium term. Second, they were evidently more concerned with the *de(con)struction* of "anticompetitive" institutions like labor unions, social-welfare programs, and interventionist arms of the governmental apparatus than with the purposeful *construction* of alternative regulatory structures. In the process of this phase of active deconstruction, however, the neoliberal offensive also helped to usher in, and to legitimize and enforce, a new regime of highly competitive interlocal relations, such that just about all local social settlements were becoming tendentially subject in one way or another to the disciplinary force of neoliberalized spatial relations. The conclusion that we drew at the time was that—in the absence of a more stable, socially/spatially redistributive, and supportive extralocal framework —the neoliberal constitution of competitive relations between localities and regions placed real limits on the practical potential of localized or "bottom-up" political action (Amin 1999). In the asymmetrical scale politics of neoliberalism, local institutions and actors were being given responsibility without power, while international institutions and actors were gaining power without responsibility: a form of regulatory dumping was occurring at the local scale, while macrorule regimes were being remade in regressive and marketized ways. This represented a deeply hostile macro- or extralocal environment, one that even the most robust of progressive localisms seemed ill placed to overturn through unilateral action. So, while there was (and is) certainly a crucial role beyond mere amelioration for progressive projects at the local scale, it seemed that any adequate response to neoliberalism had to be framed in substantially *extra*local terms. Only this could stall and circumvent the *neoliberalization of interlocal relations*—a more nebulous and a more daunting adversary.

A fundamental problem for progressive localisms—such as, for example, the Scandinavian welfare state or "high-road" regional economic initiatives—was that they did not confront neoliberalism on a level playing field of "regime competition," because neoliberalism always represented more than "just" an alternative regulatory project or program. It was not that neoliberalism was simply a creature of, say, California or the Southeast of England (although these were clearly amongst its strongholds), but that the very social and spatial relations in which such regions were embedded had *themselves* become deeply neoliberalized. Neoliberalism was therefore qualitatively different because it inhabited not only institutions and places but also *the spaces in between*. In other words, neoliberalism was playing a decisive role in constructing the "rules" of interlocal competition by shaping the very metrics by which regional competitiveness, public policy, corporate performance, or social productivity are measured—value for money, the bottom line, flexibility, shareholder value, performance rating, social capital, and so on. Neoliberalism therefore represented a form of regulation of sorts, but not a form commensurate with, say, the Keynesian-welfarism that preceded it in many (though not all) cases. In Gough's (1996:392) terms, neoliberalism was a form of "regulation by value," one that he sought explicitly to contrast with our more explicit focus on its manifest *illogics*. While there may have been more than a hint of wishful thinking on our part in the denigration of the Thatcherite project (Peck and Tickell 1995), our reading did emphasize the macrolevel disciplinary effects of neoliberalism, which were clearly part of the "logic" of the system, even whilst we may have been somewhat reluctant to acknowledge it as such (Peck and Tickell 1994b). In the final analysis, though, neoliberalism proved too robust to be brought down by the Anglo-American recessions of the early 1990s, or indeed by the Asian meltdown later in the decade. Instead, these economic crises proved to be important moments in its ongoing transformation.

Mutations of Neoliberalism

Although neoliberalism privileges the unitary logic of the market while advocating supposedly universal cures and one-best-way policy strategies, it is in reality much more variegated than such self-representations suggest. Neoliberalism remains variegated in character, certainly when assessed according to criteria like the scale and scope of state intervention, forms of capital and labor market regulation, the constitution of institutions of social regulation, patterns of political resistance and political incorporation, and so forth. However, as there are evidently powerful family resemblances, adequate conceptualizations must be attentive to *both* the local peculiarities *and* the generic features of neoliberalism. While not wishing to downplay local and national differences in the constitution of the neoliberal project, we focus here on some of the broader patterns and connections evident in the process of neoliberalization as it has taken shape in the North Atlantic zone. More specifically, we want to draw attention to what seem to us to be important *historical* shifts in the constitution of the neoliberal project in this transnational space (see also Tickell and Peck forthcoming).

The first of these shifts occurred in the late 1970s, as neoliberalism underwent a transformation from the abstract intellectualism of Hayek and Friedman to the state-authored restructuring projects of Thatcher and Reagan. This can be characterized as a movement from "proto-" to "roll-back" neoliberalism: a shift from the philosophical project of the early 1970s (when the primary focus was on the restoration of a form of free-market thinking within the economics profession and its subsequent [re]constitution as the theoretical high ground) to the era of neoliberal conviction politics during the 1980s (when state power was mobilized behind marketization and deregulation projects, aimed particularly at the central institutions of the Keynesian-welfarist settlement). The backdrop to this shift was provided by the macroeconomic crisis conditions of the 1970s, the blame for which was unambiguously laid at the door of Keynesian financial regulation, unions, corporatist planning, state ownership, and "overregulated" labor markets. In this context, the neoliberal text—freeing up markets, restoring the "right to manage," asserting individualized "opportunity rights" over social entitlements—allowed politicians the right to be both conservative and radical. It was they, not their social-democratic adversaries, who were insisting on the need for root-and-branch change; and while labor unions, social advocates, and left-of-center parties were often forced to defend (apparently failing) institutions, neoliberals made the argument for a clean break.

The second neoliberal transformation occurred in the early 1990s, when the shallow neoliberalisms of Thatcher and Reagan encountered their institutional and political limits as evidence of the perverse economic consequences and pronounced social externalities of narrowly marketcentric forms of neoliberalism became increasingly difficult to contest. However, the outcome was not implosion but reconstitution, as the neoliberal project itself gradually metamorphosed into more socially interventionist and ameliorative forms, epitomized by the Third-Way contortions of the Clinton and Blair administrations. This most recent phase might be portrayed as one of "roll-out" neoliberalism, underlining the sense in which new forms of institution-building and governmental intervention have been licensed within the (broadly defined) neoliberal project. No longer concerned narrowly with the mobilization and extension of markets (and market logics), neoliberalism is increasingly associated with the political foregrounding of new modes of "social" and penal policy-making, concerned specifically with the aggressive reregulation, disciplining, and containment of those marginalized or dispossessed by the neoliberalization of the 1980s. Commenting on this shift in the means and methods of neoliberalization, Wacquant (1999:323) pointedly observes that

> [t]he same parties, politicians, pundits, and professors who yesterday mobilized, with readily observable success, in support of "less government" as concerns the prerogatives of capital and the utilization of labor, are now demanding, with every bit as much fervor, *more* government" to mask and contain the deleterious social consequences, in the lower regions of social space, of the deregulation of wage labor and the deterioration of social protection.

This does not mean, of course, that economic policy concerns have somehow slipped off the agenda, but rather that—as modes of neoliberal economic management have been effectively normalized—the frontier of active policymaking has shifted and the process of state-building has been reanimated. More now than merely a deregulatory political mindset or a kind of ideological software, neoliberalism is increasingly concerned with the roll-out of new forms of institutional "hardware." In the neoliberal heartlands, this is associated with a striking coexistence of technocratic economic management and invasive social policies. Neoliberal processes of economic management—rooted in the manipulation of interest rates, the maintenance of noninflationary growth, and the extension of the "rule" of free trade abroad and flexible labor markets at home—are increasingly technocratic in form and therefore superficially "depoliticized," acquiring the privileged status of a taken-for-granted or foundational policy orientation. Meanwhile, a deeply interventionist agenda is emerging around "social" issues like crime, immigration, policing, welfare reform, urban order and surveillance, and community regeneration. In these latter spheres, in particular, new technologies of government are being designed and rolled out, new discourses of "reform" are being constructed (often around new policy objectives such as "welfare dependency"), new institutions and modes of delivery are being fashioned, and new social subjectivities are being fostered. In complex simultaneity, these social and penal policy incursions represent both the advancement of the neoliberal project—of extending and bolstering market logics, socializing individualized subjects, and disciplining the noncompliant— and a recognition of sorts that earlier manifestations of this project, rooted in dogmatic deregulation and marketization, clearly had serious limitations and contradictions. Consequently, what we characterize here as "roll-out" neoliberalism reflects a series of politically and institutionally mediated responses to the manifest failings of the Thatcher/Reagan project, formulated in the context of ongoing neo-liberal hegemony in the sphere of economic regulation. In a sense, therefore, it represents *both* the frailty of the neoliberal project *and* its deepening.

This is not the place to explore the historiography of neoliberalism in detail. Instead, we focus on the principal analytical and political implications of this broad movement in relation to neoliberalism's status as a regulatory project, its scalar constitution, and its sub-stantive policy foci. First, with respect to the changing character of neoliberalism as regulatory project, it should be noted that whereas its initial ascendancy during the 1970s was associated with crisis conditions "external" to the project itself, the shifts of the 1990s were substantially triggered by "internal" contradictions and tensions in the project. The macroeconomic turbulence of the 1970s, and the stresses this placed on the central institutions of Keynesian-welfarism, established both the context for neoliberalism's transition from intellectual to state project and the political conditions conducive to a decisive shift to the right. In contrast, the mutations of the 1990s essentially represented responses to previous market, state, and governance failures partly (or even largely) initiated by neoliberalism itself. While it had been ideologically presumed during the 1980s that the spontaneous operation of market forces and disciplines would alone be sufficient to the task of economic regulation as long as government got out of the way, by the 1990s it had become clear that recurrent failures of a quasisystemic nature in areas like transport, food systems, and pollution, and even in financial and labor markets, called for responses outside the narrow repertoire of deregulation and marketization. Hence the deliberate stretching of the neoliberal policy repertoire (and its associated rhetorics) to embrace a range of extramarket forms of governance and regulation. These included, inter alia, the selective appropriation of "community" and nonmarket metrics, the establishment of social-capital discourses and techniques, the incorporation (and underwriting) of local-governance and partnership-based modes of policy development and program delivery in areas like urban regeneration and social welfare, the mobilization of the "little platoons" in the shape of (local) voluntary and faith-based associations in the service of neoliberal goals, and the evolution of invasive, neopaternalist modes of intervention (along with justifications for increased public expenditure) in areas like penal and workfare policy.

Second, these shifts have been accompanied by—and partially achieved through—changes in neoliberalism's scalar constitution. These have involved complex (and often indirect) extensions of national state power, most notably in the steering and management of programs of devolution, localization, and interjurisdictional policy transfer. In welfare reform, for example, the downloading of resources, responsibilities, and risks to local administrations and extrastate agencies has occurred in the context of a close orchestration of the processes of institutional reform and policy steering by national states (Peck 2001). And while some social policies have been (superficially) decentralized and localized, just as compelling have been the movements in economic policy, where issues once deeply politicized (such as interest-rate setting, currency valuation, trade policy, corporate regulation and taxation) have since been variously parlayed into technocratic structures and routinized conventions, absorbed by transnational agencies and metaregulatory frameworks, or exposed to the "markets." At the level of the national state, neoliberalized forms of macro-economic management—based on low inflation, free trade, flexible job markets, regressive taxation, downsized government, and central-bank (relative) autonomy—now constitute the taken-for-granted context for political debate and policy development (Bluestone and Harrison 2000). Meanwhile, international institutions such as the International Monetary Fund (IMF) and the World Trade Organization (WTO) establish and police neoliberalized "rules of the road" that promulgate free(r) trade, free(r) markets, and increasingly unrestricted access to a wide range of markets (including public services under the General Agreement on Trade in Services) to transnational corporations, while potentially more progressive institutions and agreements (the International Labour Organisation, the United Nations Conference on Trade and Development, the Kyoto Protocols) are allowed to wither.

Third, in relation to the substantive foci of neoliberal policies, we draw attention to the twin processes of financialization in the realm of economic policy and activation in the field of social policy. In economic policy, the excesses of roll-back neoliberalism found vivid expressions in the financial crises of the 1990s, which took both geographical (Mexico, Russia, East Asia, Turkey) and institutional (Barings, Long Term Capital, Orange County, Equitable Life) forms. In response, new financial architectures are taking shape, under-girding a type of "global stability" by normalizing Anglo-American rationalities and, paradoxically, creating deeper systemic integration in ways that are seriously procyclical (Tickell 1999; Tickell and Clark 2001). In social policy, the (re)criminalization of poverty, the normal-ization of contingent work, and its enforcement through welfare retrenchment, workfare programming, and active employment policies represent a comprehensive reconstitution of the boundary institutions of the labor market. Following the blue-collar shakeouts of the 1980s and the white-collar downsizings of the 1990s, the attention of policymakers has focused with increasing insistency on the challenges of reproducing regimes of precarious work and mobilizing the poor for low-wage employment. Market discipline, it seems, calls for new modes of state intervention in the form of large-scale incarceration, social surveillance, and a range of microregulatory interventions to ensure persistent "job readiness" (Piven and Cloward 1998).

Of course, these shifts in the macroconstitution of neoliberalism have not been reproduced homogenously across space. In fact, they have been associated with a marked intensification of spatially uneven development, which itself has produced new opportunities for—and challenges to—the neoliberal project. Neoliberalism's persistent vulnerability to regulatory crises and market failures is associated with an ongoing dynamic of discursive adjustment, policy learning, and institutional reflexivity. As long as collateral damage from such break-downs can be minimized, localized, or otherwise displaced across space or scale, it can provide a positive spur to regulatory reinvention. One of neoliberalism's real strengths has been its capacity to capitalize on such conditions. And because little store is set by local loyalties or place commitments in neoliberalized regulatory regimes, which favor mobility over stability and short- over long-term strategies, dynamics of persistent reform and extralocal policy learning assume critical roles in the reconstruction of institutions and the maintenance of legitimacy. Such regimes are characterized, then, by the perpetual reanimation of restless terrains of regulatory restructuring. Thus, the deep neoliberalization of spatial relations represents a cornerstone of the project itself.

Spaces of Neoliberalism

Neoliberalism does indeed seem to be everywhere. And its apparent omnipresence is at the same time a manifestation of and a source of political-economic power. It is no coincidence, in this respect, that viral metaphors are so often deployed in critical analyses of the spread of neoliberalism, because notions of contagion, carrier populations, and susceptibility seem so apposite. Viruses are dangerous, of course, because they spread, and bodies politic—while they may exhibit differing degrees of resistance—are rarely immune to all the strains of neoliberalism. Crucially, any analysis of the diffusion of neoliberalism must pay attention to the nature of these movements *between* sites of incorporation and imposition, because neoliberalism cannot be reduced to an "internal" characteristic of certain institutions or polities; it also exists as an extralocal regime of rules and routines, pressures and penalties. This is not to deny the valuable role of concrete analyses of actually existing neoliberal projects—for example, in regional manifestations such as the Southeast of England (see Allen et al 1998; Peck and Tickell 1995), or in the more nebulous form of putative "reform models" like learning/flexible/networked regions or modes of zero tolerance/workfarist/activist social and penal policy (see Peck and Theodore 2001; Wacquant 1999). Rather, it is to make the point that such analyses can usefully be complemented by explorations of the webs of interlocal and interorganizational relations in which they are embedded. Moreover, these accounts of the structural contexts —which are both a product of and produced by "local" neo-liberalisms—may help to draw attention to the causally substantial connections and telling family resemblances between different forms of neoliberalization.

As David Harvey so persuasively argued of urban entrepreneurial-ism, the serial reproduction of cultural spectacles, enterprise zones, waterfront developments, and privatized forms of local governance is not simply an aggregate outcome of spontaneous local pressures, but reflects the powerful disciplinary effects of interurban competition: "[I]t is by no means clear that even the most progressive urban government can resist [social polarization] when embedded in the logic of capitalist spatial development in which competition seems to operate not as a beneficial hidden hand, but as an external coercive law forcing the lowest common denominator of social responsibility and welfare provision within a competitively organised urban system" (Harvey 1989:12). Because signature cultural events, prestige cor-porate investments, public resources, and good jobs are in such short supply, cities (perhaps the most visibly denuded victims of roll-back neoliberalism) are induced to jump on the bandwagon of urban entrepreneurialism, which they do with varying degrees of enthusiasm and effectiveness. And ultimately, their persistent efforts and sporadic successes only serve to further accelerate the (actual and potential) mobility of capital, employment, and public investment. In selling themselves, cities are therefore actively facilitating and subsidizing the very geographic mobility that first rendered them vulnerable, while also validating and reproducing the extralocal rule systems to which they are (increasingly) subjected (Cochrane, Peck and Tickell 1996). The logic of interurban competition, then, turns cities into accomplices in their own subordination, a process driven—and legitimated—by tales of municipal turnaround and urban renaissance, by little victories and fleeting accomplishments, and ultimately also by the apparent paucity of "realistic" local alternatives. Thus, elite partnerships, mega-events, and corporate seduction become, in effect, both the only games in town *and* the basis of urban subjugation. The public subsidy of zero-sum competition at the interurban scale rests on the economic fallacy that every city can win, shored up by the political reality that no city can afford principled noninvolvement in the game.

Clearly, this regime of accelerated interurban competition was not simply a product of neoliberalism, nor can it be reduced entirely to its logic, but the parallel ascendancy of neoliberalism has been crucial in reinforcing, extending, and normalizing these transurban tendencies towards reflexive and entrepreneurial city governance in (at least) seven ways:

- Neoliberalism promotes and normalizes a "growth-first" approach to urban development, reconstituting social-welfarist arrangements as anticompetitive costs and rendering issues of redistribution and social investment as antagonistic to the overriding objectives of *economic* development. Social-welfarist concerns can only be addressed *after* growth, jobs, and investment have been secured, and even then in no more than a truncated and productivist fashion.
- Neoliberalism rests on a pervasive naturalization of market logics, justifying on the grounds of efficiency and even "fairness" their installation as the dominant metrics of policy evaluation. In this analysis, urban policy measures should anticipate, complement, and in some cases mimic the operation of competitive markets.
- As the ideology of choice for both major funding agencies and "the markets," neoliberalism not only privileges lean government, privatization, and deregulation, but through a combination of competitive regimes of resource allocation, skewed municipal-lending policies, and outright political pressure undermines or forecloses alternative paths of urban development based, for example, on social redistribution, economic rights, or public investment. This produces a neoliberal "lock-in" of public-sector austerity and growth-chasing economic development.
- Neoliberalism licenses an extrospective, reflexive, and aggressive posture on the part of local elites and states, in contrast to the inward-oriented concerns with social welfare and infrastructure provision under the Keynesian era. Today, cities must actively—and responsively—scan the horizon for investment and promotion opportunities, monitoring "competitors" and emulating "best practice," lest they be left behind in this intensifying competitive struggle for the kinds of resources (public and private) that neoliberalism has helped make (more) mobile.
- Despite its language of innovation, learning, and openness, neoliberalism is associated with an extremely narrow urban-policy repertoire based on capital subsidies, place promotion, supply-side intervention, central-city makeovers, and local boosterism. The very familiarity of this cocktail is a reflection both of the coercive pressures on cities to keep up with—or get a step ahead of—the competition and of the limited scope

for genuinely novel local development under a neoliberalized environment.

- Neoliberal regimes are unforgiving in the face of incompetence or noncompliance, punishing cities that fail in the unyielding terms of competitive urbanism through equally unambiguous measures such as malign neglect, exclusion from funding streams, and the replacement of local cadres. Reinforcing these pressures, national and transnational government funds increasingly flow to cities on the basis of economic potential and governance capacity rather than manifest social need, and do so through allocation regimes that are competitively constituted (in contrast to the Keynesian pattern, where resources were secured on basis of social entitlements, bureaucratic channels, or redistributive mechanisms or through the operation of automatic stabilizers). Yet while zones of deeply impacted poverty and social exclusion may have been no-go areas for neoliberals during the 1980s, in its roll-out guise neoliberalism is increasingly penetrating these very places, animated by a set of concerns related to crime, worklessness, welfare dependency, and social breakdown.
- As key sites of economic contradiction, governance failure, and social fall-out, cities find themselves in the front line of *both* hypertrophied after-welfarist statecraft *and* organized resistance to neoliberalization. Regressive welfare reforms and labor-market polarization, for example, are leading to the (re)urbanization of (working and nonworking) poverty, positioning cities at the bleeding edge of processes of punitive-institution building, social surveillance, and authoritarian governance.

Neoliberalization cannot, therefore, be reduced to an outcome or a side effect of this after-Keynesian environment. Instead, it can be seen to have exercised a cumulatively significant and somewhat autonomous influence on the structure and dynamics of interurban competition and intraurban development. This has not been a period in which inherently competitive forces have been spontaneously "liberated" by the state's withdrawal. Rather, neoliberalism's ascendancy has been associated with the political *construction* of markets, coupled with the deliberate extension of competitive logics and privatized management into hitherto relatively socialized spheres. "Entrepreneurial" regimes of urban governance are, therefore, not simply local manifestations of neoliberalism; their simultaneous rise across a wide range of national, political, and institutional contexts suggests a systemic connection with neoliberalization as a *macro* process. In other words, the re-making of the rules of interlocal competition and extralocal resource allocation—or the deep neoliberalization of spatial and scalar relations—fundamentally reflects the far-reaching macropolitical realignment that has taken place since the 1970s. Harvey (1989:15) hints at this in remarking that the managerialist cities of the Keynesian era were rather less exposed to macropressures: "[U]nder conditions of weak interurban competition … urban governance [was rendered] less consistent with the rules of capital accumulation," while in contrast, during the subsequent phase of neoliberal entrepreneurialism, "urban governance has moved more rather than less into line with the naked requirements of capital accumulation." Yet, even stripped of its Keynesian clothing, this underlying capitalist logic does not automatically secure some kind of Hayekian order of competitive urbanism. Instead, the subsequent neoliberal "settlement" had to be *engineered* through explicit forms of political management and intervention and new modes of institution-building designed to extend the neoliberal project, to manage its contradictions, and to secure its ongoing legitimacy.

There is, then, a space for politics here, even if these are tendentially neoliberalized politics, or limited forms of resistance to this ascendant (dis)order. And where there is politics there is always the scope for geographical unevenness and path-transforming change. Somewhat paradoxically, given the strength of the coercive extralocal forces mobilized and channeled by neoliberalism, the outcome is not homogeneity, but a constantly shifting landscape of experimentation, restructuring, (anti)social learning, technocratic policy transfer, and partial emulation. Even if the overriding dynamics of neoliberalized spatial development involve regulatory undercutting, state downsizing, and races to the bottom, the outcomes of this process are more variegated than is typically assumed to be the case. Rather than some rapidly accomplished "bottoming out" of minimalist regulatory settlements, it tends to result in ongoing institutional restructuring and externally leveraged "reform" around new sets of axes.

While earlier manifestations of spatial restructuring may indeed have reflected the privileged place of destructive, "antiregulatory" moments of the neoliberalization process (emphasized in Peck and Tickell 1994a), the rather different reading outlined here has intentionally drawn attention to the complex ways in which these logics of deregulation became systematically entwined, during the 1990s, with the *roll out* of neoliberalized state forms (themselves partly the outcome of previous tensions and contradictions in the early neoliberalist project). Such forms of "deep" neoliberalization and post-Keynesian statecraft are associated with an especially restless landscape of urban competition, narrowly channeled innovation, and policy emulation, as the processes of institutional searching that have become such compelling features of the after-Fordist era have been (increasingly?) been played out at the urban and subnational scales (see Brenner 1999; Tickell and Peck 1995).

Even if the resultant repertoire of restructuring strategies is hardly more inspiring now than it was in the early 1990s—following the partial accommodations that have been engineered with various social capital, associative economy, Third-Way, and social economy approaches —it must be acknowledged that neoliberalism has demonstrated a capacity variously to spawn, absorb, appropriate, or morph with a range of local institutional (re)forms in ways that speak to its *creatively* destructive character (see Brenner and Theodore [paper] this volume). Certainly this potential has been recognized for some time, whether in the regulationist emphasis on "chance discoveries" (Jessop 2001; Lipietz 1987; Peck and Tickell 1994a), or indeed in Harvey's (1989:15) original formulation of the urban entrepreneurialism thesis:

> Competition for investments and jobs ... will presumably generate all kinds of firmaments concerning how best to capture and stimulate development under particular local conditions ... From the stand-point of long-run capital accumulation, it is essential that different paths and different packages of political, social and entrepreneurial endeavours get explored. Only in this way is it possible for a dynamic and revolutionary social system, such as capitalism, to discover new forms and modes of social and political regulation suited to new forms and paths of capital accumulation.

In contrast to the generalized skepticism that was evident a decade or so ago concerning the potentially transformative potential of neo-liberalism, which we were not alone in associating irretrievably with processes of institutional destruction and a climate of crisis politics, there has been a growing recognition of neoliberalism's potential to evolve, mutate, and even "learn." If the Greenspan boom of the 1990s tells us anything, it is surely that, under a particular configuration of geoeconomic power, neoliberal modes of growth management can be brutally effective, at least over the medium term and in the context of largely uncontested US hegemonic dominance (Peck 2002; Setterfield 2000). And the exuberance of ("new") economic growth in the US during the 1990s, in turn, served to validate American policies across a wide range of fields, not least those relating to welfare reform and labor-market flexibility (Peck 2001).

Indeed, if there is a policy-development analog for the coercive regime of interurban competition described by Harvey, it is perhaps to be found in the multifaceted process of "fast policy transfer" that has become an increasingly common characteristic of (inter)local institutional change (Jessop and Peck 2001). In concrete terms, this reflects two interconnected features of the contemporary policy development process, at least within (and between) neoliberalized national and local states. First, this process is increasingly dominated by "ideas from America," both in the direct sense of the modeling of transnational reform projects on the basis of the (technocratically stylized) experience of US cities and states (see Deacon 2000; Peck and Theodore 2001) and, more generally, in the form of the growing influence of US-inflected neoliberal restructuring strategies in fields like policing and incarceration policy, financial management, and corporate governance. Second, and in more functional terms, there is suggestive evidence that policy cycles—the elapsed time between the (re)specification of policy "problems," the mobilization of reform movements, and the selection and implementation of strategies—are being deliberately shortened in the context of a growing propensity to adopt "off-the-shelf," imported solutions in the place of the (usually slower) process of in situ policy development.

Together, these twin processes are resulting in an acceleration in policy "turnover time," as reform dynamics become effectively endemic and as extralocal learning and emulation become more or less continuous processes. This, in turn, is leading to a deepening and intensification in the process of neoliberalization, US-style. Such mechanisms of international and interlocal policy transfer— which take place along channels that have been created, structured, and lubricated by technocratic elites, think tanks, opinion-formers, consultants, and policy networks—have been rapidly established as one of the principal modes of policy development in strategically critical fields such as systemic financial stability, the management of urban "underclasses," the regulation of contingent labor markets, and the displacement of welfare entitlements with socially authoritarian packages of rights and responsibilities (Peck 2001; Tickell and Clark 2001; Wacquant 1999). For Wacquant (1999:319–320), this represents an aggressive and deliberate internationalization of a "new penal commonsense," rooted in the recriminalization of poverty and the resultant normalization of contingent labor:

> [Neoliberal nostrums] did not spring spontaneously, ready-made, out of reality. They partake of a vast constellation of terms and theses that come from America on crime, violence, justice, inequality, and responsibility—of the individual, of the "community," of the national collectivity—which have gradually insinuated themselves into European public debate to the point of serving as its framework and focus, and which owe the brunt of their power of persuasion to their sheer omnipresence and to the prestige recovered by their originators.

A conspicuously important outcome of this increased "transcontinental traffic in ideas and public policies" (Wacquant 1999:322) is the marked deepening of the process of neoliberalization on an international, if not global, scale. Crucially, this has massively enlarged the space for extensive forms of neoliberalized accumulation and policy formation, in ways that were distinctly favorable to the United States through most of the 1990s (see Wade 2001). At the same time, however, it has also shifted the scales and stakes of the attendant crisis tendencies in potentially very serious ways.

In fact, having been aggressively upscaled to the transcontinental level, the neoliberal "settlement" is now surely more, not less, vulnerable to systemic crisis. Even though the successive remaking of economic and social institutions in US-inflected forms is not leading to any kind of simple "convergence," it may nevertheless be serving to degrade the institutional "gene pool" essential for subsequent forms of neoliberal mutation and crisis containment. The (incomplete and uneven) global extension of neoliberalism may make large parts of the world more receptive (if not "safer") places for Americanized forms of accumulation and regulation, but by the same token it also amplifies their structural vulnerabilities, while reducing the scope for creative (and self-renewing) institutional learning. The specter is therefore raised that the very same channels through which the neoliberal project has been generalized may subsequently become the transmission belts for rapidly diffusing international crises of overaccumulation, deflation, and serial policy failure. Indeed, as we hover on the brink of a global recession—the first since the 1930s, when an earlier form of liberalism was the commonsense of the time—neoliberalism may be about to face its sternest test of credibility and legitimacy.

Finally, as the deleterious social consequences and perverse externalities of neoliberal economic policies become increasingly evident and widespread, the foundations may be inadvertently created for new forms of translocal political solidarity and consciousness amongst those who find themselves marginalized and excluded on a *global* basis (Hardt and Negri 2000). The globalization of the neoliberal project has therefore been tendentially (though not necessarily) associated with the partial globalization of networks of resistance. And while one of the conspicuous strengths of roll-back neoliberalism was its capacity to disorganize sources of (actual and potential) political opposition, roll-out neoliberalism is becoming just as conspicuously associated with disruption and resistance, as the process of deep neoliberalization has created new basing points, strategic targets, and weak spots. New forms of strategically targeted resistance may therefore represent both obstacles to neoliberalization and spurs to its continuing transformation.

Conclusion: Neoliberal(ism) Rules?

In many respects, it would be tempting to conclude with a teleological reading of neoliberalism, as if it were somehow locked on a course of increasing vulnerability to crisis. Yet this would be both politically complacent and theoretically erroneous. One of the most striking features of the recent history of neoliberalism is its quite remarkable transformative capacity. To a greater extent than many would have predicted, including ourselves, neoliberalism has demonstrated an ability to absorb or displace crisis tendencies, to ride—and capitalize upon—the very economic cycles and localized policy failures that it was complicit in creating, and to erode the foundations upon which generalized or extralocal resistance might be constructed. The transformative potential—and consequent political durability—of neoliberalism has been repeatedly underestimated, and reports of its death correspondingly exaggerated. Although antiglobalization protests have clearly disrupted the functioning of "business as usual" for some sections of the neoliberal elite, the underlying power structures of neoliberalism remain substantially intact. What remains to be seen is how far these acts of resistance, asymmetrical though the power relations clearly are, serve to expose the true character of neoliberalism as a *political* project. In its own explicit politicization, then, the resistance movement may have the capacity to hold a mirror to the process of (ostensibly apolitical) neoliberalization, revealing its real character, scope, and consequences.

Just as neoliberalism is, in effect, a form of "high politics" that expressly denies its political character (Beck 2000), so it also exists in a self-contradictory way as a form of "metaregulation," a rule system that paradoxically defines itself as a form of *anti*regulation. In their targeting of global rule centers like the WTO, the IMF, and the G8, resistance movements seek not only to disrupt the transaction of neoliberal business but also to draw attention to the inequities and perversities of these rule regimes themselves. At the same time, however, these rule systems cannot unproblematically be reduced to institutional condensates like the WTO, because one of the fundamental features of neoliberalism is its pervasiveness as a system of *diffused power* (Hardt and Negri 2000). Contemporary politics revolve around axes the very essences of which have been neoliberalized. As such, neoliberalism is qualitatively different from "competing" regulatory projects and experiments: it shapes the environments, contexts, and frameworks within which political-economic and socio-institutional restructuring takes place. Thus, neoliberal rule systems are perplexingly elusive; they operate between as well as within specific sites of incorporation and reproduction, such as national and local states. Consequently, they have the capacity to constrain, condition, and constitute political change and institutional reform in far-reaching and multifaceted ways. Even if it may be wrong-headed to characterize neoliberalization as some actorless force-field of extralocal pressures and disciplines—given what we know about the decisive purposive interventions of think-tanks, policy elites, and experts, not to mention the fundamental role of state power itself in the (re)production of neoliberalism—as an *ongoing ideological project* neoliberalism is clearly more than the sum of its (local institutional) parts.

Thus, it is important to specify closely—and challenge—the extralocal rule systems that provide a major source of neoliberalism's reproductive and adaptive capacity. Local resistance—especially strategically targeted local resistance—is a necessary but perhaps insufficient part of this task. Crucially, neoliberalism has been able to make a virtue of uneven spatial development and continuous regulatory restructuring, rendering the macro power structure as a whole partially insulated from local challenges. In addition, progressive local alternatives are persistently vulnerable, in this turbulent and marketized environment, to social undercutting, institutional overloading, and regulatory dumping. This is not to say that the hegemony of neoliberalism must necessarily remain completely impervious to targeted campaigns of disruption and "regime competition" from progressive alternatives, but rather to argue that the effectiveness of such counterstrategies will continue to be muted, absent a phase-shift in the constitution of extralocal relations. This means that the strategic objectives for opponents of neoliberalism must include the reform of macroinstitutional priorities and the remaking of extralocal rule systems in fields like trade, finance, environmental, antipoverty, education, and labor policy. These may lack the radical edge of more direct forms of resistance, but as intermediate and facilitative objectives they would certainly help to tip the macroenvironment in favor of progressive possibilities. In this context, the defeat (or failure) of local neoliberalisms—even strategically important ones—will not be enough to topple what we are still perhaps justified in calling "the system." It will continue to be premature to anticipate an era of "push-back" neoliberalism, let alone the installation of a more progressive regulatory settlement, until extralocal rule regimes are remade in ways that contain and challenge the forces of marketization and commodification—until there is a far-reaching *deliberalization* of spatial relations.

Acknowledgments
An earlier version of this paper was given at the seminar "Neoliberalism and the City" at the Center for Urban Economic Development, University of Illinois at Chicago, September 2001. We would like to thank all of the participants for the incisive discussion, which helped to clarify our thinking and also to thank Neil Brenner, Nik Theodore, Mark Goodwin, and Nigel Thrift for their perceptive comments and suggestions. The usual disclaimers apply.

References

Allen J, Massey D and Cochrane A, with Charlesworth J, Court G, Henry N and Sarre P (1998) *Rethinking the Region*. London: Routledge

Amin A (1997) Placing globalisation. *Theory, Culture, and Society* 14:123–137

Amin A (1999) An institutionalist perspective on regional economic development. *International Journal of Urban and Regional Research* 23:365–378

Beck U (2000) *What is Globalization?* Cambridge, UK: Polity Press

Bluestone B and Harrison B (2000) *Growing Prosperity*. Boston: Houghton Mifflin

Bond P (2000) *Elite Transition: From Apartheid to Neoliberalism in South Africa*. London: Pluto

Bourdieu P (1998) *Acts of Resistance*. Cambridge, UK: Polity Press

Bourdieu P and Wacquant L (2001) NeoLiberalSpeak: Notes on the new planetary vulgate. *Radical Philosophy* 105:2–5

Brenner N (1999) Globalisation as reterritorialisation: The rescaling of urban governance in the European union. *Urban Studies* 36:431–451

Cochrane A, Peck J and Tickell A (1996) Manchester plays games: Exploring the local politics of globalization. *Urban Studies* 33:1319–1336

Deacon A (2000) Learning from the US? The influence of American ideas upon "New Labour" thinking on welfare reform. *Policy and Politics* 28:5–18

DeMartino, G F (2000) *Global Economy, Global Justice: Theoretical Objections and Policy Alternatives to Neoliberalism*. London: Routledge

Dicken P, Peck J and Tickell A (1997) Unpacking the global. In R Lee and J Wills (eds) *Geographies of Economies* (pp 158–166). London: Arnold

Gough J (1996) Neoliberalism and localism: Comments on Peck and Tickell. *Area* 28:392–398

Hardt M and Negri A (2000) *Empire*. Cambridge, MA: Harvard University Press

Harvey D (1989) From managerialism to entrepreneurialism: The transformation of urban governance in late capitalism. *Geografiska Annaler* 71B:3–17

Jessop B (1989) *Thatcherism: The British road to post-Fordism*. Essex Papers in Politics and Government 68. Essex: Department of Government, University of Essex

Jessop B (ed) (2001) *Regulation Theory and the Crisis of Capitalism 1—The Parisian Regulation School*. Cheltenham: Elgar

Jessop B and Peck J (2001) Fast policy/local discipline. Mimeograph. Lancaster: Department of Sociology, Lancaster University

Jessop B, Bonnett K, Bromley S and Ling T (1988) *Thatcherism*. Cambridge, UK: Polity

Jessop B, Peck J and Tickell A (1999) Retooling the machine: Economic crisis, state restructuring, and urban politics. In A Jonas and D Wilson (eds) *The Urban Growth Machine* (pp 141–159). New York: SUNY Press

Larner W (2000) Theorising neoliberalism: Policy, ideology, governmentality. *Studies in Political Economy* 63:5–26

Lipietz A (1987) *Mirages and Miracles*. London: Verso

Overbeek H (1990) *Global Capitalism and National Decline*. London: Unwin Hyman

Peck J (2001) *Workfare States*. New York: Guilford

Peck J (2002) Labor, zapped/growth, restored? Three moments of neoliberal restructuring in the American labor market. *Journal of Economic Geography* 2(2): 179–220

Peck J and Theodore N (2001) Exporting workfare/importing welfare-to-work: Exploring the politics of Third Way policy transfer. *Political Geography* 20: 427–460

Peck J and Tickell A (1994a) Jungle law breaks out: Neoliberalism and global-local disorder. *Area* 26:317–326

Peck J and Tickell A (1994b) Searching for a new institutional fix: The *after*-Fordist crisis and global-local disorder. In A Amin (ed) *Post-Fordism* (pp 280–316). Oxford: Blackwell

Peck J and Tickell A (1995) The social regulation of uneven development: "Regulatory deficit," England's South East and the collapse of Thatcherism. *Environment and Planning A* 27:15–40

Peet R, with Hartwick E (1999) *Theories of Development*. New York: Guilford

Piven F F (1995) Is it global economics or neo-laissez-faire? *New Left Review* 213: 107–114

Piven F F and Cloward R (1998) *The Breaking of the American Social Compact*. New York: New Press

Polanyi K (1944) *The Great Transformation*. Boston: Beacon Press

Setterfield M (2000) Is the new US social structure of accumulation replicable? Mimeograph. Hartford, CT: Department of Economics, Trinity College

Tickell A (1999) Unstable futures: Controlling and creating risks in international money. In L Panitch and C Leys (eds) *Socialist Register* (pp 248–277). Rendleshem: Merlin Press

Tickell A and Clark G L (2001) New architectures or liberal logics? Interpreting global financial reform. Mimeograph. Bristol: School of Geographical Sciences, University of Bristol

Tickell A and Peck J (1995) Social regulation *after* Fordism: Regulation theory, neoliberalism and the global-local nexus. *Economy and Society* 24: 357–386

Tickell A and Peck J (1996) Neoliberalism and localism: A reply to Gough. *Area* 28:398–404

Tickell A and Peck J (forthcoming) Making global rules: Globalisation or neoliberalisation? In J Peck and H W-C Yeung (eds) *Making Global Connections*. London: Sage

Veltmeyer H, Petras J and Vieux S (eds) (1997) *Neoliberalism and Class Conflict in Latin America: A Comparative Perspective on the Political Economy of Structural Adjustment*. New York: St. Martin's Press

Wacquant L (1999) How penal common sense comes to Europeans: Notes on the transatlantic diffusion of the neoliberal *doxa*. *European Societies* 1:319–352

Wade R (2001) Showdown at the World Bank. *New Left Review* 7:124–137

Weiss L (1998) *The Myth of the Powerless State: Governing the Economy in a Global Era*. Ithaca, NY: Cornell University Press

Jamie Peck is a Professor of Geography and Sociology at the University of Wisconsin, Madison. He is author of *Work-Place: The Social Regulation of Labor Markets* (New York: Guilford, 1996), *Workfare States* (New York: Guilford, 2001), and a number of articles on issues related to labor-market restructuring and policy, welfare reform, urban political economy, and theories of regulation. He is currently coeditor of *Antipode* and joint editor of *Environment and Planning A*. His research at the present time is concerned with two issues: the reconstitution of temporary and low-wage labor markets and the political economy of policy transfer.

Adam Tickell is a Professor of Human Geography at the University of Bristol and has previously lectured at the universities of Leeds,

Manchester and Southampton. He is editor of *Transactions, Institute of British Geographers* and review editor of the *Journal of Economic Geography*. His work explores the geographies and politics of international financial reform, governance structures in the UK, and the reconfiguration of the political commonsense.

Chapter 3
Neoliberalism and Socialisation in the Contemporary City: Opposites, Complements and Instabilities

Jamie Gough

This paper explores some dialectics of neoliberalism and socialisation in contemporary urbanism. The significance of socialisation—nonmarket cooperation between social actors—in both production and reproduction has tended to increase in the long term. Socialisation does not always take politically progressive forms, yet it always has a problematic relation with private property and class discipline. Socialisation of diverse forms grew during the long boom, but this exacerbated the classic crisis tendencies of capitalism and resulted in increasing politicisation. Neoliberalism offered a resolution of these tensions by imposing unmediated value relations and class discipline, fragmenting labour and capital and fostering depoliticisation. However, this has led to manifest inefficiencies and failure adequately to reproduce the wage relation. Many longstanding forms of socialisation have therefore been retained, if in modified forms. Moreover, substantially new forms of urban socialisation have developed in cities. This paper examines the role of business organisations, industrial clusters, top-down mobilisation of community and attempts at "joined-up" urban governance. It is argued that these fill gaps in socialisation left by neoliberalism. Their neoliberal context has largely prevented their politicisation, in particular heading off any socialist potential. Indeed, the new forms of urban socialisation have internalised neoliberal social relations and often deepened social divisions. Thus, paradoxically, they can achieve the essential aims of neoliberalism better than "pure" neoliberalism itself. Nevertheless, these forms of socialisation are often weakened by neoliberalism. Contemporary urban class relations and forms of regulation thus reflect both opposition and mutual construction between neoliberal strategies and forms of socialisation. The paper ends by briefly contrasting this theorisation with associationalist and regulationist approaches.

Introduction

Neoliberalism poses itself as the end of the social. It seeks to unshackle social actors from social and political constraints, to enable the firm freely to maximise its profits and the individual his or her "utility". Private property is to be freed from collective rights and obligations, in particular from state interference, though the state is required all the more strongly to protect property from infringement by others. This implies particular relations between capital and labour in which the worker confronts capital as an individual rather than a member of a collective or a citizen, freeing capital both in its purchase of labour power and in the latter's consumption within the workplace.

However, this project is haunted by the logic of what I will refer to as "socialisation"—the coordination and cooperation of social actors other than through markets.[1] This logic is present both in production and in the social sphere on the grounds of the efficiency of waged and unwaged work and the satisfaction of human needs (Offe 1984). Thus, to the extent that people are able to press for the satisfaction of their needs and to the extent that business is concerned for the efficiency of production, neoliberalism faces dilemmas. The break-up of longstanding forms of socialisation within cities has caused manifest inefficiencies, not only for workers and residents but also for business. This has meant that many important forms of socialisation have not been destroyed altogether, but rather have been reformed in particular, always problematic, ways by neoliberalism. Moreover, substantially new forms of urban socialisations of production and reproduction have emerged, stamped by their neoliberal context. Brenner and Theodore highlight these deviations from "pure" neoliberalism—the messy business of "actually existing neoliberalism"—in their introduction to this volume. This paper attempts a theorisation of them.

A large left literature exists showing that neoliberalism has led to inefficient production, as well as declining standards of life of the working class (a term I use in its Marxist sense). However, this begs some questions. Why has the neoliberal offensive continued despite these palpable failures? And, on the other hand, what forms of socialisation have continued or emerged, and how are they related to their apparent opposite, neoliberalism?

Socialisation within capitalist society can take very different forms politically. It may reflect and embody a real class compromise, as in classical social democracy: an attempt to steer capital into high-productivity paths that are relatively beneficial for quality of employment and living standards. Alternatively, socialisation may simply respond to demands of capital: it can provide labour power with suitable resources and attitudes as well as other inputs to profitable production, and can organise particular paths of accumulation. Thus, socialisation in the present period, though formally opposed to neoliberal principles, may in practice reinforce the class project of neoliberalism by creating real rather than merely formal options and freedoms for capital. This paper maps some of the ways in which contemporary socialisations in cities complement and internalise neoliberalism.

Because it involves direct and explicit relations between actors, rather than relations mediated by impersonal value, socialisation of whatever political complexion can become excessively politicised from the point of view of capital (Habermas 1976; Offe 1984). Indeed, neoliberalism developed precisely as a response to such problems

(Bonefeld 1993; Bonefeld, Brown and Burnham 1995; Clarke 1988). I therefore seek in this paper to trace the historical development of the tension between the impersonal discipline of value and the political conflict immanent in socialisation in the city. This attempts to fill a gap in the literature on neoliberalism as depoliticisation (Bonefeld 1993; Bonefeld, Brown and Burnham 1995), which has underresearched the local scale and the reproduction sphere.

The paper thus seeks to interpret the contemporary city in terms of the contradictory relation between neoliberalism and socialisation—that is, both their conflict *and* their mutual construction. As this abstract dualism is developed towards historically and spatially concrete forms, I seek to show how socialisation can internalise neoliberalism and vice versa, thus complexifying the two poles. We are concerned here not only with impersonal structures but, crucially, with consciousness and political struggle and with their historical development.

I use "city" here as shorthand for the local or regional scale. This scale has a particular relevance to the neoliberalism–socialisation dialectic. On the one hand, cities contain sets of interdependencies within production and reproduction and between them facilitated by proximity, which I have termed "locally-effective structures" (Gough 1991; see also Cox 1998; Harvey 1989). On the other hand, localities are strongly subject to the pressures of capital mobility by virtue of their limited size and their formal political constitution. We shall explore how this contradiction has been developed in the present period.

The second section of the paper considers the notion of socialisation within capitalist society and its historical development. On this basis, it proposes a particular account of the origins of neoliberalism, conceived as a set of class relations. The third section examines how neoliberalism has restructured cities, but also looks at the persistence of longstanding forms of urban socialisation despite neoliberalism. The fourth considers four examples of new or substantially reworked forms of socialisation within the contemporary city, and their complex dialectics with neoliberal disciplines and fragmentations. The concluding section considers some theoretical and political issues.

The Socialisation of Capitalism and the Neoliberal Response

The core mechanisms of capitalism—capitalist production of commodities, the sale of labour power by individual workers, flows of capital governed by prospects of individual profit—have never been adequate in their pure form to ensure sustained accumulation nor, *a fortiori*, to meet the needs of the working class. Consequently, there are chronic pressures from sections of both capital and labour towards collaborative nonmarket arrangements, through both civil society and the state, to mediate the core relations. This "socialisation" relates to both production and the reproduction of people. Because the reproduction of labour power is important to capital, and because employment depends on profitability, *both* spheres are the concern of *both* classes. It is, therefore, misleading to conceive of socialisation as serving accumulation and legitimation as distinct aims: accumulation is vital for popular legitimation, and the reproduction sphere underpins accumulation. As we shall see, this greatly complicates the politics of socialisation.

Socialisation of production and reproduction can have very varied class politics. It can be conservative, as in the state-*zaibatsu* planning of production in Japan or in the public services of postwar West Germany, which were structured to encourage polarised gender roles and family stability. It can be social-democratic, as in the regulation of production and industrial bargaining in the Federation Settlement in Australia or in the classical welfare state in Scandinavia. Or it can express—and unstably embody—an offensive of labour against capital, as in the forms of workers' and residents' control of production, housing and urban services during the 1969–1970 events in northern Italy. Note, then, that socialisation does not always have a social-democratic nature. This political ambiguity will be of central concern in the argument below.

Over the very long-term development of capitalist industrialism, socialisation of both production and reproduction tends to deepen. This arises, inter alia, from an increase in capitals of long turnover times, increases in the knowledge intensity of production, and the increasing complexity and cultural content of reproduction commodities and public services, all of which produce pressures for coordination at varied scales. These pressures underlay the enormous extension of socialisation during the postwar boom in all the developed countries. Not only was demand managed by nation-states to underpin investments of long turnover time, but national, regional and local states became increasingly involved in aspects of production, including the coordination of sectoral investment, training, research and development and land and property. These interventions were typically carried out in concert with representative bodies of business, and sometimes of labour, too (de Brunhof 1978). The range and types of welfare service increased, deepening their cultural politics. State regulation of conditions of waged work and of commodity inputs to reproduction similarly increased enormously. Both the mix and the class relations of these forms of socialisation, however, varied strongly between different countries (de Brunhof 1978; Esping-Andersen 1990).

For the most part, the forms of socialisation developed in the postwar boom contributed positively to the unprecedentedly rapid rate of capital accumulation. However, this was a contradictory process.

Socialisation organised the *use values* (material processes) of production and reproduction more efficiently than would otherwise have been the case, but this had some negative impacts on *value* relations. By enhancing the accumulation of productive capital, it accelerated the growth of the organic composition of capital, hence tending to depress the rate of profit (Mandel 1978). A historically low rate of unemployment was a product both of successfully organised accumulation and, in some countries, of working-class pressure (Therborn 1986). However, in Europe in particular this cumulatively strengthened the bargaining power of labour and the size and militancy of union organisations, negatively affecting the rate of exploitation (Glyn and Sutcliffe 1972; Mandel 1978). Moreover, certain types of socialisation became accepted as (nationally specific) norms. This encouraged sections of business, of workers and of residents to organise themselves and bargain with other social actors and with the state to further their perceived interests. Sectors of business increasingly came to see various types of state support as a norm; workers sought to extend bargaining and secure legally based entitlements from employers; the nonwaged and insecurely waged won better state benefits; residents demanded improved public services and urban planning; and women and ethnic minorities, whose social positions had been fundamentally altered by the boom and whose expectations had in many cases been raised by socialisation and its rhetorics, demanded equality and resources in both production and reproduction spheres. Socialisation thus eventually contributed to a wholesale *politicisation* of waged production, reproduction relations and urban spaces. Thus, the new forms of socialisation of the boom, while having beneficial effects on accumulation, came increasingly to undermine it and to weaken capital's command over society.

The long-term decline of the average rate of profit in the major developed countries from its high point in the early 1950s reached a turning point in the late 1960s and early 1970s, resulting in decreased investment rates, increased scrapping of capacity, rising unemployment, wage limitation and restraint of state expenditures. The forms of politicisation engendered by the socialisation of the boom period had crucial impacts during this period of crisis. The civil rights movement in the US developed towards outright rebellions of African Americans, especially in the Rust Belt cities, and this movement helped to mobilise black communities in Europe. The women's and lesbian and gay movements took off, presenting a challenge to whole systems of gender, family, sexuality and social life. Trade unionists, at least at the local level, were organised and confident enough to offer strong resistance to closures and wage restraint. These revolts were closely bound up with urban crises. Populations not only resisted cuts in services but also—more offensively—demanded better-quality facilities and new types of service (around the particular needs of women and ethnic minorities, for example) and solutions to longstanding inadequacies of housing provision, and contested many large-scale projects in the built environment.

These varied forms of resistance and revolt were sometimes quite distinct, sometimes mutually reinforcing and intertwining. Their significance went beyond their immediate achievements (indeed, many were heavily defeated): the ideas and collective aspirations they generated were crucial. In North America, Australia and most of Western Europe, very substantial minorities of the population questioned the fundamental relations of class, gender, sexuality and "race", organised struggles around these issues, and episodically won majority support. The multidimensional nature of these struggles, reflecting the varied forms of socialisation addressed, reinforced an upsurge of radical optimism, a key ingredient for a systemic challenge. Through its various forums and discourses, the capitalist class was aware that this constituted a potential threat to its systems of rule, if not (yet) to its existence, the most serious since 1945–1948. A majority feeling emerged among the elite that something radical had to be done to defuse this threat.

The strategy adopted was neoliberalism. Neoliberalism addressed the two immediate, intertwined problems perceived by capital: low average rates of profit, and overpoliticisation and revolt (Bonefeld 1993; Clarke 1988). Specifically:

1) *the rate of profit.* Neoliberal policies accelerate the devalorisation of capital, reducing the mass of capital on which profit is calculated. Capital's increased power over labour enables the rate of surplus value to be increased. Privatisation enables surplus value to be extracted in new sectors. Capital is enabled to flow more easily from low- to high-profit operations, sectors and territories. Taxation falling directly or indirectly on business is reduced.

2) *depoliticisation.* Neoliberal strategy is centrally concerned with depoliticising economy and society by weakening or removing historically accumulated forms of socialisation. Existing forms of nonmarket coordination and state regulation are abandoned. Firms are encouraged and compelled to look to their own devices, rather than to the state or collaborations with other capitals. Workers' collective organisations are weakened, and their job prospects made more directly dependent on the profit rate of capitals employing or potentially employing them. Demands on public services—in particular, to address gender and "racial" inequalities—are resisted on the grounds of the need to reduce state spending "to increase competitiveness".

People are encouraged and compelled to rely on their own or their household's resources for their reproduction.

This account of the end of the boom and the genesis of a new period differs from institutionalist and regulationist accounts in several crucial respects. First, it does not locate this transition in changing dominant forms of the labour process and/or product markets. Secondly, it emphasises the role of classical Marxist value processes in lowering the rate of profit. Finally, it stresses the problem for capital of politicisation and the key role of the political consciousness of (sections of) the working class.

For capital, then, neoliberalism has a strong logic in the crisis that emerged thirty years ago. Indeed, it is hard to imagine how else capital could have reacted to this crisis in the long run. Neoliberalism, then, is not simply freeing of markets, as it is represented in neoclassical theory and in some left work.[2] Rather, it is a strategy for shifting value relations and political balance of forces and hence imposing capital's discipline on the working class and oppressed groups.[3] However, neither can it be specified simply, as it is in much urban literature, as a strategy which imposes "the interests of business" above all other social considerations: many varieties of conservative regime have done this. Neoliberalism is a *particular* strategy for accumulation, especially in its approach to socialisation, arising from a particular political conjuncture.

Breaks and Continuities in Urban Socialisation under Neoliberalism

In line with this political project, neoliberalism within cities of North America, Western Europe, Australia and New Zealand has promoted:

1) enhanced sectoral and spatial mobility of capital, freed from earlier national and local socialisations; hence deepened individualism of firms and disinclination to cooperate with others;
2) a sharper dominance of capital within the labour process and the employment relation, and an accentuation of the disciplinary rather than cooperative aspects of the employment relation;
3) sharpened competition between workers for jobs organised at varied spatial scales, from the individual to the local to the national (Gough 1992);
4) cuts in state services and increases in charges for them, widening the commodification of reproduction;
5) restructuring of local state services towards, variously, privatisation, decentralisation to quasi-autonomous agencies, fragmentation into distinct cost centres, and measurement of outputs and direct costs as a basis for allocating resources within the state;

6) inflection of local state services and regulation towards the immediately expressed or perceived demands of particular capitals, in particular to promote the competition of "the locality" against others;

7) encouragement of possessive individualism, including its expressions in urban space—walled spaces, semiprivatised public space and so on (for a graphic account see Harvey 2000: 133–156); encouragement of self-realisation through consumption of commodities, especially those with class or gender resonance;

8) arising from (4), (5) and (7), increasing appropriation of parts of state services by particular groups of residents along lines of class and ethnicity;

9) an intensification of the state's policing of private property, directed particularly against organised labour (linking to [2]) but also against the poor (linking to [7]).

Yet neoliberalism has not been able to erase the logics of socialisation: to the contrary. The new information and communication technologies have tended to intensify the technical need for socialisation by increasing the knowledge intensity of production and social life. Fordist production, with its strong demands for coordination in space and time, has continued in much of manufacturing and been extended to many consumer and business services. Non-Fordist production using task- and product-flexible methods makes even greater demands on skill, knowledge and transport infrastructures.

Neoliberalism has thus had to continue with many of the *broad* forms of socialisation that it inherited. State funding of primary and secondary education and a substantial role in higher education have continued; the state's role in health care, very different between different countries, has not changed qualitatively in any of them; collective bargaining and a role for the trade unions have remained in some sectors in all countries, even if weakened; some state regulation of working conditions and terms of employment has remained; and some form of land use planning and state input into major property developments have continued. All of these forms of socialisation have traditionally been highly differentiated between countries, and these differences have persisted to a remarkable degree. For example, Terhorst (2001) has shown the long-term continuities in the differences between urban regulation in Amsterdam and Brussels. The nationally specific class relations that were both expressed and institutionalised in forms of socialisation in the boom, and their productive logic, have not been erased, though they have been modified. These class relations are central to the national path dependencies noted by Brenner and Theodore in this volume.

The persistent logic of socialisation is reflected in the economic and social problems that have arisen in those fields where neoliberalism *has* weakened socialisation. The weakening of nonmarket coordination in fields such as training, housing and transport has led to well-documented failures to meet the needs not only of workers (Keil this volume; Weber this volume) but also of capital (Bluestone and Harrison 2000; Green 1989; Jones and Ward this volume; Peck and Tickell 1995a and this volume). Because of this immanence of social-isation, the present-day political economy of cities involves a complex interplay of neoliberal interventions, longstanding forms of socialisation and new or revived forms of coordination. Even in the characteristic-ally neoliberal urban strategies mentioned above, one finds traces of socialisation in the tropes of state–business linkages, community, local solidarity and continuing state direction and funding. The articula-tions of neoliberal and socialised relations have varied strongly between countries, depending on their inherited, institutionalised class relations (the neoliberal moment being stronger in the US and Britain, for example). One thus finds varied and impure "actually existing neo-liberalisms" (Brenner and Theodore this volume). But if neoliberalism and socialisation are formal opposites, how are these articulations realised, and what are their tensions?

New Forms of Urban Socialisation under Neoliberalism

I investigate this question by examining some new or revived forms of local socialisation that have appeared in the last twenty years or so. I consider four important instances: the role of business organisations in urban governance; the promotion of industrial clusters; community initiatives in poor areas; and attempts at "joined-up" urban govern-ment. The stylised accounts given here are based mainly on the British and US experiences.

Business Organisations in Urban Politics

The influence on local politics of local business associations, both sectoral and general, is nothing new, particularly in the US. However, it has increased since the 1980s through the setting up of growth coalitions, the spinning off by national and local states of agencies dominated by business, and the increasing role of business in small firm support, education, training, sport and culture. Neoliberalism's delegitimation of (strong) state intervention means that business has increasing legitimacy to "sort out urban problems in a businesslike way" (Eisenschitz and Gough 1993:155–158).

It is often supposed that this is a simple outcome of neoliberalism. In much of the literature on growth coalitions and "entrepreneurial cities", neoliberalism is seen as benefiting business precisely *by* handing over control of urban strategies and implementation to it. However, this is too simple: it elides collective and individual capital and makes no distinctions between different *modes* of "benefiting business".

Neoliberalism enhances capital's sectoral and social mobility and deepens interfirm competition, and thus promotes individualistic or anomic relations of firms to others. It thereby cuts against *collective* action by firms. Yet the growing role of business in the city is organised through *associations* of firms or by getting managers to sit on boards as (supposed) representatives of local business. To this extent, individual firms have to engage in debate, compromises and commitment to implement collective decisions—that is, substantial forms of socialisation (Cox 1993). Such organisation has a strong logic in the present period. Capital seeks to influence the state, given its continuing important role (see the third section of this paper). Without *collective* decisionmaking, individual capitals (firms, sectors) come to dominate urban development and services, which may not merely be "unfair" to other capitals but may actively damage them.

The transfers of urban power to business have been replete with these tensions. In some cases, the urban organisations of business have drawn in most of the major local sectors and have arrived at strategies that, at least, do not clearly disbenefit any of them. This has often been the case in the US and Australia, where city- or state-level business has had long experience and strong legitimacy in such a role. The tensions in the subsequent developments have then been largely conflicts between the business coalition and local residents, with varied reflections in formal politics. However, in many other cases— and this is typically the case in Britain—the business organisations fail to include important sections of capital operating in the locality and are unable or unwilling to develop collective strategies. The businesspeople who sit on boards then represent no one but themselves (Peck and Tickell 1995b). This mode of business involvement runs the risk of popular opposition, not to business's role as such, but to the more or less "corrupt" influence of *particular* firms. It also risks politicisation through conflicts between sections of capital that are respectively strongly and weakly represented (for the case of the British urban development corporations, see Colenutt and Tansley 1990). In Britain, it is the historic liberal traditions of business that make collective decisionmaking so difficult. Consequently, various policymakers and academics have launched a veritable crusade to get British business to "organise itself better" at the local and regional level (Bennett 1995; Evans and Harding 1997).

We see here, then, some possible complexity of the relation of neoliberalism to socialisation. Collective organisation of local business can further an aim that neoliberalism has set itself: namely, the inflection of the state towards the interests of capital as a whole. It does so by coordinating complementary elements of accumulation paths. Yet this organisation is at odds with neoliberal prescriptions; the individualism and spatial mobility of capital which neoliberalism accentuates cut against the formation of a collective local business voice. Inclusive as well as more partial involvement of business embodies reactionary class relations, and both are vulnerable to politicisation.

Local/Regional Sectoral Clusters

Localised agglomerations have been an important form of industrialisation since the industrial revolution (Storper and Walker 1989), taking their strongest form in the classical industrial district. Contemporary enthusiasts for the "new regional economy" (eg Scott 1998; Storper 1998) argue that localised sectoral clusters are now the most productive and competitive form for manufacturing and business services, due to an increasingly informational and reflexive industrialism. The ideal type cluster involves important forms of productive socialisation, including collaboration between firms, finance, research centres, sectoral support institutions, the local state and labour; these relations are *durable*, constituting a set of local "conventions" (Storper 1998). Storper's description of these elements as "nexuses of untraded dependencies" emphasises their congruence with the notion of socialisation.

While many clusters approximate this ideal type, many sectoral agglomerations do not have such strong forms of socialisation, and many sectors and local economies are not organised in this way (Amin and Robins 1990; Markusen 1996; Murray 1987). Nevertheless, "growing" clusters has become a major strategy for local economic agencies, one promoted by nation-states and international bodies (in some cases virtually their *only* strategy, as with the new English Regional Development Agencies).

Clusters are *formally* a departure from neoliberal mobility and individualism to the extent that they involve commitments between actors of substantial duration, require long-term investment in institutional supports, and are geographically immobile "assets". They differ from the characteristic industrial relations of neoliberalism in that they tend to rest on, and promote, substantially cooperative relations. However, they are also a *response* to the internationalising tendencies and sharpened competition of neoliberalism. These can best be met through the product rents and high value added by the advanced mechanisation, cooperation and use of knowledge (relative surplus value) that the strong socialisation of clusters enables. This is all the more so given that this regional socialisation can compensate for neoliberalism's weakening of socialisation at the national level (Gough and Eisenschitz 1996; Scott 1998:106).

Moreover, the class relations of the sectoral clusters can be compatible with neoliberalism. Since they are in sharp competition with each other, excessive demands and conflicts can be headed off in the interests of the cluster as a whole. To the extent that the links between firms, finance and institutions are not formalised but are developed and adjusted ad hoc, they do not need to take on a restrictive aspect (Scott 1998). This exemplifies Offe's (1984) argument that *informal* corporatism may avoid politicisation in the present period. The bargaining power of labour might seem to be dangerously large due to the substantial skills and relative immobility of the clusters, but this danger is lessened to the extent that technical surplus profits enable good wages, that cooperative and autonomous styles of working win commitment of workers, and that neoliberalism has weakened or prevented trade union organisation in the sector. Industrial bargaining can then be collective but moderate, as in the Third Italy, or demanding but individualist, as in Lipietz and Leborgne's "Californian model". Indeed, through workers' *self*-discipline, clusters can achieve the essential aim of neoliberalism—the dominance of capital over labour—more subtly and effectively than through overt coercion (Brusco 1982).

Nevertheless, the formal contradiction between local productive socialisation and neoliberal mobilities creates tensions. Even Scott (1998), who argues that regional clusters are fully congruent with neoliberal globalisation, concedes that existing clusters may be undermined by the mobility of productive capital (110), that globalised product and capital markets make it more difficult for regions to develop new clusters (69–71, 94, 134–136) and that industrial districts exacerbate uneven development within cities (72). Attempts to maintain, restructure or initiate local clusters are frequently undermined by the pursuit of individual profit by particular firms (Murray 1987) and by the absence of congruent socialisations at the national level (Gertler 1997).

The socialisation of clusters, then, has a contradictory relation to neoliberalism. Neoliberalism gives clusters a stronger raison d'être, but makes them more difficult to implement. Neoliberalism disciplines their class relations, and indeed, in the right circumstances, class discipline can be better realised by local sectoral socialisation than by neoliberalism itself.

Enhancing Reproduction of the Poor through Community

A major feature of the neoliberal city has been the remobilisation of the communities of the poor. Again, there is an antinomy here, since "community", however conceived, is a form of socialisation. Community has been mobilised by poor people themselves in an oppositional mode, resisting the impoverishment created by neoliberalism. However, poor communities have also been mobilised "from above". The state has sponsored forms of economic and social reproduction organised through voluntary community networks: community businesses which both provide employment and carry out useful work for the neighbourhood, and cooperatives for housing management, nursery provision, environmental improvements and so on. Poverty programmes have been strongly focused on neighbourhood initiatives, addressing employment, housing, education, crime, the environment and so on, either singly or holistically. In Britain, this kind of mobilisation of community developed in national-state programmes from the early 1990s. These presented themselves as having learnt from the neglect of communities in previous programmes, and proclaimed the importance of consulting with and even "empowering" poor communities. Similarly, since the late 1980s European Union local–regional programmes have required a "community" input. Business plays a substantial, though uneven, role in resourcing community-based poverty initiatives.

Radical literature since the 1960s should alert us to the fact that the term "community" is profoundly ambiguous and open-ended in class terms (Cowley et al 1977): this form of socialisation, too, can internalise very different class relations. How, then, have these top-down mobilisations of community been related to neoliberalism? Again, we find complex dialectics. In the first place, neoliberalism's creation of poverty not only leads to demands from poor communities themselves but also creates problems for capital. Not only are the poor a cost through state benefits (the institutionalised result of earlier working-class gains) and through their crime and episodic rioting, they also fail to act as effective labour power due to their domestic responsibilities and resources, location, skills, attitudes and health— that is, precisely due to the wide and complex socialisation of the reproduction of labour power. Top-down community regeneration aims to address this *socialisation* and thus not only reduce the cost overheads of the poor but reproduce the poor as effective labour power. On both counts it meets important *neoliberal* aims.

These programmes have largely been contained within the boundaries of capitalist, patriarchal and racist discipline: top-down community socialisation has fostered conservative social relations and has headed off challenges to the forms of power that create poverty (Atkinson 1999; Eisenschitz 1997). Community organisations' involvement in the running of programmes has often been token or has compromised community representatives as rationers of very limited funds. Where quasi-wage employment is involved through "training" and workfare schemes, this can function mainly as a way of socialising people into low wage labour; indeed, it achieves this better than normal employment, since community businesses can elicit greater effort, task flexibility and acceptance of insecurity because of their neighbourhood benefits and loyalties. These socialisations have tended to promote rightist forms of communitarianism in ethnic minority communities (Taylor-Gooby 1994). Many community initiatives are directed towards the disciplining of youth, not only by policing and surveillance but also through strengthening parental control. Because of their self-help mode, top-down community initiatives have largely failed to link up with struggles by trade unionists against the neoliberal degradation of public services.

This conservatism of community initiatives has been constructed by their neoliberal environment and the consciousness it generates in the poor. Neoliberalism's onslaughts against the working class as a whole have weakened any expectations that *radical* community action could make a difference: if actions by formerly strong trade unions have been smashed, if public services have been cut over and over again, if whole local industries have been lost without (effective) opposition, then what chance do organisations of the poor have? Moreover, neoliberalism has socially and culturally fragmented the working class, including the poor. People are led to rely on private resources, rather than collective actions. Many people living in poor neighbourhoods deal with their problems by relocating—or by hoping to do so (Byrne 1999). Community organisations are often split by relations of power that have been deepened by neoliberalism. "Racial" differences are the obvious example, but differences of gender have also been crucial: in the west end of Newcastle upon Tyne, the efforts of women to organise against joy-riding and to use area regeneration money have been actively, sometimes violently, opposed by men (Campbell 1993). There have certainly been community initiatives of the poor that have challenged power, but the initiatives sponsored by the state and capital have largely been able to head off such radical dynamics. Socialisation through community has thus been able to further the class aims of neoliberalism by constituting the poor as a real reserve army and by instilling self-discipline and self-reliance.

This is not to say that top-down community stimulation has been without its problems. Its strongly interventionist nature conflicts with neoliberal notions of state withdrawal and threatens politicisation. However, as Robertson and Dale (forthcoming) argue in relation to initiatives to improve the education of the poor in New Zealand, this threat may be contained by *local* targeting of the initiatives, so that they can be presented as *exceptional,* what they term "local states of emergency". Community initiatives run up against contradictions within neoliberalism concerning the articulation of women's roles in production and reproduction. Thus, policies in the US and in Tony Blair's Britain have attempted to push all women of working age into waged work while simultaneously bemoaning the weakening of the "traditional" family and parental (read maternal) socialisation. Active involvement of the poor in community initiatives is inhibited by the neoliberal context.

The individualism and sectionalism that weaken radical community action also tend to inhibit people from getting involved in state- or business-sponsored initiatives (Robertson and Dale forthcoming). For many men and some women, crime—which neoliberalism has so strongly promoted in all social layers—is a far more promising avenue than such initiatives, and people involved in this subculture keep clear of initiatives with any connection to the state (as in the Newcastle case). Moreover the moralism—whether of the Christian Right or Blair's Third Way—which so strongly infuses top-down community initiatives is contradicted by some obvious features of neoliberal life: a stronger work ethic is put in question by skyrocketing bourgeois incomes and the gains to be made from purely speculative activities (gambling and game shows for the poor), "strong families" are ridiculed by the commoditisation of sexuality, and so on. Socialisation of reproduction via community has thus been weakened, as well as subtended, by neoliberalism.

"Joined-up Government"

A final example of urban socialisation under neoliberalism is the stated aim of the current Labour government in Britain to develop "joined-up government", especially in urban policy. It is argued that urban policy has long suffered from lack of coordination of policy for education, health, transport and so on, lack of congruence between different branches of the national and local state, and lack of partnership with organisations of civil society. Divisions of government, and their links with civil society, therefore need to be better "joined up". Thus poverty has been renamed "social exclusion" to point to a holistic understanding of it as "social" and "cultural" as well as "economic", while national programmes for area regeneration have emphasised the need for "joined-up government". This, then, appears as the state taking socialisation seriously, focusing on *social* processes rather than independent actors.

In a sense, the diagnosis is right: state (and, *a fortiori*, business) urban policies have suffered from their lack of holism. This critique has, in fact, been commonplace since at least the 1960s. "Strategic planning" in the 1960s and 1970s attempted to coordinate all elements of urban systems; since the 1980s, innumerable task forces in Britain have had the remit of drawing together services and policies at local and regional levels. There have been some limited achievements of this aim. The decentralisation and semiprivatisation of state services has sometimes facilitated innovation, as the units of delivery have become less constrained by large-scale programmes and departments. For example, the transfer of social housing from local authorities to housing associations and the proliferation of training providers seem to have facilitated joined-up innovations such as the Foyers, which provide cheap rented housing for youth with training provision included.

However, on the whole, joined-up urban policy has been the exception rather than the rule. Topical areas have remained essentially separate. Even local area programmes continue to be initiated on single topics (education, health and so on). And obvious forms of socialisation have not been addressed at all: the impact of public transport deterioration on social and economic access and, via pollution, on health comes to mind. A general proximate cause of this failure is the neoliberal fragmentation of the urban state, which has made it increasingly difficult to coordinate topical areas. *Within* each policy field, the tendency to make units of delivery (individual schools, hospitals and so on) more autonomous makes it more difficult even to join up a single field.

A second key proximate cause of failure is the retreat by the state from any attempt to shape production directly. This means that would-be integrated policies have a gaping hole. In policy on social exclusion, for example, aspects of reproduction and training are addressed, but no strategy exists to provide jobs at the end. The conceptualisation of such initiatives thus stresses the causation "reproduction→production", which is an important *moment* of poverty but, taken alone, returns the debate to the crude 1960s problematic of the "culture of poverty". Thus, the introduction of social and cultural elements into the analysis of poverty ends up by being one-sided and the opposite of "joined-up".

At a more abstract level, these failures are expressions of deep constraints on the integration of policy by capital states. States are limited in the extent to which they can act holistically, however rational this might be from the point of view of technical efficiency, since this would undermine the private appropriation of profit by effectively socialising it. The delegitimation by neoliberalism of economic transfers has deepened this fundamental feature of the bourgeois state.

Other instances of new urban socialisation along the same lines could be discussed—for example the reworking of socialisation in the family, local culture and local economic policy[4]—though space does not permit this here. We can draw out a number of general points from the four examples given.

1) Neoliberalism has opened up gaps in the effective organisation of production, reproduction and their interrelation. These have been addressed through forms of socialisation that take old forms and rework them in new ways. Some of these forms have emerged only after substantial experience has shown the negative effects of neoliberalism. For example,

both community reproduction and attempts at joined-up
government have flowered in the 1990s, learning from the
"mistakes" of the 1980s (Peck and Tickell this volume).

2) The neoliberal context of these forms of socialisation has
served in most cases to prevent their politicisation. I have
emphasised that a central aim of neoliberalism has been to
overcome such politicisation. The new forms of urban socialisation have been developed under the sharp constraints of
intensified global competition. This competition is simultaneously externally imposed (the competition of local units of
production in the global arena intensified by liberalised trade
and investment flows), politically constructed at the local
scale (for example through throwing public services open to
private operation), and ideologically underpinned (as in the
discursive construction of the "competitive locality"). This
competition then provides a constant discipline on all local
actors, whether business, residents, workers or the state itself,
which stifles excessive demands and open conflicts (cf similar
processes at the national level discussed by Bonefeld, Brown
and Burnham 1995). The articulation of socialisation with
value discipline is achieved partly through relations between
spatial scales: neoliberalism at the national and international
scales provides a disciplinary framework that keeps in check
the potential politicisation of new local socialisations, whether
they be industrial clusters or community participation.

3) Urban socialisations, old and new, not only have been
compatible with neoliberal discipline but have often *enhanced*
it. Stronger integration within local clusters creates new,
profitable paths for the investment of global money capital.
The cooperative industrial relations fostered by local clusters,
community businesses and centrist local economic policy as a
whole can produce self-disciplined workers more effectively
than crude authoritarianism. Community reproduction can
create a real reserve army for the lower end of the labour market.
Thus, while formally opposed to neoliberalism, socialisation
can complement and reinforce it (cf Zuege 1999).

4) It follows that the class relations of current urban socialisations, for the most part, have no socialist dynamic. They are
implemented only to the extent that they are compatible with
(enhanced) accumulation in the locality. They tend to foster
greater cooperation between workers and residents on the one
hand and capital on the other; but this occurs on capital's
terms and requires forbearance and self-limitation on the part
of the working class. Moreover, these socialisations are often
divisive. The strategy of local clusters privileges professional

or skilled, mostly white and male, workers. Community initiatives foster postmodern social fragmentation. And, because all the new forms of socialisation are carried out under the rubric of competitiveness, they set localities against each other.

5) Despite the complementarities of neoliberalism and urban socialisations (points [2] and [3]), these socialisations are often *undermined* by neoliberalism. We saw this most sharply in the meagre outcomes of the attempts at joined-up government. We have also seen how neoliberal individualism disrupts attempts at collective engagement of both firms (the first issue discussed above) and populations (the third). Clusters can be destabilised by liberalised trade and enhanced mobility of productive and money capital. Thus, despite the substantial successes of recent urban socialisations, they are always threatened—and tendentially undermined—by neoliberal freedoms.

6) These contradictions mean that the articulation of value disciplines and socialisation can be developed in many different ways. Thus, in all of the areas of urban governance examined here, outcomes vary strongly between countries and localities. These are strongly path-dependent, resting on class relations and socialisation evolved over long historical periods.

Theoretical and Political Conclusions

My account of the contemporary city has sought to emphasise the *contradictions* of class relations, of capital accumulation and of reproduction. The fundamental contradiction examined has been that of neoliberalism and socialisation, of regulation by value and by direct coordination. This contains within it a whole number of others: mobility and fixity, money and production, value and use value, discipline and cooperation, private responsibility and politicisation, and so on. These are contradictions rather than merely conflicts, in that the two elements both undermine *and* construct each other.

This theorisation may be contrasted with two major schools within radical urban studies. In the second section of the paper, I criticised institutionalist and regulationalist accounts of the origins of neoliberalism for overplaying the technical aspects of production processes and underplaying wider contradictions of capitalist reproduction. My account of contemporary urbanism suggests further, related problems with these approaches:

1) Associationalist writers using a broadly institutionalist approach (Amin, Cooke, Healey, Scott, Storper, Thrift and so on) focus on negotiation and coordination between plural institutions of civil society, exemplified by the forms of socialisation which I considered in the fourth section of the paper,

and argue that these can promote both greater productive efficiency and a more inclusive and democratic polity. An essentially harmonious balance is thus possible between nonmarket and "market" (capitalist) relations. However, the associationalists systematically downplay the impacts of neo-liberalism and ignore its nature as a class strategy. They neglect the ways in which contemporary urban socialisations reproduce divisions by gender, "race" and skill, their spatially uneven development, and the ways in which they internalise class discipline (see the critique by Zuege 1999). The core problem is that myriad conflicts between socialisation and neoliberalism are denied.

2) I share with regulationist writers on cities (Goodwin, Jessop, Jones, MacLeod, Peck, Tickell and so on) an interest in mapping out articulations of markets and capital mobility with territorial forms of regulation. However, regulation theorists (as distinct from those who use "regulation" as a loose concept) are concerned with looking for regimes of accumulation and modes of regulation that can underpin stable and relatively conflict-free accumulation for long periods. Periods such as the present are understood as emergent regimes or as transitions from one such regime to another (Jessop this volume). In contrast, my account seeks to highlight the playing out of the abstract contradictions of capitalism in each period, including periods of *strong* accumulation. While consideration of such contradictions can be found in regulationist writing, it is generally subordinated to description of emerging patterns of regulation and specification of their functionality to accumulation (Gough 1996). Consequently, regulationists understand path dependency as inertia in *transitions between* determinate regimes, whereas in my account it is seen as the durability of class relations embodied in institutions, distributions of resources and consciousness. Politically, my focus on contradictions avoids the search pursued by many regulationists for a better capitalism (eg Lipietz 1992) and foregrounds the possibilities for working-class struggle outside of social-democratic (self-) limitations.

The associationalists are certainly right to highlight the important forms of socialisation within the contemporary city; much Left writing on cities neglects these in order to focus on clear examples of neoliberal coercion, fragmentation and austerity. However, we have seen that contemporary urban socialisations are deeply marked by neoliberalism. Can this be overcome? Despite their neoliberal cooption, these forms of socialisation have tropes that are attractive to socialists:

nonmarket relations, cooperation in production, skill and innovation, community, pluralism. We need strategies that, often, *begin from* these forms of socialisation but then take them in directions that challenge class, patriarchal and racist power.

Acknowledgements

This paper comes out of ongoing work with Aram Eisenschitz. I would like to thank the editors of this volume for inviting the paper and commenting on it, and for the very useful comments of three anonymous referees.

Endnotes

[1] What is the relation of "socialisation" to the notions of "regulation" and "governance"? Socialisation includes relations that are not usually included in the latter, such as community, neighbourhood and family ties and the moment of cooperation between workers and employers. On the other hand, regulation (though not governance) can denote regulation by markets, which I exclude from socialisation. Most importantly, socialisation is conceived as being in a *contradictory* relationship with private decision-making.

[2] For example, Allen, Massey and Cochrane (1997) conceive Thatcherism as an exacerbation of market anarchy, but neglect its central aim of disciplining labour and individual capitals. Surprisingly, Harvey's (2000:61–63) account of the principal origins of neoliberal globalisation omits any mention of its class-disciplinary intent.

[3] My assumption is that in capitalist societies gender and "racial" oppression are strongly internally related to the fundamental structures of capitalism through both production and reproduction spheres, though not reducible to them.

[4] Eisenschitz and Gough (1993) have argued that the majority of local economic initiatives are not formally neoliberal but develop mild, pragmatic forms of socialisation in varied fields through coordination between diverse social actors. This socialisation has developed under the spur of neoliberal competition and seeks to fill gaps created by neoliberal destruction. The politicisation to which this might lead has mostly been contained, because the competitive pressures on the locality incline all actors to moderate their demands, mobilising a localist loyalty. These initiatives thus realise key neoliberal aims: they sharpen the competition of localities against others, and the aspirations of labour tend to be subordinated to the profitability of local capital (Gough and Eisenschitz 1996). However, neoliberal individualism of firms and spatial mobility of capital and commodities can weaken such local initiatives (Eisenschitz and Gough 1996).

References

Allen J, Massey D and Cochrane A (1997) *Rethinking the Region*. London: Routledge

Amin A and Robins K (1990) The re-emergence of regions? The mythical geography of flexible accumulation. *Society and Space* 8:7–34

Atkinson R (1999) Discourses of partnership and empowerment in contemporary British urban regeneration. *Urban Studies* 36(1):59–72

Bennett R (1995) *Meeting Business Needs in Britain*. London: British Chambers of Commerce

Bluestone B and Harrison B (2000) *Growing Prosperity*. Boston: Houghton Mifflin

Bonefeld W (1993) *The Recomposition of the British State during the 1980s*. Aldershot: Dartmouth Publishing

Bonefeld W, Brown A and Burnham P (1995) *A Major Crisis?* Aldershot: Dartmouth
Brusco S (1982) The Emilian model: Productive decentralisation and social integration. *Cambridge Journal of Economics* 6:167–184
Byrne D (1999) *Social Exclusion.* Buckingham: Open University Press
Campbell B (1993) *Goliath.* London: Methuen
Clarke S (1988) *Keynesianism, Monetarism and the Crisis of the State.* Aldershot: Elgar
Colenutt B and Tansley S (1990) *Inner City Regeneration.* Manchester: Centre for Local Economic Studies
Cowley J, Kaye A, Mayo M and Thompson M (1977) *Community or Class Struggle?* London: Stage 1
Cox K (1993) The local and the global in the new urban politics: A critical view. *Society and Space* 11:433–448
Cox K (1998) Spaces of dependence, spaces of engagement and the politics of scale; Or, looking for local politics. *Political Geography* 17:1–24
de Brunhof S (1978) *The State, Capital and Economic Policy.* London: Pluto Press
Eisenschitz A (1997) The view from the grassroots. In M Pacione (ed) *Britain's Cities* (pp 150–178). London: Routledge
Eisenschitz A and Gough J (1993) *The Politics of Local Economic Policy.* Basingstoke: Macmillan
Eisenschitz A and Gough J (1996) The contradictions of neo-Keynesian local economic strategy. *Review of International Political Economy* 3:434–458
Esping-Andersen G (1990) *Three Worlds of Welfare Capitalism.* Cambridge: Polity Press
Evans R and Harding A (1997) Regionalisation, regional institutions and economic development. *Policy and Politics* 25:19–30
Gertler M (1997) The invention of regional culture. In R Lee and J Wills (eds) *Geographies of Economies* (pp 47–58). London: Arnold
Glyn A and Sutcliffe B (1972) *British Capitalism, Workers and the Profit Squeeze.* Harmondsworth: Penguin
Gough J (1991) Structure, system and contradiction in the capitalist space economy. *Society and Space* 9:433–449
Gough J (1992) Workers' competition, class relations and space. *Society and Space* 10:265–286
Gough J (1996) Not flexible accumulation: Contradictions of value in contemporary economic geography. Part 2: Regional regimes, national regulation and political strategy. *Environment and Planning A* 28:2179–2200
Gough J and Eisenschitz A (1996) The construction of mainstream local economic initiatives: Mobility, socialisation and class relations. *Economic Geography* 76: 178–195
Green F (ed) (1989) *The Restructuring of the UK Economy.* Hemel Hempstead: Harvester Wheatsheaf
Habermas J (1976) *Legitimation Crisis.* London: Heinemann
Harvey D (1989) *The Urban Experience.* Oxford: Blackwell
Harvey D (2000) *Spaces of Hope.* Edinburgh: Edinburgh University Press
Leborgne D and Lipietz A (1988) New technologies, new modes of regulation: Some spatial implications. *Environment and Planning: Society and Space* 6: 263–280
Lipietz A (1992) *Towards a New Economic Order.* Cambridge: Polity
Mandel E (1978) *Late Capitalism.* London: Verso
Markusen A (1996) Sticky places in slippery space: A typology of industrial districts. *Economic Geography* 72:293–313
Murray F (1987) Flexible specialisation in the "Third Italy". *Capital and Class* 33:84–95
Offe C (1984) *Contradictions of the Welfare State.* London: Hutchinson

Peck J and Tickell A (1995a) The social regulation of uneven development: "Regulatory deficit", England's South East and the collapse of Thatcherism. *Environment and Planning A* 27:15–40

Peck J and Tickell A (1995b) Business goes local: Dissecting the "business agenda" in Manchester. *International Journal of Urban and Regional Research* 19:55–78

Robertson S and Dale R (forthcoming) Local states of emergency: The contradictions of neoliberal governance in education in New Zealand. *British Journal of Sociology of Education*

Scott A (1998) *Regions in the World Economy*. Oxford: Oxford University Press

Storper M (1998) *The Regional World*. New York: Guilford Press

Storper M and Walker R (1989) *The Capitalist Imperative*. Oxford: Blackwell

Taylor-Gooby P (1994) Postmodernism and social policy. *Journal of Social Policy* 23: 385–404

Terhorst P (2001) Territorialisation of the state and urban trajectories: Amsterdam and Brussels compared. Paper delivered at the Association of American Geographers Conference, New York, US, February

Therborn G (1986) *Why Some Peoples Are More Unemployed than Others*. London: Verso

Zuege A (1999) The chimera of the Third Way. In L Panitch and C Leys (eds) *Socialist Register 2000* (pp 87–114). Woodbridge: Merlin Press

Jamie Gough has worked as an academic and policy researcher, and worked for the Greater London Council before its abolition. He is now a Senior Lecturer in Geography at the University of Northumbria at Newcastle, England. His *Work, Locality and the Rhythms of Capital*, a reconsideration of the labour process, accumulation and class relations, will be published by Continuum in 2002.

Chapter 4
New Globalism, New Urbanism: Gentrification as Global Urban Strategy

Neil Smith

This paper uses several events in New York in the late 1990s to launch two central arguments about the changing relationship between neoliberal urbanism and so-called globalization. First, much as the neoliberal state becomes a consummate agent of—rather than a regulator of—the market, the new revanchist urbanism that replaces liberal urban policy in cities of the advanced capitalist world increasingly expresses the impulses of capitalist production rather than social reproduction. As globalization bespeaks a rescaling of the global, the scale of the urban is recast. The true global cities may be the rapidly growing metropolitan economies of Asia, Latin America, and (to a lesser extent) Africa, as much as the command centers of Europe, North America and Japan. Second, the process of gentrification, which initially emerged as a sporadic, quaint, and local anomaly in the housing markets of some *command-center* cities, is now thoroughly generalized as an urban strategy that takes over from liberal urban policy. No longer isolated or restricted to Europe, North America, or Oceania, the impulse behind gentrification is now generalized; its incidence is global, and it is densely connected into the circuits of global capital and cultural circulation. What connects these two arguments is the shift from an urban scale defined according to the conditions of social reproduction to one in which the investment of productive capital holds definitive precedence.

Four sets of events in New York City at the end of the 1990s succinctly captured some of the central contours of the new neoliberal urbanism. The first concerns capital and the state. In the last days of 1998, New York Mayor Rudy Giuliani announced a huge "Christmas gift" to the city's most elite capitalists. Responding to "threats" that the New York Stock Exchange (NYSE) might relocate a mile across the Hudson River to New Jersey, Giuliani announced a $900 million taxpayer subsidy, ostensibly to keep the stock exchange in the city. This was only the latest and largest in a series of "geobribes" paid by the city to global corporations. The subsidy includes $400 million with which the city and state will build a new 650,000-square-foot Wall Street office for the NYSE. There was never any pretense that financial need was even an issue in this deal, since the subsidy came at a time when the stock exchange was siphoning unprecedented amounts of surplus capital from economies around the globe. Rather, city and state officials referred to the deal as a "partnership." There had, of course, been public–private partnerships previously, but this one was unprecedented in two ways. First—and most obvious—was the scale of the geobribe to private capital: topping $1 billion by 2001, the scale of this subsidy was wholly without precedent. Second, and more importantly, the local state in this instance eschewed all pretense of regulation or steerage of the private sector toward results it could not otherwise accomplish on its own. Instead, the subsidy was justified as an investment by the city and the state, as "good business practice." That the threat was in all likelihood hollow and that the NYSE would never seriously have considered leaving the city only confirms the point: rather than modulating the track taken by private investment, the local state simply fitted into the grooves already established by market logics, becoming, in effect, a junior if highly active partner to global capital. The destruction of the World Trade Center raises the very real possibility that the new stock exchange will occupy that site.

The second set of events concerns the social reproduction of the labor force. Earlier in 1998, the New York City Department of Education announced that it faced a shortage of mathematics teachers and as a result was importing forty young teachers from Austria. Even more extraordinary, in a city with more than two million native Spanish speakers, a shortage of Spanish teachers was to be filled by importing teachers from Spain. Annual international recruitment of high school teachers is now routine. At about the same time, it was announced that the New York City Police Department would take over responsibility for security in the city schools from the School Board. Taken together, these events connote a deep crisis, not just in the city's education system but in the wider system of social reproduction.

The third set of events speaks to a drastic heightening of social control. In 1997, the horrifying case of police brutality against Abner Louima, a Haitian immigrant, came to light. A year and a half later, unarmed Guinean immigrant Amadou Diallo was shot dead in a hail of forty-one police bullets in the vestibule of his apartment. Two of Louima's attackers were eventually imprisoned, but—like the majority of cops who gunned down innocent New Yorkers in the late 1990s—Diallo's killers were cleared of any criminal responsibility. The following year, in a move put on hold by Diallo's killing, the NYPD was issued with infamous "dum-dum" bullets, which are designed to do maximum bodily harm. Meanwhile, it was revealed that between 1994 and 1997, the city of New York had paid a record $96.8 million to settle burgeoning numbers of police-brutality lawsuits. Prior to the World Trade Center catastrophe, ordinary New Yorkers increasingly felt that their police force was out of control; even the president of the notorious police union expressed the fear that the city's repressive policing strategies of the late 1990s were "a blueprint for a police state and tyranny" (Cooper 1998: B5; Cooper 1999). These events were the direct result of Giuliani's imposition of "zero-tolerance tactics," but they were equally part of a larger shift in urban policy, from the liberalism that dominated much of the twentieth century toward what has elsewhere been called "the revanchist city" (Smith 1996; Swyngedouw 1997).

The fourth event—and possibly the most intriguing—concerns the changing political role of city government. Angry at the abandon with which United Nations (UN) diplomats seemed to flaunt local parking laws, and blaming them for much of Manhattan's gridlock, Giuliani threatened to begin towing illegally parked cars with diplomatic plates. Now openly derided for his policies of petty and not so petty repression, "Benito" Giuliani (as even the *New York Times* nicknamed him) was just as angry at the US State Department for seemingly capitulating to this UN vehicular malfeasance. Maybe it has come to the point, Giuliani huffed, where New York City needs to have its own foreign policy.[1] The larger point is that amidst a restructuring of the relationship between capital and the state, a burgeoning crisis of social reproduction, and heightened waves of political repression, there is also a rescaling of urban practices, cultures, and functions in the context of changing global relations and a dramatically altered fate of the nation-state.

These four events hint at much about the neoliberal urbanism that has been slouching toward birth since the 1980s. By neoliberalism, I mean something quite specific. Eighteenth-century liberalism, from John Locke to Adam Smith, pivoted on two crucial assumptions: that the free and democratic exercise of individual self-interest led to the optimal collective social good; and that the market knows best: that is, private property is the foundation of this self-interest, and free market exchange is its ideal vehicle. Twentieth-century American liberalism, from Woodrow Wilson to Franklin Roosevelt to John F Kennedy— emphasizing social compensation for the excesses of market and private property—is not so much a misnomer, therefore—it by no means abrogated these axioms of liberalism—but it is an outlier insofar as, in a co-optive response to the challenge of socialism, it sought to regulate their sway. The neoliberalism that carries the twentieth into the twenty-first century therefore represents a significant return to the original axioms of liberalism, albeit one galvanized by an unprecedented mobilization not just of national state power but of state power organized and exercised at different geographical scales.

Accordingly, the connections between capital and the state, social reproduction and social control have been drastically altered. And this transformation, the outlines of which we are only beginning to see, is being expressed most vividly through an altered geography of social relations—more concretely, through a rescaling of social processes and relations that creates new amalgams of scale replacing the old amalgams broadly associated with "community," "urban," "regional," "national," and "global." I focus in this paper only on neoliberal urbanism and the relationship between global and urban. I do not in any way intend to infer that other scales are less relevant in the broad scheme of things, but I do want to pick up on what seems to be a special nexus that is being forged between global and urban change. In particular, I want to make two arguments that will seem at first to be quite separate. In the first place, I want to argue that in the context of a refashioned globalism, widely (if partially) expressed via the ideological discourses of "globalization," we are also seeing a broad redefinition of the urban scale—in effect, a new urbanism—that refocuses the criteria of scale construction, in this case toward processes of production and toward the extraordinary urban growth in Asia, Latin America, and Africa. Second, focusing more on Europe and North America, I want to argue that the comparatively recent process of gentrification has been generalized as a central feature of this new urbanism. I therefore offer two threads of an argument suggesting how neoliberalism evolves new forms within the larger history of capitalist urbanization. In concluding, I hope to show that the two shifts explored here are actually interconnected.

New Urbanism
In her skillfully synthetic accounts (1992, 1998, 2000), Saskia Sassen offers a benchmark argument about the importance of local place in the new globalism. Place, she insists, is central to the circulation of people and capital that constitute globalization, and a focus on urban places in a globalizing world brings with it a recognition of the rapidly declining significance of the national economy, while also insisting that globalization takes place through specific social and economic complexes rooted in specific places. This builds on a familiar picture of globalization, defined in terms of the economic shift from production to finance. Global cities emerged when, in the 1970s, the global financial system expanded dramatically and foreign direct investment was dominated, not by capital invested directly in productive functions, but rather by capital moving into and between capital markets. This, in turn, pollinated a broad expansion of ancillary producer services concentrated in command and control posts in the financial economy, and those new urban forms are marked by extreme bifurcations of wealth and poverty, dramatic realignments of class relations, and dependence on new streams of immigrant labor. This, of course, is the paradigmatic global city. The balance of economic power has shifted since the 1970s "from production places, such as Detroit and Manchester, to centers of finance and highly specialized services" (Sassen 1992:325).

A welcome alternative to the blithe optimism of globalized utopias, Sassen's account is astute about the shifting contents of some urban economies. However, it is vulnerable on both empirical grounds, which indicate a far more complicated set of relationships connecting global cities and a wider range of cities that can be grouped under the label, global cities (Taylor 1999), and on theoretical grounds. In the end, Sassen's argument is a little vague about how places are, in fact, constructed. It does not go far enough. It is as if the global social economy comprises a plethora of containers—nation-states—within which float a number of smaller containers, the cities. Globalization brings about a dramatic change in the kinds of social and economic relations and activities carried on in these containers, a re-sorting of activities between different containers, and an increased porosity of the national containers, such that turbulence in the wider global sea increasingly buffets cities directly. However, with the exception of some national containers that may actually sink, the containers themselves remain rather rigidly intact in this vision, even as the relations between them are transformed. As Brenner (1998:11) puts it, Sassen's account remains "surprisingly statecentric." I want to argue here that in the context of a new globalism, we are experiencing the emergence of a new urbanism such that the containers themselves are being fundamentally recast. "The urban" is being redefined just as dramatically as the global; the old conceptual containers—our 1970s assumptions about what "the urban" is or was—no longer hold water. The new concatenation of urban functions and activities vis-à-vis the national and the global changes not only the make-up of the city but the very definition of what constitutes—literally—the urban scale.

Cities have historically performed multiple functions ranging from the military and religious to the political and commercial, the symbolic and the cultural, depending on the history and geography of their construction and transformation. The scale of the urban is similarly expressive of particular social geographies and histories. With the development and expansion of industrial capitalism, burgeoning cities increasingly express the powerful impulse toward the centralization of capital, while the *scale* of the urban is increasingly defined in terms of the geographical limits to daily labor migration. That is, as soon as the *social* division of labor between production and reproduction become simultaneously a spatial division, and whatever other functions the city performs and activities it embodies, the social and territorial organization of the social reproduction of labor—the provision and maintenance of a working-class population—comes to play a pivotal role in the determination of the urban scale. More than anything else, the scale of the modern city is thereby calibrated by something quite mundane: the contradictory determinations of the geographical limits of the daily commute of workers between home and work (Smith 1990:136–137).

The Keynesian city of advanced capitalism, in which the state underwrote wide swaths of social reproduction, from housing to welfare to transportation infrastructure, represented the zenith of this definitive relationship between urban scale and social reproduction. This is a consistent theme that has run through the work of European and American urban theorists since the 1960s, from urban revolution (Lefebvre 1971) to urban crisis (Harvey 1973) and Castells' (1977) explicit definition of the urban in terms of collective consumption, and has been an enduring concern of feminist urban theory (Hansen and Pratt 1995; Katz 2001; Rose 1981). Equally a center of capital accumulation, the Keynesian city was in many respects the combined hiring hall and welfare hall for each national capital. Indeed the so-called urban crisis of the late 1960s and 1970s was widely interpreted as a crisis of social reproduction, having to do with the dysfunctionality of racism, class exploitation, and patriarchy and the contradictions between an urban form elicited according to criteria of accumulation and one that had to be justified in terms of the efficiency of social reproduction.

Let us now step back and look at the question of "globalization," because if we are talking about global cities presumably their definition is implicated in the processes thereof. What exactly is globalizing at the beginning of the twenty-first century? What is new about the present? Certainly it is not commodity capital that is globalizing: Adam Smith and Karl Marx both recognized a "world market." Nor, by the same token, can it be financial capital that is globalizing. Contemporary levels of global financial interchange are only now beginning to reach again the levels of the period between the 1890s and World War I. The Bretton Woods institutions established after 1944, especially the International Monetary Fund, were intended to re-stimulate and regulate global financial flows interrupted by depression and war. Viewed in this historical light, the global expansion of stock and currency markets and broad financial deregulation since the 1980s may be more a response to globalization than its cause. The globalization of cultural images in the era of computers and unprecedented migration is also very powerful, but it is difficult to sustain a claim for the novelty of cultural globalization given the extent of pre-existing cultural cross-fertilization. Long before the 1980s, all "national" cultures were more or less hybrid. This leaves us with production capital, and I think a good case can be made that to the extent that globalization heralds anything new, the new globalism can be traced back to the increasingly global—or at least international—scale of economic production. As late as the 1970s, most consumer commodities were produced in one national economy either for consumption there or for export to a different national market. By the 1990s, that model was obsolete, definitive sites of production for specific commodities became increasingly difficult to identify, and the old language of economic geography no longer made sense. In autos, electronics, garments, computers, biomedical, and many other industrial sectors ranging from high tech to low, production is now organized across national boundaries to such a degree that questions of national "import" and "export" are supplanted by questions of global trade internal to the production process. The idea of "national capital" makes little sense today, because most global trade across national boundaries is now intrafirm: it takes place *within* the production networks of single corporations.

There is little doubt that in strictly economic terms, the power of most states organized at the national scale is eroding. This in no way invokes a "zero-sum" conception of scale (Brenner 1998; MacLeod 2001), nor is it a simplistic argument that the nation-state is withering away. In the first place, the political and cultural power of national-scale power is not necessarily eroding at all and may be hardening in many places. Second, the erosion of economic power at the national scale is highly uneven and not necessarily universal, with the US or Chinese state enjoying a quite different fate from Malaysia or Zimbabwe. For example, Mészáros (2001) has argued that the ambition of the US state seems to be its transformation into a global state, and the conduct of the brutal "war on terrorism"—in reality a war for global hegemony (Smith forthcoming)—seems to confirm this analysis. Yet the sources of increased economic porosity at the national scale are undeniable: communications and financial deregulation have expanded the geographical mobility of capital; unprecedented labor migrations have distanced local economies from automatic dependency on home grown labor; national and local states (including city governments) have responded by offering carrots to capital while applying the stick to labor and dismantling previous supports for social reproduction; and finally, class and race-based struggles have broadly receded, giving local and national governments increased leeway to abandon that sector of the population surplused by both the restructuring of the economy and the gutting of social services. The mass incarceration of working-class and minority populations, especially in the US, is the national analogue of the emerging revanchist city. Comparatively low levels of struggle were crucial in the virtual nonresponse by government to the Los Angeles uprisings after 1992, which stand in dramatic contrast to the ameliorative—if paternalistic—response after the uprisings of the 1960s.

Two mutually reinforcing shifts have consequently restructured the functions and active roles of cities. In the first place, systems of production previously territorialized at the (subnational) regional scale were increasingly cut loose from their definitive national context, resulting not just in the waves of deindustrialization in the 1970s and 1980s but in wholesale regional restructuring and destructuring as part of a reworking of established scale hierarchies. As a result, production systems have been downscaled. The territorialization of production increasingly centers on extended metropolitan centers, rather than on larger regions: the metropolitan scale again comes to dominate the regional scale, rather than the other way round. In place of the American Northeast or Midwest, the English Midlands, and the German Ruhr, for example—classic geographical fruits of modern industrial capitalism—we have São Paulo and Bangkok, Mexico City and Shanghai, Mumbai and Seoul. Whereas the traditional industrial regions were the backbone of national capitals in the nineteenth and much of the twentieth centuries, these new, huge urban economies are increasingly the platforms of *global* production. This rescaling of production toward the metropolitan scale is an expression of global change; at the same time, it lies at the heart of a new urbanism.

The corollary is also taking place, as national states have increasingly moved away from the liberal urban policies that dominated the central decades of the twentieth century in the advanced capitalist economies. In the US, President Ford's refusal to bail out New York City amidst a deep fiscal crisis (immortalized in the famous *Daily News* headline: "Ford to City: Drop Dead"), followed by the failure of President Carter's attempted urban plan in 1978, gave the first intimation of a national economy increasingly delinked from and independent of its cities. The wholesale demise of liberal urban policy followed in fits and starts, working toward Clinton's cynical slashing of the social welfare system in 1996. If the effects are often more muted and take myriad forms, the trajectory of change is similar in most of the wealthiest economies, although Italy—the transfer of some national state power to the European Union notwithstanding—may be an exception.

The point here is not that the national state is necessarily weakened or that the territoriality of political and economic power is somehow less potent. This argument—that global power today resides in a network of economic connections rather than in any particular place—is embodied in the influential treatment of *Empire* by Hardt and Negri (2000), but it is flawed by a certain necromancy with finance capital and a blindness to the contradictions of power that comes with the necessary fixing of economic activities and political control in space. Certainly, specific functions and activities previously organized at the national scale are being dispersed to other scales up and down the scale hierarchy. At the same time, however, national states are reframing themselves as purer, territorially rooted economic actors in and of the market, rather than external compliments to it. Social and economic

restructuring is simultaneously the restructuring of spatial scale, insofar as the fixation of scales crystallizes the contours of social power—
who is empowered and who contained, who wins and who loses—into
remade physical landscapes (Brenner 1998; Smith and Dennis 1987;
Swyngedouw 1996, 1997).

As various contributions to this volume suggest, neoliberal urbanism is an integral part of this wider rescaling of functions, activities,
and relations. It comes with a considerable emphasis on the nexus of
production and finance capital at the expense of questions of social
reproduction. It is not that the organization of social reproduction no
longer modulates the definition of the urban scale but rather that its
power in doing so is significantly depleted. Public debates over suburban sprawl in Europe and especially the US, intense campaigns in
Europe promoting urban "regeneration," and the emerging environmental justice movements all suggest not only that the crisis of social
reproduction is thoroughly territorialized but, conversely, that the
production of urban space has also come to embody that crisis. A
connection exists between the production of the urban scale and
the efficient expansion of value, and a "mis-scaled" urbanism can
seriously interfere with the accumulation of capital. The crisis of daily
commuting lies at the center of this crisis. I once surmised (Smith
1990:137) that where the geographical expansion of cities outstripped
their ability to get people from home to work and back again, the
result was not just urban chaos but a "fragmentation and disequilib-
rium in the universalization of abstract labour" that went to the heart
of economic cohesion. While this contradiction between geographical
form and economic process no doubt endures, the evidence from cities
in many parts of Asia, Africa, and Latin America presents a rather
different picture. The daily commute into São Paulo, for example, can
begin for many at 3:30 a.m. and take in excess of four hours in each
direction. In Harare, Zimbabwe, the average commuting time from
black townships on the urban periphery is also four hours each
way, leading to a workday in which workers are absent from home for
sixteen hours and sleeping most of the rest. The economic cost of
commuting for these same workers has also expanded dramatically, in
part as a result of the privatization of transportation at the behest of
the World Bank: commutes that consumed roughly 8% of weekly
incomes in the early 1980s required between 22% and 45% by the mid
1990s (Ramsamy 2001:375–377).

Why is this happening? Many well-meaning planners indict the lack
of suitable infrastructure, and that is undeniably an issue. However, if
we step back one level of abstraction, there is a fundamental geographical contradiction between the dramatically increased land
values that accompany the centralization of capital in the core of these
metropolises and the marginal, exurban locations where workers are

forced to live due to the pitiful wages on which that capital central-ization is built. Yet, extraordinarily, chaotic and arduous commutes have not yet led to an economic breakdown; the impulses of economic production—and, especially, the need to have workers turn up at the workplace—have taken precedence over any constraints emanating from the conditions of social reproduction. The rigors of almost un-bearable commuting have not yet compromised economic production. Instead, they have elicited a "desperate resilience" and been absorbed amidst the wider social breakdown that Katz (forthcoming) calls "disintegrating developments."

Thus, the leading edge in the combined restructuring of urban scale and function does not lie in the old cities of advanced capitalism, where the disintegration of traditional production-based regions and the increasing dislocation of social reproduction at the urban scale is certainly painful, unlikely to pass unopposed, but also partial. Rather, it lies in the large and rapidly expanding metropolises of Asia, Latin America, and parts of Africa, where the Keynesian welfare state was never significantly installed, the definitive link between the city and social reproduction was never paramount, and the fetter of old forms, structures, and landscapes is much less strong. These metropolitan economies are becoming the production hearths of a new globalism. Unlike the suburbanization of the postwar years in North America and Europe, Oceania, and Japan, the dramatic urban expansion of the early twenty-first century will be unambiguously led by the expansion of social production rather than reproduction. In this respect, at least, Lefebvre's announcement of an urban revolution redefining the city and urban struggles in terms of social reproduction—or indeed Castells' definition of the urban in terms of collective consumption—will fade into historical memory. If "capitalism shifted gears" with the advent of Keynesianism "from a 'supply-side' to a 'demand-side' urban-ization," as Harvey (1985:202, 209) once observed, twenty-first-century urbanism potentially reverses this shift.

This restructuring of scale and the cautious re-empowerment of the urban scale—Giuliani's ambition for a five-borough foreign policy—represents just one thread of neoliberal urbanism. It dovetails with the more culturally attuned assessment of political geographer Peter Taylor (1995:58), who argues that "[C]ities are replacing states in the construction of social identities." Cities like São Paulo and Shanghai, Lagos and Bombay, are likely to challenge the more traditional urban centers, not just in size and density of economic activity—they have already done that—but primarily as leading incubators in the global economy, progenitors of new urban form, process, and identity. No one seriously argues that the twenty-first century will see a return to a world of city-states—but it *will* see a recapture of urban political prerogative vis-à-vis regions and nation-states.

Finally, the redefinition of the scale of the urban in terms of social production rather than reproduction in no way diminishes the importance of social reproduction in the pursuit of urban life. Quite the opposite: struggles over social reproduction take on a heightened significance precisely because of the dismantling of state responsibilities. However, state abstention in this area is matched by heightened state activism in terms of social control. The transformation of New York into a "revanchist city" is not an isolated event, and the emergence of more authoritarian state forms and practices is not difficult to comprehend in the context of the rescaling of global and local geographies. According to Swyngedouw (1997:138), the substitution of market discipline for that of a hollowed-out welfare state deliberately excludes significant parts of the population, and the fear of social resistance provokes heightened state authoritarianism. At the same time, the new urban work force increasingly comprises marginal and part-time workers who are not entirely integrated into shrinking systems of state economic discipline, as well as immigrants whose cultural and political networks—part of the means of social reproduction—also provide alternative norms of social practice, alternative possibilities of resistance.

In summary, my point here is not to argue that cities like New York, London, and Tokyo lack power in the global hierarchy of urban places and high finance. The concentration of financial and other command functions in these centers is undeniable. Rather, I am trying to put that power in context and, by questioning the common assumption that the power of financial capital is necessarily paramount, to question the criteria according to which cities come to be dubbed "global." If there is any truth to the argument that so-called globalization results in the first place from the globalization of production, then our assessment of what constitutes a global city should presumably reflect that claim.

Urban Regeneration: Gentrification as Global Urban Strategy

Let me now shift scales and focus toward the process of gentrification. If one dimension of neoliberal urbanism in the twenty-first century is an uneven inclusion of Asian and Latin American urban experiences, especially at the forefront of a new urbanism, a second dimension concerns what might be called the generalization of gentrification as a global urban strategy. At first glance these surely seem like two quite different arguments, the one about luxury housing in the centers of global power, the other about new models of urbanism from the integrating peripheries. They certainly express contrasting experiences of a new urbanism, but that is precisely the point. Neoliberal urbanism encompasses a wide range of social, economic, and geographical

shifts, and the point of these contrasting arguments is to push the issue
of how varied the experience of neoliberal urbanism is and how these
contrasting worlds fit together.

Most scholars' vision of gentrification remains closely tied to the process as it was defined in the 1960s by sociologist Ruth Glass. Here
is her founding 1964 statement (Glass 1964:xviii), which revealed
gentrification as a discrete process:

> One by one, many of the working-class quarters of London have
> been invaded by the middle classes—upper and lower. Shabby,
> modest mews and cottages—two rooms up and two down—have
> been taken over, when their leases have expired, and have become
> elegant, expensive residences. Larger Victorian houses, downgraded
> in an earlier or recent period—which were used as lodging houses or
> were otherwise in multiple occupation—have been upgraded once
> again ... Once this process of "gentrification" starts in a district it
> goes on rapidly until all or most of the original working-class
> occupiers are displaced and the whole social character of the district
> is changed.

Almost poetically, Glass captured the novelty of this new process
whereby a new urban "gentry" transformed working-class quarters.
Consider now an updated statement thirty-five years later, again from
London. The following is an excerpt from the 1999 decree for "Urban
Renaissance" (DETR 1999) released by a special Urban Task Force
appointed by the UK Department of the Environment, Transport and
the Regions (DETR):

> The Urban Task Force will identify causes of urban decline ... and
> practical solutions to bring people back into our cities, towns, and
> urban neighborhoods. It will establish a new vision for urban regen-
> eration ... [Over the next twenty-five years] 60% of new dwellings
> should be built on previously developed land ... [W]e have lost con-
> trol of our towns and cities, allowing them to become spoilt by poor
> design, economic dispersal, and social polarisation. The beginning of
> the 21st century is a moment of change [offering] the opportunity for
> an urban renaissance.

This language of urban renaissance is not new, of course, but it takes
on far greater significance here. The scale of ambitions for urban
rebuilding has expanded dramatically. Whereas state-sponsored postwar urban renewal in Western cities helped to encourage scattered
private-market gentrification, that gentrification and the intensified
privatization of inner-city land and housing markets since the 1980s
has, in turn, provided the platform on which large-scale multifaceted
urban regeneration plans, far outstripping 1960s urban renewal, are
established. The current language of urban regeneration, particularly

in Europe, is not one-dimensional, but it bespeaks, among other things, a generalization of gentrification in the urban landscape.

Consider some key differences in the visions presented by Glass and the DETR. Whereas, for Glass, 1960s gentrification was a marginal oddity in the Islington housing market—a quaint urban sport of the hipper professional classes unafraid to rub shoulders with the unwashed masses—by the end of the twentieth century it had become a central goal of British urban policy. Whereas the key actors in Glass's story were assumed to be middle- and upper-middle-class immigrants to a neighborhood, the agents of urban regeneration thirty-five years later are governmental, corporate, or corporate-governmental partnerships. A seemingly serendipitous, unplanned process that popped up in the postwar housing market is now, at one extreme, ambitiously and scrupulously planned. That which was utterly haphazard is increasingly systematized. In scale and diversity, the process of gentrification has evolved rapidly, to the point where the narrowly residential rehabilitation projects that were so paradigmatic of the process in the 1960s and 1970s now seem quaint, not just in the urban landscape but in the urban-theory literature.

Most importantly, perhaps, a highly local reality, first identified in a few major advanced capitalist cities such as London, New York, Paris, and Sydney, is now virtually global. Its evolution has been both vertical and lateral. On the one hand, gentrification as a process has rapidly descended the urban hierarchy; it is evident not only in the largest cities but in more unlikely centers such as the previously industrial cities of Cleveland or Glasgow, smaller cities like Malmö or Grenada, and even small market towns such as Lancaster, Pennsylvania or České Krumlov in the Czech Republic. At the same time, the process has diffused geographically as well, with reports of gentrification from Tokyo to Tenerife (Garcia 2001), São Paulo to Puebla, Mexico (Jones and Varley 1999), Cape Town (Garside 1993) to the Caribbean (Thomas 1991), Shanghai to Seoul. In some kind of irony, even Hobart, the capital of Van Diemen's Land (Tasmania), where dispossessed British peasants turned poachers and rebels were exiled in the nineteenth century and where, in turn, the local people were annihilated, is also undergoing gentrification.

Of course, these experiences of gentrification are highly varied and unevenly distributed, much more diverse than were early European or North American instances of gentrification. They spring from quite assorted local economies and cultural ensembles and connect in many complicated ways to wider national and global political economies. The important point here is the rapidity of the evolution of an initially marginal urban process first identified in the 1960s and its ongoing transformation into a significant dimension of contemporary urbanism. Whether in its quaint form, represented by Glass's mews, or in its socially organized form in the twenty-first century, gentrification portends a displacement of working-class residents from urban centers. Indeed, the class nature of the process, transparent in Glass's version of gentrification, is assiduously hidden in the verbiage of the British Labour government. That symptomatic silence says as much about the city's changing social and cultural geography, twinned with a changing economic geography, as do its more visible and voluble signs.

In the context of North America and Europe, it is possible to identify three waves of gentrification (Hackworth 2000). The first wave, beginning in the 1950s, can be thought of as sporadic gentrification, much as Glass observed it. A second wave followed in the 1970s and 1980s as gentrification became increasingly entwined with wider processes of urban and economic restructuring. Hackworth (2000) labels this the "anchoring phase" of gentrification. A third wave emerges in the 1990s; we might think of this as gentrification generalized. Of course, this evolution of gentrification has occurred in markedly different ways in different cities and neighborhoods and according to different temporal rhythms. In Mexico City, for example, the process is nowhere as highly capitalized or widespread as in New York, remaining confined to the city's central district, in addition to Coyoacán, and the demarcation of three identifiable waves of gentrification has little if any empirical validity there. In Seoul or São Paulo, the process is geographically isolated and in its infancy. In the Caribbean, the increasing connections between gentrification and global capital generally filter through the tourist industry, giving it its own distinct flavor. By the same token, the transformation of mile after mile of old wharf and warehouse properties along both banks of the Thames suggests that gentrification in London is more expansive than in most North American cities. Insofar as it is an expression of larger social, economic, and political relations, gentrification in any particular city will express the particularities of the place in the making of its urban space.

And yet, to differing degrees, gentrification had evolved by the 1990s into a crucial urban strategy for city governments in consort with private capital in cities around the world. Liberal urban policy, which in Europe dated back in some places to the end of the nineteenth century and in North America to the transition from the Progressive Era to Roosevelt's New Deal, was systematically defeated beginning with the political economic crises of the 1970s and the conservative national administrations that followed in the 1980s. From Reagan to Thatcher and, later, Kohl, the provisions of that liberal urban policy were systematically disempowered or dismantled at the national scale, and public policy constraints on gentrification were replaced by subsidized private-market transformation of the urban built environment. This transformation was intensified by the coterie of neoliberal leaders that followed—Clinton, Blair, Schröder—and the new phase of gentrification therefore dovetails with a larger class conquest, not only of national power but of urban policy. By the end of the twentieth century, gentrification fueled by a concerted and systematic partnership of public planning with public and private capital had moved into the vacuum left by the end of liberal urban policy. Elsewhere, where cities were not governed by liberal urban policy during much of the twentieth century, the trajectory of change has been different, yet the embrace of a broadly conceived gentrification of old centers as a competitive urban strategy in the global market leads in a similar direction. In this respect, at least, turn-of-the-century neoliberalism hints at a thread of convergence between urban experiences in the larger cities of what used to be called the First and Third Worlds.

The generalization of gentrification has various dimensions. These can be understood in terms of five interrelated characteristics: the transformed role of the state, penetration by global finance, changing levels of political opposition, geographical dispersal, and the sectoral generalization of gentrification. Let us examine each of these in turn. First, between the second and third waves of gentrification, the role of the state has changed dramatically (Hackworth and Smith 2001). In the 1990s, the relative withdrawal of the national state from subsidies to gentrification that had occurred in the 1980s was reversed with the intensification of partnerships between private capital and the local state, resulting in larger, more expensive, and more symbolic developments, from Barcelona's waterfront to Berlin's Potsdamer Platz. Urban policy no longer aspires to guide or regulate the direction of economic growth so much as to fit itself to the grooves already established by the market in search of the highest returns, either directly or in terms of tax receipts.

The new role played by global capital is also definitive of the generalization of gentrification. From London's Canary Wharf to Battery Park City—developed by the same Canadian-based firm—it is easy to point to the new influx of global capital into large megadevelopments in urban centers (Fainstein 1994). Just as remarkable, however, is the extent to which global capital has percolated into much more modest, neighborhood developments. Emblematic in this regard is a new sixty-one-unit condominium building in New York's Lower East Side, two miles from Wall Street, where every apartment is wired with the latest high-speed Internet connections. This is a small development by global city standards, but it was built by nonunion immigrant labor (a stunning development in New York in the 1990s), the developer is Israeli, and the major source of financing comes from the European American Bank (Smith and DiFilippis 1999). The reach of global capital down to the local neighborhood scale is equally a hallmark of the latest phase of gentrification.

Third, there is the question of opposition to gentrification. From Amsterdam to Sydney, Berlin to Vancouver, San Francisco to Paris, gentrification's second wave was matched by the rise of myriad homeless, squatting, housing, and other antigentrification movements and organizations that were often loosely linked around overlapping issues. These rarely came together as citywide movements, but they did challenge gentrification sufficiently that, in each case, they were targeted by city politicians and police forces. Apart from anything else, the heightened levels of repression aimed at antigentrification movements in the 1980s and 1990s testified to the increasing centrality of real-estate development in the new urban economy. Cities' political regimens were changing in unison with their economic profile, and the dismantling of liberal urban policy provided as much a political opportunity as an economic one for new regimes of urban power. The emergence of the revanchist city (Smith 1996) was not just a New York phenomenon: it can be seen in the antisquatter campaigns in Amsterdam in the 1980s, attacks by Parisian police on homeless (largely immigrant) encampments, and the importation of New York's zero-tolerance techniques by police forces around the world. In São Paulo, highly repressive tactics applied to the city's street people are rationalized in terms of the "scientific" doctrine of "zero tolerance" emanating from New York. In all of these cases, the new revanchism was explicitly justified in terms of making the city safe for gentrification. The new authoritarianism both quashes opposition and makes the streets safe for gentrification.

The fourth characteristic of this latest phase is the outward diffusion of gentrification from the urban center. This is far from a smooth or regular process, but as gentrification near the center results in higher land and housing prices, even for old, untransformed properties, districts further out become caught up in the momentum of gentrification. The pattern of diffusion is highly variable and is influenced by everything from architecture and parks to the presence of water. Above all, it is geared to the historical patterns of capital investment and disinvestment in the landscape. The more uneven the initial outward growth of capital investment and the more uneven the disinvestment in these newer landscapes, the less even will be the diffusion of gentrification. By the same token, in cities where the majority of spatial expansion has occurred in recent years and where the opportunities for sustained disinvestment have been circumscribed, the diffusion of gentrification may be similarly limited.

Finally, the sectoral generalization that typifies this most recent phase goes to the heart of what distinguishes the new gentrification. Whereas urban renewal in the 1950s, 1960s, and 1970s sought a full-scale remaking of the centers of many cities and galvanized many sectors of the urban economy in the process, it was highly regulated and economically and geographically limited by the fact that it was wholly dependent on public financing and therefore had to address issues of broad social necessity, such as social housing. In contrast, the earliest wave of gentrification that followed urban renewal proceeded with considerable independence from the public sector. Despite considerable public subsidy, the full weight of private-market finance was not applied until the third wave. What marks the latest phase of gentrification in many cities, therefore, is that a new amalgam of corporate and state powers and practices has been forged in a much more ambitious effort to gentrify the city than earlier ones.

Retaking the city for the middle classes involves a lot more than simply providing gentrified housing. Third-wave gentrification has evolved into a vehicle for transforming whole areas into new landscape complexes that pioneer a comprehensive class-inflected urban remake. These new landscape complexes now integrate housing with shopping, restaurants, cultural facilities (cf Vine 2001), open space, employment opportunities—whole new complexes of recreation, consumption, production, and pleasure, as well as residence. Just as important, gentrification as urban strategy weaves global financial markets together with large- and medium-sized real-estate developers, local merchants, and property agents with brand-name retailers, all lubricated by city and local governments for whom beneficent social outcomes are now assumed to derive from the market rather than from its regulation. Most crucially, real-estate development becomes a centerpiece of the city's *productive* economy, an end in itself, justified by appeals to jobs, taxes, and tourism. In ways that could hardly have been envisaged in the 1960s, the construction of new gentrification complexes in central cities across the world has become an increasingly unassailable capital accumulation strategy for competing urban economies. Herein lies a central connection to the larger outline of a new urbanism, and we shall return to it shortly.

The strategic appropriation and generalization of gentrification as a means of global interurban competition finds its most developed expression in the language of "urban regeneration." Consonant with the importance of the state in the new wave of urban change, it is not in the US that this process has proceeded furthest, but rather in Europe. Tony Blair's Labour administration may be the most outspoken advocate of reinventing gentrification as "urban regeneration," but gentrification is a Europe-wide movement. Denmark, for example, made regeneration official policy in 1997 with a separate National Secretariat for Urban Regeneration, and Berlin bureaucrats have come to view the entire period of rebuilding after 1991 as one of "urban regeneration." A major conference was held in Paris in December 2000 on the theme of "Convergence in Urban Regeneration and Housing Policy in Europe." The conference was attended by senior policy directors and advisors representing all governments of the European Union, together with some neighboring states aspiring to EU membership; its brochure signaled the intent to push the "debate on housing and regeneration ... beyond the narrow span of physical development to examine the institutional arrangements which have to be put into place" in order to make "urban regeneration" a reality. The mission of those attending the conference was practical and comprehensive: large-scale urban transformation will require solid links between "the providers of social housing, private investors, [and] those responsible for training or policing" as well as between "local regeneration agencies, local authorities, and national governments." Regeneration policies are multifaceted and include various efforts that would not normally be included under the label of "gentrification," yet it also makes sense to see these initiatives—the British urban regeneration manifesto, European state policies, and the efforts to establish a Europe-wide urban regeneration strategy—as the most ambitious attempts to incorporate gentrification into the heart of transnational urban policies.

There are a number of striking aspects of these new "urban regeneration" agendas. First is a question of scale. The coordination of urban "regeneration" strategies across national boundaries is unprecedented. While various international sources certainly contributed to the rebuilding of European cities after World War II, the subsequent urban renewal programs were resolutely national in origin, funding, and scope. Today, by contrast, Europe-wide initiatives on urban regeneration are pioneering cross-national gentrification at a scale never before seen. A central concern lies with efforts to integrate housing initiatives with "other regenerative activities." Thus, as the title of the Paris conference conveys, this transition from housing-centered gentrification policy to a broad-based multisectoral "regeneration" is still in process—and, unlike the situation in the US, the question of social housing cannot be entirely excluded from the vision of regeneration. While a Europe-wide state-centered strategy of urban regeneration is by no means yet in place, therefore, for Eureaucrats, developers, and financiers throughout the continent, it is very much in sight. A crucial connection to the earlier discussion of the new urbanism becomes clear: third-wave gentrification is increasingly expressive of the rescaling of the urban vis-à-vis national and global scales.

Second is the question of geographical focus. The 1999 British regeneration manifesto, apparently watchful of the environmental consequences of continued suburban sprawl, declares that over the next twenty-five years, 60% of new housing provision should occur on "brownfield" sites—that is, on urban land that has already gone through one or more cycles of development. Clearly, this initiative will be aimed at older urban areas that have undergone sustained disinvestment, and while these can be scattered throughout metropolitan areas, it is reasonable to expect that they would be concentrated in or near urban centers. Enveloped as regeneration, gentrification is thus recast as a positive and necessary environmental strategy.

Connected is the question of "social balance" and the need, as the regeneration strategy puts it, to "bring people back into our cities" (DETR 1999). "Social balance" sounds like a good thing—who could be against social balance?—until one examines the neighborhoods targeted for "regeneration," whereupon it becomes clear that the strategy involves a major colonization by the middle and upper-middle classes. To the politician, planner, or economist, social balance in London's Brixton means bringing "back" more of the white middle classes. Advocates of "social balance" rarely, if ever, advocate that white neighborhoods should be balanced by equal numbers of people of African, Caribbean, or Asian descent. Thus, it is not "people" in general who are to be brought "back into our cities"; this appeal is not aimed at Welsh coal miners, Bavarian farm workers, or Breton fisher folk. Rather, the appeal to bring people back into the city is always a self-interested appeal that the white middle and upper-middle classes retake control of the political and cultural economies as well as the geography of the largest cities. Probing the symptomatic silence of who is to be invited back into the city begins to reveal the class politics involved.

Then there is the question of the anodyne language of "regeneration" in itself. In the first place where does this language come from? A biomedical and ecological term, "regeneration" applies to individual plants, species, or organs—a liver or a forest might regenerate—and insinuates that the strategic gentrification of the city is actually a natural process. Thus, the advocacy of regeneration strategies disguises the quintessentially social origins and goals of urban change and erases the politics of winners and losers out of which such policies emerge. Gentrification generally involves displacement, yet neither the British manifesto for "urban regeneration" nor the agenda of the Europe-wide Paris conference registers any recognition of the fate of those people displaced by the proposed reconquest of the city.

The language of regeneration sugarcoats gentrification. Precisely because the language of gentrification tells the truth about the class shift involved in "regeneration" of the city, it has become a dirty word to developers, politicians, and financiers; we find ourselves in the ironic position that in the US, where the ideology of classlessness is so prevalent, the language of gentrification is quite generalized, whereas in Europe it is suppressed. Thus even seemingly progressive planners and local councillors from Bochum to Brixton, who still think of themselves as socialists and who may be keenly aware of the dangers of displacement, have become captured by the bureaucratic promise of "regeneration" to such an extent that the integral agenda of widespread gentrification of urban centers is largely invisible. Not only does "urban regeneration" represent the next wave of gentrification, planned and financed on an unprecedented scale, but the victory of this language in anesthetizing our critical understanding of gentrification in Europe represents a considerable ideological victory for neoliberal visions of the city.

The point here is not to force a one-to-one mapping between regeneration and gentrification strategies, or to condemn all regeneration strategies as Trojan horses for gentrification. Rather, I want to insist that gentrification is a powerful, if often camouflaged, intent within urban regeneration strategies and to mount a critical challenge to the ideological anodyne that sweeps the question of gentrification from sight even as the scale of the process becomes more threatening and the absorption of gentrification into a wider neoliberal urbanism becomes more palpable. Gentrification as global urban strategy is a consummate expression of neoliberal urbanism. It mobilizes individual property claims via a market lubricated by state donations.

Conclusion

In this paper, I present two rather different arguments. On the one hand, I challenge the Eurocentric assumption that global cities should be defined according to command functions rather than by their participation in the global production of surplus value. On the other hand, I want to highlight the ways in which gentrification has evolved as a competitive urban strategy within the same global economy. The post-1990s generalization of gentrification as a global urban strategy plays a pivotal role in neoliberal urbanism in two ways. First, it fills the vacuum left by the abandonment of twentieth-century liberal urban policy. Second, it serves up the central- and inner-city real-estate markets as burgeoning sectors of *productive* capital investment: the globalization of productive capital embraces gentrification. This was neither inevitable nor accidental. Rather, as cities became global, so did some of their defining features. The emerging globalization of gentrification, like that of cities themselves, represents the victory of certain economic and social interests over others, a reassertion of (neoliberal) economic assumptions over the trajectory of gentrification (Smith and DiFilippis 1999).

Even where gentrification per se remains limited, the mobilization of urban real-estate markets as vehicles of capital accumulation is ubiquitous. A further symptom of the intense integration of the real-estate industry into the definitional core of neoliberal urbanism comes from cities such as Kuala Lumpur, Singapore, Rio de Janeiro, and Mumbai, where real-estate prices in the 1990s have multiplied many-fold. The same processes of capital centralization that accentuate the contradiction between production and social reproduction also enhance the gentrification process, although of course this works out in very different ways in different places. In Mumbai, in particular, market deregulation and global competition in the mid-1990s led to "extravagantly high prices" that briefly eclipsed even those in New York, London, and Tokyo (Nijman 2000:575). The highly volatile extremes of 1996 have receded, but the upper end of the Mumbai real-estate market now forever finds itself in competition with real estate in cities across the world, a condition which has brought small-scale but very real gentrification to some neighborhoods.

Whereas the major territorial axis of economic competition prior to the 1970s pitted regional and national economies against each other, by the 1990s the new geographical axis of competition was pitting cities against cities in the global economy. This competition takes place not simply in terms of attracting and keeping industrial production but also in the marketing of cities as residential and tourist destinations. This has been explicit in British regeneration policies such as the City Challenge in the 1990s (Jones and Ward this volume), and equally explicit from New York to Atlanta to Vancouver, where antihomeless policies have been justified in terms of an enhanced tourist industry. *Travel and Leisure* magazine now hosts a regular feature that appropriates the language of "emerging economies" to put a spotlight on "emerging cities." Montevideo is renowned for its "thriving café society"; Tunis "has a grandeur that calls to mind Prague and Vienna"; "Panama City is fashioning itself as the culturally savvy gateway" to the Canal Zone: "[O]nce you've settled in, get out and shop"; and "Cracow is experiencing a renaissance" (On the Town 2000:50). Similar aspirations scripted Mayor Giuliani's intense urban boosterism following the World Trade Center catastrophe: "[G]o out and lead a normal life," he exhorted three days after September 11. "Go to restaurants, go to plays and hotels, spend money."

Lefebvre (1971) once argued that urbanism had supplanted industrialization as the motive force of capitalist expansion: industrialization might have bred systemic urbanization, but urbanization now engendered industrialization. That claim has not withstood the test of time, especially in light of the globalization of industrial production and the expansion of East Asia that was well in tow as Lefebvre wrote. And yet, he seems to have anticipated something very real. In a global sense urbanization has not, of course, supplanted industrialization; all of the products that fuel urbanization are made somewhere in the global economy. Nonetheless, urban real-estate development—gentrification writ large—has now become a central motive force of urban economic expansion, a pivotal sector in the new urban economies. An adequate theoretical understanding of neoliberal urbanism will have to revisit Lefebvre's argument and differentiate its insights from its exaggerations.

Acknowledgments

I am very happy to acknowledge the comments and support of Julian Brash, Eliza Darling, Jeff Derksen, and David Vine, in addition to comments by the editors and reviewers of this piece.

Endnotes

[1] This notion of city-based foreign policies with global reach was quite illiberally lifted from social democratic proposals made at a concurrent New York-based international conference organized by the ex-mayor of Barcelona, Pasqual Maragal. Giuliani refused to attend, but appropriated their ideas anyway.

References

Brenner N (1998) Global cities, glocal states: Global city formation and state territorial restructuring in contemporary Europe. *Review of International Political Economy* 5:1–37

Castells M (1977) *The Urban Question*. London: Edward Arnold

Cooper M (1998) Study says stricter oversight of police would save city money. *New York Times* 16 November:B1, B5

Cooper M (1999) Vote by PBA rebukes Safir and his policy. *New York Times* 15 April: B3.

Department of the Environment, Transport and the Regions (DETR) (1999) Towards an Urban Renaissance. http://www.regeneration.detr.gov.uk/utf/renais/ (last accessed 9 February 2002)

Fainstein S (1994) *City Builders: Property, Politics, and Planning in London and New York*. Oxford: Basil Blackwell

Garcia L M (2001) Gentrification in Tenerife. Paper presented to the ISA Group 21 Conference, Amsterdam, June

Garside J (1993) Inner-city gentrification in South Africa: The case of Woodstock, Cape Town. *GeoJournal* 30:29–35

Glass R (1964) *London: Aspects of Change*. London: Centre for Urban Studies and MacGibbon and Kee

Hackworth J (2000) "The Third Wave." PhD dissertation, Department of Geography, Rutgers University

Hackworth J and Smith N (2001) The state of gentrification. *Tijdschrift voor Economische en Sociale Geografie* 92(4):464–477

Hansen S and Pratt G (1995) *Gender, Work, and Space*. London: Routledge

Hardt M and Negri A (2000) *Empire*. Cambridge, MA: Harvard University Press

Harvey D (1973) *Social Justice and the City*. London: Edward Arnold

Harvey D (1985) *The Urbanization of Capital*. Oxford: Basil Blackwell

Jones G and Varley A (1999) The reconquest of the historic centre: Urban conservation and gentrification in Puebla, Mexico. *Environment and Planning A* 31:1547–1566

Katz C (2001) Vagabond capitalism and the necessity of social reproduction. *Antipode* 33:708–727

Katz C (forthcoming) *Disintegrating Developments: Global Economic Restructuring and Children's Everyday Lives*. Minneapolis: University of Minnesota Press

Lefebvre H (1971) *La Révolution Urbaine*. Gallimard: Paris

MacLeod G (2001) New regionalism reconsidered: Globalization and the remaking of political economic space. *International Journal of Urban and Regional Research* 25:804–829

Mészáros I (2001) *Socialism or Barbarism: From the "American Century" to the Crossroads*. New York: Monthly Review

Nijman J (2000) Mumbai's real estate market in the 1990s: Deregulation, global money and casino capitalism. *Economic and Political Weekly* 12 February:575–582

On the Town. Emerging Cities (2000) *Travel and Leisure* January 42–50

Ramsamy E (2001) "From Projects to Policy: The World Bank and Housing in the Developing World." PhD dissertation, Department of Urban Planning, Rutgers University

Rose D (1981) Accumulation versus reproduction in the inner city. In M Dear and A Scott (eds) *Urbanization and Urban Planning in Capitalist Society* (pp 339–382). London: Methuen

Sassen S (1992) *The Global City*. Princeton, NJ: Princeton University Press

Sassen S (1998) *Globalization and Its Discontents*. New York: New Press

Sassen S (2000) *Cities in the World Economy*. Thousand Oaks, CA: Pine Forge Press

Smith N (1990) *Uneven Development: Nature, Capital, and the Production of Space*. Oxford: Basil Blackwell

Smith N (1996) *New Urban Frontier: Gentrification and the Revanchist City*. London: Routledge

Smith N (forthcoming) Scales of terror: The manufacturing of nationalism and the war for US globalism. In S Zukin and M Sorkin (eds) *After the World Trade Center*. New York: Routledge

Smith N and W Dennis (1987) The restructuring of geographical scale: Coalescence and fragmentation of the northern core region. *Economic Geography* 63:160–182

Smith N and J DiFilippis (1999) The reassertion of economics: 1990s gentrification in the Lower East Side. *International Journal of Urban and Regional Research* 23: 638–653

Swyngedouw E (1996) Reconstructing citizenship, the rescaling of the state, and the new authoritarianism: Closing the Belgian mines. *Urban Studies* 33:1499–1521

Swyngedouw E (1997) Neither global nor local: "Glocalization" and the politics of scale. In K Cox (ed) *Spaces of Globalization: Reasserting the Power of the Local* (pp 137–166). New York: Guilford

Taylor P (1995) World cities and territorial states: The rise and fall of their mutuality. In P Knox and P Taylor (eds) *World Cities in a World System* (pp 48–62). Cambridge, UK: Cambridge University Press

Taylor P (1999) So-called "world cities": The evidential structure within a literature. *Environment and Planning* 31:1901–1904

Thomas G (1991) The gentrification of paradise: St John's, Antigua. *Urban Geography* 12:469–487

Vine D (2001) "Development or Displacement?: The Brooklyn Academy of Music and Gentrification in Fort Greene." Unpublished paper presented at the conference on Gotham: History of New York, CUNY Graduate Center, 7 October

Neil Smith is Distinguished Professor of Anthropology and Geography at the Graduate Center of the City University of New York (CUNY) and Director of the Center for Place, Culture and Politics. He works on the broad connections between space, social theory and history, and his books include *New Urban Frontier: Gentrification and the Revanchist City* (New York: Routledge, 1996) and *Uneven Development: Nature, Capital and the Production of Space* (Oxford: Blackwell, 1991). He is author of more than 120 articles and book chapters and sits on numerous editorial boards. His newest book is *Mapping The American Century: Isaiah Bowman and the Prelude to Globalization*

(Berkeley: University of California Press, forthcoming). He has received Honors for Distinguished Scholarship from the Association of American Geographers and has been a John Simon Guggenheim Fellow. He is also an organizer of the International Critical Geography Group.

Part 2 Cities and State Restructuring: Pathways and Contradictions

Chapter 5
Liberalism, Neoliberalism, and Urban Governance: A State-Theoretical Perspective

Bob Jessop

This paper discusses the recurrence and the recurrent limitations of liberalism as a general discourse, strategy, and regime. It then establishes a continuum of neoliberalism ranging from a project for radical system transformation from state socialism to market capitalism, through a basic regime shift within capitalism, to more limited policy adjustments intended to maintain another type of accumulation regime and its mode of regulation. These last two forms of neoliberalism are then related to a broader typology of approaches to the restructuring, rescaling, and reordering of accumulation and regulation in advanced capitalist societies: neoliberalism, neocorporatism, neostatism, and neocommunitarianism. These arguments are illustrated in the final part of the paper through a critique of the *World Report on the Urban Future 21* (World Commission 2000), both as an explicit attempt to promote flanking and supporting measures to sustain the neoliberal project on the urban scale and as an implicit attempt to naturalize that project on a global scale.

The novelty of recent neoliberal projects lies in their discursive, strategic, and organizational reformulation of liberalism in response to three recent developments: the increasing internationalization and/or globalization of economies; the interconnected crises of the mixed economy and the Keynesian welfare national state associated with Atlantic Fordism, of the guided economy and developmental state in East Asia, and of the collapse of the Soviet bloc; and the rise of new social movements in response to the economic, political, and social changes associated with the preceding two changes. Although neoliberal projects are being pursued on many different and often tangled scales, it is in cities and city-regions that the various contradictions and tensions of "actually existing neoliberalism" (Brenner and Theodore [paper] this volume) are expressed most saliently in everyday life. It is also on this scale that one can find major attempts to manage these contradictions and tensions in the hope of consolidating the neoliberal turn through supplementary and/or flanking strategies and policies.

Liberalism and Neoliberalism

Liberalism is a complex, multifaceted phenomenon. It is: a polyvalent conceptual ensemble in economic, political, and ideological *discourse*; a strongly contested *strategic concept* for restructuring market-state relations with many disputes over its scope, application, and limitations; and a recurrent yet historically variable pattern of economic, political, and social *organization* in modern societies. Liberalism rarely, if ever, exists in pure form; it typically coexists with elements from other discourses, strategies, and organizational patterns. Thus, it is better seen as one set of elements in the repertoire of Western economic, political, and ideological discourse than as a singular, univocal, and internally coherent discourse in its own right. Likewise, it is better seen as a more or less significant principle of economic, political, and social organization in a broader institutional configuration than as a self-consistent, self-sufficient, and eternally reproducible organizational principle. Thus, the meaning and import of liberalism can vary considerably. It can be a hegemonic or dominant theme in some periods and movements, subaltern or subordinate in others. In addition, the actual practices of self-described liberal (or neoliberal) regimes may depart significantly from underlying ideologies and programs.

Ideologically, liberalism claims that economic, political, and social relations are best organized through formally free[1] choices of formally free and rational actors who seek to advance their own material or ideal interests in an institutional framework that, by accident or design, maximizes the scope for formally free choice. Economically, it endorses expansion of the market economy—that is, spreading the commodity form to all factors of production (including labor power) and formally free, monetized exchange to as many social practices as possible. Politically, it implies that collective decisionmaking should involve a constitutional state with limited substantive powers of economic and social intervention, and a commitment to maximizing the formal freedom of actors in the economy and the substantive freedom of legally recognized subjects in the public sphere. The latter is based in turn on spontaneous freedom of association of individuals to pursue any social activities that are not forbidden by constitutionally valid laws. These three principles may conflict regarding the scope of anarchic market relations, collective decisionmaking, and spontaneous self-organization as well as the formal and substantive freedoms available to economic, legal, and civil subjects. And, as Marx (1996:243) noted, "Where equal rights exist, force decides." In other words, within the matrix of liberal principles, the relative balance of economic, political, and civic liberalism depends on the changing balance of forces within an institutionalized (but changeable) compromise.

As a new economic project oriented to new conditions, neoliberal-ism calls for: the liberalization and deregulation of economic transactions, not only within national borders but also—and more importantly—*across* these borders; the privatization of state-owned enterprises and state-provided services; the use of market proxies in the residual public sector; and the treatment of public welfare spending as a cost of international production, rather than as a source of domestic demand (see below). As a political project, it seeks to roll back "normal" (or routine) forms of state intervention associated with the mixed economy and the Keynesian welfare national state (or analogous forms of intervention in the developmental state or socialist plan state) as well as the "exceptional" (or crisis-induced) forms of inter-vention aimed at managing, displacing, or deferring crises *in* and/or *of* accumulation regimes and their modes of regulation in Atlantic Fordism, East Asia, and elsewhere. It also involves enhanced state intervention to roll forward new forms of governance (including state intervention) that are purportedly more suited to a market-driven (and, more recently, also allegedly knowledge-driven) globalizing economy. This typically involves the selective transfer of state capacities upwards, downwards, and sideways, as intervention is rescaled in the hope of securing conditions for a smoothly operating world market and to promote supply-side competitiveness on various scales above and below the national level. Urban and regional governments and growth coalitions may gain a key role as strategic partners of business in this changed context. A shift also occurs from government to market forces and partnership-based forms of governance, reflecting the neoliberal belief in the probability, if not inevitability, of state failure and/or the need to involve relevant stakeholders in supply-side policies. And policy regimes are internationalized under the aegis of the institutions of the neo-liberal Washington Consensus promoted by the US government and leading international economic organiza-tions in the hope of harmonizing (if not standardizing) economic and social policy and their supporting institutions so that the liberal world market can work more effectively (on this and other readings of the Washington Consensus, see Williamson 2000). The economic, social, and political measures pursued in support of the neoliberal project generally seem to involve a paradoxical increase in intervention. However, neoliberals claim this is temporary and legitimate, for, after a brief transitional period, the state can retreat to its proper, minimal role, acting only to secure the conditions for the continued expansion of the liberal market economy and a self-organizing civil society (the illusory nature of this claim is illustrated by the contributions of Jones, Keil, and Peck and Tickell to this volume). Finally, as a project to reorganize civil society, neoliberalism is linked to a wider range of political subjects than is typical of orthodox liberalism. It also tends to promote "community" (or a plurality of self-organizing communities) as a flanking, compensatory mechanism for the inadequacies of the market mechanism. This is yet another area where cities or city-regions acquire significance in the neoliberal project, since they are major sites of civic initiative as well as of the accumulating economic and social tensions associated with neoliberal projects.

The resurgence of liberalism in the form of neoliberalism is often attributed to a successful hegemonic project voicing the interests of financial and/or transnational capital. Its recent hegemony in neoliberal regimes undoubtedly depends on the successful exercise of political, intellectual, and moral leadership in response to the crisis of Atlantic Fordism—a crisis that the rise of neoliberalism and neoliberal policies has exacerbated. However, its resonance is also rooted in the nature of capitalist social formations. Liberalism can be seen as a more or less "spontaneous philosophy" within capitalist societies—that is, as a seemingly natural, almost self-evident economic, political, and social imaginary that corresponds to specific features of bourgeois society. In particular, it is consistent with four such features.

The first of these is the institution of private property—that is, the juridical fiction of "private" ownership and control of the factors of production. This encourages individual property owners and those who dispose over fictitious commodities such as labor-power and natural resources to see themselves as entitled to use or alienate their property as they think fit, without due regard to the substantive interdependence of activities in a market economy and market society. In this realm "rule Freedom, Equality, Property and Bentham, because both buyer and seller of a commodity, say of labor-power, are constrained only by their own free will" (Marx 1996:186). Second, and relatedly, there is the appearance of "free choice" in consumption, where those with sufficient money choose what to buy and how to dispose over it. Third, the institutional separation and operational autonomies of the economy and state make the latter's interventions appear as external intrusions into the activities of otherwise free economic agents. This may initially be an unwelcome but necessary extraeconomic condition for orderly free markets, but if pushed beyond this minimum night-watchman role it appears as an obstacle to free markets and/or as direct political oppression. Fourth, there is the closely related institutional separation of civil society and the state. This encourages the belief that state intervention is an intrusion into the formally free choices of particular members of civil society once the conditions for social order have been established.

Opposition to liberalism may also emerge "spontaneously" on the basis of four other features of capitalist social relations that are closely related to the former set. First, growing *socialization of the forces of production* despite continued *private ownership of the means of production* suggests the need for ex ante collaboration among producer groups to limit market anarchy, through top-down planning and/or various forms of self-organization. Second, there are the strategic dilemmas posed by the *shared interests of producers* (including wage-earners) in maximizing total revenues through cooperation and their *divided and potentially conflictual interests* over how these revenues are distributed. Various nonmarket governance mechanisms have a role here helping to balance cooperation and conflict. Third, there are the contradictions and conflicts posed by the coexistence of *the institutional separation and mutual dependence* of the economic and state systems. This leads to different logics of economic and political action, at the same time as it generates a need to consult on the economic impact of state policies and/or on the political repercussions of private economic decisionmaking. And fourth, there are problems generated by the nature of civil society as a sphere of *particular interests* opposed to the state's supposed embodiment of *universal interests*. This indicates the need for some institutional means of mediating the particular and universal and, since this is impossible in the abstract, for some hegemonic definition of the "general interest" (on the always imperfect, strategically selective nature of such reconciliations, see Jessop 1990).

This suggests that, if liberalism can be interpreted as a more or less "spontaneous philosophy" rooted in capitalist social relations, one should also recognize that it is prone to "spontaneous combustion" due to tensions inherent in these same relations. This was noted in Polanyi's critique of late nineteenth-century liberalism, which argued that, in response to crisis-tendencies in laissez-faire capitalism, many social forces struggled to re-embed and re-regulate the market. The eventual compromise solution was a *market economy* embedded in and sustained by a *market society* (Polanyi 1944). The same point applies to neoliberal capitalism. Thus, after the efforts of "roll-back neoliberalism" (Peck and Tickell this volume) to free the neoliberal market economy from its various corporatist and statist impediments, attempts are now being made to secure its medium-term viability by embedding it in a neoliberal market society. This involves measures to displace or defer contradictions and conflicts beyond the spatio-temporal horizons of a given regime, as well as supplementary measures to flank, support, and sustain the continued dominance of the neoliberal project within these horizons (on the key concept of "spatiotemporal fix" in this regard, see Jessop 2001).

This line of argument should not be restricted to liberalism and neoliberalism, for the other modes of governance characteristic of capitalist social formations are also contradictory and tension-ridden. Indeed, there are strange complementarities here. On the one hand, while liberalism tends to regenerate itself "spontaneously" on the basis of key features of capitalist societies, this regeneration meets obstacles from some of the other key features of such societies. On the other hand, while the latter provide the basis for the resurgence of other discourses, strategies, and organizational paradigms, such as corporatism or statism, their realization tends to be fettered in turn by the features that generate liberalism. Overall, these mutually related tendencies and countertendencies produce oscillations in the relative weight of different kinds of coordination and modes of policymaking.

This said, different principles of governance seem more or less well suited to different stages of capitalism and/or its contemporary variants. Thus, liberalism was probably more suited to the pioneering forms of competitive capitalism than to later forms—though Polanyi and others would note that it has clear limitations even for competitive capitalism —and it is more suited to uncoordinated than coordinated market economies, for which statism and corporatism are better (see Coates 2000; Hall and Soskice 2001; Huber and Stephens 2001). Thus, different stages and forms of capitalism may have distinctive institutional attractors (or centers of gravity) around which oscillation occurs. This makes it imperative to study "actually existing neoliberalisms" to understand how their dynamic and viability are shaped by specific path-dependent contexts, competing discourses, strategies, and organizational para-digms, and the balance of forces associated with different projects.

The Neoliberal Turn and Its Implications

The initial rise of neoliberalism as a wide-ranging economic and political strategy was associated with the *neoliberal regime shift* in Britain and the US in the late 1970s. This reflects the fact that their uncoordinated market economies were less well equipped organization-ally and institutionally than were coordinated economies to manage the crisis-tendencies of Atlantic Fordism, and that they provided more fertile ground for the rise of neoliberalism. This was followed by similar shifts in Canada, New Zealand, and Australia, with New Zealand showing, in many ways, the least impure form of neoliberal-ism. An increasing number of coordinated economies (including the "Rhenish" cases and the social democratic economies of Scandinavia) initiated *neoliberal policy adjustments* during the 1980s and continued them into the 1990s. Then, with the collapse of the Soviet bloc in 1989–1990, Western neoliberal forces and international institutions under US leadership (with strong British backing) launched their program for a *neoliberal system transformation* for the postsocialist economies in Eastern and Central Europe, with rather equivocal (or cynically opportunistic) support from domestic *nomenklatura* capitalists. Given the political, intellectual, and moral climate from the late 1970s to early 1990s and the dominance—if not hegemony— of a transatlantic neoliberal power bloc, such disparate sets of changes were often lumped together and misinterpreted (enthusiastically or despairingly) as proof of the general triumph of neoliberalism. (See Table 1 for these different degrees or forms of neoliberalism.)

However, this impression was seriously misleading, since it failed to distinguish the different forms and degrees of neoliberalism, even in this heady period, and ignored the extent to which each of its three types was subject to challenge and prone to failure. Thus, major alternatives to neoliberal system transformation were already being promoted in the 1990s. These included Germany's attempt to mold postsocialism by integrating its eastern neighbors and the Balkans into an expanded German economic bloc reminiscent in scope (but not methods of coordination) of the fascist *Großraumwirtschaft* (large space economy), and Sweden's efforts to extend its social democratic model into the postsocialist societies and create a Baltic Sea economic region. Moreover, outside Poland, the Czech Republic, Slovakia, and Hungary, the much-hyped transformation increasingly took the form of a parasitic *nomenklatura* capitalism presiding over a generalized economic collapse. Meanwhile, capitalist societies undertaking a neoliberal regime shift also began to face problems in the 1990s with their pursuit of pure market forces and promoted a "Third Way" to support and flank their own neoliberal projects. This is the significance of Major (and then Blair) in Britain and of Clinton in the US (on New Labour's urban policy in this respect, see Jones and Ward's contribution to this volume).

Conversely, those economies that embarked on neoliberal policy adjustment rarely moved on to a neoliberal regime shift. Indeed, attempts to do so were rejected by electors and/or opposed by leading economic and political forces with vested interests in maintaining the prevailing production regimes. Here, adjustment took the form of rolling back the exceptional (or crisis-induced) aspects of state intervention that had been introduced to displace or defer Atlantic Fordism's crisis-tendencies in favor of neoliberal measures to reduce inflation and government deficits. However, there has been no comparable roll-back of the normal (routine) forms of intervention associated with the postwar mode of growth. Instead, they have been

Table 1: Forms of Neoliberalism

Policy Adjustment	Modulation of policies to improve performance of an accumulation regime and mode of regulation
Regime Shift	Paradigm shift in accumulation and regulation, introducing new economic and political principles
Radical System Transformation	Neoliberalism as strategy for moving from state socialism to capitalist social formation

modified to promote greater flexibility and innovation and to reinforce the welfare state's role in aiding adjustment to global pressures in small open economies. This is reflected in the greater continuity in institutions and modes of policymaking, even as distinctive national variants of a new mode of regulation are emerging with a mix of neostatist, neocorporatist, and some neoliberal features (see below).

Looking Beyond Neoliberalism to Interpret Recent Changes

If the above account is correct, one should not conflate the global neoliberal turn with the broader set of recent changes in economic, political, and social life. For, although the rise of neoliberal discourse and the pursuit of neoliberal strategies has helped to shape the form and content of these changes, the latter have more general (and deeper) roots in the broader political economy of Atlantic Fordism and its articulation with the wider world system and have also prompted responses quite different from the attempt to establish a global neoliberal market economy. Various labels have been proposed by different theoretical approaches to describe these changes, and no single approach could hope to capture them in all their complexity. This is certainly not my aim here. Instead I want to explore the value of a state-theoretical regulationist approach to some changes that affect capital accumulation and its regulation in North America, Europe, and Australasia. In particular, I suggest that these changes can be analyzed in terms of the Schumpeterian workfare postnational regime (or SWPR).

This regime has four key features that distinguish it in ideal-typical terms from the Keynesian welfare national state (or KWNS). First, it seeks to promote international competitiveness and sociotechnical innovation through supply-side policies in relatively open economies. Thus, with Keynes's symbolic dethronement, today's emblematic economist is Schumpeter, the theorist of innovation, enterprise, long waves of technological change, and creative destruction (on this last aspect, see Brenner and Theodore [paper] this volume). The economic policy emphasis now falls on innovation and competitiveness, rather than on full employment and planning. Second, social policy is being subordinated to economic policy, so that labor markets become more flexible and downward pressure is placed on a social wage that is now considered as a cost of production rather than a means of redistribution and social cohesion. In general, the aim here is to get people from welfare into work, rather than resort to allegedly unsustainable welfare expenditures, and, in addition, to create enterprising subjects and overturn a culture of dependency. Third, the importance of the national scale of policymaking and implementation is being seriously challenged, as local, regional, and supranational levels of government and social partnership gain new powers. This is reflected in the concern to find creative "postnational" solutions to current economic, political, social, and environmental problems, rather than relying primarily on national institutions and networks. The urban level is important here for economic and social policy. And, fourth, there is growing reliance on partnership, networks, consultation, negotiation, and other forms of reflexive self-organization, rather than on the combination of anarchic market forces and top-down planning associated with the postwar "mixed economy" or on the old tripartite corporatist arrangements based on a producers' alliance between big business, big labor, and the national state.

There are various forms of the SWPR, different routes can be taken towards them, and there are significant path-dependent as well as path-shaping aspects to trajectories and outcomes alike. A neoliberal regime shift is only one of many possibilities. To facilitate a comparative analysis of "actually existing" neoliberalization (Peck and Tickell this volume), it is useful to contrast neoliberalism with three other ideal-typical strategies that can lead from some form of the KWNS to some form of the SWPR: neocorporatism, neostatism, and neocommunitarianism. Before elaborating on these particular concepts in more detail, however, I will explain the general theoretical purposes of ideal types and their possible role(s) in empirical analysis.

Ideal types are so called because they involve thought experiments, not because they represent some normative ideal or other. They are theoretical constructs formed by the one-sided accentuation of empirically observable features of social reality to produce logically coherent and objectively feasible configurations of social relations. These configurations are never found in pure form, but their conceptual construction may still be useful for heuristic, descriptive, and explanatory purposes. The four variants of the SWPR are constructed around six interdependent, partly overlapping aspects of economic regulation. These comprise: the dominant form of competition; the form and extent of external regulation of private economic actors; the size of the public sector; the form and extent of state-owned production of goods and services; the articulation between national economies and the state's role in managing international economic relations; and the tax regime. However, given this interdependence and overlap, the six features listed for each ideal type are not exactly equivalent. Seeking complete equivalence would privilege one type (probably neoliberalism) as the benchmark for comparison and so risk losing sense of what gives each type its own distinctive coherence. The prefix "neo" highlights important discontinuities with the liberal, corporatist, and statist variants of the KWNS linked to Fordism and/or their contemporary communitarian alternatives. While specific economic, political, and intellectual forces are often closely identified with one or other response, the types are best seen as poles around which different solutions could develop. Each has contrasting implications for economic and social policy. Individual mixes depend on institutional legacies, the balance of political forces, and the changing economic and political conjunctures in which different strategies are pursued. The four types are presented in summary in Table 2 and elaborated in the following paragraphs.

Neoliberalism promotes market-led economic and social restructuring. In the public sector, this involves privatization, liberalization, and imposition of commercial criteria in the residual state sector; in the private sector, deregulation is backed by a new juridicopolitical framework that offers passive support for market solutions. This is reflected in: government measures to promote "hire-and-fire," flexitime, and flexiwage labor markets; growth of tax expenditures steered by private initiatives based on fiscal subsidies for favored economic activities;

Table 2: Strategies to Promote or Adjust to Global Neoliberalism

Neoliberalism
1. Liberalization—promote free competition
2. Deregulation—reduce role of law and state
3. Privatization—sell off public sector
4. Market proxies in residual public sector
5. Internationalization—free inward and outward flows
6. Lower direct taxes—increase consumer choice

Neostatism
1. From state control to regulated competition
2. Guide national strategy rather than plan top-down
3. Auditing performance of private and public sectors
4. Public–private partnerships under state guidance
5. Neomercantilist protection of core economy
6. Expanding role for new collective resources

Neocorporatism
1. Rebalance competition and cooperation
2. Decentralized "regulated self-regulation"
3. Widen range of private, public, and other "stakeholders"
4. Expand role of public–private partnerships
5. Protect core economic sectors in open economy
6. High taxation to finance social investment

Neocommunitarianism
1. Deliberalization—limit free competition
2. Empowerment—enhance role of third sector
3. Socialization—expand the social economy
4. Emphasis on social use-value and social cohesion
5. Fair trade not free trade; Think Global, Act Local
6. Redirect taxes—citizens' wage, carers' allowances

measures to turn welfare states into means of supporting and subsidizing low wages and/or to enhance the disciplinary force of social security measures and programs; and a more general reorientation of economic and social policy to the private sector's "needs." In addition, social partnership is disavowed in favor of managerial prerogatives, market forces, and a strong state. Neoliberals also support free trade and capital mobility. They expect innovation to follow spontaneously from freeing entrepreneurs and workers to seize market opportunities in a state-sponsored enterprise culture.

Neocorporatism involves a negotiated approach to restructuring by private, public, and third-sector actors and aims to balance competition and cooperation. It is based on commitment to social accords as well as the pursuit of private economic interests in securing the stability of a socially embedded, socially regulated economy. However, whilst Atlantic Fordist corporatism involved cooperation between big business, mass unions, and an interventionist state to promote full employment and overcome stagflation, neocorporatism reflects the diversity of policy communities and networks relevant to innovation-driven growth, as well as the increasing heterogeneity of labor forces and labor markets. It is also more directly and explicitly oriented to innovation and competitiveness. Thus, neocorporatist networks include policy communities representing functional systems (eg science, health, and education), and policy implementation becomes more flexible through the extension of "regulated self-regulation" and public-private partnerships. Compliance with state policies is voluntary or depends on self-regulating corporatist organizations endowed with public status. And—whether at local, national, or supranational level—states use their resources to support decisions reached through corporatist negotiation. Corporatist arrangements may also become more selective (eg excluding some entrenched industrial interests and marginal workers, integrating some "sunrise" sectors and privileging core workers); and, reflecting the greater flexibility and decentralization of the post-Fordist economy, the centers of neocorporatist gravity shift to firms and localities and away from centralized macroeconomic concertation.

Neostatism involves a market-conforming but state-sponsored approach to economic and social restructuring whereby the state seeks to guide market forces in support of a national economic strategy. This guidance depends heavily on the state's deployment of its own powers of imperative coordination, its own economic resources and activities, and its own knowledge bases and organizational intelligence. Compared with the statist form of the KWNS, however, there is a changed understanding of international competition. This is a Schumpeterian view based on dynamic competitive advantage rather than Ricardian static comparative advantage or Listian dynamic growth based on catch-up investment in a protected, mercantilist economy. There is a mixture of state-driven decommodification, state-sponsored flexibility, and other state activities to secure the dynamic efficiency and synergistic coherence of a core productive economy. This is reflected in an active structural policy that sets strategic targets relating to new technologies, technology transfer, innovation systems, infrastructure, and other factors affecting international competitiveness broadly understood. The state also favours an active labor market policy to re-skill labor power and encourages a flexiskill rather than flexiprice labor market. It guides private–public partnerships to ensure that they serve public as well as private interests. Whilst the central state retains key strategic roles, parallel and complementary activities are also encouraged at regional and/or local levels. However, the central state's desire to protect the core technological and economic competencies of its productive base is often associated with neomercantilism at the supranational level.

Neocommunitarianism is a fourth approach to building an SWPR. It emphasizes the contribution of the "third sector" and/or the "social economy" (both located between market and state) to economic development and social cohesion, as well as the role of grassroots (or bottom-up) economic and social mobilization in developing and implementing economic strategies. It also emphasizes: the link between economic and community development, notably in empowering citizens and community groups; the contribution that greater self-sufficiency can make to reinserting marginalized local economies into the wider economy: and the role of decentralized partnerships that embrace not only the state and business interests but also diverse community organizations and other local stakeholders. The neocommunitarian strategy focuses on less competitive economic spaces (such as inner cities, deindustrializing cities, or cities at the bottom of urban hierarchies) with the greatest risk of losing from the zero-sum competition for external resources. Against the logic of a globalizing capitalism, the social economy prioritizes social use-value. It aims to redress the imbalance between private affluence and public poverty, to create local demand, to re-skill the long-term unemployed and reintegrate them into an expanded labor market, to address some of the problems of urban regeneration (eg in social housing, insulation, and energy-saving), to provide a different kind of spatiotemporal fix for small and medium-sized enterprises, to regenerate trust within the community, and to promote empowerment. This involves co-ordinated economic and social strategies across various scales of action and, ideally, a minimum income guarantee—whether as citizens' wage, basic income, or carers' allowances.

The changes associated with these different strategies typically involve some rescaling of the mode of economic regulation. Nonetheless, different strategies may be pursued on different scales. For example, a retreat of state intervention at the national level may be linked to its rolling forward at local or supranational levels (cf Gough and Eisenschitz 1996). This has obvious implications for the urban level, where key issues of competitiveness, labor market flexibility, and social policy intersect, and where new supply-side orientations may permit differential economic and social policies and perhaps— notably under neoliberalism—encourage uneven development. Thus, even where both the national and international levels are dominated by attempts to promote a neoliberal regime shift, the urban level may be characterized more by neocorporatism, neostatism, and neocommunitarianism. Indeed this last pattern is particularly linked to attempts to manage issues of social exclusion and social cohesion at the urban level even in the most strongly neoliberal cases. The resurgence—or (in southern Europe) the emergence—of "social pacts" in European Union member states also reflects the multiscalar nature of the changing world economy and its repercussions on national economic and social policy (on social pacts, see Ebbinghaus and Hassel 1999; Grote and Schmitter 1999; Regini 2000; Rhodes 1998). Overall, this requires attention to how these four alternative approaches to post-Fordist restructuring are combined in "actually existing" strategies or projects and, in particular, how different approaches may acquire different weights at different scales within the same strategy or project. There is certainly no good reason to expect the same broad approach to dominate at all levels, and there are several good reasons why more complex and complicated pictures might emerge.

Neoliberalism and Cities

Some of the implications of neoliberalism for cities (and some of the above-noted complications) can be discerned in a recent report entitled *World Report on the Urban Future 21* (World Commission 2000). This is a specially prepared report that was written by a distinguished fourteen-member "World Commission" moderated by Sir Peter Hall, the renowned professor of urban planning, and serviced by Ulrich Pfeiffer, a professional urban planning consultant, for Urban21. Urban21 was a prestigious international conference held in Berlin in June 2000, sponsored by the German government, with additional support from the governments of Brazil, South Africa, and Singapore. The world commissioners who prepared the report are drawn from "the great and the good" and have been involved in a range of public, parastatal, professional, and private activities. Allowing for some overlap in experience and positions, they included: academic policy entrepreneurs, mayors, an ambassador, a vice president and ex-vice president of the World Bank, a senior civil servant, architects, jurists, ministers, senior UN officials, former parliamentary deputies, and leaders of national and international nongovernmental organizations

(NGOs). Sponsors of some of the conference symposia included international producer service firms, a major software house, a construction firm, and a major German regional bank. Whilst no single report should be taken as wholly representative of current thinking on urban governance, this one does provide some useful insights into the naturalization of neoliberalism and its implications for sustainable cities in an era of the globalizing, knowledge-driven economy. It has since been published in book form as Hall and Pfeiffer (2000).[2]

All four of the above-noted distinctive features of the SWPR are clearly discernible in the *World Report*, even though they are not fully examined. Of special interest for present purposes is how these features are related to cities and their future. First, cities are clearly regarded as engines of economic growth, key centers of economic, political, and social innovation, and key actors in promoting and consolidating international competitiveness. Moreover, with the transition to a postindustrial era, the rise of the knowledge-driven economy, and the increasing importance of the information society with its requirements for lifelong learning, cities are seen as even more important drivers for innovation and competitiveness than before. Admittedly, the authors identify different types of cities—based on informal hypergrowth, based on dynamic innovation and learning, or the declining cities of an outmoded Fordist model of growth—and recommend different responses for each. However, these represent different adaptations of the overall neoliberal program to the same set of challenges.

Second, in line with the familiar neoliberal critique, welfare states are seen as costly, overburdened, inefficient, incapable of eliminating poverty, overly oriented to cash entitlements rather than empowerment, and so on. The report argues that, where it already exists, the welfare state should be dismantled in favor of policies that emphasize moving people from welfare into work, that link social and labor market policy, and that provide incentives to learn and/or prepare for a new job. Likewise, where they have not yet developed, welfare states should be firmly discouraged. Instead, arrangements should be instituted to encourage family, neighborhood, informal, or market-based and market-sustaining solutions to the problems of social reproduction. States should not attempt to provide monopoly services but should contract them out or at least introduce internal competition. In hypergrowth cities, for example, this translates into a call to revalorize the informal economy and/or the social economy and neighborhood support mechanisms as a means of tackling social exclusion. In more dynamic or mature cities, the report recommends other projects to produce "active and productive citizens" who will not burden the state or demand entitlements without accepting corresponding responsibilities. Thus, education and informal self-help are the key to survival and sustainability and, in principle, education should be made available to all. Cities should develop their stock of indigenous "human capital" and their local labor markets in order to promote local well-being as well as international competitiveness.

Third, the *World Report* clearly recognizes the emerging crisis of the national scale of economic, political, and social organization, the increased importance of the global level (especially in the form of a still emerging "single global urban network" that cross-cuts national borders), and the resurgence of the local and regional levels. Its response is to promote the principles of subsidiarity and solidarity. Problems should be resolved at the lowest level possible, but with capacity-building and financial support from the national administration. This requires integrated action between various levels of government, with an appropriate allocation of responsibilities and resources. Unsurprisingly, the report envisages a key role for cities in managing the interface between the local economy and global flows, between the potentially conflicting demands of local sustainability and local well-being and those of international competitiveness, and between the challenges of social exclusion and global polarization and the continuing demands for liberalization, deregulation, privatization, and so on.

Fourth, there is a strong emphasis on partnership and networks rather than top-down national government. Thus, in addition to sub-sidiarity and solidarity across different scales of economic, political, and social organization, the report also calls for partnership between the public and private sectors and between government and civil society. Public–private partnerships should nonetheless work *with* the grain of market forces, not against it. In addition, partnerships should involve not only actors from the private economic sector but also NGOs, religious groups, community-action groups, or networks among individuals. Promoting partnerships requires a retreat of the state (especially at national level) so that it can do well what it alone can do. Nonetheless, the latter tasks do include steering partnerships and moderating their mutual relations in the interests of "the maximum welfare of all the people." This is reflected in the *World Report*'s call for "good governance, seen as an integrated effort on the part of local government, civil society and the private sector."

In noting how the *World Report* fits in with the neoliberal project, I am not arguing that its principal authors, the commissioners, their professional, academic, and lay consultants, or the principal speakers at the Urban21 conference are necessarily conscious agents of neo-liberalism in either its initial "red in tooth and claw" version or its current "Third Way" variant. Some may be; others are not. More important for my purposes is how this document implicitly endorses neoliberalism in the ways it describes recent economic and political changes, ascribes responsibility for them, and prescribes solutions for the problems they create. In this sense, it is a deeply ideological document and contributes to the "New World Order" by sharing in a "new *word* order" (Luke 1994:613–615) For ideology is most effective when ideological elements are invisible, operating as the background assumptions which lead the text producer to "textualize" the world in a particular way and lead interpreters to interpret the text in a particular way (Fairclough 1989:85).

Indeed, alongside its diagnosis of the various failures of previous modes of economic growth and urban governance in different types of city, said in each case to justify neoliberalism, the *World Report* recognizes that neoliberalism has its own limits and also generates major social tensions. Its authors accept the recently perceived need to re-embed neoliberalism in society, to make it more acceptable socially and politically, and to ensure that it is environmentally sustainable. Here, Polanyi lives! Yet they make as few concessions as possible to the forces that oppose the program, protagonists, and driving forces of neoliberalism. Hence, the *World Report* also identifies and advocates different sets of strategies to support and complement the neoliberal project in different regions and/or types of cities. Its proposals for the informal, weakly regulated, and vulnerable hypergrowth cities of the developing world combine neoliberalism with a strong emphasis on mobilizing popular energies, the informal or social economy, and communitarian values. In these cities, then, it ascribes a key role to neocommunitarianism in sustaining neoliberalism. In contrast, no such dilution is recommended for the mature but declining cities of the Atlantic Fordist regions: they must take their neoliberal medicine. A different prescription again is offered for the dynamic cities of East Asia. This comprises a mix of neoliberalism with public–private partnerships to improve the infrastructure and policy environment for international as well as local capital. Here the developmental state is allowed to remain proactive, provided that it is rescaled and becomes more open to world-market forces. In no case is there a challenge to the wisdom of the "accumulated knowledge and experience" noted by the *World Report* that market forces provide the best means to satisfy human wants and desires and that, provided they are steered in the right direction through good governance, they can also solve the most pressing problems facing humankind in the new century.

Naturalizing Neoliberalism

The *World Report* also illustrates another key feature of neoliberalism. The latter's success depends on promoting new ways of representing the world, new discourses, new subjectivities that establish the legitimacy of the market economy, the disciplinary state, and enterprise culture. The language of the *World Report* shares in this tendency to naturalize the global neoliberal project, most notably in its concern with renewing and consolidating neoliberal principles at the urban scale. Thus, the many changes associated with this project are variously represented in the *World Report* as natural, spontaneous, inevitable, technological, and demographic. It takes technological change and globalization as given, depersonalizes them, fetishizes market forces, and fails to mention the economic, political, and social forces that drive these processes.

Moreover, the very same processes that cause the problems identified in the report will also solve them: technological change will provide solutions to emerging problems, democratization will occur, population growth will decline, economic growth will continue, the informal sector will expand to deal with social problems. No one could infer from the report that technological change and globalization are deeply politicized processes and objects of struggles within the dominant classes, within states, and within civil society. Instead, it presumes an equality of position in relation to these changes: *they* are objective and inevitable, *we* must adapt to them. Thus, whereas globalization, technological change, and competition are depersonalized, human agency enters in through the need for survival and sustainability. It is, above all, local communities, women, and workers who must adapt to these impersonal forces. They must be flexible, empower themselves, take control of their pensions by self-funding them, undertake lifelong learning, put democratic pressure on urban administrations to support their informal initiatives, and so on. Likewise, cities can become competitive, take control of their economic destinies, develop their local markets, especially the localized labor markets, their local infrastructure and their stock of housing, develop good governance, and become attractive places for working and living. Moreover, on the rare occasions where blame is attributed for economic and social problems, it tends to be localized. Thus, urban poverty results not so much from capitalism as from ineffective local administration—which a judicious combination of mobilization from below and capacity-building from above can correct.

The *World Report* contains no analysis of capitalism and its agents. The dynamic of the knowledge-driven economy is described in objective, factual terms. The report contains only one reference to "the present economic system" (undefined), and this admits that it is massively suboptimal and inefficient—but does not pause to ask why. The only economic actors it identifies are local urban networks of small-scale producers and service, small firms, private companies, and (clearly benign) "world-class companies." The only capital identified is human capital. The only social actors are: people around the world with shared or common aspirations; the weak, the old, and the young; the rich and the poor; women; families; informal neighborhood support networks; and members of civil society. The only political actors mentioned are urban leaders, citizens, and city administrations.

There is no reference at all to the economic, political, or ideological roles of multinational companies, transnational banks, strategic alliances among giant companies, the military-industrial complex, an emerging transnational class, the World Economic Forum, or the overall dynamic of capitalism. There is no reference to popular movements, new social movements, grass-roots struggles, trade unions, or even political parties—good governance is, apparently, above party politics. Also unmentioned are the crucial roles of the International Monetary Fund, the World Bank, the Organization for Economic Cooperation and Development, the World Trade Organization, and other international economic agencies; and the efforts of the US and its allies to promote globalization or redesign political and social institutions to underwrite and complement neoliberalism. Presumably, these must be left to operate above the national level (at which ultimate responsibility for social justice and redistribution is apparently to be located) and to define (technocratically) the framework within which cities pursue sustainable development. Pollution and environmental destruction appear to be facts of nature, rather than products of specific sets of social relations. The empowerment of women appears to be a key mechanism of social transformation, but patriarchy figures nowhere as a mechanism of domination or oppression—and neither states nor firms, neither political nor business leaders, seem to have vested interests in sustaining it.

In short, here is a text that simulates egalitarianism (that of a "we," a collectivity of individuals, families, and communities all equally confronted with objective, inevitable changes and challenges) and lacks any explicit reference to power and authority, exploitation and domination. It is no surprise, then, that these challenges can be met in ways that will reconcile international competitiveness with local autonomy, economic growth with sustainability, market forces with quality of life, the needs of the highly skilled with the economic development of the entire city. This harmonization of contradictions and antagonisms is to be achieved at the urban level through a rallying of the good and the great, the movers and shakers, the rich and the poor, shanty dwellers and property capital, men and women, to the banner of "good governance." And that they will so rally is, it appears, assured through the same "accumulated knowledge and experience" that has recognized the virtues of multidimensional sustainable development. Adequate forms of urban governance are thus central to securing the neoliberal project as it is pursued in different forms and to different degrees in different local, regional, national, and transnational contexts.

Conclusion

This sort of search for a new spatiotemporal fix for neoliberalism is unsurprising, for attempts to spread the neoliberal economic project globally have experienced major setbacks in recent years. This is especially clear in the massive failure of the militant free-marketeers' initial neoliberal project to promote radical system transformation in postsocialist societies. Despite a very steep learning curve and substantial foreign support, there is still no successful paradigmatically neoliberal regime in the ex-Soviet bloc. Likewise, in the case of the attempt to impose neoliberal regime shifts in East Asia and Latin America, failure is evident in unexpected financial and industrial crises and a financial contagion that threatened to spread through an increasingly integrated world market. In the neoliberal regime shifts in the former heartlands of Atlantic Fordism, failure can be seen in unexpected social costs with serious political repercussions, such as growing economic polarization and social exclusion rather than the promised "trickle-down" effects of liberated market forces. In addition, countries that embarked on neoliberal policy adjustment did not move on to a neoliberal regime shift, but instead sought alternative paths of economic, social, and political restructuring. More generally, new forms of resistance have developed on a global scale (eg the Multilateral Agreement on Investments, Seattle, Genoa).

Although such setbacks have not triggered a major reversal of the global neoliberal project, they have led many key protagonists to re-evaluate strategies and tactics. This explains the growing concern with how best to present the project, to coordinate actions to promote and consolidate it on different scales, to manage its social and environmental costs and their adverse political repercussions, and to identify and pursue flanking measures that would help to re-embed the recently liberated market forces into a well-functioning market society. If getting the international institutional architecture and international regimes right is one key aspect of attempts to stabilize neoliberalism, intervention at the urban scale is equally essential, because this is where neoliberalism has its most significant economic, political, and social impacts on everyday life. Whether or not such projects will succeed is another matter. I have already advanced some general reasons why the various modes of governance associated with capitalism all tend to encounter contradictions, tensions, and obstacles. Only time and struggles will tell whether sufficient flanking and supporting measures can be introduced to stabilize neoliberalism as the basis for regulation of a glocalized knowledge-driven economy.

Acknowledgements
This paper has benefited from discussions with Neil Brenner, Gordon MacLeod, Martin Jones, Jamie Peck, Adam Tickell, and Nik Theodore, comments by other participants in the "Neoliberalism and the City" conference at the University of Illinois in Chicago, September 2001, and the suggestions of three *Antipode* referees. The usual disclaimers apply.

Endnotes

[1] I use the concept of "formal freedom" here to draw an implicit contrast with the lack of full *substantive* freedom due to the multiple constraints that limit free choice. The institutionalization of formal freedom is nonetheless a significant political accomplishment and a major element in liberal citizenship, as well as a precondition for market economies.

[2] This report provoked a response from a Berlin-based tenants' organization, drawing on its own range of national and international policymakers, advisors, and academic experts, which attempted to denaturalize what the *World Report* attempted to naturalize. See Eick and Berg (2000).

References

Coates D (2000) *Models of Capitalism: Growth and Stagnation in the Modern Era*. Cambridge, UK: Polity

Ebbinghaus B and Hassel A (1999) The role of tripartite concertation in the reform of the welfare state. *Transfer* 5:64–81

Eick V and Berg R (eds) (2000) *Und die Welt wird zur Scheibe ... Reader zum Weltbericht (Für die Zukunft der Städte—URBAN 21)*. Berlin: Berliner MieterGemeinschaft

Fairclough N (1989) *Language and Power*. London: Longmans

Grote J and Schmitter P C (1999) The renaissance of national corporatism: Unintended side-effect of European economic and monetary union or calculated response to the absence of European Social Policy? *Transfer* 5:34–63

Gough J and Eisenschitz A (1996) The construction of mainstream local economic initiatives: Mobility, socialization, and class relations. *Economic Geography* 72: 175–192

Hall P and Pfeiffer U (2000) *Urban Future 21: A Global Agenda for Twenty-First-Century Cities*. London: Federal Ministry of Transport, Building and Housing/E & F N Spon

Hall P A and Soskice D (eds) (2001) *Varieties of Capitalism: The Institutional Foundations of Comparative Advantage*. Oxford: Oxford University Press

Huber E and Stephens J D (2001) *Development and Crisis of the Welfare State: Parties and Politics in Global Markets*. Chicago: University of Chicago Press

Jessop B (1990) *State Theory*. Cambridge, UK: Polity

Jessop B (2001) The crisis of the national spatiotemporal fix and the ecological dominance of globalizing capitalism. *International Journal of Urban and Regional Studies* 24:273–310

Luke T (1994) Placing power/siting space: The politics of global and local in the New World Order. *Environment and Planning D: Society and Space* 12:613–628

Marx K (1996) *Capital*. Vol 1. London: Lawrence and Wishart

Polanyi K (1944) *The Great Transformation*. New York: Rinehart

Regini M (2000) Between deregulation and social pacts: The responses of European economies to globalization. *Politics and Society* 28:5–33

Rhodes M (1998) Globalization, labor markets, and welfare states: A future of "competitive corporatism"? In M Rhodes and Y Mény (eds) *The Future of European Welfare: A New Social Contract?* (pp 178–203). Basingstoke: Macmillan

Williamson J (2000) What should the World Bank think about the Washington Consensus? *World Bank Research Observer* 15:251–264

World Commission (2000) *Weltbericht für die Zukunft der Städte Urban 21* (World report on the urban future 21). English-language version formerly available at http://www.urban21.de/english/04-objective/world-report.htm; link no longer functioning. German-language version available at http://www.urban21.de/german2/weltbericht/weltbericht.pdf (last accessed 18 February 2002)

Bob Jessop is a Professor of Sociology in Lancaster University. He is best known for his contributions to state theory, the regulation approach, the analysis of postwar British political economy, welfare-state restructuring, and, most recently, governance failure and meta-governance. Among his publications are *The Capitalist State* (Oxford: Blackwell, 1982), *Nicos Poulantzas* (London: Macmillan, 1985), *Thatcherism* (Cambridge, UK: Polity Press, 1988; coauthored with Kevin Bonnett, Simon Bromley, and Tom Ling), *State Theory* (Cambridge, UK: Polity Press, 1990), *Strategic Choice and Path-Dependency in Post-Socialism* (Aldershot: Edward Elgar, 1996; coedited with J Hausner and K Nielsen), and *The Future of the Capitalist State* (forthcoming).

Chapter 6
Excavating the Logic of British Urban Policy: Neoliberalism as the "Crisis of Crisis-Management"

Martin Jones and Kevin Ward

This paper suggests that crisis theories provide a framework for analyzing the urban spaces of neoliberalism. Drawing on crisis-theoretic approaches to state theory, we examine the path-dependent links between neoliberalism, urban policy, and Britain's cyclical and crisis-prone cities through three tendencies: the geographies of state regulation, the institutionalization of interurban competition, and rescaling as the "crisis of crisis-management." These are used to explore the argument that Britain's cities are hosts to ineffectual regulatory strategies because urban policy appears to be a response to the sociopolitical and geographical contradictions of *previous* rounds of urban policy, and not the underpinning contradictions of accumulation.

> Whether state power is able to manage and reproduce the highly oppressive, irrational, and self-contradictory capitalist system is of course an open question. (Offe 1984:257)

Introduction

Despite over twenty years of state experimentation involving billions of pounds of public expenditure and resulting in an Amazonian jungle of institutions, policies, programs, and acronyms, the "urban problem" is becoming *more* deeply entrenched. Britain's cities remain centers of low economic activity, possess high (but at times hidden) unemployment and welfare dependency, contain large areas of physical dereliction, and are witness to increased crime and social disorder. While optimistic media and political accounts of Britain's urban areas suggest that we are "turning the corner"—emerging from industrial decline to become key postindustrial centers of economic growth (DETR 2000; Urban Task Force 1999)—more systematic analysis is a little more somber (Turok and Edge 1999). As if to demonstrate the fragile and extremely partial nature of any so-called urban renaissance, several of England's northern cities have given birth to a spate of race riots, the scale of which have not been seen since the early 1980s. Although racial tension is undoubtedly an influence here, we suggest that in Oldham, Bradford, and Burnley significant connections exist between ethnicity and poverty (cf Sardar 2001). In all three cities, the numerous "rounds of regeneration" since the late 1970s have had only a marginal impact on local economies, which have been subjected to intense economic restructuring and now face a depressing postindustrial landscape of deepening inequalities and entrenched social polarization.[1]

However, this paper is concerned neither with providing a review of the various institutional and policy twists and turns in Britain's cities since the late 1970s nor with reviewing the changing state of the UK urban economy. These tasks have been performed at length elsewhere (see Atkinson and Moon 1994; Eisenschitz and Gough 1993; Gough and Eisenschitz 1996a) and highlight the competing aims and objectives of urban policy and the longer-term British "modernizing" project of which contemporary economic development is an intricate component (Gough and Eisenschitz 1996b). And yet, Labour's recent urban white paper (DETR 2000)—yet *another* statement on the need for holistic regulatory mechanisms and appropriate patterns of intervention—presents us with a unique opportunity to stand back from the "practicalities of policy" (Robson 1988) and to open up for analysis the *neoliberalization* of British cities. In this paper, we argue that the seemingly unconnected processes of state restructuring and policy formation detailed in such policy audits and trawls are, in fact, outcomes of the same process of ideologically infused political decision-making that *cannot* be separated from the inherent contradictions of capital accumulation (cf Fainstein and Fainstein 1982; Harloe 1977; Rees and Lambert 1985).[2]

Working within the political economy tradition, this paper suggests that crisis theories offer a useful lens for excavating the regulatory logic of British neoliberal urban policy. We recognize that the "word crisis is used with less precision and greater frequency than most others in analyses of political ... change" (Goodwin and Painter 1996:638), but disagree with claims that crisis is the "old horse" that has been flogged "to death" (Walker 1995) and that crisis theory itself is in crisis because it produces a "crisis talk" (Holton 1987) with no analytical value. Concurring with Goodwin and Painter (1996), we agree that critics of crisis theory often equate crisis with a "permanent" crisis and not with a series of periodic crises of varying intensity and duration. Capitalism, of course, has always been in some form of crisis. In contrast to Marxist and regulation theory readings of crisis, which (to varying degrees) have a tendency to read off institutional and policy development from the economic logic of accumulation, this paper argues that there is considerable mileage left in the Frankfurt school's notion of political crisis found in the work of Habermas and, in particular, of Offe.

We are, of course, fully aware of the limitations attached to political theories of crisis. By focusing on the ideological and political contradictions of state policy, this perspective inevitably separates state-led policy developments from shifts in the economy (Cochrane 1989). Given that trying to find an appropriate way of conceptualizing the state within its economic/accumulation context is a mammoth task, and part of a bigger research agenda that we can only touch upon here, our contribution should be read alongside the work that explores the restructuring of UK urban areas and the economic failures of neoliberalism (Gough and Eisenschitz 1996b). As part of this project, three arguments are offered that should be seen as extensions of the regulation approach and that we feel capture timely and important events taking place in Britain with respect to the *spaces of neoliberalism*.

- First, at a general level, we suggest that under neoliberalism the contradictions of capitalist accumulation cannot be resolved through the state. If anything, the contemporary irrationalities of capitalism are being intensified through state interventions at a number of different spatial scales. And we agree with the prognosis of Peck and Tickell (1994:292), who claim that neoliberalism is "part of the problem, not part of the solution."
- Second, given that urbanization is an integral feature of late capitalist accumulation (Harvey 1985; Rees and Lambert 1985)—to the extent that in Britain, for example, 80% of the population live in cities and towns, and urban areas provide 91% of national output and 89% of employment (DETR 2000) —under neoliberalism cities are being presented as both the sites of, and the solutions to, various forms of crisis (see also Begg 1999; Brenner and Theodore [paper] this volume; Clarke and Gaile 1998; Peck and Tickell this volume).
- Third, in undertaking this crisis-management role under neo-liberalism (the site-and-solution relationship), it appears that Britain's cities host ineffectual and contradictory regulatory strategies, with initiatives often being introduced as a direct responses to the contradictions created by *previous* state-led interventions—in other words, the state's *own* contradictions— and not the economic contradictions of capitalist accumulation. Thus, the British neoliberal urban condition is an actually existing example of the "crisis of crisis-management" (Offe 1984:36). The implementation of urban policy is frequently associated with crises, which are diffused—temporarily, but at the same time continuously and serially—through a centrally orchestrated reorganization of the policy area and/or a rework-ing of the state apparatus, to reappear at a later date and require "new" urban policies that, in turn, create further contradictions and crisis. Thus, contemporary urban policy provides a good

illustration of how the "regulatory process" can become "an object of regulation in its own right" (Goodwin and Painter 1996:638).

Taking forward this argument, the next section of the paper briefly summarizes theories of crisis as a means of establishing a framework for analyzing contemporary variants of urban neoliberalism and to highlight the connections that exist between capitalism, crisis, the state and the city, and urban policy formation. This conceptual agenda is explored in a further section, which points to how such an approach allows us to analyze the logic at the heart of the neoliberalization of Britain's cities. Specifically, we examine the path-dependent links between neoliberalism, urban policy, and Britain's cyclical and crisis-prone cities through three tendencies: the geographies of state regulation, the institutionalization of interurban competition, and re-scaling as the crisis of crisis-management. These tendencies are deployed in the paper as fluid categories through which a number of crisis-theoretic informed arguments are assembled.

Crisis Theory: Retrospect and Prospect
Marxist and Neo-Marxist Developments in Crisis Theory
The term "crisis" is associated with periods of both destruction *and* creation (Brenner and Theodore [paper] this volume; Hay 1996; O'Connor 1987). Because notions of crises are analogous with the existence and "metamorphosis" of capitalism, orthodox accounts tend to be found within Marxist political economy. These take the economic imperatives and contradictions of accumulation as their starting point, and a number of crises and crisis tendencies are identified in relation to changes in profitability, economic growth, and the business cycle. We do not have the space to discuss these here; in brief, debates within Marxist political economy over the past twenty-five years have been occupied with notions of overaccumulation, underconsumption, and the theory of the falling rate of profit (for discussion, see Webber and Rigby 1996).

In contrast to Marx's prediction that capitalism would sow the seeds of its own destruction through the continued search for surplus value through exploitation, neo-Marxist theories of crisis suggest that capitalism can *temporarily* resolve its internal (economic) contradictions through processes of "switching" (Harvey 1999) or "displacement" (Hay 1996). For instance, in *The Limits to Capital* (1999) Harvey explores the inner logic of capitalism through three different but interrelated "cuts." The "first-cut" theory of crisis relates to the general instability of capitalist production and to the ways in which this is resolved through a sector-based switching of investment. By contrast, "second-cut" theory stresses a temporal displacement of crisis through new forms of circulation involving financial and monetary arrangements. Harvey's "third-cut" theory of crisis attempts to stress both the temporal and the spatial displacement of crisis—the historical geography of capitalism—by way of "spatial fixes." For Harvey, then, the survival of capitalism is dependent on the reproduction of uneven development, which should be seen as both a temporary resolution to *and* a cause of crisis.

In a similar vein, regulation approaches suggest that social, political, cultural, and institutional structures play key roles in the (social) reproduction of capitalism, despite its inherent tendency towards forms of crisis. Regulationists do not deny the underlying (or necessary) contradictory tendencies inherent in the process of accumulation. Their unique contribution rests on claims that capitalism does not possess its own "self-limiting mechanisms" (Aglietta 1998:49), and research subsequently explores the regularization or normalization of economic life in its broadest sense (Jessop 1997). In this respect, modes of regulation act as "mediating mechanisms" (Aglietta 1998:49), and regulation can be interpreted as a geographically specific set of regulatory "processes" and "practices," revolving around key institutional sites and scales (Goodwin and Painter 1996). Regulationists suggest that only when a relatively coherent phase of capital accumulation exists (where the inherent contradictions and crisis tendencies are temporarily internalized and stabilized) can stability occur and modes of development exist.

There are, of course, weaknesses with the ways in which these literatures deal with the role of the state in relation to crisis. In emphasizing economic explanations of crisis, neo-Marxists often understate political and social crises (O'Connor 1987), and ongoing developments within the extra-economic coordinating or mediating mechanisms of capitalism are frequently "read off" from changes in the economy (Florida and Jonas 1991; Hay 1995). Marx, of course, did not develop a fully-fledged theory of the state, and *The Limits to Capital* (Harvey 1999) identifies the state's role in crisis management as a conceptual "problem." Likewise, notwithstanding the emphasis placed on sociopolitical struggle within the regulation approach, the state and its politics remain key "missing links" (Tickell and Peck 1992). However, neo-Marxist literatures maintain that states do not have (unbridled) capacity to internalize further the contradictions of capitalist accumulation through their apparatuses, without a price.

In this paper, we do not pretend to offer a full treatment of the state. Rather, we are interested in *expanding* the regulation approach to focus more explicitly on the regulatory mechanisms and policy frameworks in and through which crisis tendencies are internalized and "mediated" (Aglietta 1998) as an exercise of state power and political practice. To further this agenda, we turn not to the sociology of Bourdieu (cf Painter 1997), or to the discourse-theoretic writings of Jenson (1991), but to some of the neglected and rich insights of the Frankfurt school and political readings of crisis.

Habermas and the Logic of Crisis Displacement

In *Legitimation Crisis* (1976) Habermas identifies two distinct forms of crises: "systems" crises and "identity" crises. Systems crises are associated with structural features of a system and the internal contradictions related to socioeconomic and political processes. "Steering problems" are said to exist when "crisis effects cannot be resolved within the range of possibilities that is circumscribed by the original principles of the society" (7). In contrast, identity crises occur when those in civil society experience the effects of crisis such that identities and systems of meaning are questioned. Habermas creates two additional subdivisions of crisis to produce four distinct levels of capitalist crisis.

In the useful summary provided by Hay (1996), systems crises are divided into "economic crises" (crises of economic systems) and "rationality crises" (crises of the state's political administrative system and its steering mechanisms). A rationality crisis is one in which the "administrative system does not succeed in reconciling and fulfilling the imperatives received from the economic system" (Habermas 1976:46). Identity crises are divided into "legitimation crises" (of the political system) and "motivational crises" (within the sociocultural system). For Habermas (75), motivational crises relate to the breakdown of the sociocultural system when it becomes "dysfunctional for the state and the systems of social labour." Legitimation crises are linked to crises of rationality and the state's operation. However, they differ in that, while rationality crises emerge out of the objective inability of the state to manage socioeconomic systems, legitimation crises are an "input crisis" that result from the failings of the state as perceived by the society from which the state obtains its political legitimacy (Habermas 1976:46).

Notwithstanding some limitations (see Held 1996), Habermas's (1976) highly original and innovative presentation of crisis theory points to how the forms of crisis and the tendencies in advanced capitalism correlate (Hay 1996). Habermas maintains that the interactions taking place between various moments of crisis through state intervention within the economy can be interpreted through the *logic of crisis displacement*. This powerful insight suggests that forms of crisis that originate from within the economy (such as market failure and the flight of capital) can be transferred into the political realm of the state. Through its multifarious modes of intervention and policy repertoires, the state has the strategic capacity to transform economic crises into crises of political management or rationality within new modes of governance. States can, therefore, displace economic problems into politically mediated institutional projects, and, to facilitate easier decisionmaking, new forms of representation are often sought that support the ideological and material effects of state intervention (cf Jessop 1990; Jones 2001). If the economy is not successfully regulated, Habermas argues, crises of state rationality can become legitimation crises. It is out of such circumstances that the destruction of the liberal democratic political system through a disorganized state apparatus is predicted.

Offe and the Crisis of Crisis-Management

The work of Offe is crucial for taking forward our argument on the logic of crisis displacement and its consequences. For Offe (1984), the capitalist state, because it is essentially capitalist, is dependent on, but not reducible to, accumulation. For this reason the state is, by design, continually snared within the multiple contradictions of capitalism. On the one hand, states have to ensure the continued accumulation of capital; on the other, they have to appear neutral arbiters of interests to preserve their legitimacy. As a consequence, the state depends on stability in accumulation for its own functioning, but because it is not an "instrument of the interest of capital," a selective "sorting process" is deployed to incorporate certain interest groups into (and exclude others from) the state apparatus and policymaking process to protect accumulation and ensure (relatively) crisis-free stabilization (51).

To provide the basis for our arguments, we are less interested in the internal differentiation of the state apparatus and more interested in the ways in which multiple contradictions are *managed* by the state as a consequence of its ongoing involvement in accumulation through urbanization. Based on observations on the Keynesian welfare state and its limits, Offe (1985:223–227) highlights the need to distinguish between two different types of state strategy, which reflect crisis responses through "modes of political rationality." "Conjunctural" strategies look for a resolution to crisis within pre-existing state structures, political administrative systems, and institutional practices. This represents "minor tinkering" (Hay 1996:94). In contrast, "structural" modes of political rationality are adopted in response to conditions of economic and political crisis and require a structural transformation of the state apparatus and its relationship with the economy. For Jessop (1990:345–346; 1998), this involves a continual reworking of the state's "internal structures" (the scalar architecture of the state and its power networks), "patterns of intervention" (distinctions between public and private and economic versus social projects), "representational regimes" (territorial-based forces, interest groups, state managers), and "state projects" (modes of policymaking) to create *spaces for maneuver*. The contradictions of capitalism can therefore be further internalized (albeit temporarily) by the state through the exercise of *political strategy*.

Reinforcing these propositions, Offe (1984) argues that in its perpetual political management of crisis, the state under "late capitalism" (and, we would argue, neoliberalism) will frequently *not* be a response to structural economic crises, such as the crisis of Fordist/Keynesian accumulation, but to *crises in the rationality and legitimacy of the state and its intervention*. This occurs because the increasing complexity of state functions—and, more importantly, the introduction of supply-side institutional strategies and policy mechanisms (as opposed to demand-side interventions)—bring with them coordination problems within both the administrative and political systems. In other words, "although (arguably) the state aims for crisis-free stabilization and integration in capitalist economies, the *expanded functions* of the state are *themselves* a source of dysfunction and crisis" (Dear and Clark 1978:179; emphasis added). This leads to a crisis of "administrative rationality" or governance failure *if* there is "an inability of the political-administrative system to achieve a stabilization of its internal 'disjunctions'" (Offe 1984:58). And because the state generates unintended consequences out of what might appear to be ostensibly rational interventions, which *sharpen* the contradictions of accumulation, it becomes embroiled in a "crisis of crisis-management" (Offe 1984). This much-quoted phrase describes the way in which state strategies, modes of intervention and policy repertories are "recycled" (Hay 1996; Hudson 2001) through an eternal process of political crisis-management best described as "muddling through" (Offe 1984:20). Here, despite a multitude of "steering problems" encountered by the state, its interventions are carefully managed by a continued ability to design and redesign the policy field (Offe 1975:141–142). New mixes are made from old recipes.

Urban Spaces of Neoliberalism: Four Crisis-Theoretic Propositions

We would suggest that this conceptual insight has four important implications for the state's institutional architecture and modes of policymaking under neoliberalism:

- First, in contrast to Habermas's (1976) notion of legitimation crisis, we suggest that crises are being *further* displaced, through a complex and contradictory process of state rescaling (see Brenner 1998; Lipietz 1994; MacLeod and Goodwin 1999), from the political sphere of the state onto civil society's "vulnerable groups" (such as the unemployed and the homeless), "vulnerable regions," and—more generally—regional and local states (Held and Krieger 1982; Swyngedouw 2000).

Each one is then blamed, in a social-pathological sense, for its own economic failings and made to shoulder the responsibility for a *devolved rationality crisis*.

- Second, and related to this, neoliberal regulatory experiments and crisis management tactics appear to be bringing with them a number of contradictions. Several ramifications are worth noting: there are problems of accountability and a blurring of policy responsibility (Jones and Ward 1997); difficulties of co-ordination exist both within and across different spatial scales, due to an emerging system of intergovernmental relations associated with "multilevel governance" (Scharpf 1997); conflicting time horizons are present between those formulating and those implementing policy initiatives; and policy failure is frequently blamed on devolved institutional structures and their state managers, and not on central government (Jones 1999).

- Third, building on the above, there is an exhaustion of policy repertories under neoliberalism. Old policies are recycled and "new" ones are borrowed from elsewhere through speeded-up policy transfer. Here, Offe (1996:52) makes an important distinction between "institutional gardening" and "institutional engineering." The latter term captures the idea of an institutional design open to policy influences from external forces. By contrast, "gardening" implies working with the grain of path-dependency through homegrown regulatory mechanisms. In the latter case, policymaking is not driven by the business cycle and/or the need to address sector-based crises; rather, it is pushed along by the electoral cycle and the primacy of politics (Jessop and Peck 1998).

- Fourth, many of these regulatory strategies and their emerging urban contradictions are being presented as necessary requirements for securing a competitive advantage under globalization (compare Brenner and Theodore [paper] this volume; Gough this volume; Jessop this volume; Leitner and Sheppard this volume; Smith this volume). Our interpretation of the entrepreneurial direction of contemporary urban policy suggests that the (il)logics and discourses of globalization represent a *further* scalar crisis displacement political strategy in and through which to legitimize the "reshuffling of the hierarchy of spaces" (Lipietz 1994:36).

Rereading British Urban Policy

This section explores these crisis-theoretic propositions through three "cuts," or tendencies, that seek to capture the ongoing restructuring of British urban policy. We feel that, together, these go some way towards addressing Offe's (1984:37) concern that crisis must be conceived of "not at the level of events but rather at the superordinate level of mechanisms that generate 'events.'" First, we draw on recent urban policy developments to analyze the changing geographies of state regulation (or sites for crisis containment). Second, we explain the ascendance of the competitive mode of policy intervention, as the state distributes resources through its institutionalized interurban competitions. Third, we argue that the contemporary emphasis on coordination (witness the growing usage of terms such as "governance" and "partnership") in urban policy reveals much about the state's *construction* of the problem as one not just of economic decline but rather as one of failed management. We discuss the recent history of coordinating and "steering" mechanisms, through which the state appears to be engaged in the crisis of crisis-management (Offe 1984).

Geographies of State Regulation
The 1980s—and the period of "consolidated" and "radical" Thatcherism—marked something of a turning point in British urban policy. Of course, the 1968 and the 1977 white papers marked significant "moments" in the evolution of policy (Atkinson and Moon 1994; CDP 1977), and it has been argued that "the program for the national economy carried out by the British government since 1975 is essentially neoliberal" (Gough and Eisenschitz 1996b:183). And yet, only when the New Right's critique of the welfare state crystallized at the beginning of the 1980s did it become clear that cities would became important sites through which the response to the Fordist-Keynesian crisis of accumulation would be assembled (Deakin and Edwards 1993). In these formative days of urban neoliberalism, a number of "nested hierarchical structures" (Harvey 1999:428–429) were introduced to manage crisis, each one representing a site for internalizing the contradictions of accumulation. Institutional creations such as urban development corporations (UDCs) and training and enterprise councils (TECs) were introduced to regulate urban property markets and urban labor markets (cf Cochrane 1999; Jones 1999). And, through a process of centrally orchestrated localism, certain functions were devolved from the nation-state downwards and delivered through an increasingly complex suite of flanking territorial alliances. New institutions were created to bypass the perceived bureaucratic modes of intervention associated with locally embedded and scale-dependent structures of local government. Through this strategy, the assumptions of how and for whom urban policy should be delivered were challenged. Put another way, the rules of the rationality game were rewritten.

The growth in new urban-based institutions to deliver economic redevelopment marked the emergence of what some termed a "new localism," although this concept—in particular, how it related to other changes in the scalar modus operandi of the state—was never fully defined (Lovering 1995). Marking a break from the Keynesian welfare settlement, where, although local government acted as the dominant regulatory mechanism (Goodwin and Painter 1996) its role was structured by the actions of the nation-state, it appeared to some that this was the dawn of a new age of central–local relations (Hall and Jacques 1989). Viewed more broadly, this apparent restructuring of the "representational regime" (Jessop 1990) was symptomatic of an altogether more complex series of shifts in the ways in which a "rationality crisis" was being managed through the rescaling of the state apparatus and the containment of conflict through instituting forms of representation. Across a range of policy areas, the scale of intervention shifted, as the taken-for-granted primacy of the nation-state was challenged and flanking mechanisms at the local level were introduced (Jessop this volume).[3]

Set within the context of responding to the so-called needs of globalization, the local was, therefore, constructed alongside the national as a primary scale for the delivery of economic and social policies (DoE 1993). More critically, with this reorganization of the internal structures of the state (Jessop 1990) went a critical reframing of the modes and the methods of state intervention. As Oatley (1998:31) argues, "[T]he government tried to establish locally based business-driven regeneration agencies during the 1980s as a way of constructing an organisational basis for local neoliberalism; in the 1990s neoliberal objectives have been pursued through new institutional forms at the local level." With the discursively mediated "failure" of these local innovations, the state again set about reorganizing the scale at which it regulated economic development. Reflecting the logic underpinning the first wave of *after*-national changes in the contours of state activity, and with the progression of devolution across western Europe in the 1990s, "the region" emerged (perhaps more through political practice that an underpinning territorial economic necessity) as *the* strategically important scale at which the state needed to manage a rescaled rationality crisis (Jones 2001). Accordingly, the creation of regional development agencies (RDAs) in 1999 marked a substantial centrally prescribed reinscription of the state's regional regulatory capacity. While the nation-state retained its orchestrating capabilities, the region (following on from the local) became constructed as the site at which to address globalization and mediate successful economic restructuring. Mirroring the deregulatory and procapital logic that was present in the genes of urban development corporations, RDAs were charged with regulating a "probusiness" approach to regional development (Deas and Ward 2000).

In both the first and second wave of state scalar restructuring, then, the creation of new institutions was performed as part of a systemic "rolling back" of the welfare state, and with it, how it regulated socio-economic contradictions through the creation of a "rationality crisis" and the "rolling out" of a new type of state shell for a new method of crisis management (cf Peck and Tickell this volume). As part of this emergence of a neoliberal urban policy, we suggest, the logic upon which the new state shell was premised—namely, competition and the market—required codification and institutionalization.

Institutionalizing Interurban Competition

A cornerstone of neoliberalism has been the state's internalizing and subsequent creation in institutional form of interurban competition. This has been achieved by removing the (national) regulatory management of uneven development and also by encouraging more speculative forms of accumulation through the promotion of place, rather than meeting the needs of discrete territories (Harvey 1989). In part through a critique of local government's methods of decision-making, the state established the parameters within which "territorial alliances" and "local coalitions" had to operate to be eligible to bid for state expenditure when City Challenge and the Single Regeneration Budget Challenge Funds were introduced at the beginning of the 1990s. Both redevelopment programs are allocated through a competition between localities.[4] While the creation of new subnational institutions through a rescaling of the patterns of intervention might have been the first part of this process, its complimentary "other" was the redefining of the political economic context within which these institutions—and their elected predecessors, local government—had to function and maneuver.

In 1991, the British government announced a "revolution in urban policy" (DoE 1991). The first example of this new stance on an old problem was City Challenge. Initially only those cities and towns that had been eligible for state grants under the old Urban Programme could bid for City Challenge status. The competition was tightly parameterized. More than simply a change in policy, the introduction of what became known as the Challenge Fund model marked the rolling-out of a whole new way of performing, of evaluating, and even of talking about urban development. As Oatley (1998:14) explains, "Challenge initiatives have focused on opportunities rather than problems." Illustrating the adoption of neoliberal promarket language by the state, this model has evolved to become an important mechanism through which the state distributes redevelopment money. Whether in terms of training (through the TEC Challenge, in which each TECs competed against each other for extra revenue) or business investment (through Sector Challenge, in which some sectors were privileged over other for state monies), the process through which issues/places are identified as needing state funds and how this expenditure is then evaluated has been realigned through *neoliberalization*. This change in how resources are allocated reflect the new logic that underscores the state's financing of urban redevelopment. This rests on four principles, which together help to reproduce the neoliberalization process:

- the introduction of the market (and the creation of a "market proxy" where no market exists) into the funding and the delivery of local state services;
- the incorporation into the state apparatus of members of local business communities in the regulation of regeneration projects;
- the redesigning of the internal structure of the state through the formation of public–private partnerships to decide program goals, the best means of achieving them, the institutional configuration most suited to meet them, and how their successes/ failures should be evaluated;
- and the creation of new institutions, combining business representatives with state officials to oversee and to deliver all forms of economic and social policy.

What runs through these different areas of program redesign is the concern with introducing some notion of "the market" into the state system, both through the formal resource allocation model, as in the case of Compulsory Competitive Tendering (CCT), and through the co-opting of business leaders, as in the example of TECs and their successor bodies. In their wake, however, the changing geographies of state regulation and the institutionalization of interurban competition leave a series of unsolved political and economic contradictions. One response has been to introduce a number of new institutions to coordinate the interurban competitions/scalar reconfigurations, as part of a long line of attempts by the state to manage the contradictions of earlier programs.

Rescaling as the Crisis of Crisis-Management
Building upon the above analysis, it is clear that the two tendencies in British urban policy constitute a significant effort by the state to construct and regulate crisis at the urban scale. The construction of a "new" scale of regulation, whether it be the "local" or the "regional," on which to begin to assemble neoliberal regulatory mechanisms and the codification of interurban institutional competition illustrates how the state apparatus has determined the parameters for "doing" urban redevelopment (Ward 2001). We would suggest that these endeavors indicate the ways in which a "rationality crisis" has been created through the displacement of economic crises of accumulation into problems for political and policy management, which, in turn, are having to reconcile their *own* internal contradictions.[5] Repeatedly, then, the

recent history of British urban policy can be read as being one in which the institutions and the programs *themselves*, and not the economy, become objects of regulation (cf Goodwin and Painter 1996). In order to understand and explain the demands on current urban policy, it is necessary to examine how the political sphere has been used as a means of managing ongoing urban economic difficulties.

In 1985, City Action Teams (CATs) were formed and charged with the local management of national programs. However, this was not a technocratic process; instead, it was a political one, ensuring the melding of local deliverables with the parameters set through national political strategies, which at the time revolved around the dismantling of a number of the central pillars of the Fordist-Keynesian settlement. It is not altogether surprising that these attempts to mobilize private-sector expertise through the urban state apparatus were created in Birmingham, Liverpool, London, Manchester, and Newcastle. These were (for the most part) large (Labour-led) urban city-regions and were at the front line of economic restructuring and its resistance. With the exception of the Community Development Projects, which wound down in the late 1970s, this initiative constituted perhaps the first effort to regulate the *previous* years of state intervention, and in particular, to ensure that all programs designed and introduced prior to the election of Thatcher in 1979 could be realigned, rationalized, or simply abolished. Rather than setting about reorganizing the national level of policy design and implementation, the creation of city-based institutions had the advantage of effectively devolving the management of crisis downwards, not to local government but to a group of state and business representatives. The remit of CATs was to minimize the overlap between different programs. Organized along the lines of the fast-action response teams favored by contemporary businesses, the CATS were, by design, presented as the "flexible" alternative to local government. Operating outside the formal local state machinery, CATs could wring out so-called efficiency gains from existing programs and systemically influence the nature of urban development politics.

A year later, eight Task Forces were rolled out across the English localities. London was the site for two, while the other six were established in Birmingham, Bristol, Leeds, Leicester, Manchester, and Middlesbrough. Again the emphasis was on the local coordination of national institutions and national state grants. Both CATs and associated programs—such as Enterprise Zones, which were local experiments in creating a deregulation/antitaxation space in which inward investment would relocate—were under the auspices of the Task Forces.

After this period of experimentation in designing urban institutions to manage crisis, more recent state strategies involved the creation of national institutions (such as Action for Cities) and national expenditure programs (such as the Single Regeneration Budget, or SRB) to manage the effects and contradictions of previous rounds of state intervention. In the first of these, the government attempted to "airbrush out" past policy and political failures. It sought to reaffirm the dominant ideology within which discrete policies were situated by calling for a more coordinated approach (where the scope for local resistance might be less). This concern was driven in part by concerns that neoliberal urban policy had created a "patchwork quilt of complexity and idiosyncrasy" (Audit Commission 1989:4). However, instead of addressing this problem, late-Thatcherite state interventions were far from coordinated. Action for Cities, and to an extent the SRB, presented a "rag-bag of policies with ill-defined objectives" (Imrie and Thomas 1999:39).

The election of Labour in 1997 did not disrupt the neoliberalization project under way in Britain's cities. During the first few months of the new Labour administration, the SRB was discredited as a strategy for "ensuring coordination" (DETR 1997a). However, it was retained and later modified to respond to contradictions created by a previous lack of community involvement. Even the recent programmatic changes in city-region redevelopment governance—the creation of RDAs— have in their policy genes the "effective and proper ... co-ordinat[ion] of regional economic development" (DETR 1997b:1). However, to rationalize the policy messes and tangled hierarchies created by the RDAs, Labour created a Regional Co-ordination Unit, after a hard-hitting report concluded that "better Ministerial and Whitehall *co-ordination* of policy initiatives and communication" was needed (Performance and Innovation Unit 2000:5; emphasis added). Such endeavors have been somewhat complicated by the national reorganization of the state apparatus, involving the abolition of the Department for Environment, Transport and the Regions (DETR) and its replacement by the Department for Transport, Local Government and the Regions (DTLR). As a consequence, city-region redevelopment is the responsibility of several branches of the state, which only fuels a crisis of crisis-management through further problems of coordination (Tomaney 2001).

These national scale maneuvers have been followed by *further* attempts to cope with a crisis of state rationality through centrally driven state administrative reorganization at a local level. During the summer of 2001, Local Strategic Partnerships (LSPs) were introduced to *rationalize* the partnership overload created by twenty years of localized public policy developments. As part of a *national* strategy for Neighborhood Renewal, and reporting to the Government Offices for the Regions (ie central government), LSPs present single bodies charged with joining up the "different parts of the public sector as well as the private, business, community and voluntary sectors so that different initiatives and services support each other and work together" (DETR 2001:10). Illustrating the multifarious contradictions created by neoliberalism and the state's need to respond to its own scalar and strategic contradictions, this strategy is *not* concerned with rationalization per se; there is no mention of LSPs replacing the myriad of partnerships currently in place for education, employment, crime, health, and housing. Instead, each LSP "should work with and *not replace* neighbourhood-level partnerships" (DETR 2001:11; emphasis added). This strategy appears to be less about cutting out local duplication and bureaucracy than about a recentralizing of the right to manage rationality crises with the state apparatus. Recognizing this, we would concur with those commentators on British urban policy who maintain that the "challenge … is to establish a national-to-local framework for enabling the exercise of subsidiarity in a strategic fashion" (Robson et al 2000:5).

Critically, we suggest that attempts by the state to regulate the political crisis invoked through its own contradictions are continuing to emerge on the policy landscape, to the point that policymakers are running out of "new" repertoires and a "circularity of policy responses" is occurring (Wilks-Heeg 1996:1263). Take, for instance, the latest urban white paper, *Our Towns and Cities: The Future* (DETR 2000), in which the British state embraces "third-way" politics as the friendly face of neoliberalism, but in the process exacerbates the contradictions of capitalism through its own interventions. This "revolutionary" framework calls for a "new vision for urban living" largely founded on modernist assumptions on the need to get the "design and quality of the urban fabric right" (Urban Task Force 1999:ch 2). This is not "revolutionary" at all; its policy gene is a document (with a similar title) published twenty years ago (DoE 1980) and key elements of the "urban renaissance" are heavily reminiscent of the last urban white paper, *Policy for the Inner Cities* (HMSO 1977). In this endeavor to promote a cultural mode of urban interventionism with a heightened emphasis on cities as sites for consumption and living, and despite continual emphasis placed on further coordination, no attempt is being made to rationalize the institutional and policy matrix of the city and no measures are being taken to address the ongoing problems created by private-sector mobilization and the thorny issue of market failure. No, in fact, the opposite is happening, through the formation of "Urban Regeneration Companies" that want to insert the private sector into the city—a move driven by the contradictions caused by community-led initiatives (see DETR 1998)—and the recent reorganization of the Department for Trade and Industry to increase the business voice in economic policy formulation and its implementation (a "first in Whitehall") through a Strategy Board (see DTI 2001).

Last, recently it has been possible to discern crisis management being shifted out of the political sphere of the state and into the social sphere once more. This response by the state to "failure" consists of two strands of strategic selectivity. First, in turning to civil society the state has invoked notions of "neighbourhood" and "community" (see DETR 1997a, 2000). These terms are invoked as part of an attempt to shift (through scale) the onus for addressing deepening social inequalities. The second theme is the recent individualization or atomization of policies, marking in part a return to the "social pathology" approach that dominated British urban policy in the late 1960s (CDP 1977) and also demonstrating the influences of "fast policy transfer" (Jessop and Peck 1998) or "worldwide ideological marketing" (Wacquant 1999:321–323). Through the construction of "the individual" as the problem, "the individual" also becomes constructed as the solution. Economic and financial risk is being shifted from the state and onto the individual through welfare-to-work policies such as the various "New Deal" initiatives. Crisis management then becomes one part of a complicated comprise consisting of a restructured scalar architecture of the state, through which we appear to be witnessing what Harvey (1999:431) terms "a crisis in the co-ordinating mechanisms" of capitalism.

Concluding Comments

Having assembled a theoretical framework for making sense of the recent process of the urbanization of neoliberalism, this paper has suggested that crisis-theoretic work reveals much about the last two decades of urban policy in Britain, and beyond (cf Leitner and Sheppard this volume). There is, of course, further mileage in this perspective; elsewhere, we have discussed the need to consider a "fourth-cut" theory of crisis (Jones 2001; Jones and Ward 2001) as part of a longer excavation of the logic underscoring "mainstream local economic initiatives" (Gough and Eisenschitz 1996a:178), making a modest contribution to Harvey's (1999) unfinished project.

For the purposes of this paper, in structuring our empirical analysis around three interrelated tendencies—the geographies of state regulation, the institutionalizing of interurban competition, and the crisis of crisis-management—we have sought to provide a "deep" reading of urban political and policy change. Urban policies pursued by the state in Britain during the 1990s were bound, *by design*, to intensify the internal contradictions of capital accumulation. We have maintained throughout the paper that Britain's cities host ineffectual regulatory strategies because urban policy appears to be a response to the sociopolitical and geographical contradictions of *previous* rounds of urban policy, not the underpinning contradictions of accumulation. We would further suggest that the "entrepreneurial turn" of nation, regional, and local states, and of the discourses within which policies are couched, has a series of implications for socio-spatial polarization and deepening financial inequality (see also Home Office 2001). Additionally, urban policy that codifies the underlying logic of inter-urban competition leads to an inefficient use of public money, separates communities, and has the capacity to trigger a fiscal crisis of the state. Despite these potential impending crises, the ability of neoliberalism to morph must not be underestimated, and—at least in the short term —the rules of neoliberalism look set to remain in place.

Acknowledgments

An earlier version of this paper was presented at the seminar "Neoliberalism and the City", at the University of Illinois at Chicago (September 2001). We would like to thank the organizers (Neil Brenner and Nik Theodore), who did an outstanding job organizing and hosting the event, and the enthusiastic participants and referees for their comments on the paper. Mark Whitehead, Gordon MacLeod, Bill Edwards, and Mark Goodwin have helped us to clarify the arguments offered here. The usual disclaimers apply.

Endnotes

[1] This point is a central concern within the Cantle report on the disturbances in the northern cities (Home Office 2001:10), which states that "The plethora of initiatives and programmes, with their baffling array of outcomes, boundaries, timescales and other conditions, seemed to ensure divisiveness and a perception of unfairness in virtually every section of the communities we visited."

[2] Our paper is less concerned with defining neoliberalism (on which see Brenner and Theodore [paper] this volume; Jessop this volume) and more concerned with conceptualizing its operation in relation to Britain's cities. However, we see neoliberalism as a multifaceted project based on institutionalizing and normalizing competitive deregulation, and this frequently involves periods of re-regulation at different spatial scales (see Peck and Tickell this volume). This represents something of a departure from the argument that constructs national government as neoliberal and local economic initiatives as centrist (Eisenschitz and Gough 1993; Gough and Eisenschitz 1996a: 209–210; Gough and Eisenschitz 1996b:179–180). We suggest that urban policy since the late 1970s have been increasingly neoliberalized across a number of spatial scales.

[3] This is not to argue that "the local" is a recent political strategic concern. As Gough and Eisenschitz (1996a:206) make clear, "There is a long history of local initiatives for modernisation." Rather, the argument is that through a qualitative reorganization of the state, the local has become of increasing importance because of the scalar transformation of the national state (Jones 1999; MacLeod and Goodwin 1999).

[4] This constitutes the internalization and deepening of key aspects of the socialization process under capitalism emphasized by Gough and Eisenschitz (1996b:192).

[5] This is not to argue that the UK is not suffering from an ongoing urban economic crisis (see Robson et al 2000; Turok and Edge 1999).

References

Aglietta M (1998) Capitalism at the turn of the century: Regulation theory and the challenge of social change. *New Left Review* 232:41–90

Atkinson R and Moon G (1994) *Urban Policy in Britain: The City, the State, and the Market*. London: Macmillan

Audit Commission (1989) *Urban Regeneration and Economic Development: The Local Government Dimension*. London: HMSO

Begg I (1999) Cities and competitiveness. *Urban Studies* 36:795–809

Bourdieu P and Wacquant L (2001) NeoLiberalSpeak: Notes on the new planetary vulgate. *Radical Philosophy* 108:2–5

Brenner N (1998) Between fixity and motion: Accumulation, territorial organization, and the historical geography of spatial scales. *Environment and Planning D: Society and Space* 16:459–481

Clarke S E and Gaile G L (1998) *The Work of Cities*. London: University of Minnesota Press

Cochrane A (1989) Britain's political crisis. In A Cochrane and J Anderson (eds) *Politics in Transition* (pp 34–66). London: Sage

Cochrane A (1999) Just another failed urban experiment? The legacy of the Urban Development Corporations. In R Imrie and H Thomas (eds) *British Urban Policy: An Evaluation of the Urban Development Corporations* (pp 246–258). London: Sage

Community Development Project (CDP) (1977) *Gilding the Ghetto: The State and the Poverty Experiments*. London: CDP Inter-Project Team

Deakin N and Edwards J (1993) *The Enterprise Culture and the Inner City*. London: Routledge

Dear M and Clark G (1978) The state and geographical process: A critical review. *Environment and Planning A* 10:173–183

Deas I and Ward K (2000) From the "new localism" to the "new regionalism"? The implications of regional development agencies for city-regional relations. *Political Geography* 16:273–292

Department of the Environment (DoE) (1980) *Urban Renaissance: A Better Life in Towns*. London: Department of the Environment

Department of the Environment (DoE) (1991) Michael Heseltine outlines new approach to urban regeneration. Press Release 138, 11 March. London: Department of the Environment

Department of the Environment (DoE) (1993) *Single Regeneration Budget: Notes on Principles*. London: Department of the Environment

Department of the Environment, Transport and the Regions (DETR) (1997a) *Regeneration Programmes—The Way Forward*. Discussion paper. London: Department of the Environment, Transport and the Regions

Department of the Environment, Transport and the Regions (DETR) (1997b) *Building Partnerships for Prosperity: Sustainable Growth, Competitiveness and Employment in the English Regions*. Cm 3814. London: Department of the Environment, Transport and the Regions

Department of the Environment, Transport and the Regions (DETR) (1998) *Community-Based Regeneration Initiatives*. Working Paper. London: Department of the Environment, Transport and the Regions

Department of the Environment, Transport and the Regions (DETR) (2000) *Our Towns and Cities: The Future. Delivering an Urban Renaissance*. Cm 4911. London: Department of the Environment, Transport and the Regions

Department of the Environment, Transport and the Regions (DETR) (2001) *Local Strategic Partnerships: Government Guidance*. London: Department of the Environment, Transport and the Regions

Department of Trade and Industry (DTI) (2001) DTI reviews: Structure and priorities and business support. Press notice 22 November. London: Department of Trade and Industry

Eisenschitz A and Gough J (1993) *The Politics of Local Economic Policy: The Problems and Possibilities of Local Initiative*. London: Macmillan

Fainstein N and Fainstein S (1982) *Urban Policy under Capitalism*. London: Sage

Florida R and Jonas A (1991) US urban policy: The postwar state and capitalist regulation. *Antipode* 23:349–384

Goodwin M and Painter J (1996) Local governance, the crises of Fordism, and the changing geographies of regulation. *Transactions of the Institute of British Geographers* 21:635–648

Gough J and Eisenschitz A (1996a) The construction of mainstream local economic initiatives: Mobility, socialization, and class relations. *Economic Geography* 72: 178–195

Gough J and Eisenschitz A (1996b) The modernization of Britain and local economic policy: Promise and contradictions. *Environment and Planning D: Society and Space* 14:203–219

Habermas J (1976) *Legitimation Crisis*. London: Heinemann

Hall S and Jacques M (eds) (1989) *New Times: The Changing Face of Politics in the 1990s*. London: Lawrence and Wishart

Harloe M (ed) (1977) *Captive Cities: Studies in the Political Economy of Cities and Regions*. Chichester: Wiley

Harvey D (1985) *The Urbanization of Capital*. Oxford: Blackwell

Harvey D (1989) From managerialism to entrepreneurialism: The transformation in urban governance in late capitalism. *Geografiska Annaler* 71b:3–17

Harvey D (1999) *The Limits to Capital*. New ed. London: Verso

Hay C (1995) Restating the problem of regulation and re-regulating the local state. *Economy and Society* 24:387–407

Hay C (1996) *Restating Social and Political Change*. Buckingham: Open University Press

Held D (1996) *Models of Democracy*. Cambridge, UK: Polity

Held D and Krieger J (1982) Theories of the state: Some competing claims. In S Bornstein, D Held and J Krieger (eds) *The State in Capitalist Europe* (pp 1–20). London: Allen & Unwin

Her Majesty's Stationery Office (1977) *Policy for the Inner Cities*. Cmnd 6845. London: HMSO

Holton R J (1987) The idea of crisis in modern society. *British Journal of Sociology* 38:502–520

Home Office (2001) *Community Cohesion: A Report of the Independent Review Team Chaired by Ted Cantle*. London: Home Office

Hudson R (2001) *Producing Places*. New York: Guilford Press

Imrie R and Thomas H (1999) Assessing urban policy and the Urban Development Corporations. In R Imrie and H Thomas (eds) *British Urban Policy: An Evaluation of the Urban Development Corporations* (pp 3–39). London: Sage

Jenson J (1991) All the world's a stage: Ideas, spaces, and times in Canadian political economy. *Studies in Political Economy* 36:43–72

Jessop B (1990) *State Theory: Putting Capitalist States in Their Place*. Cambridge, UK: Polity

Jessop B (1997) Survey article: The regulation approach. *The Journal of Political Philosophy* 5:287–326

Jessop B (1998) The rise of governance and the risks of failure: The case of economic development. *International Social Science Journal* 155:29–45

Jessop B (2001) Good governance and the urban question: On managing the contradictions of neoliberalism. Mimeograph. Lancaster: Department of Sociology, University of Lancaster

Jessop B and Peck J (1998) Fast-policy/local discipline: The politics of time and scale and the neoliberal workfare offensive. Mimeograph. Lancaster: Department of Sociology, University of Lancaster

Jones M (1999) *New Institutional Spaces: Training and Enterprise Councils and the Remaking of Economic Governance.* London: Jessica Kingsley/Regional Studies Association

Jones M (2001) The rise of the regional state in economic governance: "Partnerships for prosperity" or new scales of state power? *Environment and Planning A* 33: 1185–1211

Jones M and Ward K (1997) Crisis and disorder in British local economic governance: Business Link and the Single Regeneration Budget. *Journal of Contingencies and Crisis Management* 5:154–165

Jones M and Ward K (2001) Urban policy under capitalism: Towards a "fourth-cut" theory of crisis. Mimeograph. Aberystwyth: Institute of Geography and Earth Sciences, University of Wales

Lipietz A (1994) The national and the regional: Their autonomy vis-à-vis the capitalist word crisis. In R P Palan and B Gills (eds) *Transcending the State-Global Divide: A Neostructuralist Agenda in International Relations* (pp 23–44). London: Lynne Rienner

Lovering J (1995) Creating discourses rather than jobs: The crisis in the cities and the transition fantasies of intellectuals and policymakers. In P Healey, S Cameron, S Davoudi, S Graham and A Madani-Pour (eds) *Managing Cities: The New Urban Context* (pp 109–126). Chichester: Wiley

MacLeod G and Goodwin M (1999) Reconstructing an urban and regional political economy: On the state, politics, scale, and explanation. *Political Geography* 18:697–730

Oatley N (1998) Cities, economic competition, and urban policy. In N Oatley (ed) *Cities, Economic Competition, and Urban Policy* (pp 3–20). London: Paul Chapman

O'Connor J (1987) *The Meaning of Crisis: A Theoretical Introduction.* Oxford: Blackwell

Offe C (1975) The theory of the capitalist state and the problem of policy formulation. In L N Lindberg, R Alford, C Couch, and C Offe (eds) *Stress and Contradiction in Modern Capitalism* (pp 125–144). London: Lexington Books

Offe C (1984) *Contradictions of the Welfare State.* London: Hutchinson

Offe C (1985) *Disorganized Capitalism: Contemporary Transformations in Work and Politics.* Cambridge, UK: Polity

Offe C (1996) *Modernity and the State: East, West.* Cambridge, UK: Polity

Painter J (1997) Regulation, regime, and practice. In M Luria (ed) *Reconstructing Urban Regime Theory: Regulating Politics in a Global Economy* (pp 122–143). London: Sage

Peck J and Tickell A (1994) Searching for a new institutional fix: The *after*-Fordist crisis and the global-local disorder. In A Amin (ed) *Post-Fordism: A Reader* (pp 280–315). Oxford: Blackwell

Performance and Innovation Unit (2000) *Reaching Out: The Role of Central Government at Regional and Local Level.* London: Cabinet Office

Rees G and Lambert J (1985) *Cities in Crisis: The Political Economy of Urban Development in Post-War Britain.* London: Edward Arnold

Robson B (1988) *Those Inner Cities: Reconciling the Social and Economic Aims of Urban Policy.* Oxford: Clarendon

Robson B, Parkinson M, Boddy M and Maclennan D (2000) *The State of English Cities.* London: DETR

Sardar Z (2001) A dying body attracts vultures. *New Statesman* 4 June:10–12

Scharpf F (1997) The problem-solving capacity of multilevel governance. *Journal of European Public Policy* 4:520–538

Swyngedouw E (2000) Authoritarian governance, power, and the politics of rescaling. *Environment and Planning D: Society and Space* 18:63–76

Tickell A and Peck J (1992) Accumulation, regulation, and the geographies of post-Fordism: Missing links in regulationist research. *Progress in Human Geography* 16:190–218

Tomaney J (2001) Reshaping the English regions. In A Trench (ed) *The State of the Nations 2001* (pp 107–133). Exeter: Imprint Academic

Turok I and Edge N (1999) *The Jobs Gap in Britain's Cities*. Bristol: Policy Press

Urban Task Force (1999) *Towards an Urban Renaissance. Final Report*. London: E & FN Spon

Wacquant L (1999) How penal common sense comes to Europeans: Notes on the transatlantic diffusion of the neoliberal *doxa*. *European Societies* 1:319–352

Walker R (1995) Regulation and flexible specialization as theories of capitalist development: Challenges to Marx and Schumpeter. In H Liggett and D C Perry (eds) *Spatial Practices: Critical Explorations in Social/Spatial Theory* (pp 144–208). London: Sage

Ward K (2001) "Doing" regeneration: Evidence from England's three second cities. *Soundings* 17:22–24

Webber M and Rigby D (1996) *The Golden Age Illusion: Rethinking Postwar Capitalism*. New York: Guilford Press

Wilks-Heeg S (1996) Urban experiments limited revisited: Urban policy comes full circle? *Urban Studies* 33:1263–1279

Martin Jones is Reader in Human Geography at the University of Wales, Aberystwyth. Author of *New Institutional Spaces* (London: Jessica Kingsley, 1999) and numerous journal articles, his research interests are in post-Marxist state theory, urban and regional political economy, the governance of economic development, and labor market policy. He is currently codirecting an ESRC-funded research project on the impacts of UK devolution and constitutional change on economic governance.

Kevin Ward is a Lecturer in Human Geography at the University of Manchester. Author of numerous journal articles, his research interests are in urban and regional governance, urban regeneration, and labor geographies. He is currently working on issues of urban entrepreneurialism, the negotiation of the work/nonwork divide in urban Britain and on a study of the globalization and localization of the temporary staffing industry.

Chapter 7
"The City is Dead, Long Live the Net": Harnessing European Interurban Networks for a Neoliberal Agenda

Helga Leitner and Eric Sheppard

A network discourse has emerged during the last two decades, representing networks as self-organizing, collaborative, nonhierarchical, flexible, and topological. Progressive scholars initially embraced networks as an alternative to markets and hierarchies; neoliberal thinkers and policymakers have reinterpreted them in order to serve a neo-liberal agenda of enhanced economic competitiveness, a leaner and more efficient state, and a more flexible governance. The European Commission and the German state have initiated and financially supported interurban network programs, broadly framed within this neoliberal network discourse, despite their long traditions of regulated capitalism. Really existing interurban networks depart, however, from these discourses. Embedded within pre-existing processes of uneven development and hierarchical state structures, and exhibiting internal power hierarchies, really existing networks are created, regulated, and evaluated by state institutions, and often exclude institutions and members of civil society, making them effective channels for disseminating a neoliberal agenda. At the same time, they create new political spaces for cities to challenge existing state structures and relations and are of unequal potential benefit to participating cities, both of which may catalyze resistance to neoliberalization.

With the headline "Die Stadt is tot, es lebe das Netz" (The city is dead, long live the net), in August 1997 the renowned German newspaper *Die Welt* introduced to the German public a new way of thinking about cities. In this vision, cities cannot make it on their own in an era of globalization and increased interurban competition, but need to cooperate. Networks, in the form of public–private partner-ships and interurban cooperation even across national borders, are thus presented as the key to urban futures. *Die Welt* was drawing on an emergent trend in both public policy and academic discourse that con-strues networks as a preferable mode of coordination and governance for coping with the vagaries of globalization and internationalization, facilitating a more efficient use of public resources, increasing com-petitiveness, generating economic growth, and resolving social problems. Networks and networking have become particularly fashionable in the European Union, embracing scientific collaboration, telecommunications and transportation, and policy networks, as well as collaboration within and between localities. With respect to urban and regional policy, the European Commission has been promoting networks as new modes of governance at scales ranging from the local to the transnational: between firms, between public and private sectors, and between cities and regions (Amin and Thrift 1995; Cooke and Morgan 1993; European Commission 1994; Leitner and Sheppard 1998, 1999). This has been replicated within some member states. Germany in particular has made interurban networking integral to its regional policy (Bundesamt für Bauwesen und Raumordnung 1999). Networks are also popular among academics who, inter alia, have portrayed local interfirm networks as a preferred organizational strategy for localities, catalyzing economic efficiency, flexibility in response to changing market conditions, collaborative innovation, and robustness in the face of global production and finance networks.

Certain aspects of networks are emphasized when they are promoted as an alternative to markets and hierarchies: their self-organizing, collaborative, nonhierarchical, and flexible nature. This representation has proved attractive to progressives and neoliberals alike (Barry 1996). Whereas progressives conceive of networks as an alternative to markets, neoliberals have come to embrace them as a vehicle for promoting free markets (cf Brenner and Theodore [paper] this volume; Jessop this volume).

In this paper, we trace how, and the extent to which, interurban networks have become enrolled into the neoliberalization of spatial policies in Europe. We first examine how network discourses have represented networks as having certain properties, and how these properties have proven attractive to and been given distinctive interpretations by both progressive and neoliberal perspectives. We then show how neoliberal interpretations have become central to policy discourses framing the promotion of interurban networks in the EU and Germany. Finally, we compare these discourses with practices of interurban networking, examining the degree to which really existing networks depart from the discursive claims, reasons for this, and their role within European neoliberalization.

Network Discourses

By definition, networks are relational: the conditions of possibility and actions of network participants are defined by their relationship with other participants, rather than by their own inherent characteristics. During the last two decades, however, network discourses have emerged that go beyond this broad definition to represent networks as possessing a particular set of "natural" properties (cf Castells 1996; Cohendet et al 1998; Latour 1993; Leitner, Pavlik and Sheppard forthcoming; Powell

1990). This representation is contested, particularly in social network analysis, but is now broadly accepted in the interdisciplinary writing on this topic (Leitner, Pavlik and Sheppard forthcoming).

First, networks are *self-organizing*. Networks evolve a relational organizational structure that is bottom-up, rather than externally imposed. Self-organizing systems are path-dependent and evolutionary, and unpredictable in the medium run because network dynamics can be dramatically affected by small changes in external conditions. In this sense, networks are often thought of as archetypical complex systems. Second, networks are *collaborative*: "modes of transaction which presume some form of *mutual orientation* and usually *obligation*" (Amin and Thrift 1997:152; emphasis in original). Third, networks are *nonhierarchical*. Network participants are linked by two-way, horizontal relationships that give each participant a voice over the collective outcome. Fourth, networks are *flexible*. Two aspects of flexibility are typically invoked: (1) network linkages are continually subject to change, and network structures are periodically restructured; (2) network boundaries are fuzzy: participants can leave networks and potential participants can join. Fifth, the spatiality of networks is *topological*. By this, we mean that networks evolve by creating linkages between participants who were not previously connected, thereby constructing mutuality between previously isolated actors. They connect actors, or places, that previously seemed distant from one another. "Technological networks ... are nets thrown over spaces, and they retain only a few scattered elements of those spaces. They are connected lines, not surfaces" (Latour 1993:118).

Many also impute desirable performance characteristics to networks, bestowing a general spirit of optimism on network discourses (Hay 1998). In this view, networks minimize the destructive aspects of market-based competition and encourage collaboration by facilitating tacit mutuality and trust between participants. The rigid bureaucracies of the state and corporate capital break down in networks, making them "lighter on their feet" (Powell 1990:302) than hierarchies. Their flexibility and self-organizing properties promote learning and innovation. As a consequence they are more robust and efficient and less bureaucratic than markets or hierarchies. Geographically, local networks facilitate the survival of localities (and of the nation-states to which they belong) in the face of the uncertainties of global capital mobility (Amin and Thrift 1994; Storper 1997), and interurban networks allow localities to participate in alliances with a geographical scope better matching that of corporations and state agencies (Leitner and Sheppard 1999).

As yet, however, the evidence linking performance with network characteristics is weak. The common approach has been to examine successful places, to identify network characteristics of those places, and to assert that their success is due to these characteristics and that less successful places either lack network characteristics or lack the right balance of network characteristics. To date, little has been done to demonstrate that less successful places indeed do not have the right kinds of networks, or to show exactly how network characteristics translate into success. Such claims thus run the danger of functionally attributing the success of a place to its network characteristics without demonstrating exactly how this works (Hay 1998; Leitner, Pavlik and Sheppard forthcoming).

Both progressive and neoliberal thinkers and policymakers have been attracted to these network discourses. In the remainder of this section we discuss these contrasting interpretations of network discourses, why network discourses have this degree of ideological flexibility, and why neoliberalism is now appropriating network discourses.

Progressive Interpretations

The importance of local urban networks was initially recognized by progressive scholars seeking a "third way" for European urban and regional policy, an alternative to a managed economy and neoliberalism. Cooke and Morgan (1993, 1998) and Amin and Thrift (1992, 1995, 1997), in particular, provide programmatic statements about how local urban and regional networks can serve a progressive agenda in a globalizing world.[1] Table 1 summarizes this interpretive grid.

Local networks are seen as drawing on the advantages of proximity for facilitating nonroutine interactions, which can advance the prospects for cities and regions adopting a network approach. Spatial proximity enhances relationships between firms in ways that promote innovation and learning, between the public and private sectors in ways that direct economic restructuring in positive directions and improve labor market information and training, and between the state and civil society in ways that deepen political participation. The result is what Storper (1997) has termed the creation of local "relational assets."

The self-organizing nature of networks promotes continual innovation in the private sector, complemented by local political processes enhancing institutional thickness—the development of territorially based cultural complexes that underwrite trust and support associative democracy. Collaboration should reduce destructive competition in the private sector, antagonism between capital and labor, and fissures between local civil society, the state, and the private sector. Amin and Thrift (1995:61) call for "a flatter, more permeable state ... for which it is much more difficult to draw a dividing line between state institutions and institutions of civil society." Full participation in governance makes local networks nonhierarchical: Marshallian industrial districts give all firms a voice, and associative

Table 1: Progressive and Neoliberal Interpretations

Network Properties	Progressive Interpretation	Neoliberal Interpretation
Self-organizing	Dynamic economic clusters; bottom-up associational democracy	Dynamic economic clusters; bottom-up professionalized network modes of governance
Collaborative	Democratization of the economy; collaboration between firms, workers, and the state; democratization of the state, empowering civil society	Strategic alliances between firms promote innovation; workers collaborate with capitalists within firms; public–private partnerships foster state entrepreneurialism
Nonhierarchical	Full participation: many small firms disperse economic power; equal voice given to all	Full competition: no favoritism for firms, industries; no state monopolies; no unions; political pluralism
Flexible	Open information exchange between firms, state, civil society; inclusive governance	Flexible workforce, flexible capital, flexible governance
Topological spatiality	Integrating firms, workers, civil society, and the state within place-based alliances; fostering collaboration among cities	Local and extralocal interfirm networks and public–private partnerships; fostering flows of commodities, capital, information, and people within and among cities
Performance characteristics	Innovative, learning-intensive, strongly democratic; promoting social justice, respect for difference, and societal and ecological sustainability	Efficient, innovative, entrepreneurial; promoting a competitive local economy and state, good profits and wages, and sustainable development

Source: Authors; Amin and Thrift (1995).

democracy gives all residents a voice. Flexibility is achieved through both an open information exchange between firms, the state, and civil society, and an inclusive governance structure.

The topological spatiality of networks is primarily envisioned as a local process, drawing more local residents into governance. Amin and Thrift (1995) stress the difficulties of opening the boundaries of currently existing networks to include new voices, however. They express concern that this kind of opening up is too important and too difficult to be left in the hands of networks themselves, and may require intervention from higher levels of the state.

The strong performance of places like Silicon Valley, Emilia-Romagna, and Baden-Württemberg is seen as exemplifying the benefits of such networks, although analysts of these examples often stress the economic advantages of network (or "learning") cities and regions without looking too closely at the inequalities evolving within such regions (Amin 1989). A more radical democratic agenda seeks broader performance criteria (Amin and Thrift 1995:60). Central to all these discussions of network performance is the geographical claim that local networks empower cities and regions (particularly those residents whose voices have typically been ignored). Networked regions will be more democratic, economically vibrant, and more secure from the vagaries of globalization than other regions. This can be extended to claim that cities and regions can further empower themselves, relative both to mobile finance capital and the hierarchical power structures of territorial states, by joining interurban networks (Church and Reid 1996; Leitner, Pavlik and Sheppard forthcoming). Cities in competition with one another are easier targets for capital than are interurban collaborative networks, and networks transcending the boundaries of political territories create new political spaces for challenging existing territorial state structures.

Neoliberal Interpretations

Neoliberalism falls squarely on the free-market end of the long and complex tradition of liberal thought. Its advocacy of more market and less state has run into difficulty, however, in academic and policy circles. New institutional economists find that firms may rationally prefer a hierarchical organizational structure to markets. Economic sociologists and industrial-district theorists argue that networks provide the mutuality and trust necessary for markets to function. Simplifying a complex argument, such networks enable economic agents to trust one another, to engage in strategic alliances to take advantage of economies of scope, and to avoid writing contractual agreements for every conceivable economic transaction and eventuality (Granovetter 1985; Hodgson 1994; Saxenian 1994; Scott 1989; Storper 1997). In the policy arena, the practical experience of market failure and criminal capitalism in transitional economies such as Russia and the chaos of the 1999 Asian financial crisis have convinced some influential proponents of neoliberalism that really existing capitalism can be destructive and exploitative unless it is embedded in an appropriate institutional context. As a consequence, a modified neoliberal position has emerged, accepting aspects of this criticism while still arguing that free market capitalism, appropriately catalyzed, is the best guarantee of prosperity for all (Sachs 1999).

Michael Porter (1989, 1995, 1996) exemplifies this position, with recommendations that have been widely adopted by urban policy-makers around the world. He argues that the key to urban prosperity lies in developing a competitive advantage, and that the key to competitive advantage is to be found in clusters of firms forming industrial districts, networking with one another in ways that promote dynamic external economies, innovation, and growth. These clusters should be in leading-edge industries that take advantage of a locality's strengths. In principle, every location can identify such a cluster and rely on it to generate good (high-wage and interesting) jobs and an improved physical environment. Porter envisages a role for the state, but one confined to helping cities identify their appropriate competitive advantage and to correcting market imperfections (for a critique see, inter alia, Sheppard 2000).

More generally, contemporary neoliberal thought emphasizes the importance of efficient and professionalized governance. While state institutions have a role to play, policy networks can ensure that political decisionmaking is flexible, dynamic, and efficient (Martin and Mayntz 1991). Policy networks, such as local public–private partnerships and those linking different localities, are seen as capable of ensuring competitiveness and innovation. Neoliberal governance is content to delegate authority to experts insulated from the democratic process, located in urban development agencies and the like, who can be relied on to develop best practices. Neoliberal policy networks are thus accompanied by a de-democratization of the political process.

In this neoliberal view, self-organization is best left to networked firms and professionalized network modes of governance; collaboration prioritizes entrepreneurial values; hierarchies are eliminated to free up economic and political competition; and flexibility in the economy and in political governance is crucial. Topologically, networks promote new collaborations and facilitate the flow of production factors within and among cities. In short, neoliberal networks are supposed to enhance urban competitiveness, allow workers and capitalists to prosper together, and not degrade the environment (Table 1).

The ability of network discourses to be retrofitted with interpretations spanning the political spectrum is testimony to the attractiveness of the properties highlighted in this discourse. Network discourses, like those of sustainability, are unobjectionable at this level of abstraction. Few are opposed to bottom-up initiatives, learning, innovation, collaboration, the elimination of power hierarchies, flexibility, or connecting social actors and places together in novel ways. The claim that networks also perform better only reinforces the attractiveness of this discourse. Real differences remain, however, in what is included and valued in progressive and neoliberal interpretations (Table 1), and particularly in whether the values of the marketplace should dominate those of political participation and social justice. These differences create a space where the implementation of networks can be contested. In the following, we examine which interpretations are prioritized in interurban network discourses in the EU and Germany.

Interurban Network Discourses in the European Union and Germany

During the past decade the emerging interurban network discourse in Europe has been spearheaded by two principal institutions: the European Union (EU) and the German state.[2] While neither institution can be described simply as neoliberal, we seek to show that the representations of networks in these discourses are primarily framed within neoliberal goals.

European Union Interurban Networks[3]

Since the late 1980s, the European Commission has promoted and encouraged transnational interurban networks as a part of its structural funds. Reading across an enormous range of EU policy documents, it is possible to glean the following overarching goals for these networks:

- improving local responsiveness to challenges posed by an increasingly European and global economy, making cities and regions more competitive;
- achieving a more efficient use of public resources;
- facilitating the spread of innovative "best-practice" economic development practices; and
- strengthening economic and social cohesion by reducing economic and social disparities within EU territory.

To a large extent, these goals are framed by the neoliberal economic policy emphasis on competition, innovation, and efficient use of state resources. Improving competitiveness values activities in terms of their contribution to profit-making. A more efficient use of state resources implies the existence of public sector waste that needs to be reduced. The meaning of the third goal depends on how innovativeness is interpreted. Yet, if valued in terms of the first two goals, innovative practices should serve neoliberal goals. Unlike the other three, however, the fourth goal departs from a strictly neoliberal agenda. Its inclusion reflects the EU's own ambivalent position on economic policy. Whereas the Single Market resonates closely with neoliberal thinking, the EU continues to emphasize its structural-funds programs on the grounds that state intervention is necessary for addressing inequality—a position closer to state-regulated capitalism than to neoliberalism (Bache 2000).

Networks are presented as capable of achieving these four goals because they promote collaboration, involve bottom-up initiative (anyone can initiate or join, and networks are sensitive to participants' needs), promote learning through the dissemination of information and experiences and the diffusion of best practices, and link distant and nearby participants (particularly more and less successful regions) (Commission of the European Communities 1992). An enormous variety of EU-sponsored networks now exists, with all kinds of individual agendas, including economic development, environment, energy and resources, health and social policy, youth employment, urban planning, public administration, transport, technology, and research. Such agendas are shaped by the interpretive frame outlined above.

Neoliberal thinking has clearly diffused through Commission policymaking, but the views of individual commissioners and bureaucrats within the EU range from neoliberal to social democratic. This leaves room for the development of EU-sponsored networks that may depart substantially from a neoliberal agenda, depending on the goals and beliefs held by the participants, by those offering sponsorship, and by those evaluating the program's performance.

German Interurban Networks

Although discussion dates back to 1993, the German "Städtenetze" pilot project was formally launched by the federal state in 1998. To gain official recognition, German interurban networks must involve at least three cities and must go beyond such pro forma interactions as city twinning. Ten criteria are listed for an effective network (Bundesamt für Bauwesen und Raumordnung 1999:38). These criteria (Table 2)

Table 2: Ten Criteria for Interurban Networks in Germany

1. **Voluntary**—participation is voluntary. Networks may change over time, as cities join or leave
2. **Equality**—all cities are equal partners
3. **Common goal**—everybody in the network contributes to and expects to benefit from this goal
4. **Common interest**—each city expects that cooperation will help fulfill its goals within the network
5. **Pluralism**—competition is not eliminated, but should not negatively affect the benefits of cooperation
6. **Multidimensionality**—cooperation should involve multiple initiatives in multiple areas, resulting in medium- and long-term improved performance
7. **Not a new scale of governance**—networks create a network structure among existing governance bodies, instead of shifting governance functions from one scale to another or creating a new scale of governance
8. **Concrete tasks**—networks must go beyond routine interactions, contribute to improved performance of certain functions, and provide benefits for residents of participating cities
9. **Territorial**—urban networks must be territorial, connecting cities within a region and fostering regional identity
10. **More effective spatial development**—networks should maximize the potential of the region and use its territory more effectively

Source: Bundesamt für Bauwesen und Raumordnung (1999).

represent networks as flexible (criterion 1), nonhierarchical (criterion 2), collaborative (criteria 3 to 5), self-organizing (criteria 6 and 8), and topologically connecting separate cities into new relational partnerships (criterion 9).

The nature and goals of the interurban network project are succinctly presented in Bundesamt für Bauwesen und Raumordnung (1999). The project is conceived as an additional instrument for regional policy to address the new exigencies of globalization and increased interterritorial competition. Two overall goals are highlighted, within the broader requirement that regional planning should promote national unity after 1989:

- "Standort Deutschland": Secure the competitiveness of Germany and its regions by creating more effective counterweights to other major EU metropolitan areas.
- Increase the potential and efficiency of resource use within a network.

These goals stress the neoliberal performance characteristics of competitiveness and a more efficient state. They are also consistent with changes in national policy priorities. Economic competitiveness, rather than sociospatial cohesion, is becoming the core priority of German national spatial planning, thus redefining regional policies primarily as an instrument for fostering locational competitiveness rather than reducing spatial inequalities (Brenner 2000). Strengthening the endogenous growth potential and capacities of cities and regions is seen as key to national competitiveness. It is assumed that interurban networks are effective tools for enhancing regional and national competitiveness, in contrast to centralized regulation or local initiative.

Networks are also presented as avoiding duplication across cities and as economizing on land and other resources. In addition, more cooperation is seen as fostering sustainable economic and ecological development. The pooling of resources and know-how allows communities to create a high-quality environment for residents and businesses and to increase competitiveness, thereby promoting sustainable development (Töpfer 1997). Instead of creating new state structures, regulation, and bureaucratization, networks' flexibility and relatively unregulated character stimulates creativity and expands the scope of action (Bundesamt für Bauwesen und Raumordnung 1999:37): "Wir brauchen keine neue Bürokratie. Wir brauchen nicht mehr, sondern weniger Staat" (Melzer 1997:498).[4]

In summary, despite their long traditions of corporate or regulated capitalism, the European Commission and the German federal government emphasize neoliberal goals of competitiveness and an efficient state in their interurban network discourses. Notwithstanding Germany's long and recently renewed tradition of corporate or regulated capitalism, these goals are more central to interurban network discourses in Germany than to those in the EU. The German discourse even goes so far as to explicitly state that the naturalized properties of networks are sufficient to make them a superior mode of governance for securing competitiveness and increased resource potential and efficiency. This construes interurban networks as ideally suited to neoliberalization. There remains a dearth of empirical studies to support these claims, however, and the pre-existing conditions under which networks emerge, as well as their own internal dynamics, may conspire to create really existing networks that depart substantially from their discursive representation.

Really Existing Interurban Networks

Really existing interurban networks in Germany and the EU inevitably differ from their representation in network discourses. First, their development is embedded within pre-existing conditions: capitalist processes characterized by uneven development, and hierarchical state structures with a tradition of strong territorial regulation. Critics express concern that "Beneath ... the celebratory discourses of 'learning,' 'knowledge' and 'innovation' that permeate academic and policy-related analyses hovers a capricious scenario of combined and uneven development, intense interterritorial competition, devaluation, and overaccumulation" (Jones and MacLeod 1999:308). Second, many networks exhibit tendencies towards hierarchy, inequality, and exclusion, in contrast to the claims made in the network discourse. In this section, we examine whether and how actual networks differ from the discursive claims, and the implications of this for their actual role in the neoliberalization of urban policy in Europe.

Interurban Networks and Neoliberalizing State Structures
Regulating Interurban Networks

The majority of currently existing interurban networks in Europe are not bottom-up self-organizing modes of governance, but owe their existence to discourses and practices of the EU Commission and individual member states. There is thus a disjuncture between neoliberal discourses of a smaller state, less regulation, and more efficient networked governance structures and the reality of new regulation and bureaucracies. This exemplifies the paradox, noted by others, that neoliberalization has resulted in new institutional sites of regulation coordinated by an activist state, rather than a rolling back of state power (Brenner and Theodore [paper] this volume; Jessop this volume; Peck and Tickell this volume). Of particular importance are state supervision over the creation of networks and evaluation of their performance.

The EU Commission offers substantial funding to interurban networks through a variety of network programs, supporting several thousand transnational network projects. The Directorate General for Regional Policy and Cohesion (DGXVI) alone has introduced four major network programs: PACTE, OUVERTURE and ECOS, RECITE, and INTERREG (Leitner forthcoming).[5] The Commission actively encourages cities to join interurban networks, even arranging "fairs" where representatives of cities can seek network partners. As part of a competitive bidding process, groups of cities are free to apply to (and gain funding from) a particular EU network program as a new network, proposing an agenda and budget consistent with network program directives. The stated goals of EU interurban network programs thus largely circumscribe both the broad agenda and the forms of cooperation pursued by networks within those programs.

Network programs also define the membership criteria (geographic in the case of territorial networks and socioeconomic in the case of thematic networks) that are used in decisions about whether a proposed network is eligible for support from that program. The ECOS program, for example, was designed to foster the exchange of information and experience between local authorities in the EU and in Central and Eastern Europe and particularly encouraged EU structural problem regions to participate. Networks supported by the ECOS program, therefore, had to include cities from Central and Eastern Europe and favored structural problems regions in the EU. Individual ECOS networks tackle a wide variety of local development issues (from service provision to economic development, tourism, and sustainable development), but forms of cooperation are similar. Cooperation concentrates on exchange of information and experience, particularly the transfer of know-how from highly developed localities in the EU to less developed ones (eg the MARKETS network) (ECOS-Ouverture 1998).

By contrast, the INTERREG and RECITE programs were designed to go beyond this more routine cooperation to include comparative research, pilot projects, and the implementation of joint development projects (European Commission 1997). Membership criteria also differ, involving the geographic criterion of contiguous regions spanning national boundaries for INTERREG (which was designed to develop cross-border cooperation in the EU's internal and external border regions), and various socioeconomic criteria matching individual thematic network goals for RECITE. For example, the RECITE "Demilitarized" thematic network connects sixteen cities and regions, in five member states, affected by the restructuring of defense-related industries and the closure of military bases (Figure 1).

In Germany, where interurban networks are being promoted by the federal (and Länder) governments, membership is based on regional

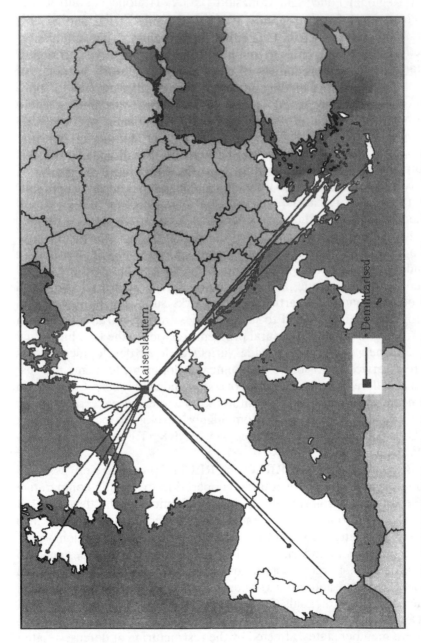

Figure 1: The EU RECITE "Demilitarized" network. Source: European Commission (1997)

location. Interurban networks have to be territorial, connecting cities within a region. Even though this is a national program, six of the twenty-six interurban networks currently under way extend across national borders to include nearby cities in the Netherlands, Luxembourg, and Austria (Figure 2). These interurban networks are in various stages of development, with a variety of specific agendas reflecting regional conditions (Bundesamt für Bauwesen und Raumordnung 1999), although the vast majority focuses on economic development. Forms of cooperation and network agendas are less regulated than in the EU case, in part because the networks developed in a more bottom-up manner: a number of them were already in existence and had developed their own approaches prior to the formalization of the federal program.

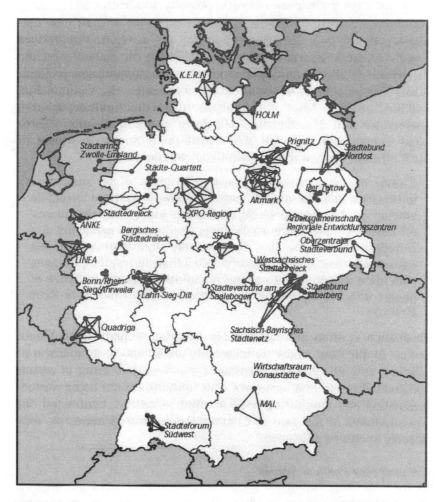

Figure 2: German "Städtenetze" (interurban networks). Source: Forum Städtenetze

State regulation is also exerted through the ongoing monitoring and evaluation of European Commission- and German state-sponsored interurban networks. Interestingly, evaluation is based on a belief that networks, once established, will achieve their expected goals. This is stated quite explicitly in the German case, where the assumption is made that interurban networks will achieve the stated goals of securing competitiveness and increasing resource potential and efficiency, and that evaluation should thus emphasize identifying what is needed to accomplish cooperation (Bundesamt für Bauwesen und Raumordnung 1999). In both the EU and Germany, evaluations focus primarily on documenting activities, outputs, and products of cooperation.

Much time, effort, and money are devoted to network evaluation of the EU-sponsored networks. The EU hires external consultants to evaluate each individual network project, and Eurocrats produce voluminous reports summarizing the achievements of individual networks and programs. Each network leader also is required to produce regular progress reports in a format specified by the Commission and to provide detailed summary statements of all expenditures. Expenditures may be subject to audits by member states, the Commission, and the European Court of Auditors, to ensure that funds are spent in accordance with the objectives laid down in the application (European Commission 1996:40). The considerable burden is evident to local officials. As one Irish local official commented,

> Europe has gone absolutely bananas in terms of the amount of information that it wants. It's incredibly slow, it wants an incredible amount of documentation. My god, when you go claiming money off them—it's unreal the whole thing: you have the possibility of a European auditor, you have the possibility of an Irish auditor, you have to get a local auditor to certify stuff. I think the way they are going with these things they are going to end up killing the initiative of people who will decide not to become involved. (quoted in Rees 1997:41)

Evaluation is often presented as an essential element of neoliberal policy. In this view, states are inherently inefficient by comparison to markets, and independent assessment is necessary in order to ensure accountability and that taxpayers' contributions are not being wasted. Evaluation and monitoring itself is often privatized, contracted out to consultants in the case of Commission-sponsored networks, supposedly to ensure efficiency.

Creating New Political Spaces
Notwithstanding top-down regulation, interurban networks provide new political spaces for localities. By creating space for cooperation among cities, and by operating across the boundaries of territorially

based political systems, such networks present participating cities with the opportunity to challenge extant state structures and relations. Interurban networks are also implicated in a complex neoliberal rescaling of political governance in Europe.

Interurban networks have created and enhanced communication among cities. Interviews with network participants in Germany reveal that the experience of cities discussing development issues with one another was novel, since it is rare that administrators in adjacent cities regularly communicate with one another (Strauss 1999). Initially there was widespread unwillingness to cooperate, but examples of success-ful collaboration within some early networks helped overcome this resistance (Bundesamt für Bauwesen und Raumordnung 1999). Simi-larly, the opening up of dialogue and exchange of information and experience among network participants has been cited as the most important positive effect in surveys and evaluations of EU network programs. According to Rees (1997:36), "At the very least there is more dialogue and exchange between the regions and cities in the EU as a result of the programmes ... the regions themselves have become international in their outlook and in their willingness to become involved in regions with similar characteristics/ problems."

Once in existence, interurban networks have the potential to enhance the power and authority of cities and contribute to the transformation of extant state power. By providing resources and political legitimacy for collaboration, EU interurban networks can empower local and regional authorities vis-à-vis the national government (Leitner forthcoming; Rees 1997). In Church and Reid's (1996) study of three cross-border networks between French and British local authorities, British local officials saw transnational networks as strengthening their political autonomy, especially in areas of local economic policy. "This was not viewed as such an important issue in the French urban authorities since their autonomy had been strengthened by the gov-ernmental reforms of the early 1980s" (Church and Reid 1996:1310).

EU interurban networks also have influenced Commission policy-making in their areas of interest (Benington and Harvey 1998). For example, collective efforts by the Demilitarized network played an important role in the creation of KONVER II, a Community Initiative providing EU funding for regions attempting to counter the effects of the decline in the defense industry, to promote industrial conversion, and to find ways to reuse military facilities. The European Action for Mining Communities (EURACOM) and EuroCities networks, bypassing their respective national governments, each successfully lobbied the EU Commission and the European Parliament for the introduction of new Community Initiatives (RECHAR II and URBAN, respectively).[6]

In sum, really existing interurban networks not only hinge upon but are also part of the transformation of extant state power and the complex rescaling of political power that are currently unfolding in the EU and its member states. By stretching across space and transcending the territories of hierarchical state structures, interurban networks present opportunities for participating cities to strengthen their power and authority vis-à-vis the national and supranational scales. The European Commission utilizes these networks not only to push its own neoliberal policy agenda of enhancing economic growth and competitiveness, but also to increase its power over member states. These tendencies, consistent with a hollowing out of the nation-state, have not gone unchallenged. The German state is reasserting its power to pursue a national neoliberal project of enhancing Standort Deutschland by promoting its own interurban networks. The British government has blocked some EU network initiatives and direct access of UK cities to EU funding (Benington and Harvey 1998).

Network Dynamics: Exclusion, Inequality, and Imitation

In contrast to the representation of networks as flexible and nonhierarchical, certain potential stakeholders have not been given a voice within the organizational structures of the EU- and German government-sponsored interurban networks. Many Commission-sponsored interurban networks are dominated by nonelected public officials, professionals (academics, state planners), and business interests (business organizations, business representatives) from participating cities. There is often little input from organizations of civil society such as unions, citizens' groups, and issue-oriented nongovernmental organizations (NGOs), and even local elected officials (Strauss 1999). Those who are included decide on network agendas and the allocation of resources, within regulatory parameters, generally taking their decisions behind closed doors. Church and Reid (1996) suggest that the absence of elected officials or citizens' representatives creates a democratic deficit, and that international cooperation for economic development, such as city marketing, may conflict with the ability of elected officials to provide local social services. A further concern of local politicians, they note, is that the complexity of participating in EU initiatives increases their dependency on professionals.

In Germany, Strauss's (1999) analysis shows that nine of eleven interurban networks studied focus exclusively on economic develop-ment. Despite considerable rhetoric about sustainable development, ecological concerns are given less weight unless they are crucial for harnessing the tourist potential of an area. Strauss attributes this in part to the exclusion of environmental and nature conservancy groups from both the initial federal planning group and individual networks. Even proponents of interurban networks have recognized dangers of exclusion: "The challenge is to seek and use the input of the private sectors but ensure that they don't dominate the network agenda" (Melzer 1997:506).

The forms that exclusion takes, with discussions dominated by networked local elites relying on professionalized governance and decision-making processes, can facilitate implementation of a neoliberal agenda of competitiveness and innovation. The democratic deficit and the prioritization of competition over social redistributive issues are reminiscent of the public–private partnerships and growth coalitions characterizing urban entrepreneurialism in the 1980s (Leitner 1990), themselves an important aspect of "roll-out" neoliberalization (Peck and Tickell this volume). The principal difference is that competition is now at the interurban rather than the urban scale.

Unequal power relations among the cities within a network are also common, unlike discourses representing networks as nonhierarchical. Even where a network's organizational structure gives all participants equal voice in principle, initial differences in bargaining power can result in a correspondingly unequal distribution of the benefits of network participation. Because of uneven development, the cities joining a network bring very different resources and conditions of possibility to the collaboration. Differences in wealth and resources among network cities can make richer cities reluctant to share information or spread the wealth, placing poorer cities in a disadvantaged position. Asymmetric power relations may also be constituted as a result of the organizational structure governing networks. For example, EU regulations require that each interurban network have a lead institution/coordinator. This coordinator generally wields more power and control and may attempt to impose a dominant conception of network interest on other network members.

Power hierarchies within networks have been extensively analyzed in social network analysis, which focuses on aspects of networks left out of the emergent network discourses. In this view, internal network structures create power hierarchies: as a consequence of their distinct positions within networks, participants have unequal influence over network outcomes. Really existing networks may then experience hegemonic struggles to define the dominant conception of network interest. Cities at the center of interurban networks have more power, undermining the idea that all participating cities benefit equally. Indeed, the complexity of the linkages connecting network members makes it difficult even to measure the interurban distribution of costs and benefits within a network (Strauss 1999).

Unequal power relations among network participants have complex implications for neoliberalization. When inequality is a persistent feature of interurban networks, discursive claims that neoliberalism creates a level playing field are undermined. Disaffection among

disadvantaged participating cities may then threaten the attractiveness of networks as a channel for neoliberalization. Yet networks that
compete successfully may increase the wealth of each member city,
even though the intranetwork distribution of costs and benefits is
uneven. In such cases, disadvantaged participants may also support
neoliberalization.

Network discourses of self-organization promoting innovation are
also problematic. Routine information-sharing dominates cooperation
in EU-sponsored interurban networks (Leitner and Sheppard 1999:
240). Participating cities share knowledge and experiences, construct
common databases, and learn about "best practice." The ECOS-
Ouverture network program, for example, emphasizes all of these,
within the overall goal of transmitting knowledge to localities in Central
and Eastern Europe that facilitates their economic transition. Yet
"the real transfer of skills and development tools ... has certainly not
been widespread" (Rees 1997:45). This is perhaps not surprising in
geographically extensive networks that bring distant partners from
quite different national and cultural contexts together for the first
time. This makes it harder to achieve the kinds of tacit understandings
argued to facilitate self-organization and innovation in local networks,
whereas routine communication is easier.

Routine interactions may not be particularly innovative. Indeed, the
emphasis is on adopting the same best practices in all cities, rather
than on valuing innovation and difference as a source of change.
The very idea of "best practice" assumes that practices exist that
are best in every local context and should be adopted everywhere. The
idea also gives interurban EU networks the potential to facilitate
international fast policy transfer among cities, making them very
effective channels for the propagation of new neoliberal urban
policies. Paradoxically, their effectiveness for this purpose emphasizes
a reality of imitation and adoption, contradicting discourses that
emphasize self-organization and innovation.

Conclusion

Neoliberalism has successfully appropriated network discourses for its
own purposes. The ability to give network properties and performance
characteristics a distinctly neoliberal interpretation has enabled
neoliberalism to take on board significant critiques from economic
sociology and geography about the unrealistic nature of pure markets.
The possibility of drawing on neoliberal network interpretations as a
vehicle for promoting neoliberal goals of competitiveness and flexible
governance has been realized in the EU and Germany, where such
interpretations dominate interurban network policy prescriptions.

Really existing interurban networks depart in some significant ways
from the properties emphasized in network discourses. They have, to

a large extent, been driven and shaped by top-down state-initiated actions, rather than by bottom-up self-organization; they exhibit tendencies towards hierarchies and exclude members and institutions of civil society, rather than being nonhierarchical and inclusionary; they show little promise of overcoming inequalities and uneven development; and their capacity for innovation, rather than imitation, is limited to date. This is not surprising, since network discourses ignore the embeddedness of networks in hierarchical state structures and capitalist markets. Networks evolve under pre-existing conditions where territorial state regulation, unequal power relations, and uneven development are pervasive. In addition, networks themselves exhibit tendencies towards hierarchy, inequality, imitation, and exclusion, each of which departs from the naturalized network properties.

In some ways, these differences between network discourses and really existing networks have helped make interurban networks into channels of neoliberalization. They have facilitated the top-down spread of the neoliberal gospel of competitiveness and flexible governance, as well as the promotion of professionalized elite decisionmaking, insulated from the democratic process, and fast policy transfer. At the same time, however, really existing interurban networks have created new collaborative possibilities and new political spaces for cities to challenge extant state structures and relations.

Yet this possibility that interurban networks can increase the power and authority of cities need not result in a significant challenge to the neoliberal agenda promoted by higher tiers of the state. Further research is needed to identify under what conditions interurban networks might become arenas of progressive political struggle. It is not encouraging that interurban networks are so closely embedded in state structures, and it is perhaps more likely that such challenges to the neoliberal agenda will come from outside the types of interurban networks discussed here.

Indeed, there is evidence that other networks, pursuing a progressive/social justice agenda, are challenging neoliberalization. Within cities, the possibilities of local-exchange trading schemes (local currency networks) that seek to realize local exchange outside the regular market have received much attention, notably from the British state and the EU (North 2000). In the United States living-wage movement, grass-roots activists from many different cities have developed an interurban network that has helped force some local states to take steps towards raising the minimum wage (Pollin and Luce 1998). At the international scale, activist networks moving beyond borders have received much recent publicity for their successes in challenging neoliberal discourses, although questions remain about the degree to which these transnational network discourses will be able to shape policy outcomes. From a progressive perspective, the nonhierarchical character of networks, their flexibility, and their capacity to jump scale and challenge corporations and states, remain attractive. At the same time, however, progressives should not be seduced by this network ideal. There are innumerable examples of progressive social movements, pursuing ideals of unity and collective action, whose effectiveness has been undermined by realities of internal power hierarchies, rigidity and exclusion.

Acknowledgements

The authors are grateful for insightful comments from Neil Brenner, Bob Jessop, Nik Theodore, Jamie Peck, Kevin Ward and an anonymous reviewer, none of whom bear responsibility for the arguments of this paper.

Endnotes

[1] Nonlocal networks, interurban, interregional and translocal activist issue networks have been neglected by progressive urban scholars until recently (Church and Reid 1996; Keck and Sikkink 1998; Leitner and Sheppard 1998, 1999; Leitner, Pavlik and Sheppard forthcoming).

[2] To our knowledge, Germany is the only EU member state that has formally adopted urban networks as a new regional policy instrument.

[3] See also Leitner, Pavlik and Sheppard (forthcoming).

[4] "We do not need any new bureaucracy. We need less rather than more state" (authors' translation).

[5] OUVERTURE, ECOS, and INTERRES are detailed below. PACTE has provided opportunities for the exchange of know-how and experiences between local and regional communities of the EU on a wide range of issues. RECITE (Regions and Cities for Europe) seeks to promote collaboration among local and regional communities on economic development and the sharing of experiences.

[6] The thematic EURACOM network links 450 local authorities in seven EU member states for collective lobbying of the EU on coalfield issues. EuroCities represents over 40 "second-tier" EU cities, lobbying EU directorates and promoting joint concerns. Unusually, it began as a bottom-up initiative by Rotterdam in 1986. RECHAR provides EU support for areas affected by coal-industry decline. URBAN provides EU support to revitalize the economy and social fabric of urban areas.

References

Amin A (1989) Flexible specialization and small firms in Italy: Myths and realities. *Antipode* 21:13–34

Amin A and Thrift N (1992) Neo-Marshallian nodes in global networks. *International Journal of Urban and Regional Research* 16(4):571–587

Amin A and Thrift N (1994) Holding down the global. In A Amin and N Thrift (eds) *Globalization, Institutions, and Regional Development in Europe* (pp 257–260). Oxford: Oxford University Press

Amin A and Thrift N (1995) Institutional issues for the European Regions: From markets and plans to socioeconomics and powers of association. *Economy and Society* 24:41–66

Amin A and Thrift N (1997) Globalization, socioeconomics, territoriality. In R Lee and J Wills (eds) *Geographies of Economies* (pp 147–157). London: Arnold

Bache I (2000) *Europeanization and Partnership: Exploring and Explaining Variations in Policy Transfer*. Belfast: Queen's University. http://www.qub.ac.uk/ies/onlinepapers/poe8.pdf (last accessed 18 February 2002)

Barry A (1996) The European network. In J Berland and S Kember (eds) *Technoscience: New Formations 29* (pp 26–37). London: Lawrence and Wishart

Benington J and Harvey J (1998) Transnational local authority networking within the European Union: Passing fashion or new paradigm? In D Marsh (ed) *Comparing Policy Networks* (pp 149–166). Philadelphia: Open University Press

Brenner N (2000) Building "Euro-regions": Locational politics and the political geography of neoliberalism in postunification Germany. *European Urban and Regional Studies* 7(4):319–345

Bundesamt für Bauwesen und Raumordnung (1999) *Modellvorhaben "Städtenetze." Neue Konzeptionen der interkommunalen Kooperation*. Bonn: Bundesminesterium für Verkehr, Bau- and Wohnungswesen

Castells M (1996) *The Rise of the Network Society*. Oxford: Blackwell Publishers

Church A and Reid P (1996) Urban power, international networks, and competition: The example of cross-border cooperation. *Urban Studies* 33:1297–1318

Cohendet P, Llerena P, Stahn H and Umbauer G (1998) *The Economics of Networks*. Berlin: Springer-Verlag

Commission of the European Communities (1992) *Urbanisation and the Functions of Cities in the European Community*. Luxembourg: Office for Official Publications of the European Communities

Cooke P and Morgan K (1993) The network paradigm: New departures in corporate and regional development. *Environment and Planning D: Society and Space* 11: 543–564

Cooke P and Morgan K (1998) *The Associational Economy: Firms, Regions, and Innovation*. Oxford: Oxford University Press

ECOS-Ouverture (1998) *External Interregional Co-operation 1991–1998*. 2nd ed. Glasgow: ECOS-Ouverture, European Commission, DGXVI

European Commission (1994) *Europe 2000+: Cooperation for European Territorial Development*. Brussels: European Union

European Commission (1996) *RECITE II—Interregional Co-operation Projects Information Pack*. Brussels: European Commission, DGXVI:1–44

European Commission (1997) *Review of Interregional Cooperation*. Review no. 13. Brussels: European Commission, DGXVI

Forum Städtenetze. http://www.staedtenetzeforum.de (last accessed 1 February 2002)

Granovetter M (1985) Economic action and social structure: The problem of embeddedness. *American Journal of Sociology* 91:481–510

Hay C (1998) The tangled webs we weave: The discourse, strategy, and practice of networking. In D Marsh (ed) *Comparing Policy Networks* (pp 33–51). Philadelphia: Open University Press

Hodgson G (1994) Hayek, evolution, and spontaneous order. In P Mirowski (ed) *Natural Images In Economic Thought: Markets Read in Tooth and Claw* (pp 408–447). Cambridge, UK: Cambridge University Press

Jones M and MacLeod G (1999) Towards regional renaissance? Reconfiguring and rescaling England's economic governance. *Transactions of the Institute of British Geographers* 24:295–313

Keck M and Sikkink K (1998) *Activists beyond Borders*. Ithaca, NY: Cornell University Press

Latour B (1993) *We Have Never Been Modern*. Cambridge, MA: Harvard University Press

Leitner H (1990) Cities in pursuit of economic growth. *Political Geography Quarterly* 9(2):146–170

Leitner H (forthcoming) Geographical scales and networks of spatial connectivity: Transnational inter-urban networks and the rescaling of political governance in Europe. In E Sheppard and R B McMaster (eds) *Scale and Geographic Inquiry*. Oxford: Blackwell

Leitner H, Pavlik C and Sheppard E (forthcoming) Networks, governance, and the politics of scale: Interurban networks and the European Union. In A Herod and M Wright (eds) *Geographies of Power: Placing Scale*. Oxford: Blackwell

Leitner H and Sheppard E (1998) Economic uncertainty, interurban competition, and the efficacy of entrepreneurialism. In T Hall and P Hubbard (eds) *The Entrepreneurial City* (pp 285–308). London: John Wiley & Sons

Leitner H and Sheppard E (1999) Transcending interurban competition: Conceptual issues and policy alternatives in the European Union. In A Jonas and D Wilson (eds) *The Growth Machine: Critical Perspectives Twenty Years Later* (pp 227–246). Albany: State University of New York Press

Martin B and Mayntz R (eds) (1991) *Policy Networks: Empirical Evidence and Theoretical Considerations*. Frankfurt: Campus

Melzer M (1997) Schlüsselfragen einer zukunftsfähigen Standortpolitik mit Städtenetzen. *Informationen zur Raumordnungspolitik* 7:495–508

North P (2000) Is there space for organization from below within the UK Government's action zones? A test of collaborative planning. *Urban Studies* 37(8):1261–1278

Pollin R and Luce S (1998) *The Living Wage: Building a Fair Economy*. New York: The New Press

Porter M (1989) The competitive advantage of nations. *Harvard Business Review* 68(2):73–93

Porter M (1995) The competitive advantage of the inner city. *Harvard Business Review* 74(3):55–71

Porter M (1996) Competitive advantage, agglomeration economies, and regional policy. *International Regional Science Review* 19(1):85–90

Powell W (1990) Neither market nor hierarchy: Network forms of organization. *Research in Organizational Bahviour* 12:295–334

Rees N (1997) Interregional co-operation: An effective means towards sustained economic development? In *Review of Interregional Cooperation*. Review no. 13. Brussels: European Commission, DGKVT

Sachs J D (1999) Twentieth-century political economy: A brief history of global capitalism. *Oxford Review of Economic Policy* 15(4):90–101

Saxenian A (1994) *Regional Advantage: Culture and Competition in Silicon Valley and Route 128*. Cambridge, MA: Harvard University Press

Scott A J (1989) *Metropolis: From the Division of Labor to Urban Form*. Berkeley, CA: University of California Press

Sheppard E (2000) Competition in space and between places. In E Sheppard and T J Barnes (eds) *Companion to Economic Geography* (pp 169–186). Oxford: Blackwell

Storper M (1997) *The Regional World: Territorial Development in a Global Economy*. New York: Guilford

Strauss K (1999) Städtenetze—Erwartungen und Wirklichkeit aus ökologischer Sicht. *Raumforschung und Raumordnung* 4:284–290

Töpfer K (1997) Das Neue denken. *Die Welt* WR1:1–2

Helga Leitner is a Professor of Geography and a faculty member in the Institute of Global Studies and the Interdisciplinary Center for the Study of Global Change at the University of Minnesota. She has published two books and has written numerous articles and book chapters on the political economy of urban development and urban entrepreuneurialism, the politics of citizenship and immigrant incorporation, and the politics of scale. Her current research interests include geographies of governance and citizenship, and interurban policy and activist networks.

Eric Sheppard is a Professor of Geography and member of the Interdisciplinary Center for the Study of Global Change and the Institute for Social, Ecological and Economic Sustainability at the University of Minnesota. He is a former editor of *Antipode* and currently coeditor of *Environment and Planning A*. His current research interests include interurban policy and activist networks, the spatiality of globalization, and geographies of the information society. He is coauthor of *The Capitalist Space—Economy* (Unwin and Hyman, 1990), *A World of Difference* (New York: Guilford Press, 1998), and *A Companion to Economic Geography* (London: Blackwell, 2000).

Chapter 8
Extracting Value from the City: Neoliberalism and Urban Redevelopment

Rachel Weber

How do states make the built environment more flexible and responsive to the investment criteria of real estate capital? Spatial policies, such as urban renewal funding for slum clearance or contemporary financial incentives, depend on discursive practices that stigmatize properties targeted for demolition and redevelopment. These policies and practices have become increasingly neoliberalized. They have further distanced themselves from those "long turnover" parts of the city where redevelopment needs are great but where the probability of private investment and value extraction is slight. They have become more entwined in global financial markets seeking short-term returns from subsidized property investments. They have shifted their emphasis from compromised use values (embodied in the paternalistic notion of "blight") to diminished exchange values (embodied in the notion of "obsolescence"). I argue that obsolescence has become a neoliberal alibi for creative destruction and, therefore, an important component in contemporary processes of spatialized capital accumulation.

Introduction
The promise of durability has attracted kaisers, kings, mayors, and other megalomaniacs to the built environment. The physical-technical ensemble of the city—buildings, sewers, roads, monuments, transport networks—conveys a sense of fixity and obduracy that appeals to the political desire to make strong, lasting statements. However, these same characteristics often throw up challenges for the private capital that undergirds and enables urban development policies. The accumulation process experiences uncomfortable friction when capital (ie "value in motion") is trapped in steel beams and concrete. For example, property "exposure" requires elaborate and expensive schemes for offsetting risks. Prior investments create path dependencies that, because of the difficulties inherent in modifying physical structures, constrain future investments. The temporal horizons of investors, developers, and residents rarely coincide. The very materiality of the built environment sets off struggles between use and exchange values, between those with emotional attachments to place and those without such attachments.

In order to reconcile the political imperative to build with the capitalist demand for liquidity, states have developed mechanisms to make the built environment more flexible and responsive to the invest ment criteria of real-estate capital. At the national scale in Europe and North America, these efforts include everything from funding for postwar urban renewal to neoliberal policy moves such as deregulating financial markets, commodifying debt (eg through mortgage securitization), destroying certain credit shelters for housing, and providing increasing support for real-estate syndications. Local states have produced their own set of directives, most aimed at absorbing the risks and costs of land development so capitalists do not have to do so. Municipalities justify such interventions by strategically stigmatizing those properties that are targeted for demolition and redevelopment. These justifications draw strength from the dual authorities of law and science in order to stabilize inherently ambiguous concepts like blight and obsolescence and create the appearance of certitude out of the cacophony of claims about value.

This research examines the changing role of states in property devaluation in the United States, searching in the detritus of the built environment for clues about regime shifts. States respond to the needs of capital in historically and geographically contingent ways. The degree of "epoch-making" change that took place in the early 1970s is hotly contested (Amin 1994): neither capitalist development nor associated state forms can be so thoroughly transformed as to lack any resemblance to former incarnations. Nevertheless, certain commonalities among Western industrial nations can be detected and periodized in order to draw out dominant principles. The policies and practices used to prepare real estate for the extraction of value in the last two decades, such as tax increment financing (TIF), are in many ways representative of the neoliberal turn theorized in more depth by others in this volume. Neoliberalism is a hypermarketized style of governance (ie government *through and by* the market) that denigrates collective consumption and institutions. It is also an ideological fetishization of pure, perfect markets as superior allocative mechanisms for the distribution of public resources (see, for example, Brenner and Theodore [paper] this volume). Although recent neoliberal policy moves draw from earlier tactics and discourses, they also refashion them in certain critical ways. This study attempts to avoid crude binarisms (ie Fordism/post-Fordism) while exploring both the changes and the continuities in the state financing strategies and associated discourses that influence value in urban property.

Value in the Built Environment
Capital circulates through the built environment in a dynamic and erratic fashion. At various points in its circulation, the built environment

is junked, abandoned, destroyed, and selectively reconstructed. The physical shells of aging industrial orders may sit dormant for decades before being cleared for a new high-tech "campus," while efficiencies near the central business district come down efficiently to be reborn as luxury condominiums within a year. Marx saw the tendency of solid material to decompose and melt as a basic fact of modern life (Berman 1988). Contemporary scholars have gone a step further, analyzing the progression of time-space-structured transformations that revalorize devalued landscapes (Bryson 1997; Harvey 1989b; Smith 1996; Zukin 1982). In this section, I briefly trace the cycle of value creation and destruction in real estate before addressing the less-frequently analyzed role of the state in this cycle.

As a spatially embedded commodity, real estate embodies a crucial paradox. Real estate has always attracted a range of investors, from the small-scale speculator-next-door to the largest insurance companies, because the investment produces an alienable commodity whose association with a particular location makes it scarce and valuable (Fainstein 1994). Fee-simple ownership accords the owners the legal right to capture any socially produced increases in ground rent plus the value of the improvements. If returns from rents and future sales are sufficient to pay off the initial development costs and also meet the fees and time horizons of creditors and investors, new cycles of investment can be set in motion.

On the other hand, the fact that capital invested in the built environment is immobilized for long periods of time detracts from real estate's attractiveness as an investment instrument. Real estate is illiquid, entails high transaction costs upon sale, requires security, and is not easily divisible. Longer turnover periods create barriers to further accumulation, as capital gets tied up *in situ* until it returns a profit. The obduracy of real estate resists frequent modification (Hommels 2000). These qualities make the commodity of real estate very sensitive to devalorization, especially in contrast to machinery and other forms of fixed capital (Harvey 1982).

Once a structure is built, its ability to generate rents depends on the fluctuating value of two distinct elements: its improvements and location in space. Ground rents depend on demand for a particular location. They may increase as new development surrounds a building or the cachet of the neighborhood improves. They may decrease as demand wanes or if a location becomes overbuilt. For this reason, spatialized capital, unlike derivatives or corporate equities, has the unique (dis)advantage of having its value held hostage by the vagaries of proximity and its relationship to other properties (Fainstein 1994; Logan and Molotch 1987).

The value of the physical structure is similarly context-dependent. As soon as a building is constructed, it begins to age. Buildings will suffer from physical depreciation over time, which, *ceteris paribus*, reduces their market value. In this sense, the wear and tear on a building is not so different from a piece of machinery or other kinds of fixed capital. The tax code and private-appraisal industry account for the value change by recognizing depreciation in both capital equipment and building improvements (land does not depreciate) as a function of a building's "economic life."

However, a structure's value is a function not only of elapsed calendar time, but also of the conscious decision to invest and maintain or, conversely, to undermaintain and disinvest. Although the value of land does not depend on its upkeep, improvements require ongoing maintenance. Beyond routine reproduction of the circuit of capital, new investments will only be made if owners can capture rents or create surplus profit through innovation (Schumpeter 1942). Property may be revalorized through innovation in construction materials, design, and amenities. Some innovations may improve the efficiency of building operations, for example by lowering ceilings to reduce heating costs. Other innovations bank on an increase in sign values associated with a modern aesthetic. Schumpeter's notion of "creative destruction" captures the way in which capital's restless search for profits requires constant renewal through galelike forces that simultaneously make way for the new and devalue the old.

What is left behind by innovation is considered "obsolete." Obsolescence implies something out of date—a product, place, or concept displaced by modernization and progress. Appraisers divide property conditions into "functional" and "economic" obsolescence, categories that correspond roughly to value changes in location and improvements. Functional obsolescence results from changes in modern building practices and the manner in which buildings are utilized (Appraisal Institute 2001). Indicators of functional obsolescence in housing include

> structures of an overly large size; poor central utilities, especially hot water systems without circulating pumps; central hallways, which increase utility costs; high ceilings; inconvenient layout; out-of-date plumbing; electrical figures including square sinks and inadequate numbers of electrical outlets; old light fixtures; inadequate hot water capacity; pre-1973 aluminum electrical wiring. (Bullock 1996:36)

Economic or external obsolescence relates to factors outside of the property that reduce demand and negate its value. Buildings may become obsolete as the adjacent properties are rezoned and the buildings become unsuited to their new surroundings.

Obsolescence tends to suppress rental income and exchange values, but it may not diminish utility or use values. For example, an older building's structural components and configurations may meet the expectations and needs of tenants. If its owners cannot capture sufficient rents to encourage upkeep or additional investment, however, obsolescence may produce a lower level of physical maintenance and eventual deterioration. Utility and exchange value move in concert if the building becomes so structurally deteriorated as to be uninhabitable and abandoned (Cohen 2001; Sternlieb and Burchell 1973). The building's owners, seeing scant prospects for immediate redevelopment in the neighborhood, may continue to disinvest.

Capitalists triage devalued buildings into their own temporal categories. If the building in question is located in an area of concentrated poverty, it may become marginalized as "long-turnover" because the short-term rent gap is not sufficiently wide to warrant rehabilitation.[1] Its carcass may be left for scavengers and illegal uses as it falls into ruin and capital moves out to other more lucrative opportunities. When the value of the structure declines faster than the ground rents increase, however, it becomes "short-turnover," and demolition—a potent spatial fix—prepares the land for gentrification and building upgrading. Spatial-temporal boundaries "restrict the effects of devalorization, economic decline, and asset loss to clearly circumscribed neighborhoods and protect the integrity of mortgages in other areas" (Smith 1996:192). Uneven development sets the stage for the movement of capital in the relatively fixed built environment as new opportunities for value arise from the ashes of the devalued.

States and Creative Destruction

The calculus employed by capitalists to identify value in the built environment is neither standardized nor unchanging. They rely heavily on the determinations made by communities of technical experts, such as appraisers and market analysts, but speculation, luck, political influence, and class resistance also conspire to transform the process of value creation and destruction into one of intense sociopolitical struggle (Brenner and Theodore [paper] this volume). It would also be a mistake to view the creative destruction of the built environment as purely market-determined, a disembodied and overdetermined process that progresses in a linear fashion and is catalyzed by every withdrawal and subsequent injection of capital. The price mechanism alone does not determine if and when buildings will be devalued, demolished, or reborn. The private real-estate market often cannot supply all the conditions necessary for the extraction of value (Feagin 1998). Within each locale, a lattice of state and nonstate institutions— thick and hierarchal in some places, thin and ephemeral in others— influence value in the built environment.

Interventions into real-estate markets require states to juggle two contradictory imperatives: "to maintain or create the conditions in which profitable capital accumulation is possible," while at the same time managing the potential political repercussions (O'Connor

1973:6). Balancing accumulation and legitimation is a difficult task: the extension of the state into the market renders the political, economic, and legal bases of corporate legitimacy visible and thus vulnerable to interrogation and resistance (Habermas 1973). State actors may "mystify (their) policies by calling them something they are not," or "try to conceal them (eg by making them administrative, not political, issues)" (O'Connor 1973:6). They may solicit mass support for growth-oriented policies by ensuring some trickle-down benefits (eg jobs, expanded tax base, or lower taxes) and fostering a more collaborative political culture.

Beyond obfuscation and redistribution, states may neutralize some of the conflict surrounding value in the built environment by bringing different kinds of expertise to bear on divisive issues in hopes of achieving some semblance of ideological "closure." States have historically relied on the collaborating authorities of law and science to legitimize different regulatory regimes. Both law and science share a general commitment to resolving conflict through the discovery of truths. Laws convert state power into deeply embedded routines, the legitimacy of which depends on the perceived rationality of established procedures, the appearance of neutral administration, and the *de facto* acceptance of an order of authority by its subjects (Weber 1978). Science promises a similar mastery over the irrational, contested, and ambiguous. To the extent that the knowledge justifying state policies can be construed as natural, scientific "truths" perform the task of reproducing the values and credibility of state institutions (Callon, Law and Rip 1986; Wynne 1989).

Finding value or a lack thereof in the built environment is an arbitrary and inconsistent process in which the state, particularly the local state, offers its assistance. States discursively constitute, code, and order the meaning of place through policies and practices that are often advantageous to capital (Beauregard 1993). Because the presence or absence of value is far from straightforward, states attempt to create a convergence of thinking around such critical issues as the economic life of buildings, the priority given to different components of value, the sources of devaluation, and interrelationships between buildings and neighborhoods. By emphasizing the discursive nature of state interventions, I do not mean to imply that the discourse of devaluation is a mere fiction, distinct from both the objectively lowered value in the built environment that I described in the previous section and the policies I will describe in the following sections. Narratives often become indistinguishable from the basic empirical identities of buildings, neighborhoods, and entire cities (Shields 1991).[2]

Moreover, the discourse mutates in tandem with the changing market logics of real estate (dis)investment, as words take on new meanings and new themes shape spatial tactics. The Keynesian welfare state of the immediate postwar era allowed specific forms of financial regulation to predominate at the national scale, which influenced both the nature and availability of capital in local real-estate markets as well as the redevelopment priorities of municipalities. With varying degrees of assuredness, scholars have identified a rupture in the mode of capital accumulation in the early 1970s, a break that underpinned important changes in real-estate finance and its governance (Aglietta 1979; Amin 1994). Banks, for example, found their primacy challenged by new sources of fast-moving, globalized capital, while innovations in securitization and trading technologies have made the product of real estate more liquid and alienable. Although Fordist modes of production and Keynesian state forms were dismantled, it still remains to be seen exactly what forms of accumulation and financial governance will take their place. Some have classified the period following the crisis in Fordism as one of institutional searching and temporary fixes (Peck and Tickell this volume). Neoliberalism either has filled the void as a successor regime or represents new crisis tendencies acting out. In the following pages, I consider how these changes have shaped the urban spatial practices of the state.

Urban Blight and Renewal

In the postwar period, the national state provided a protected harbor in which domestic suppliers of real-estate capital (primarily banks) provided long-term mortgage loans at fixed interest rates to developers, investors, builders, and homebuyers (Downs 1985). Credit availability, relatively high wages, and national subsidies—particularly to the growing ranks of the white middle classes in the form of insurance (for bank deposits and mortgages) and defense contracts—helped fuel a postwar building expansion in the suburbs. Depopulated of their middle- and upper-income residents, cities became home to concentrations of poor immigrants and African-American migrants who lived and worked in a decaying built environment. In the middle of the century, the federal government possessed the tax revenue and the political will necessary for robust, national-level interventions (Teaford 1990). Starting with the Housing Act of 1949 and the amending Housing Act of 1954, cities received a growing stream of federal aid to purchase inner-city property for urban redevelopment and renewal. To receive the federal funds for land acquisition, they were required to draw up plans for development, form renewal agencies emboldened with new legal powers, and create mechanisms to quickly appropriate devalued property (von Hoffman 2000). Massive amounts of federal funds flowed into US cities through the 1970s, subsidizing developers and unionized construction workers with cleared prime land at bargain-basement prices (ie "write-downs").

To dispose of devalued properties during this era and prepare space for new rounds of investment, the national state collaborated with the local state to create quasiscientific methods for identifying "blight." The language of urban destruction evolved from the vice-obsessed teens and twenties into its own technical language in roughly the middle third of the century. Historic accounts of urban policy during this period point to blight as the primary justification for creative destruction (Beauregard 1993; Fogleson 2001; Page 1999). In the local renewal ordinances and state statutes of this period, the definition of blight is vague: it is framed as both a cause of physical deterioration and a state of being in which the built environment is deteriorated or physically impaired beyond normal use. The discourse of blight appropriated metaphors from plant pathology (blight is a disease that causes vegetation to discolor, wilt, and eventually die) and medicine (blighted areas were often referred to as "cancers" or "ulcers"). The scientific basis for blight drew attention to the physical bodies inhabiting the city, as well as the unhygienic sanitary conditions those bodies "created."

Federal and local officials crafted standards of urban rebuilding that were drafted into the law. As preconditions for the use of local eminent-domain powers, these standards allowed them to triage what was worth preserving from what demanded immediate destruction. Armed with checklists of the spatial-temporal qualities that constituted blight (ie "blighting factors"), some of which had been developed in the 1950s by the American Public Health Association, planners' standardized techniques hid underlying motives and biases. The checklists included factors like the age of buildings (their "useful life," in most cases, was considered to be forty to fifty years), density, population gain or loss, overbuilding on lots, lack of ventilation and light, and structural deterioration. The criteria for blight designation sometimes referred to public health statistics such as the death rates from tuberculosis and syphilis (see, for example, *Morris v. District of Columbia Redevelopment Land Agency* 117 F. Supp. 705, 1953). Many of the blight indicators involved some sort of mixing or blurring of boundaries: a mixture of land uses or of the race and ethnicity of residents. As Swartzbaugh (2001) notes in her historical study of race in Chicago, even though buildings on the black South Side were not as old as those on the north and west sides of that city, they were more frequently categorized as unfit or substandard. Blight was disproportionately found in nonwhite areas; one checklist even included "percentage of Negroes" (Chicago Plan Commission 1942, quoted in Swartzbaugh 2001:9) as one of three indications of blight.

The early redevelopment legislation and city ordinances are notable for three areas of emphasis: first, the compromised use-values of residents living in blighted neighborhoods and buildings; second, a focus on building new low-income housing to replace the deteriorated stock; and third, justifications for managerial state intervention in order to eliminate or prevent conditions injurious to the public health, safety, morals, or welfare. In the legal challenges that followed, blight was perceived as a legitimate precondition for demolition and new housing construction because it produced hardships for residents and bred crime and disease (Quinones 1994). Obsolescence, on the other hand, primarily limited the profitability of property owners and was a more questionable justification for the use of urban police powers (ie "public purpose"). Although the downtown business interests and their friends in City Hall defined blight as an economic condition in which the market value of property is lost (Beauregard 1993), the courts tried—unsuccessfully, in many cases—to draw a line between use and exchange values to keep cities from indiscriminately assisting capital. In its attempt to defend an older neighborhood from the bulldozer, one court went so far as to note:

> Its fault is only that it fails to meet what are called modern standards. Let us suppose that it is backward, stagnant, not properly laid out, economically Eighteenth Century—anything except detrimental to health, safety, or morals. Suppose its owners and occupants like it that way. Suppose they are old-fashioned, prefer single-family dwellings, like small flower gardens, believe that a plot of ground is the place to rear children, prefer fresh to conditioned air, sun to fluorescent light. In many circles all such views are considered "backward and stagnant." Are those who hold them therefore blighted? Can they not, nevertheless, own property? Choice of antiques is a right of property ... The slow, the old, the small in ambition, the devotee of the outmoded have no less right to property than have the quick, the young, the aggressive, and the modernistic or futuristic. (*Morris v. District of Columbia Redevelopment Land Agency* 1953, 38)

In the context of American-style welfare capitalism, targeting blight instead of obsolescence allowed the state to destroy with a public purpose—the laudable goal of "healthy" cities—as the moral overtones of blight blurred the boundaries between public and private responsibility.

The proffered solutions for dealing with this problem changed midcentury. Before the Housing Act of 1954, the bulldozer approach prevailed. Like teams of surgeons, city governments removed the concentrations of blight while the federal government assumed the role of the insurance company, absorbing the costs of demolition and land preparation. Cutting off the possibility of other alternatives, local states and real-estate interests campaigned against the "evil" of rehabilitation, labeling it wrong-headed and illegitimate. "Guard Against Unwarranted Rehabilitation," read one slogan of the time, for it would "only perpetuate bad land patterns" and "provide no lasting solution" (Swartzbaugh 2001:14). Property could be better sanitized and revalorized in its empty state, thus eliminating the possibility of the blight returning. From liberal-technocratic mayors in cities like Chicago and San Francisco to the construction trades and public employees unions, from master builders like Robert Moses and Ed Logue to local banks, disparate groups were enrolled in the project of justifying the destruction and rebuilding. Local governments expanded their workforces to accommodate the increase in activity and extend the webs of patronage, while the federal government protected them from serious legal challenges from residents and their advocates.

The 1954 act substituted the term "urban renewal" for "urban redevelopment" to indicate the federal government's more comprehensive approach and signal its acceptance of the conservation of existing structures as a means of stemming blight (von Hoffman 2000). As cities shifted away from slum clearance and housing construction, they also expanded the meaning of blight to include those areas and properties that had the *potential* to become deteriorated. Blight was portrayed as an epidemic—dysfunctional, corrosive, and inherently mobile. This move allowed cities to cater to the cultural elite with commercial projects like Lincoln Center in New York City and subsidize conspicuously profitable private office space for corporate headquarters and manufacturing districts to stem the white flight to the suburbs (Ranney 2001). Federal funds were supplemented by the local taxpayers, who supported large amounts of municipal debt finance, much of which was used for public institutions—urban campuses of state universities, hospitals, government facilities—that lacked their own exchange values but pulled up those of surrounding properties. In this sense, municipal Keynesianism depended on cities as nodes of production, where rising industrial productivity and close ties to the federal government would ensure sustained growth.

Urban renewal pulverized the inner city in the middle of the century, funneling billions of federal dollars into costly downtown commercial projects, highways, and sanitized streetscapes. Between 1949 and 1965, one million people, mostly low-income, were evicted in the name of eliminating and containing blight (Hall 1996). Ultimately, rent strikes, widespread protests, Black Power, Jane Jacobs, and several crucial lawsuits helped to replace renewal funds with Community Development Block Grants and diffuse the power of the renewal agencies to a broader network of neighborhoods and state actors. Renewal opposition was successful partly because organizations and lawsuits challenged the scientific and legal basis of blight, unhinging the signifier from the referent. Friedman (1968:159) observed, "Finding blight merely means defining a neighborhood that cannot effectively fight back, but which is either an eyesore or is well-located for some particular construction project that important interests wish to build." Blight was maligned as a convenient incantation to justify the use of redevelopment powers for projects that were already planned.

However, although resistance to the demolition and redevelopment plans was organized and powerful enough to slow the federal bull-dozer, efforts to undermine the legitimacy of "blight" did not entirely remove the term or its legacy from the lexicon of urban policymaking.

The Neoliberalization of Devalued Property

The 1970s brought high inflation, an increasingly global context for investment, and a flood of capital from basic manufacturing into real estate and other speculative investments. The same phenomena that hastened the demise of Fordism also lowered the risk-adjusted returns on capital invested in the built environment vis-à-vis other asset categories. On the demand side, capitalists found that accumulation was better served by keeping financial resources churning rapidly within the system, rather than making sunk costs that would expose capital to great risks (Dow 1999).

Since the 1970s, capital deployment and turnover times have sped up, as have flows of information and signs in general (Lash and Urry 1987; Virillio 1986). On the supply side, in order to attract capital looking for large, liquid trading markets, the commodity of real estate has become progressively dematerialized and deterritorialized. Real estate has lost its status as a distinct and quirky asset class, in the process becoming more detached from place and more subject to the disciplining power and accelerated schedules of global capital markets.

The federal government actively accommodated the drive for liquidity in real estate by creating new forms of property and incentives to invest in real estate through tax policies, such as shelters, deductions, and tax credits. By creating a secondary mortgage market through quasipublic institutions (eg Fannie Mae, formed in 1968), the state has increased the total size of capital flows with the unattainable aim of reducing cyclical instability of real-estate capital. These institutions buy mortgages, package them, and guarantee their payments with government backing on mortgage-backed securities held by other insti-tutions, such as pension funds. Securitization connects real-estate credit markets to the nation's general capital markets and creates more liquidity in the system (Budd 1999). The secondary mortgage market also enables investors in one part of the country to invest in mortgages originated in another region, effectively ending the geographic segmen-tation of credit (Schill 1999). These innovations, mediated by the development of new electronic trading technologies, have increased the pace of financial transactions so that capital does not get grounded for too long.

The federal government also deregulated the thrifts in the 1970s and lifted the ceilings on interest rates. Less regulated institutional investors (eg mutual and pension funds) and insurance companies became engaged in bank-like activity displaced banks from the credit markets they formerly dominated. Enacting a change in tax shelters in 1981, the Reagan administration effectively bolstered the role of equity syndicators, such as real-estate investment trusts (REITs), flooding the markets with capital. The resulting overaccumulation resulted in the overbuilding of the 1980s (Fainstein 1994), particularly in the Sunbelt office sector, and led the real-estate industry into its worse crisis since the Great Depression.

Clearly, finance does not just "hang above the rest of the political economy, as it were, as a dominating and abstract force whilst forming part of an order ... of neoliberalism" (Gill 1997:72). New aspects of finance and the money form at the national and global scales are directly relevant to local governance, setting the market rules for (dis)investment in the built environment (Christopherson 1993). Financial deregulation and the increasing securitization of real estate removes owners from actual structures and moves locally determined value away from the underlying property. Determining a property's true value requires detailed knowledge of the local real-estate market (Warf 1999). Distant capitalists will only invest if the property is recognizable beyond its unique character embedded in space and if it can provide short-term returns. When these conditions are met, the particularity of a building is transformed into the uniformity of a financial "instrument," and place becomes subordinated to "a higher realm of ordering beyond territorialism: speed" (Douglas 1999:146).

If these conditions are not met, disinvestment may occur. Distant investors that operate in many jurisdictions often lack in-depth knowledge of and familiarity with the markets in which they operate. For this reason, the spatial distancing of real-estate investments may encourage the demolition of devalued properties over their rehabilitation. Although each location in space is unique and requires place-specific knowledge (eg of the demand for local real estate, zoning regulations) to assess its value, land that is devoid of improvements is more recognizable to the abstracting, utilitarian logic of capital markets. Rehabilitation and upgrading requires additional knowledge (of contractors and building materials) that distant investors often lack. In comparison, space is more malleable and potentially more valuable to investors when it is empty. If higher degrees of local knowledge are required, either profits will have to be higher in order to compensate for these inflexibilities (Clark and O'Connor 1997) or other parties, such as the state, will have to assume a portion of these additional costs.

The globalization of real-estate capital and the dematerialization of property have created new challenges for the local state. Municipalities are subject to a highly territorialized fiscal dependency, and they operate in a more delimited and competitive space than do national regimes. Moreover their ability to raise the revenues with which to bid for private investment is controlled by higher orders of government, such as state-government-imposed debt caps. Rather than retreat from policymaking, the last two decades have witnessed a proliferation of municipal regimes increasingly active in creating landscapes amenable to the quick excavation of value (Swyngedouw 1997). Cutting back national sources of assistance, such as urban renewal dollars and development block grants, has only aggravated interjurisdictional competition, raising the stakes and encouraging more desperate efforts to pin down increasingly fleet-footed capital.

Whereas the national and local bureaucracies of the Keynesian state formed a thick structure of organized power around urban renewal, local strategies now emanate from a hollowed-out, "contract" state (Jessop 1998; Strange 1996). Local government functions have been sold to the lowest-cost bidders: to private consulting firms (who draft neighborhood plans), bond underwriters (who help municipalities privatize infrastructure development and management and then underwrite the bonds to pay for those activities), and nonprofits (who build and manage housing and social services for those displaced from public housing). Whereas cities were beholden to the temporal pressures of the federal government during urban renewal, they are now dependent on the short-term horizons of REITs and those institutional investors who purchase municipal bonds. The contract state operates through decentralized partnerships with real-estate capitalists, and what remains of the local state structure has been refashioned to resemble the private sector, with an emphasis on customer service, speed, and entrepreneurialism. Indeed, the narrative of entrepreneurialism has underpinned city management practices since the late 1980s, as local governments attempt to project modern self-images and embrace innovative tactics to remake old spaces in the face of global competition (see MacLeod this volume).[3]

The marketized ideologies of neoliberalism as articulated in the entrepreneurial practices of cities stress different justifications for the stigmatization of space necessary for its revalorization. Agricultural and medical metaphors may have been appropriate for the rapidly urbanizing society of the mid-20th century, with its rural roots and relative bureaucratic legitimacy. However, the civil rights movement, dissolution of Keynesian managerialism, and numerous legal challenges forced cities to be more cautious about recalling the paternalism of the welfare state. Cities have attempted to sidestep this ideological minefield in two related ways. First, they have further distanced themselves from those "long-turnover" parts of the city where redevelopment needs are great but where the probability of private investment and extracting additional value is low. Second, although cities continue to identify blight in order to stigmatize space, I would argue that some of the concept's welfarist associations have been neutralized by the overarching narrative of municipal entrepreneurialism and its antithesis, the narrative of obsolescence. Obsolescence has become a neoliberal alibi for creative destruction, and therefore an important component in contemporary processes of spatialized capital accumulation.

There is nothing new about obsolescence. Concerns that the city as a settlement form was obsolete were voiced in earlier parts of the century (Beauregard 1993), and obsolescence is frequently cited as one of many "blighting factors" in redevelopment from the 1930s onward. Obsolescence poses a greater threat to exchange values than to use values, whereas blight threatens both. An obsolete building, eg one that has overly high ceilings, is not physically unusable but rather cannot be used as profitably as one with lower ceilings and modern heating systems. A recent legal suit over a redevelopment agency's activities noted that "Whether the building has become nonfunctional or obsolete for its use under current market conditions does not indicate whether the building is unsafe or uninhabitable for human purposes ... [Such buildings] do not breed disease or crime; they fail to measure up to their maximum potential use in terms of economic, social, architectural, or civic desirability" (*Friends of Mammoth v. Town of Mammoth Lakes Redevelopment Agency* 98 Cal. Rptr. 2d 334, 2000:553).

Proof of obsolescence, therefore, requires the purveyor to demonstrate an objective loss of exchange value, rather than to subjectively comment on the loss of utility for a building's current residents. Appraisers, developers, and local officials point to certain indicators, such as rental values that are less than either the cost of demolition or accumulated depreciation (Urban Land Institute 1996). Obsolete office buildings can then be reclaimed as lofts, obsolete zoning and building codes can be revamped so that they are more user-friendly, and obsolete manufacturing space can be demolished to increase the supply of potentially developable land. Or, as one excited journalist noted about New York City, "after languishing on the sidelines as the wallflowers of the real-estate industry, outmoded industrial buildings, vacant for years, are being pursued by investors and developers who are profiting by dressing them up and dancing them around again" (Charles 1998:1).

Couching justifications for redevelopment in the language of obsolescence allows entrepreneurial cities to evade responsibility for the less commodified components of welfare, such as health, safety, and morals, previously assumed (at least discursively) by the early managerialist state. On the surface, obsolescence appears morally and racially neutral, as if the social has been removed from an entirely technical matter. Whereas the Keynesian state framed slum clearance as a government responsibility to aid victim-residents, entrepreneurial urban policies use discursive frames that assign neither blame nor responsibility. What is responsible for obsolescence? Time, for one. Buildings age in what is framed as a natural, inevitable, and irreversible process. They are replaced by successively more modern structures. Functional obsolescence is simply the spatialization of turnover time; it is time given material expression in physical space. Obsolescence takes the agency from the owner-investor-tenant and relocates it in the commodity itself.

Markets are also responsible for obsolescence, although, by virtue of their lack of agency, they are cleared of any moral charge for the outcome of uneven development. Innovation and changing consumer demand, the logic goes, will create excess capacity in any market as new commodities become desirable and older ones fall out of favor (eg suburban greenfield versus urban brownfield sites). Markets are the straightforward expression of the popular will, and "since markets are the product of our choices, we have essentially authorized whatever the market does to us" (Frank 2001:5). As the correlate of gentrification, obsolescence appeals to the individualist notions of taste and preference that guide consumption and trump any structural or social explanations for wide-scale devaluation (Smith 1996). The market is viewed as an omniscient and neutral arbiter of value, with consumer sovereignty as the link between freedom and capitalism.

Entrepreneurial Interventions

Although markets drive obsolescence, state institutions continue to provide assistance in identifying its presence and reclaiming it. Real-estate executives insist that "[T]here is no alternative to extensive government intervention to encourage renovation or replacement of obsolete structures" (Lueck 1994:C3), and many of these same executives sit on the committees that design the strategies meant to provide such assistance. Urban renewal was very successful in laying the foundation for the devalorization and revalorization of capital, and many of its tactics, such as land write-downs, remain in use today. However, the neoliberal governance of urban development has allowed other spatial practices to flourish and new politicized and marketized relationships to convene around financing, constructing, destroying, and reconstructing the built environment.

One of the most interesting developments has been the resurgence of sublocal fiscal enclaves within the city limits that have access to sources of finance beyond the reach of the city as a whole and compete among themselves for the attention of private investment and the bond market. These enclaves include tax increment financing districts (TIF), business improvement districts (BID), and special-purpose development corporations, all of which have their roots in

older special assessment districts to some extent. TIF forms the focus
of the remainder of this paper, for, as a rescaled form of city power, it
is both heavily invested in the classification of obsolescence and
particularly illustrative of the neoliberal turn.

TIF evolved out of a method used to match federal block grants in
the 1950s, but it was only used by a few states (particularly those on
the West Coast) until the 1970s. By the 1990s, TIF had become the
most popular means of financing redevelopment in the US (Briffault
1997). TIF creates a special taxing jurisdiction around an area targeted
for redevelopment and earmarks future property tax revenues to
pay for the up-front costs of development. The area in question must
meet the definition of "blight" found in the state enabling legislation.
However, the existence of blight is most frequently demonstrated by
the presence of obsolete structures and land uses and by property
values that have not grown as quickly as some benchmark (usually the
average growth rate of the municipality as a whole).[4] Developers and
consultants, in concert with the municipality, draft a study to document the deterioration, the age of the building stock, zoning and land-
use designations, vacancies, and changing property values. These
criteria resemble some of those used to identify blight during urban
renewal, although they have been purged of any reference to race,
health, or hygiene.

When municipalities have attempted to demonstrate blight in
recent years by pointing to compromised use-values, as they did
during urban renewal, they have been challenged by popular protests
and legal suits. For example, the Chicago suburb of Addison tried to
demonstrate blight by pointing to "dust on windowsills, missing toilet
paper roll holders, small cracks in linoleum floor … and unwashed
dishes in kitchen sinks" (*Hispanics United of DuPage County v. Village
of Addison* 958 F. Supp 1320, 1994:27). The municipality planned to
use TIF to demolish 827 units in two poor and predominantly Latino
neighborhoods, but they only brought down eight four-unit apartments
before a lawsuit and three years of intense negotiations forced them
to stop. Municipalities have had better luck demonstrating blight and
engaging in redevelopment activities when they do not seek to implicate
use values but instead focus on those areas where rent gaps are wide
and where potential for revalorization is great. This is because TIF
depends, not on absolute levels of property taxes, but on the "increment"
or difference between property taxes in the year of designation and
subsequent years (in Illinois, the time period is twenty-three years).
In other words, surplus value only accrues to the local state and, by
extension, the market when assets are repriced upwards. Introducing
property that was publicly owned (eg a public housing complex),
acquired through eminent domain, or destroyed through demolition
into a sufficiently hot real-estate market creates the huge spike in

property values necessary to justify the up-front expenditure and pay off the bonded debt.

As a result, cities have used TIF primarily for large-scale downtown redevelopment projects and in gentrifying neighborhoods, bypassing the slow-turnover parts of the city where there is little hope of generating additional property taxes. TIF has supported the entrepreneurial state's involvement in place marketing, tourism, historic preservation, and beautification. Such efforts often seek to alter the sign value of devalued buildings and places through the commodification of a sanitized kind of nostalgia. Chicago, for example, has spent $60 million in TIF funds to renovate several downtown theatres (Neighborhood Capital Budget Group 1999). These historic structures could be considered obsolete because by the 1970s they no longer hosted Broadway musicals but instead showed martial arts movies for a low-income audience.

Timing the intervention is key to its success or failure. If TIF designation occurs at both (a) the nadir of the value curve and (b) when there is initial speculative interest in the properties, TIF can maximize the surplus appropriated from the property. Only a coalition of municipal officials and affiliated real-estate capitalists possesses both the local knowledge and the police powers to be the first movers in such a small window of opportunity. Conflict typically ensues as these coalitions attempt to keep other speculators out (because they may cause assessments to rise prematurely) until the TIF process can be put securely into motion. After designation, the city borrows against the potential stream of future revenues in order to absorb the present cost of land development, infrastructure improvements, property assembly, and demolition so that developers do not have to do so.

Co-constructing obsolescence allows the state and private developers to both write down property values and speed the turnover of capital in the built environment. When particular properties experience significant devaluation, the local state may draw on its own expertise and legal authority to initiate a "quick-take" use of its eminent domain power. Tax-delinquent, "nuisance," and abandoned properties—often grouped together as "temporarily obsolete, abandoned or derelict sites," or "TOADS"—then become part of the city's extensive inventory of real estate (Greenberg, Popper and West 1990).

However, neoliberal ideology dismisses most forms of public ownership as socially and privately unproductive. When ownership resides with the government, the logic goes, the property is fiscally barren, and there is no profit motive or institutional check on the dissipation of potential value by manager-bureaucrats. Indeed, neoliberal urban development strategies, including TIF, have sought to privatize the city's property holdings and increase the pace at which they are acquired and subsequently disposed. Cities, like the finance capital that enables them, tend to resist the role of landlord over long periods of time. Devalued properties typically do not stay in public hands for long before being reintroduced into circulation. They are gifted or auctioned off to private developers, scavengers, or speculators. Once the public housing came down and titles to the formerly tax-delinquent properties were safely transferred, cities in the 1990s found themselves sitting on a goldmine of value that was sold to the highest bidders.[5] In this way, as Smith (1996:70) notes, "assembling properties at a fair market value and returning them to developers at lower assessed prices, the state bears the cost of last stages of capital devalorization, thereby ensuring that developers recoup high returns without which rehabilitation or redevelopment would not occur." The city plays a critical role in the circulation of capital as a short-term holding tank for devalued properties.

Property-tax dollars are not simply granted to firms as abatements or deductions, as they were during an earlier "dismantling" phase of urban policy (Peck and Tickell this volume). Instead, TIF creates new institutions to put tax revenues "in play" in global capital markets, where they are bonded and arbitraged beyond recognition. For example, the City of Chicago has placed a TIF around its most notorious public housing complex, Cabrini Green, in preparation for its demolition and redevelopment as mixed-income housing in an extremely expensive real-estate submarket (Ranney 2001). The City developed a complex financing scheme to secure the TIF bonds because of the political risks inherent in the project (ie at the time of the bond sale, a lawsuit that was filed on behalf of the residents and sought to halt the redevelopment was pending). It paid a large fee to the Bank of Canada to provide bond guarantees and arranged for Nations Bank to engage in an interest-rate swap that gave Nations Bank the right to invest the tax increments. Only with these costly guarantees to nullify the political risk would the insurance funds purchase the TIF bonds.

Just as flexible accumulation looks more to finance capital than the Fordist firm did, entrepreneurial states rely more heavily on the markets in public debt and private equities in real estate than did the Keynesian state. Dependence on financial markets contributes to the public sector's loss of time sovereignty, as investors have much shorter time horizons than states. A small cadre of highly specialized underwriting shops for TIF deals have become important agents in the networks of urban fiscal governance. These boutiques are able to charge higher spreads for TIF debt because of the speculative risks involved. Meanwhile, cities woo bond-rating agencies with exaggerated claims of performance in hopes of securing better grade—and therefore less expensive—debt. Despite the bull market, however, several TIF bonds defaulted in the 1990s, and for every default, there were a hundred close calls that strained the contract state's capacity for fiscal management (Johnson 1999).

Conclusion

As the federal-grants economy that funded urban renewal efforts has been dismantled, entrepreneurial cities have sought to distance themselves from prior welfarist commitments, reclaim obsolete spaces, and find innovative ways to make costly redevelopment projects "pay for themselves." Devolution increased cities' dependence on own-source revenues, namely property tax revenues, which in turn made them more dependent on those that create value: the private real-estate market. Neoliberal redevelopment policies amount to little more than property speculation and public giveaways to guide the place and pace of the speculative activity. In this way, the miniaturization of fiscal space through strategies like TIF assists the local state in preparing urban property for the deep excavation of value.

The local state's dependence on its own property base and its willingness to subject that base to market rule accounts for the renewed zeal with which it stigmatizes space. Obsolete buildings melt into air, making it easier for the state to match distant investors with the empty, deterritorialized spaces left behind. However, reliance on the erratic capital markets to reinvigorate devalued properties often jeopardizes the fiscal health of cities. Nowhere is this more evident than with TIF, where cities front huge sums for land acquisition and development based on tenuous promises of future value generation. Such speculative risks expose the fact that control is costly in neo-liberal regimes where value in the built environment depends on the circulation of fast, fictitious money and an unruly web of politicized and marketized relationships.

Acknowledgments

For their comments on previous drafts, the author wishes to thank participants in the Neoliberalism and the City workshop and three anonymous reviewers. Laura Swartzbaugh, John Slocum, Lisa Perez, Marc Doussard, Dave Ranney, Neil Brenner, and Nik Theodore also contributed substantially to the final product.

Endnotes

[1] Rent gaps materialize when current property values do not fully capitalize their potential ground rent.

[2] For an example of this, one need look no further than the case of depreciation, which both describes a real loss of value from age and use and also represents a discursive figment of a tax system that rewards property ownership with deductions for "expected" devaluation. Appraisers, the private gatekeepers of value, use standards informed by the federal tax code to identify actual depreciation in buildings.

[3] Entrepreneurialism is defined broadly as a combination of competitive, growth-oriented local economic development strategies, intimate public–private collaborations, and boosterism (Harvey 1989a; Jessop 1998).

[4] Indiana's TIF legislation, for example, states that municipalities must demonstrate that "normal development and occupancy are undesirable or impossible due to a lack of development, cessation of growth, dearth of improvements, character of occupancy, substandard buildings or the presence of other factors that impair values or prevent normal use of development of property" (cited in Michel 1996:460).
[5] In Chicago, local officials admit that the city's excessive use of TIF (with over 113 districts in which over 12% of the city's tax base is tied up) places pressure on them to return as many properties as possible to the tax rolls, preferably in a more highly valued state (interview with City of Chicago Department of Buildings, July 2001).

References

Aglietta M (1979) *A Theory of Capitalist Regulation*. London: New Left Review
Amin A (1994) *Post-Fordism: A Reader*. Oxford: Blackwell
Appraisal Institute (2001) *The Appraisal of Real Estate*. 12th ed. Chicago
Beauregard R (1993) *Voices of Decline*. Cambridge, MA: Blackwell
Berman M (1988) *All That Is Solid Melts into Air*. New York: Penguin Books
Briffault R (1997) The law and economics of federalism: The rise of sublocal structures in urban governance. *Minnesota Law Review* 82:503–534
Bryson J (1997) Obsolescence and the process of creative reconstruction. *Urban Studies* 34(9):1439–1458
Budd L (1999) Globalization and the crisis of territorial embeddedness in international financial markets. In R Martin (ed) *Money and the Space Economy* (pp 115–138). London: Wiley
Bullock S (1996) Appraising low-investment grade apartments. *Appraisal Journal* 64:34–43
Callon M, Law J and Rip A (eds) (1986) *Mapping the Dynamics of Science and Technology: Sociology of Science in the Real World*. Basingstoke: Macmillan
Charles E (1998) With space tight, outdated factories find new roles. *The New York Times* 4 January:11–1
Christopherson S (1993) Market rules and territorial outcomes: The case of the United States. *International Journal of Urban and Regional Research* 17:274–288
Clark G and O'Connor K (1997) The informational content of financial products and the spatial structure of the global finance industry. In K Cox (ed) *Spaces of Globalization: Reasserting the Power of the Local* (pp 89–114). New York: Guilford
Cohen J (2001) Abandoned housing: Exploring lessons from Baltimore. *Housing Policy Debate* 12:415–448
Douglas I (1999) Globalization of governance: Toward an archeology of contemporary political reason. In A Prakash and J Hart (eds) *Globalization and Governance* (pp 134–160). New York: Routledge
Dow S (1999) The stages of banking development and the spatial evolution of financial systems. In R Martin (ed) *Money and the Space Economy* (pp 31–48). London: Wiley
Downs A (1985) *The Revolution in Real-Estate Finance*. Washington, DC: Brookings Institution
Fainstein S (1994) *The City Builders: Property, Politics, and Planning in London and New York*. Cambridge, MA: Blackwell
Feagin J (1998) *The New Urban Paradigm*. Lanham, MD: Rowman and Littlefield
Fogleson R (2001) *Downtown: Its Rise and Fall, 1880–1950*. New Haven, CT: Yale University Press
Frank T (2001) The god that sucked. *The Baffler* 14 (Spring):1–9
Friedman L (1968) *Government and Slum Housing: A Century of Frustration*. Chicago: Rand McNally

Gill S (1997) Finance, production, and panopticism: Inequality, risk, and resistance in an era of disciplinary neoliberalism. In S Gill (ed) *Globalization, Democratization, and Multilateralism* (pp 51–76). New York: St. Martins

Greenberg M, Popper F and West B (1990) The TOADS: A new American epidemic. *Urban Affairs Quarterly* 25:435–54

Habermas J (1973) *Legitimation Crisis.* Boston: Beacon Press

Hall P (1996) *Cities of Tomorrow.* Oxford: Blackwell

Harvey D (1982) *The Limits to Capital.* Oxford: Basil Blackwell

Harvey D (1989a) From managerialism to entrepreneurialism: The transformation of urban governance in late capitalism. *Geographiska Annaler* 71B:3–17

Harvey D (1989b) *The Urban Experience.* Baltimore: Johns Hopkins Press

Hommels A (2000) Obduracy and urban sociotechnical change: Changing Plan Hoog Catharijne *Urban Affairs Review* 35:649–676

Housing Act (1949) Public Law no. 81–171, 63 Stat. 413 (1950)

Housing Act (1954) Public Law no. 83–560, 68 Stat. 590 (1955)

Jessop B (1998) The narrative of enterprise and the enterprise of narrative: Place marketing and the entrepreneurial city. In T Hall and P Hubbard (eds) *The Entrepreneurial City* (pp 77–99). West Sussex: Wiley

Johnson C (1999) TIF debt finance: An analysis of the mainstreaming of a fringe sector *Public Budgeting and Finance* 19(1):46–67

Lash S and Urry J (1987) *The End of Organized Capitalism.* Madison: University of Wisconsin Press

Logan J and Molotch H (1986) *Urban Fortunes.* Berkeley: University of California Press

Lueck T (1994) Giuliani plans inducements to revive Wall Street area. *The New York Times* 16 December:A1

Michel C (1996) Brother, can you spare a dime: Tax increment financing in Indiana. *Indiana Law Journal* 71:457–479

Neighborhood Capital Budget Group (1999) *Chicago TIF Encyclopedia.* Chicago: NCBG

O'Connor J (1973) *The Fiscal Crisis of the State.* New York: St. Martin's

Page M (1999) *The Creative Destruction of Manhattan, 1900–1940.* Chicago: University of Chicago Press

Quinones B (1994) Redevelopment redefined: Revitalizing the central city with resident control *University of Michigan Law Review* 27:689–734

Ranney D (2001) "Global Decisions, Local Collisions: Combating the New World Order." Unpublished manuscript

Schill M (1999) The impact of the capital markets on real estate law and practice. *John Marshall Law Review* 32:269–312

Schumpeter J (1942) *Capitalism, Socialism, and Democracy.* New York: Harper and Row

Shields R (1991) *Places on the Margin: Alternative Geographies of Modernity.* London: Routledge

Smith N (1996) *The New Urban Frontier: Gentrification and the Revanchist City.* New York: Routledge

Sternlieb G and Burchell R (1973) *Residential Abandonment: The Tenement Landlord Revisited.* New Brunswick, NJ: Rutgers University Center for Urban Policy Research

Strange S (1996) *The Retreat of the State: The Diffusion of Power in the World Economy.* Cambridge, UK: Cambridge University Press

Swartzbaugh L (2001) "Sifting, Sorting, and Relocating: Racial Formation in Early 20th-Century Chicago." Unpublished manuscript

Swyngedouw E (1997) Neither global nor local: "Glocalization" and the politics of scale. In K Cox (ed) *Spaces of Globalization* (pp 137–166). New York: Guilford

Teaford J (1990) *The Rough Road to Renaissance: Urban Revitalization in America, 1940–1985.* Baltimore: Johns Hopkins Press

Urban Land Institute (1996) *New Uses for Obsolete Buildings*. Washington, DC: ULI

Virillio P (1986) *Speed and Politics*. New York: Semiotexte

von Hoffman A (2000) A study in contradictions: The origins and legacy of the Housing Act of 1949. *Housing Policy Debate* 11:299–326

Warf B (1999) The hypermobility of capital and the collapse of the Keynesian state. In R Martin (ed) *Money and the Space Economy* (pp 227–240). London: Wiley

Weber M (1978) *Economy and Society*. Ed G Ross and C Wittich. Berkeley: University of California Press

Wynne B (1989) Establishing the rules of laws: Constructing expert authority. In R Smith and B Wynne (eds) *Expert Evidence: Interpreting Science in the Law* (pp 23–55). New York: Routledge

Zukin S (1982) *Loft Living: Culture and Capital in Urban Change*. Baltimore: Johns Hopkins Press

Rachel Weber is an Assistant Professor in the Urban Planning and Policy Program of the University of Illinois at Chicago. Her current research focuses on the design and effectiveness of financial incentives to private businesses and developers. She is the author of the book *Swords into Dow Shares: Governing the Decline of the Military Industrial Complex* (Boulder: Westview Press, 2000), which explores the relationship between financial markets and corporate restructuring in the defense industry.

Part 3 New Geographies of Power, Exclusion and Injustice

Chapter 9
Neoliberal Urbanization in Europe: Large-Scale Urban Development Projects and the New Urban Policy

Erik Swyngedouw, Frank Moulaert and Arantxa Rodriguez

This paper summarizes the theoretical insights drawn from a study of thirteen large-scale urban development projects (UDPs) in twelve European Union countries. The project focused on the way in which globalization and liberalization articulate with the emergence of new forms of governance, on the formation of a new scalar gestalt of governing and on the relationship between large-scale urban development and political, social and economic power relations in the city. Among the most important conclusions, we found that:

- Large-scale UDPs have increasingly been used as a vehicle to establish exceptionality measures in planning and policy procedures. This is part of a neoliberal "New Urban Policy" approach and its selective "middle- and upper-class" democracy. It is associated with new forms of "governing" urban interventions, characterized by less democratic and more elite-driven priorities.
- Local democratic participation mechanisms are not respected or are applied in a very "formalist" way, resulting in a new choreography of elite power. However, grassroots movements occasionally manage to turn the course of events in favor of local participation and of modest social returns for deprived social groups.
- The UDPs are poorly integrated at best into the wider urban process and planning system. As a consequence, their impact on a city as a whole and on the areas where the projects are located remains ambiguous.
- Most UDPs accentuate socioeconomic polarization through the working of real-estate markets (price rises and displacement of social or low-income housing), changes in the priorities of public budgets that are increasingly redirected from social objectives to investments in the built environment and the restructuring of the labor market.
- The UDPs reflect and embody a series of processes that are associated with changing spatial scales of governance; these changes, in turn, reflect a shifting geometry of power in the governing of urbanization.

Large-Scale Urban Development Projects as Urban Policy

Over the past fifteen years or so, local authorities—alone or in concert with the private sector—have strongly relied on the planning and implementation of large-scale urban development projects (UDPs), such as museums, waterfronts, exhibition halls and parks, business centers, and international landmark events, as part of an effort to re-enforce the competitive position of their metropolitan economies in a context of rapidly changing local, national, and global competitive conditions. In many cases, these projects were supported by a majority of the local constituency, or at least by a silent majority. In other cases, they were initiated by means of "exceptionality" measures, such as the freezing of conventional planning tools, bypassing statutory regulations and institutional bodies, the creation of project agencies with special or exceptional powers of intervention and decision-making, and/or a change in national or regional regulations. On occasion, national governments became the main developers, setting aside both local authorities and constituencies.

This paper will examine the dynamics that have accompanied the implementation of large-scale UDPs in thirteen European cities within the European Union (EU). The analysis is based on research undertaken as part of a Targeted Socioeconomic Research Action (Framework IV program of the EU), "Urban Restructuring and Social Polarization in the City" (URSPIC). URSPIC examined whether large-scale UDPs, as emblematic examples of neoliberal forms of urban governance, contribute to accentuating processes of social exclusion and polarization, or whether they foster social integration and promote integrated urban development.[1] The project intended to contribute to the analysis of the relationship between urban restructuring and social exclusion/integration in the context of the emergence of the new regimes of urban governance that parallel the Europe-wide—albeit geographically uneven and, on occasion, politically contested—consolidation of a neoliberal and market-driven ideology and politics. The selected UDPs embody and express processes that reflect global pressures and incorporate changing systems of local, regional, and/or national regulation and governance. These projects, while being decidedly local, capture global trends, express new forms of national and local policies, and incorporate them in a particular localized setting. The selected UDPs are listed in Table 1 according to their city's ranking in the world urban hierarchy and their stage of development at the start of the research project in 1997.

Reordering the Urban: Large-Scale UDPs and the "Glocalization" of the City

Cities are, of course, brooding places of imagination, creativity, innovation, and the ever new and different. However, cities also hide in their underbelly perverse and pervasive processes of social exclusion and marginalization and are rife with all manner of struggle, conflict, and often outright despair in the midst of the greatest

Table 1: The Thirteen Case-Study Projects of the URSPIC Project

Type of City	Stage of the Project—1997		
	Design	Construction	Commercialization
World cities		**ROTTERDAM** (RANDSTAD HOLLAND) KOP VAN ZUID **LONDON** THE SOUTH BANK	**BRUSSELS** ESPACE LEOPOLD/EU DISTRICT
Euro-city	**BERLIN** ADLERSHOF		
Big town	**COPENHAGEN** ORESTADEN **DUBLIN** DOCKLANDS -INTERN. FINANCIAL SERVICES CENTRE **ATHENS** OLYMPIC VILLAGE	**LISBON** EXPO 1998 **VIENNA** DONAU CITY	
Secondary town		**BILBAO** ABANDOIBARRA **BIRMINGHAM** CENTRAL BUSINESS DISTRICT (CBD)	**NAPLES** CENTRO DIREZIONALE **LILLE** EURALILLE

Source: http://www.ifresi.univ-lille1.fr (select Programmes de Recherche and then select URSPIC).

affluence, abundance, and pleasure. These dynamics that define the urban experience have, if anything, taken on a heightened intensity over the past two decades or so. There is no need to recount here the tumultuous reordering of urban social, cultural, and economic life that has rampaged through the city. Many urban communities have been left in the doldrums of persistent decline and permanent upheaval and are still faced with the endless leisure time that comes with lasting unemployment. Others have risen to the challenge that restructuring sparks off and have plunged into the cracks and fissures that have opened up a vast arena of new possibilities of action and intervention, as governments and economies desperately seek out new niches for revitalizing the urban fabric.

These urban transformations, exhaustively documented in many academic research and governmental documents, have invariably been situated in the context of a transforming spatial political, sociocultural, and economic system. While economic processes were rapidly globalizing and cities were trying to carve out their niche within the emerging new divisions of labor, of production, and of consumption, political transformations—pursued by local, regional, and national governments of all ideological stripes and colors—were initiated in an attempt to align local dynamics with the imagined, assumed, or real requirements of a deregulated international economic system, whose political elites were vigorously pursuing a neoliberal dogma. Heralded by some as the harbinger of a new era of potential prosperity and vilified by others as the source of enduring restructuring and accentuated social polarization and marginalization, the urban arena became a key space in which political-economic and social changes were enacted. The new urban policy, developing in parallel with the new neoliberal economic policy, squarely revolved around re-centering the city. Old forms and functions, traditional political and organizational configurations, had to give way to a new urbanity, a visionary urbanity that would stand the tests imposed by a global and presumably liberal world order. Repositioning the city on the map of the competitive landscape meant reimagining and recreating urban space, not just in the eyes of the master planners and city fathers and mothers, but primarily for the outsider, the investor, developer, businesswoman or –man, or the money-packed tourist.

The urban turned into ruin in the devastating restructuring of the 1970s and 1980s. Rebuilding the city—as in the aftermath of a war— became the leitmotif of urban policy. Large-scale and emblematic projects were the medicine the advocates of the new urban policy prescribed. Accommodation of the EU's encroaching office expansion in Brussels, the Guggenheim museum in Bilbao, the new financial district in the Dublin docklands, the science-university complex Adlershof in Berlin, Copenhagen's Orestaden project, and the 1998

World Expo in Lisbon, among many other examples that are dotted over the map of urban Europe, testify to the unshakeable belief of the city elites in the healing effects that the production of new urban complexes promises for the city's vitality.

While we agree that large-scale UDPs have indeed become one of the most visible and ubiquitous urban revitalization strategies pursued by city elites in search of economic growth and competitiveness, we also insist that it is exactly this sort of new urban policy that actively produces, enacts, embodies, and shapes the new political and economic regimes that are operative at local, regional, national, and global scales. These projects are the material expression of a developmental logic that views megaprojects and place-marketing as means for generating future growth and for waging a competitive struggle to attract investment capital. Urban projects of this kind are, therefore, not the mere result, response, or consequence of political and economic change choreographed elsewhere. On the contrary, we argue that such UDPs are the very catalysts of urban and political change, fuelling processes that are felt not only locally, but regionally, nationally, and internationally as well. It is such concrete interventions that express and shape transformations in spatial political and economic configurations. They illustrate the actual concrete process through which postmodern forms, post-Fordist economic dynamics, and neoliberal systems of governance are crafted and through which a new articulation of regulatory and governmental scales is produced. UDPs are productive of and embody processes that operate in and over a variety of scales, from the local to the regional, the national, the European, and the global scale. From our vantage point, the urban project becomes the lens that permits the casting of light on (1) how the scalar interplay is etched into particular urban schemes; (2) how these projects, in turn, express the way forces operating at a variety of geographical scales intersect in the construction of new socioeconomic environments; and (3) how social polarization and exclusion/integration, as well as processes of empowerment/disempowerment, are shaped by and work through these forms of sociospatial restructuring.

This paper attempts to provide a panoramic view of changes in urban development strategies and policies in some of Europe's greatest cities. While being sensitive to the formative importance of local and national configurations, the case studies also suggest a series of similarities that point to a more general process of urban socioeconomic restructuring and of reorganization of the system of governance. The localization of the global and the globalization of the local become crafted in place-specific forms, yet they show perplexing—and often disturbing—common threads. In many ways, therefore, urban environments as constructed places are the condensed expression and incarnation of the transformation of sociospatial processes that operate on a variety of articulated geographical scales.

Urban Redevelopment Strategies in the European City: Autocratic Governance, Monumental Spaces, and Mythical Imaginations

A New Urban Policy (NUP)? The Search for Growth and Competitive Restructuring

Despite the differences between the case-study projects and the distinct political-economic and regulatory regimes of which they are part, they share a new approach in urban policy that strongly expresses, at the scale of the urban, the main ingredients of a New Economic Policy (NEP). New Economic Policy is the policy platform of conservative liberalism. Contrary to what its ideology sustains, conservative liberalism has always maintained a very special and intimate relationship with state intervention (see Keil this volume). It seeks to reorient state intervention away from monopoly market regulation and towards marshaling state resources into the social, physical, and geographical infra- and superstructures that support, finance, subsidize, or otherwise promote new forms of capital accumulation by providing the relatively fixed territorial structures that permit the accelerated circulation of capital and the relatively unhindered operation of market forces. At the same time, the state withdraws to a greater or lesser extent from socially inclusive blanket distribution-based policies and from Keynesian demand-led interventions and replaces them with spatially targeted social policies and indirect promotion of entrepreneurship, particularly via selective deregulation, stripping away red tape, and investment "partnerships" (see Peck and Tickell this volume). The relationship between NEP, New Urban Policy (NUP), and UDPs is summarized in Figure 1 and will be explored further in the subsequent sections of this paper.

One of the key components of the new mode of socioeconomic regulation in cities has been a gradual shift away from distributive policies, welfare considerations, and direct service provision towards more market-oriented and market-dependent approaches aimed at pursuing economic promotion and competitive restructuring. In most cities, urban revitalization is presented as an opportunity to change economic hierarchies and functions within the urban region, creating new jobs and strengthening the city's position in the urban division of labor. In this way, the search for growth turns urban renewal into a mediated objective, a necessary precondition for economic regeneration. Although this general trend takes quite distinct forms in different cities (see Table 2 for a description of six of these projects), project-based urban interventions generally involve critical changes in priorities

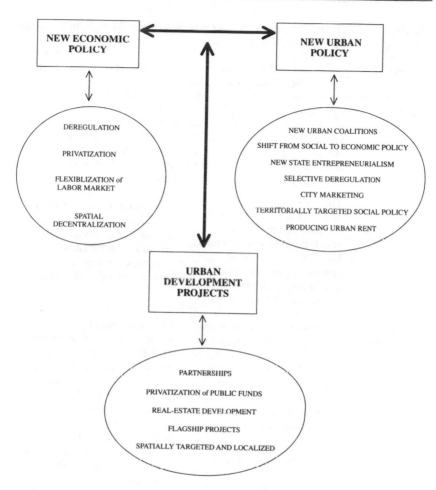

Figure 1: Relationship between NEP, NUP, and UDPs

and the ascent of a more assertive, dynamic, and entrepreneurial style of urban governance. Planners and local authorities adopt a more proactive and entrepreneurial approach aimed at identifying market opportunities and assisting private investors to take advantage of them. Table 2 also summarizes the developmental view promoted by the city's economic and political elites and the associated boosterist discourses that legitimize the projects and the associated institutional and regulatory framework.

State-led or State-based: The Myth of the Absent State
In contrast to discourses of market-led and entrepreneurial activity (risk taking, market-led investments), the UDPs are decidedly and almost without exception state-led and often state-financed. In a context of a liberalizing European metagovernance by the European

Table 2: The Role of UDPs in the City's Growth Strategy: Main Functions and Development Logic for Six Projects

Project	Size and Location New Functions	Main Development Logic
Berlin Adlershof	The development area is located in an outlying district (*Treptow*) in the Southeast of Berlin, 12 km from the center. It is connected to the suburban rail network. The area encompasses approximately 420 ha, with a site for science (R&D activities), a business area, a Media City, a university campus, a park, sites for trade and industry, and several residential areas.	Urban renewal logic. Its main objectives are the restructuring of old industrial areas, the promotion of a future vision for an improved labor market based around high-technology and advanced services, and supporting the formation of small innovative businesses in the field of technology, to create new urban mix of science, economy, media services, living, and leisure.
Bilbao Abandoibarra	Abandoibarra is a waterfront site of 345.000 m² located in the heart of the city of Bilbao. Situated strategically on the edge of the 19th-century expansion of the city, one of the highest-income neighborhoods. The site is presented as the new cultural and business center for Bilbao. Two major sites, the Guggenheim Museum and the Euskalduna Conference and Concert Hall, are the key landmarks of a project that also includes the construction of 80.000 m² for office space, a 27.000-m² shopping center, a luxury hotel, university facilities, and 800 housing units, as well as an additional 122.000 m² of green areas.	Urban renewal logic. The project aims to create a new directional center to lead economic regeneration in a declining industrial region/city; promote a postindustrial and international city, create a new economic structure, foster diversification of the urban sectoral mix, and support job creation in new and presumably dynamic and growth-oriented sectors such as culture and leisure.
Brussels Leopold Quarter (Quartier Leopold)	The Leopold quarter is a site of approximately 1 square km north-east of the city center. It was the first extension of Brussels (1837) beyond its medieval walls.	*From the developers' point of view*: capital accumulation facilitated by the rapid Europeanization and internationalization of Brussels.

Table 2: Continued

Project	Size and Location New Functions	Main Development Logic
	Originally conceived as an upper-class residential area, it is now one of the main office areas of Brussels and the central area for the expansion of a proliferating EU-related administration. It is served by an underground line and two railway stations.	*From the perspective of local government*: to assure the continuing presence and facilitate the further expansion of the European Union and related international institutions. Main objectives are: to provide office space to the EU and to whatever clients are attracted by Brussels' status as European capital; to reaffirm Brussels' role as Europe's capital and to cash in on the economic impact this has; and to raise the political and cultural position of the city in the European urban hierarchy.
Dublin Docklands Development Project (with International Financial Services Centre [IFSC] as flagship)	Original area covered 11 ha of downtown docklands on the north side of the river, which runs through the city center. This was subsequently widened to 29 ha and was recently extended to cover all 500 ha of the port area on both sides of the river. Development of IFSC on the north side of the river; continued mix of residential, business, service and cultural activities on both sides of the river.	Economic growth for original site; social and economic growth and physical regeneration for extended 500-ha site (of which only about 100 ha are in need of redevelopment).
Naples Centro Direzionale (CD)	110 ha immediately east of the city center. The area is adjacent to the main railway station and well connected via major roads to the city harbor, airport, and motorway network. Only half of the area has actually been developed. Mixed uses: mainly offices for public institutions (courts, regional parliament and related functions, Public Register, fire-brigade headquarters, church,	Discourse of modernization to create a postindustrial city. Because of its mixed use, the CD is supposed to contribute to the economic regeneration of the city and to improve its urban quality. As host location of public and private service activities, the CD is also supposed to decrease congestion in the historical city center.

Table 2: Continued

Project	Size and Location New Functions	Main Development Logic
	school, etc), but also offices for business, commercial activities, and sport facilities. Residence accounts for 30% of the total built volume.	
Vienna Donau City	The Donau-City (a multifunctional UDP) is located near the Danube, covering a subcenter with a size of about 17.4 ha. The housing projects on the same riverside cover 41,507 m². The development axis—Lasallestrasse—runs across the Danube and connects the Donau-City with the inner city and the surrounding microregions on both riversides.	Presented as a "bridge to the future," fostering economic growth and the formation of an international image for Vienna; strong emphasis on symbolic capital formation.
	Commercial and residential development: housing (1500 subsidized flats), offices, shopping, leisure and cultural facilities, school and university buildings, research and development park, apartment hotel.	The Donau-City (including the Viennese site of the United Nations Organization (UNO)) is regarded as a flagship for Vienna, aimed at strengthening its role as an "international meeting place." The development axis is supposed to attract international business and foster and act as pivotal point in East-West (European) trade and investment; it offers housing for upper classes.

Commission, of national deregulation, of shrinking or stable social redistributional policies, of the outright exclusion of some groups at the national or EU level (for example, immigrants), and of an often narrowing fiscal basis for local urban intervention, UDPs are marshaled as panaceas to fight polarization, to reinvigorate the local economy, and, most importantly—an explicit goal of these projects— to improve the tax basis of the city via a sociospatial and economic reorganization of metropolitan space. In some cases—such as Lille, Rotterdam, Brussels, Copenhagen, or Birmingham—a mix of projects is presented. Regardless of the efficacy of such a mix, the main objective of these projects is to obtain a higher social and economic return and to revalue prime urban land. The production of urban rent is central to such urban redevelopment strategies. Closing the rent gap and cashing in on the produced revalorization of the development land is a clear leitmotiv in most projects. Table 3 summarizes this for three of the case studies, but it is also clearly evident in Copenhagen, Brussels, Dublin, Bilbao, Athens, Vienna, and Birmingham.

Urban redevelopment is considered to be a central strategy in re-equilibrating the problematic fiscal balance sheet of local government. Spatially focused policies aimed at producing increasing rent income, altering the socioeconomic tax basis, and producing profitable economic activities are among the few options available, particularly in a context in which the structure of fiscal revenues is changing rapidly. As the financial-services sector and profit-making via global speculative transactions drain major financial means and investments, such activities simultaneously escape government control and generate very limited local fiscal returns. In such context, the revaluation of urban land remains one of the few means open to local governments to increase tax returns. Of course, closing rent gaps or producing high-rent-yielding spaces requires a production of built environments that permit significant surplus-value creation and/or realization. Yet the politics of rent-production through the production of the built environment has remained elusive in much of the recent literature on urban change.

Despite the rhetoric of market-led and privately covered investments, the state is invariably one of the leading actors in the process: in ten of the thirteen cases discussed in this paper, its role is outspoken. Risks are taken by the state, shared on occasion with the private sector, but given the speculative, real-estate-based nature of the projects, deficits are likely to occur. Traditional and well-documented processes of socialization of cost and risk and privatization of the possible benefits are central characteristics of most UDPs. While, in the past, invoking the social return of the projects legitimized such practices, they are now usually hidden behind a veil of creative accounting or by means of channeling funds via quasigovernmental organizations or mixed private/public companies. As can be gleaned from Table 3, in the cases of Berlin's Adlershof and Lisbon's Expo 1998, the state became increasingly involved in covering deficits, a condition true in many of the other cases. It is only in the redevelopment of London's South Bank that no state guarantee is involved and that the state only contributes through spending on social programs, training, and the provision of basic infrastructure.

A common theme is that most of the projects are decidedly rent-extraction-based. Their success rests fundamentally on (1) the production of potential extra rent and (2) the subsequent realization of the produced land rent. The employment and economic activity generating consequences of the projects, however important they may turn out to be, are all subject to the successful appropriation of the "manu-factured" land rent embodied in the new built environment. The

Table 3: The Financial Risks of the UDP and the Role of the State in Three UDPs

UDP	Original Financial Construction (1997)	Financial Risks for the State
Berlin Adlershof	*Developers:* BAAG (Berlin Adlershof Aufbaugesellschaft mbH) is a developer with a trusteeship and negotiates between the public administration and the private investors. Main functions: public relations, consultation, coordination. A control group of seven state secretaries decides the development and the economic plan, as well as timing and funding. WISTA Management GmbH is the operating company and has been founded for the development and the marketing of the science and commercial technology site. It is a 100% subsidiary of the City of Berlin. *Financing:* The main idea of the planning instrument applied in Adlershof is to use means from the trust fund to develop and open up the area to make it available for building. Property values are frozen for a set number of years, and a portion of profits is recaptured by the city when the land is sold to investors. This legal tool and its self-financing philosophy are highly dependent on an increase of the land-value levels, which makes them vulnerable to changes in the real-estate market. Since land prices have been declining since 1994 in Berlin and consequently in the development area, there is less turnover than expected, and the income from selling the land is too low for this plan to work out. As a consequence, BAAG receives loans in order to prefinance the development measures. Thus, the development of Adlershof depends mainly on public funding. Until now, there have been no financially strong investors. Furthermore, regional and national financial support is combined with money from the European	BAAG estimates that up to the year 2010, private and public investment will amount to 2.81 billion Euro in Adlershof. Of that, 2.19 billion Euro is estimated to come from private sources, while 610 million Euro will be public investments. Until 2000, only 23,1% of these resources were committed or already spent. By the end of 2001, 560 million Euro had been invested in Adlershof, mainly public funding. The debts of BAAG's trust fund reached 122.9 million Euro in December 1999, for which the state is liable. By September 2000, the level of indebtedness had risen to 127.3 million Euro. This growing debt puts a great burden on the public budget. The financial committee of the parliament agreed in June 1998 to invite the Auditor-General's Office to inspect the financial situation of the Adlershof project and of other development areas in the city. Today, in 2002, Berlin's financial situation causes great concern. The greatest number of large urban development projects (Adlershof is only one among several)—constitute a long-term drain on public finances. This is especially the case in the five development areas where the deficits have continuously risen. The commitment to the long-term financial scheme of the big projects is not matched by the

Table 3: Continued

UDP	Original Financial Construction (1997)	Financial Risks for the State
	Structural Funds to build up the infrastructure on the science and technology site (WISTA); the non-university research institutions are supported by the state; most companies rely on subsidized rents and on different aid programs; the construction of the campus depends on funds from the federal government and the regional government (Land) of Berlin.	expected tax income or the returns of sales of public land. They absorb financial resources that could be used for much-needed improvements in other areas. The impending fiscal stress was discussed at the beginning of the 1990s, but the policy-makers failed to reduce the projects to a reasonable number and size.
Lisbon Expo 1998	*Developers:* Parque EXPO 98 SA (a newly created state company) has extensive development powers and is underwritten by the Portuguese government; the social capital is entirely public; the main shareholders are the state and the municipalities of Lisbon and Loures. Parque Expo is the main shareholder of six other companies constituted to run the real-estate operation (Expo Urbe), Exposition 1998, and some of the facilities remaining after the exposition (the Oceanarium, the multipurpose pavilion, the refuse treatment plant, and the transport terminal, train, and metro). *Financing:* The financial model was designed to implement the exposition at zero cost, not including the external operations supported by EU funds. The main revenues for implementing the Expo and the urban project came from the exposition and the sale of the land. However, the expected returns were not achieved. *Parque Expo 1997 budget:* • Exposition (ticket sales, publicity, sponsors): 309 million Euro • Sale of land and property: 653 million Euro	Apart from being the main shareholder, the state guaranteed and provided the conditions for releasing the land at no cost to Parque Expo and for allocating EU funding of the project. The amount allocated directly to the Expo under the Urban Renovation Program of the EU's Community Support Framework was about half of the total sum for urban renovation for the whole country for five years—around 240 million Euro. The final balance between costs and revenues is still unknown. It was estimated that accumulated expenses until the year 2009 would make a total of 1850 million Euro, of which 375 million Euro were financial costs (Parque EXPO 98, Budget Report, Lisbon, March 1999). The main changes to the initial budget were the higher building and infrastructure costs and lower-than-expected revenue from the sale of tickets and sponsors (250 million Euro). In addition, Parque Expo will receive revenues (60 million Euro) from the sale of a few of the Expo pavilions to the state for the installation of administrative activities and cultural facilities.

Table 3: Continued

UDP	Original Financial Construction (1997)	Financial Risks for the State
	• Other companies (sale of company shares): 77 million Euro • European Funding (ERDF and Cohesion Fund): 304 million Euro (includes funding for primary infrastructure works inside the Expo site and for external operations: transport infrastructure, metro and train station, multipurpose pavilion, and environmental works) • State-direct funding (social capital): 87 million Euro • Other (renting of spaces): 51 million Euro.	In order to make up for the increasing deficit, Parque Expo raised land prices and changed previous costs and agreements. It is expected that revenue from land sales will bring an income of 850 million Euro by 2009—an increase of 30 percent from the initial estimate. These trends pushed property values up at the Expo site: Expo flats are now, on average, the most expensive in Lisbon. Thus, the state, through a public developer, is competing with the local market for raising house prices. Accounts have also to be settled with the municipalities of Lisbon and Loures for the investment in infrastructure works (the equivalent of 187 million Euro) when the site is handed back to the city.
London South Bank	*Developers*: The developers are public institutions and not-for-profit companies that have initiated the regeneration schemes. Some private developers are also active in the area. *Financing*: housing schemes are mainly financed by loans (Hambros Bank), revenues from rents (car park, shops) and grants from the Housing Corporation Grant. Public space improvements are financed by grants from the Single Regeneration Budget, local councils, the National Lottery, and the businesses' own funds. Public funds are used for new transport infrastructures. Private investors have turned the County Hall into a hotel and leisure center. Part of the Shell offices has been turned into luxury apartments by private investors.	No state guarantees. National state involvement through Single Regeneration Budget subsidies. The consequences for public budget are negligible. The consequences for other spending sectors (social, education, training, basic urban infrastructure, and so on) are negligible.

public-private or public-public initiatives rework the urban fabric such that the potential rent from new developments is significantly higher than existing rent levels. Sinking capital and investment into the production of a new built environment revalues, at least potentially, the monetary value of the land and the built environment—benefits that are almost always reaped by the private sector. This is particularly noticeable in the cases of Dublin, Brussels, Bilbao, Berlin, Athens, Copenhagen, and Naples (for greater detail on these cases, see sources cited in the acknowledgments).

Institutional Fragmentation and "Pluralistic" Governance

The newly emerging regimes of governing urban revitalization involve the subordination of formal government structures to new institutions and agencies, often paralleled by a significant redistribution of policy-making powers, competencies, and responsibilities. In the name of greater flexibility and efficiency, these quasi-private and highly auto-nomous organizations compete with and often supersede local and regional authorities as protagonists and managers of urban renewal. Moreover, the fragmentation of agencies and the multiplicity of institutions, both formal and informal, are often portrayed as positive signs, suggesting enabling institutional thickness, a considerable degree of local embeddedness, and significant social capacity-building. In addition, these institutional and regulatory configurations are celebrated as a new form of governing, signaling a better and more transparent articulation between government (state) and civil society. The "stakeholder" participation on which partnerships are based becomes a normative model that is presented as a democratic forum that permits open and nondistorted communication and action.

Yet the actual configuration of such project-based institutions reveals an extraordinary degree of selectivity. Although a varying choreography of state, private sector, and nongovernmental organization (NGO) participation is usually present (see Table 4 for a comparative over-view), these forms of urban governance show a significant deficit with respect to accountability, representation, and the presence of formal rules of inclusion or participation. Indeed, accountability channels are often gray, nonformalized, and nontransparent, frequently circumventing traditional democratic channels of accountability (eg to a repre-sentative elected body). As Table 4 suggests, the structures of representation of the participating partners are diffuse and unregu-lated. There are rarely formalized mechanisms of representation, and it is often difficult, if not impossible, to identify who represents what, who, and how. Finally—and most importantly—participation is rarely statutory, but operates through co-optation and invitation, usually by the key power brokers within the institutions. This invariably influences the regulatory environment, shapes the interventions, and produces a

Table 4: From Planning to Projects: Exceptionality Measures and Local Democracy

UDP	Territorial Fragmentation	Exceptionality Measures/ Accountability	Inclusion of Neighborhood Population in Decision-making	Institutional Complexity	Social Returns
Rotterdam Kop van Zuid	Attempt to construct physical link/bridge with central city	No exceptionality measures, but erosion of trust in political process. Elected borough councils	In later stage of project and in an indirect way	Highly complex. Independent State-Municipal Partnership for Kop van Zuid. Involvement of private investors. Complex of policies for urban regeneration and social renewal difficult to coordinate	Yes, but very limited and in adjacent neighborhoods. 1990s: stronger stress on social projects in adjacent neighborhoods
London The South Bank	Detachment from adjacent wards. Bridge with central London	One of the most democratic models in URSPIC sample	Yes	Not complex: from grassroots organization to partner-dominated planning	Yes
Berlin Adlershof	Detachment; filling gaps	Democratic control on public overspending	No	Partnership between the public sector (Berlin) and semiprivate developer. Little state/municipality coordination	Indirect
Brussels Espace Leopold (EU)	Detachment	Permissive attitude of authorities towards private developers	No	Proliferating number of private developers and of "informal" public/private relations	No (negative social returns)
Lisbon Expo 1998	Few or no links with oriental zones of Lisbon	Discretionary planning agency	No	No relations with overall planning in Lisbon; no links with other UDPs in Lisbon	Ambiguous

Table 4: Continued

UDP	Territorial Fragmentation	Exceptionality Measures/ Accountability	Inclusion of Neighborhood Population in Decision-making	Institutional Complexity	Social Returns
Copenhagen Oerestaden	Attempt to connect Oerestaden to the city	Linked to the Oeresund Regionalization Strategy. Democratic deficit in the initial phase	No. No linkages to community empowerment programs in deprived districts of Copenhagen	Very complex. Independent state-municipal partnership/ company. In reality, controlled by the Ministry of Finance in Denmark	Ambiguous. Perhaps social returns to the city as a whole and in the long run
Dublin Dublin Docklands Development Project with IFSC as flagship	Detachment in early phase— attempt to create new sector to the east of existing CBD. Attempt to build bridges and fill gaps in latest phase	Development Authority: responsible to national government. Local government and local communities initially excluded from decision-making. Now the most democratic model in the URSPIC sample	Initially No, but subsequently Yes: local neighborhood excluded in first phase but now directly represented on the Governing Council of the Urban Development Corporation (UDC).	Initially an exclusive, executive-style Quango with own complete planning powers. Changed to local social-partnership model of regeneration in 1997 with own planning powers coexisting alongside those of local government. Dual planning regime (local authority and UDC) now yielding complex development scenarios	Local: none in the initial stage of the project but local social programs now well developed and other initiatives coming on stream (including social housing); a major contributor through IFSC activities and tax revenues to gross domestic product and exchequer resources
Bilbao Abandoibarra	Filling gaps; building bridges	Combination of statutory planning instruments and discretionary	No	No, but innovations in managing structures and public-public partnerships for "concerted" urbanism	Ambiguous. Benefits for adjacent areas but no trickle-down effects

Table 4: Continued

UDP	Territorial Fragmentation	Exceptionality Measures/ Accountability	Inclusion of Neighborhood Population in Decision-making	Institutional Complexity	Social Returns
		management by a special purpose urban development company (mixed economy firm)			
Athens Olympic Village	Detachment; undermining social and economic coherence of surrounding localities	Central state level controls the redevelopment process and contains involvement of the local authorities and population	No. Virtually nothing has been done to involve neighborhood populations in the decision-making process	The development project depends on two governance/government systems, a "normal" and an "exceptional" one. The normal system deals with regular developmental issues, while the "exceptional" is the system that prepares and administers the Olympics	Ambiguous. The project's social returns include some potential gains in employment during the construction phase. The Olympic Village also includes a public housing scheme for the post-Olympic era. No central commitment exists that guarantees housing for local population
Vienna Donau-City	Filling gaps; bridge to central city	Only superficial democracy: hearings without power	Ambiguous	Proliferation of private developers and public authorities	Negative social returns: institutionalization of public-private partnerships, high-income groups as clientele of social democracy

Table 4: Continued

UDP	Territorial Fragmentation	Exceptionality Measures/ Accountability	Inclusion of Neighborhood Population in Decision-making	Institutional Complexity	Social Returns
Naples Centro Direzionale	The project has increased fragmentation in the city	The private developer had a dominating influence on national, regional, and local government	No: only through formal political representation in the city council. No provision of information and/or direct consultation	No coordination with other projects. No relations with planning in the city and metropolitan area	Improvements of public transport infrastructures
Birmingham CBD	Filling gaps	Urban machine politics. Costs hidden from council and public	No	The City Council diverted finance from their education and housing budgets through a private sector company that they own. This was used as matched funding for EU Regional Funds	Negligible for deprived communities in the immediate area
Lille Euralille	Filling gaps	Use of special structure for development company	Formally, consultation with citizens	Coordination with other UDPs only on paper	Some trickle-down effects. Improved public transport system

Key: Territorial fragmentation: functional and physical separation from adjoining poorer neighborhoods; building bridges with neighborhoods; filling gaps in abandoned, deindustrialized, or emptied-out zones. Exceptionality measures: special laws, special planning tools, new non- or quasigovernmental systems or agencies, avoidance of democratic control, and so on.

particular imagination of the urban in line with the demands, dreams, and aspirations of the included, while marginalized or otherwise excluded groups remain symptomatically absent. This process has become the dominant mode of institutional organization and suggests a shift from a system of representative urban government to one of stakeholder urban governance that is centered on newly established institutional arrangements. In our case studies (and this is especially clear in Berlin, Athens, Brussels, Lisbon, and Bilbao—see Table 4), a complex range of public, semipublic, and private actors shape an interactive system in which different, but allied, views and interests are "negotiated." Public-private partnerships epitomize the ideal of this cooperative and coordinated mode of "pluralistic" governance.

The emergence of a more fragmented and pluralistic mode of urban governance has also contributed to the redefinition of roles played by local authorities. In particular, it has served to reinforce the tendency towards a more proactive approach, letting local authorities act simultaneously as enablers, partners, and clients. At the same time, the new structures of governance also express the outcomes of an ongoing renegotiation between the different levels of government—local, regional, and national—regarding competencies and powers in the management of urban revitalization. These institutions are bunkered against popular participation and influence by local community groups and, indeed, against democratic control and accountability. The cases of London, Lisbon, Brussels, and Bilbao reveal an extraordinary degree of autonomy and impermeability of the managing organizations. Often, this organic autonomy has helped to reinforce the tendency to avoid a social and political debate over alternative paths and strategies.

Of course, as Table 4 illustrates, the level and degree of institutional reorganization of the systems and institutions of urban governance is highly variegated and context-dependent. Moreover, as the process of planning and implementation is confronted with social protest or critique, institutional and organizational forms adjust or transform in order to maintain legitimacy, social cohesion, and sufficient political support. Despite the great diversity of local, regional, and national changes in the forms of urban governance and despite their often very different agendas (ranging from merely economic growth-based initiatives to integrated projects aimed at improving social conditions in the city), the project-based nature of these interventions is accompanied by new institutional configurations, characterized by power geometries that differ from those of the traditional arenas of government. A veil of secrecy pre-empts criticism and discussion, and a highly selective leaking of information is justified on the grounds of commercial confidentiality and technical impartiality. Indeed, a conspicuous feature of these large-scale projects is the relatively low resistance and conflict they generate. With the exception of Dublin and Brussels, there has been no major "grassroots" contestation of the UDPs. In this sense, the role of local growth coalitions is critical in framing a discourse of renewal, innovation, achievement, and success.

From Planning to Projects

Large-scale urban projects are often presented as project-focused market-led initiatives, which have replaced statutory planning as the primary means of intervention in cities. Planning through urban "projects" has indeed emerged as the main strategy to stimulate economic growth and to "organize innovation," both organizationally and economically (see Table 4). Large-scale projects and events are perceived as strategic instruments aiming at reshaping the city. Against the crisis of the comprehensive *Plan*—the classic policy instrument of the Fordist age—the large, emblematic *Project* has emerged as a viable alternative, allegedly combining the advantages of flexibility and targeted actions with a tremendous symbolic capacity. Essentially fragmented, this form of intervention goes hand in hand with an eclectic planning style where attention to design, detail, morphology, and aesthetics is paramount. The emblematic *Project* captures a segment of the city and turns it into the symbol of the new restructured/ revitalized metropolis cast with a powerful image of innovation, creativity, and success. And yet, despite the rhetoric, the replacement of the *Plan* by the *Project* has not displaced planning from the urban arena. In fact, the case studies reveal that in most examples there is a strong strategic component and a significant role for planning. However, in the process, there has been a drastic reorganization of the planning and urban policy-making structures and a rise of new modes of intervention, planning goals, tools, and institutions.

Urban Projects and the Neoliberal Urban Order

Visioning the City as an Elite Playing Field

The UDPs included in our study have a variety of characteristics, but their sheer dimensions elevate them to central icons in the scripting of the image of the future of the cities in which they are located. Invariably, the main aspiration is to turn the city into a global competitive actor in the domain in which the elites feel it has some competitive advantage. Needless to say, the imagin(eer)ing of the city's future is directly articulated with the visions of those who are pivotal to the formulation, planning, and implementation of the project. Consequently, these projects have been and often still are arenas that reflect profound power struggles and position-taking of key economic, political, social, or cultural elites. The scripting of the project highlights and reflects the aspirations of a particular set of local, regional, and national—and sometimes also international—actors that shape, through the exercise of their socioeconomic, cultural, or political power, the development trajectories of each of the areas. As such, the UDPs can be considered as "elite playing fields," on which the stake is to shape an urban future in line with the aspirations of the most powerful segment(s) among the participants.

Clearly, the association of coalitions of elite players changes over time and from place to place, and alliance formation and break-up redefines development trajectories in important ways. Struggles for inclusion in or exclusion from the elite circles become pivotal in shaping wider process of social, cultural, political, and economic integration or exclusion. Each case study narrates the sociohistorical dynamics of alliances in the choreography of social-power struggles (for detailed accounts, see sources listed in acknowledgments). In conjunction with structural socioeconomic changes, these are instrumental in shaping the fortunes of urban environments, as they decide fundamental rights to housing, access to services, access to land and the like. Again, the role of the state, the system of governance, and the position of the citizens vis-à-vis these institutional forms will be central in determining the mechanisms of inclusion/exclusion that are shaped by the new urban development trajectories. Yet, the underlying motive is to reinvigorate a successful accumulation strategy and accompanying hegemony of vision that revolves around the requirement to turn the projects into viable—that is, profitable—economic ventures.

From a Social to a Spatial Definition of Development: Targeting Places rather than People

Almost all of the case-study projects pay at least rhetorical attention to social issues associated with the planning and implementation of the project. The assumed trickle-down mechanisms, occasionally accompanied by targeted policies to facilitate social inclusion processes (see Table 4), are considered of sufficient strength to permit a socially balanced and successful development. However, in contrast to the universal, inclusive, and blanket support policies that characterized Keynesian and welfare-state interventionism, economic regeneration is now primarily achieved via place-bound and spatially targeted redevelopment schemes. While national funding and incentives are diminishing, private development capital (of local, national, or extranational origin) is being mobilized for the implementation of territorially defined urban projects. In addition, given the reduction in universal welfare programs, the "territorial" approach or "targeted"-area approach have replaced universal support structures. Moreover, the slimming-down of national social redistribution is accompanied by policies that direct funds and attention to particular social groups, identified on the basis of their location, their place, and the characteristics of their living environment. Similarly, the EU's urban social programs take on an outspoken, spatially focused character.

In sum, there has been a shift from universalist to spatially targeted and place-focused approaches in the 1990s. Targeting policies/interventions to geographically circumscribed areas and to economically dynamic or promising activities is presented as a path to remedy socioeconomic exclusion. Indeed, in the policy discourse, UDPs are presented as instruments that can also help to overcome social exclusion. The official rhetorical attention to social issues is mobilized politically to legitimize projects, while the underlying and sometimes explicit objective is different. The assumption of trickle-down, however, does not hold true in a context characterized by an absence of regulatory (labor, financial, and income) standards or income redistribution systems at the national or EU level. This accounts, of course, for the significant differences in sociospatial inequality between, for example, Denmark, with its long social-democratic tradition, and the UK, with its much more liberal-conservative legacy. The targeting of spaces for "development" permits recasting particular social groups as problematic, excluded, marginalized, and nonintegrated. Consequently —so the official argument goes—strategies of integration and inclusion should be pursued by means of territorial, place-based policies, rather than through national or European-wide socioeconomic measures, redistribution, and political-economic strategies. From the perspective of this NUP, it is places that need to be integrated, not citizens; it is places that need redevelopment, not people that require jobs and income. Of course, the above is not a plea for dismissing community capacity-building and local-level initiatives, but they need to be framed in more general redistribution and regulatory polices at higher-scale levels—those of the national state and, more importantly, the European Union.

Interurban Competition for National or European Funds

As most of the UDPs are nationally or EU (co-)funded (see Table 3), municipalities or other forms of local governance compete for targeted funding. In general, the concentration of public investments in these large-scale project locations involves redistributing resources away from other uses and areas. In addition, funds are allocated on a project-formulation basis, not on the basis of social needs or considerations of fostering the social economy. Either explicitly or implicitly, the competitive tendering process by national or international organizations favors projects that have a sound institutional and organizational basis capable of engaging in the complex tasks of project formulation, lobbying, negotiation, and implementation. This requires not only a set of sophisticated skills, but also significant financial resources, as well as easy access to the centers of power. All of this is usually not available to the weaker social groups and areas in the city, which are consequently falling behind and are dependent on ad hoc measures imposed from above. Moreover, given the need to foster alliances between often-rival economic and political elite groups to create the necessary hegemony of vision to compete successfully for state support and private investment, the development activities are often masked in a web of secrecy and hidden behind a screen of commercial confidentiality.

In the context of more targeted interventions and reduced universal social support, which is increasingly organized and conducted by and through elite coalition formation, public resources are drained from universal programs to targeted territorial projects geared at supporting a particular social configuration—a process that itself harbors exclusionary mechanisms. The misty organizational structures in Brussels, the exclusive elite coalitions of Birmingham, and the shifting alliances in Copenhagen and Naples illustrate the variety of processes through which this takes place.

Authoritarian Management, Exclusion, and Client Formation

The new systems of urban governance—the quasigovernmental institutional framework based upon forging synergies between the public sector and the elite fractions of civil society—also justify the adoption of discretionary forms of management. Thus, the way the process develops creates the conditions for the establishment of centralized and more autocratic management, which privileges direct appointments. Thus, the role of lobbies, family ties, business connections, and forms of "clientelism" become dominant. These forms of coalition-formation at the level of project formulation and implementation accentuate a growing gap between actual governance and civil society, intensify processes of political exclusion, and promote a dual society in terms of a coalition of public/private interests on the one hand and a growing group of disenfranchised on the other. While the above suggests that growth machines, elite coalitions, and networks of power are centrally important in shaping development trajectories, it is evident from our case studies that different growth machines are associated with different interests and lead to different mechanisms of inclusion/exclusion.

Nonetheless, the "coalitions" of public and semipublic actors invariably produce an exclusive group involved in a common discourse on the progress of the project, a discourse that is not easily opened to public scrutiny or that would invite or permit dissidence. Important decisions and arrangements are made by steering committees, boards of directors of operating companies, nonaccountable quasigovernmental organizations, and the like, and are often kept away from public scrutiny. Outsiders are usually not tolerated. There is, at best, only a highly formalized form of public participation that maintains key power in the hands of the existing elite structure and even prevents newly emerging elites (such as, for example, immigrant entrepreneurs and an emerging group of sociocultural elites in the transnational communities in cities like Brussels or Vienna) to enter the established networks of governance and dominant elite coalitions. These coalitions create a public discourse on the importance of the project and define it as a particular milestone in the shaping of the future of the city, and their interventions are presented as essential to maintaining a viable position in the interurban competition at a pan-European or global scale.

The reactions of the local state to exogenous and endogenous pressures manifest in the establishment of these new forms of urban governance (public-private partnerships, development co-operations, new administrative structures, and new political forums) that circumvent, bypass, ignore, or marginalize certain social groups. The national state itself is often instrumental in shaping and organizing such exclusive growth coalitions and in providing the extraordinary regulatory environment in which they can operate outside a system of public accountability. In some cases, such as Copenhagen, Brussels, and Vienna, such growth-coalitions reproduce or re-enforce existing but threatened corporatist forms of governance. Informal networks of a relatively small number of individuals occupying key positions in public administration, business, or design/architecture form a new field of power. In the tendering of large-scale projects, these networks are of crucial importance. Needless to say, the projects are therefore closely associated with the interests of the particular coalition sets (and their clients); they are usually self-referential, closed circles that consolidate their power while preventing access to others.

UDPs, Speculation, and the Production of Land Rent

As producers of urban space, UDPs are inherently speculative and hence highly risky, in the sense that their financial and economic viability depends on the future realization of the produced increased urban rents. Of course, the latter depend not only on the particular characteristics of the project or the vitality of the local economy, but also on national and international economic conditions. In addition, such projects provide opportunities to extract from the state (at a local, national, or EU level), in addition to its direct contributions, further resources in terms of public investment for infrastructures, services, and buildings. Most of the project's development costs are supposed to be met from the sale or renting of land or buildings— the value of which has been jacked up through state support, re-regulation, zoning changes, infrastructure investment, and the like.

All this suggests that it is financially very attractive for real-estate developers to concentrate on developing projects for the more well-to-do customers, for housing as well as for businesses. In fact, the financial viability of market-driven urban revitalization projects is, of course, invariably predicated upon closing existing rent gaps by means of the production of a new built environment that is at least potentially capable of generating high income. The uncertain and, hence, intrinsically speculative character of the production of new land rent points towards the key role of the state as the preferred interlocutor for carrying the financial risks associated with such real-estate-based urban restructuring (see also the chapters by Smith and Weber this volume).

Whether successful or not, the dependence on rent returns for the feasibility of UDPs invariably targets high-income segments of the population or potentially high-productivity-based economic activities and makes the success of the project dependent on the dynamics of the real-estate sector (see Table 5). This does not contribute to alleviating the process of social segmentation and exclusion and often leads to the creation of islands of wealth in an impoverished environment, resulting in the city becoming a patchwork of socioeconomically highly diversified and more mutually exclusive areas. To the extent that low-cost or social housing is included in the project, the lower revenue from such targeted housing policy undermines the financial feasibility of the project and requires, in turn, considerable state support or subsidies. Table 5 summarizes the relationships between real-estate development, the production of high rental returns, and a project's financing structure. Moreover, given the real-estate-based nature of these projects, the public funding is, through private rent appropriation, transferred to the private sector. Consequently, there is a flow of capital from the public to the private sector via the built environment, often without mediation by means of socially targeted policies or instruments.

The City as Patchwork

Given the often radically new socioeconomic functions associated with UDPs, a process of transfer and of dislocation of jobs inevitably takes place. Spatial labor markets become out of joint or are mismatched. Targeted labor-market policies might remedy some of this disjuncture, but the sheer scale of labor-market restructuring often implies prolonged stress on the labor market combined with painful processes of adaptation and, frequently, a growing separation between remaining local communities and the incoming new workforce. This separation is often accentuated through now-generalized processes of deregulation of labor markets at national and EU levels. This leads to a double-edged dualization of labor markets. Increasingly, dual or

Table 5: Relationship between Dynamics in the Real-Estate Market and UDP
Development: Nine Cases

Project	Real-Estate Market, the Production of Rent, and the Development of the UDP
Berlin Adlershof	The reunification of Germany was decisive for the development of Berlin's real-estate market and triggered a sudden rush of initiatives from international and national investors and developers. This was reinforced by a strong competition for attractive sites. Today, the Berlin real-estate market shows increasing supply-side reserves and demand structures that fall short of expectation. These developments have had a major impact on the progress and pace of the project implementation in Adlershof. Here, a high volume of office and housing sites has been planned without considering the decreasing demand. Due to the restraint of private investors, project development has slowed down in Adlershof.
Bilbao Abandoibarra	As in most other cities throughout Spain, since the mid-1980s, the real-estate market in Bilbao has experienced an extraordinary boom. During the 90s, housing prices in the city continued to rise, although the rate of growth decreased in the last third of the decade. Real-estate prices in Abandoibarra both benefited from and contributed to this boom. In the less than four years that separated the beginning of redevelopment works and the marketing of the first housing land slots, land prices in Abandoibarra more than doubled (2.3 times). Real-estate price increases have spread throughout the city, but they tend to be proportionally higher in Abandoibarra's adjoining neighborhoods. And, while it cannot be said that land price increases in the city are exclusively related to Abandoibarra's redevelopment, it is nonetheless certain that this scheme is contributing significantly to this trend as well as to the alteration of housing prices differentials among different neighborhoods across the city.
Brussels Leopold Quarter	Due to the continuous demand for additional office space in the Leopold Quarter—a demand led by the EU institutions, but also by both national and international banking and insurance sectors—rental values have systematically increased over the past decades. Rents in the Leopold Quarter are now amongst the highest in the country (up to 200 Euro per m²). The increasing demand for office space has also generated speculative activities in the area: remaining residential blocks are systematically bought by property developers and eventually demolished and replaced with offices, regardless of land-use planning regulations. Other residential pockets have been upgraded and made available for wealthy (international) residents, or are now de facto (and illegally) used as offices for smaller organizations (for example, lobby groups and law firms). Globally operating real-estate agents (such as Jones Lang Wootton and Healey & Baker) have come to dominate the Leopold Quarter market, while construction and property development remains mainly in Belgian (and French) hands.

Table 5: Continued

Project	Real-Estate Market, the Production of Rent, and the Development of the UDP
Copenhagen Orestaden	In general, the prices in the housing market skyrocketed during the second half of the 1990s and the social geography within the city has become more polarized. There still exists an important social-housing sector, but the role of this sector has gradually declined, because housing construction subsidized by the municipality and the state has almost stopped since the beginning of the nineties. The municipal housing policy has increasingly been used as a tool to regulate the tax base of Copenhagen, favoring the middle classes. The UDP follows this trend.
Lille Euralille	Euralille and other UDPs in the Lille agglomeration did not lead to skyrocketing increases of land and housing prices. However, inside the agglomeration, real-estate market dynamics have produced a displacement of lower-middle-class and working-class population to "cheaper" areas. Gentrification projects in particular (first Vieux Lille, then Euralille, Wazemmes, and Moulins) with more offices, exquisite services, and middle- to upper-class housing estates, led to local price rises, driving deprived population groups to other neighborhoods, especially to the south of Lille or even outside the agglomeration. The UDP has contributed to this growing spatial differentiation of real-estate and rental values.
Vienna Donau-City	Rents skyrocketed in the second half of the 1980s and have been stagnating since then. This can be explained by a contradictory movement. On the one hand, there still exists an important public-housing sector. Housing construction subsidized by the municipality was intensive until 1996, and restrictive rent laws were applied until 1982. On the other hand, liberal regulation is advancing: subsidies for construction of housing have been dramatically reduced over the last years. Furthermore, publicly subsidized housing is increasingly oriented towards the upper middle classes. The UDP is a paradigmatic case illustrating these changes.
Naples Centro Direzionale	During the 1980s, prices in the real-estate market grew dramatically to reach record levels in 1991 and 1992, particularly in selected central areas. They subsequently declined almost as fast as they had previously risen, continuing to fall until 1997, when the first signs of recovery appeared and prices stabilized or began to increase again. Apartments in the Centro Direzionale di Napoli (CDN) became available at the peak of the market price for prime location units and thus could be expected to yield quite significant returns. The developer, however, sold 90% of the residential units to a state-run pension fund for the employees of public companies and guaranteed his return. By law, only families working for state agencies are entitled to rent those apartments, and rental prices are set lower than the market price according to the rules of the

Table 5: Continued

Project	Real-Estate Market, the Production of Rent, and the Development of the UDP
	1978 Fair Rent Act. This decision removed these units from the sale and rental markets, creating a separate segment that is somewhat insulated from market dynamics. The project had also a depressing effect on the value of building land for other office projects in the city.
Dublin Docklands Development Project (with IFSC as flagship)	Property demand in both the housing and office markets, both within the UDP site and in the surrounding neighborhoods, has grown rapidly in the 1990s and land prices in the area have soared due to the presence of the IFSC. With companies queuing to get into the successful IFSC site as the economy boomed in the 1990s, the intense demand for office space squeezed other real-estate markets, most notably the provision of social and affordable housing within and around the UDP. Average house prices tripled between 1989 to 1999, while the provision of social housing evaporated due to the post-1986 retrenchment of public-sector welfare spending. The housing situation is particularly acute in the docklands UDP and neighboring areas. Local residents cannot compete with investors or the predominantly young professionals who purchase or rent the limited supply of private residential units available in the area. The result has been gentrification of the initial UDC site and the exclusion from the life of the area, through the property market, of many of the latest generation of the indigenous population.
London South Bank	The real-estate market on the South Bank is subject to contradictory tendencies. On the one hand, the South Bank is one of the most expensive spots in central London because of its central location opposite the City and Westminster. In terms of real-estate prices, it is exceeded only by those two areas. On the other hand, the South Bank's community development group, Coin Street Community Builders, owns 6.5 acres of land on the South Bank, which is designated for the construction of co-operative housing schemes and public spaces. This has a certain downward effect on real-estate prices. However, the recently opened new underground line (the Jubilee Line) has significantly improved the South Bank's connections with the rest of Central London and will certainly have an upward effect on real-estate prices. Furthermore, the successful "reimagineering" efforts through public space improvements and consistent place marketing, together with the opening of major nearby attractions such as the new Tate Gallery, will also have an effect on real-estate prices. Meanwhile, the housing market remains strongly dominated by Local Authority housing (38%), housing co-operatives (28%), and semipublic institutions (17%). Only 15% of residents live in privately owned houses and 2% in privately rented flats. Another estimated 2000 adults live in hostels, on the streets, and in other nonpermanent accommodation (estimates for 1994).

segmented labor markets are seen, with a group of highly paid and skilled executives on the one hand and large groups of less secure—often informal—workers on the other, and many other categories in between. The segmentation of labor markets, which is facilitated by the national deregulation of labor-market rules and other changes in the national regulatory frameworks, becomes cemented in and expressed by the socioeconomic composition of the UDPs. The inclusion of the existing labor pool proves difficult or impossible, while retraining and targeted labor-market entry policies tend not to be very successful, despite the prolonged support for such programs.

This socioeconomic restructuring, combined with a mosaic of newly constructed built environments with their associated increased rents, produces urban islands, a patchwork of discrete spaces with increasingly sharp boundaries (gated business centers, leisure, or community spaces). This is reinforced through a combination of physical, social, and cultural boundary formation processes. The overall result is the consolidation of a fragmented city, which accompanies the reorganization of the sociospatial fabric of the urban agglomeration (see also MacLeod this volume). In some cases, this mosaic takes the form of suburbanization of poverty, while internal differentiation accentuates sociospatial differentiation and polarization, a process that often takes outspoken racialized forms (notably in Brussels, Berlin, Rotterdam, and Vienna).

Conclusion: Neoliberal Urbanism and Democratic Deficit

Urban regeneration and development policies in the European city, in the context of national and EU-wide tendencies towards the implementation of neoliberal socioeconomic policies, brought about critical shifts in domains and levels of intervention and in the composition and characteristics of actors and agents, institutional structures, and policy tools. Over the last decade and a half, urban regeneration policy has become an increasingly central component of urban policy. For the most part, urban regeneration schemes based on large-scale UDPs have emerged as a response to urban restructuring processes associated with the transformation of production and demand conditions locally, nationally, and globally; they generally combine physical upgrading with socioeconomic development objectives. In particular, such projects have become an integral part of neoliberal policies to replace more traditional redistribution-driven approaches. The search for growth and competitive redevelopment has become the leading objective of the NUP in an attempt to reassert the position of cities in the emerging global economy. Enhancing the competitive advantage of cities is seen as largely dependent on improving and adapting the built environment to the accumulation strategies of a city's key elites. Therefore, physical reconstruction and economic recovery tend to go hand in hand and, very often, are perceived as quasi-simultaneous processes: megaprojects are viewed as providing a solid foundation for fostering future growth and functional transformation. At the same time, urban revitalization is projected beyond the cities' limits and linked to regional recovery and internationalization strategies.

How do the various UDPs reflect this NUP? Figure 1 already summarized various critical dimensions of this policy. Most UDPs have caused increased physical and social fragmentation in the city. Notable exceptions include Kop van Zuid in Rotterdam, which established a physical-functional—but not a social—"bridge" with the rest of the city, and Oerestaden in Copenhagen, which has—after prolonged protest—recovered some housing and service functions that would otherwise have been lost. The other projects have primarily filled gaps for the (higher) middle-class real-estate and consumption-good markets, but not for other, usually poorer and/or immigrant sections of the urban population. While economic gaps have been "plugged," greater social disparities and sociospatial fragmentation have been produced.

A central issue involved in urban regeneration policies is the relation of UDPs to existing planning instruments and regulations. While these projects are generally inserted into existing statutory planning guidelines, the initial conception, design, and implementation lies at the margins of formal planning structures. The framework of "exceptionality" associated with these initiatives favors a more autonomous, if not autocratic, dynamic marked by special plans and projects that relegate statutory norms and procedures to a secondary and subordinated place. Many local authorities and national governments justify the exceptionality of a UDP on the basis of different factors: scale, the emblematic character of the operation, timing pressures, the need for greater flexibility, efficiency criteria, and the like. "Exceptionality" is a fundamental feature of the new urban policy, based on the primacy of project-based initiatives over regulatory plans and procedures. These changes involve, among other things, the emergence of new policy tools, actors, and institutions, and they have important consequences for urban policy-making in general and for local democracy in particular. These projects exemplify like no other the trends towards a new local mode of regulation of urban (re)development and management shaped by the pressures of competitive restructuring and changing social and economic priorities, as well as by major political and ideological shifts. Indeed, the emergence of the NUP rests significantly on the establishment of new forms of intervention at the local level that, to a large extent, constitute a rupture with traditional forms. Entrepreneurialism is about the public sector running cities in a more businesslike manner, in which institutions of local governance operate like the private sector or are replaced by private-sector-based systems. Indeed, the NUP is closely associated with fundamental shifts from traditional government structures to a more diffused, fragmented, and flexible mode of governance. The combination of different spatial and administrative scales in urban policy-making and the increasing fragmentation of competencies and responsibilities is one of its most striking aspects. In most cities, the full dimension of urban regeneration cannot be adequately apprehended without reference to the multiplicity of agents, the articulation of spatial scales at which they operate, and the fragmentation of agency responsibility within the urban arena. In some cases, this trend seems to be linked to a shift from hierarchical relationships (in terms of the traditional territorial hierarchy of statutory planning procedures) to a more collaborative and stakeholder-based, but often socially highly exclusive, scheme in which partnerships between and networks of a variety of elites play a key role. However, at the same time, fragmentation and diversity are also accompanied by tendencies towards the exclusion of certain groups and collectives from participating in the decision-making process. A democratic deficit emerges as a central element of this strategic approach.

The fragmentation of the mode of governance redefines the role and position of local authorities. Indeed, in the name of greater flexibility and efficiency, these new institutions compete with and often supplant local and regional authorities as protagonists and managers of urban renewal. In fact, the new governance structures express the outcomes of an ongoing renegotiation between the different levels of government—local, regional, national, and European—and between public and private actors over competencies, decision-making powers, and funding. The establishment of these new structures frequently involves massive redistribution of policy-making powers, competencies, and responsibilities away from local governments to often highly exclusive partnership agencies, a process that can be described as the "privatization of urban governance."

The fragmented character of many of the UDPs—which are often self-contained, isolated, and disconnected from the general dynamics of the city—contrasts sharply with the strong emphasis on coordinated action of different actors, the encouragement of partnerships, and the building of networks and support coalitions. These are presented as providing a potentially superior form of urban management, more flexible and efficient, and thus better adapted to the competitive trends of global urban change. The trend towards a more flexible and network-oriented approach is often perceived as a validation of "bottom-up," less hierarchical, and more participatory dynamics. However, participation is often limited to selected professionals—architects, planners, economists, engineers, and so on—who have become increasingly influential, while the nonprofessional sector and less powerful social groups are largely excluded.

In the same way, the shift from centralist, formalized, bureaucratized, hierarchical, top-down planning approaches to decentralized, more horizontal, informal, flexibilized, bottom-up, and network planning approaches has gone hand in hand with increasing inequality in access to decision-making. The role of experts is strengthened at the expense of a diminishing role of the public in general and of traditional organized groups in particular, with a consequent loss of democratic accountability. Yet these new forms of governance are often legitimized on the basis of their superior ability to offer a more inclusive, non-hierarchical, and participatory approach to planning. However, the realities of a network based on the primacy of the expert and dominated by the fusion of technical, economic, and political elites suggest a selective exclusion of major sections of civil society in terms of access to decision-making processes.

As is succinctly summarized in the Viennese case study, "the advantage of these personalized networks is mutual trust and high adaptability; its disadvantage is a decrease of public accountability, a weakening of civil society and an erosion of the existing parliamentary democracy." In those cases in which neighborhood movements reacted to the initial lack of local democracy (Rotterdam, Dublin), participation had to be partly restored, and neighborhood demands, as well as concerns about social issues, climbed a few notches up the policy priority list. Nevertheless, the limited and spatially targeted interventions associated with project-based urban restructuring policies prevent these movements from transcending the localized issues associated with a project's implementation and from translating these social demands into more generalized policy models at higher spatial scales. This is arguably the most significant implication of the NUP. The downscaling of urban policies to place-specific interventions in a context in which traditional redistributional policies are being reduced at higher-scale levels forces social movements to operate through localized actions. This, in turn, militates against the urgent need to translate these place-specific actions and demands into more general social and economic programs articulated at the national, EU, or international scale.

Acknowledgments and References

The analysis presented in this paper draws upon the results of a thirty-month research project on Urban Redevelopment and Social Polarization in the City (URPIC). The support of the European Union's IVth Framework Program is gratefully acknowledged.

The project was co-ordinated by Frank Moulaert, Arantxa Rodriguez, and Erik Swyngedouw. Although the present paper cannot provide full empirical details on each of the thirteen city cases, detailed case-study results have been published in the following journals: *Journal of European Urban and Regional Studies* 8(2) 2001, *Geographische Zeitung* 89 (2 and 3), 2002, *Rassegna Italiana di Sociologia* 41(4), 2001, and *Ciudad y Territorio—Estudioas Territoriales (CiTET)*, November 2001 and forthcoming 2002.

Case studies will also be published in *Urbanising Globalisation*, by F Moulaert, A Rodriguez, and E Swyngedouw, Oxford University Press, forthcoming 2002.

The project reports, images and further details on each of the projects can be found on the World-Wide Web at http://www.ifresi.univ-lille1.fr (select Programmes de Recherche and then select URSPIC).

Many of the insights reported in this paper come from a large number of participants in this project. We would like to acknowledge our debt in writing this contribution to all those who worked with us on this project. Their fieldwork, data collection, interviews, and surveys provided the foundation and material and many of the insights for this project, and their thoughts and writings were used extensively in the preparation of this paper. We are very much indebted to: Serena Vicari and Lucia Cavoli (Naples), Pavlos Delladetsimas (Athens), João Cabral (Lisbon), Elodie Salin and Thomas Werquin (Lille), Elena Martinez (Bilbao), Guy Baeten (London and Brussels), Louis Albrechts (Brussels), Hartmut Hauserman and Katja Simons (Berlin), Andreas Novy, Vanessa Redak, and Johachim Becker (Vienna), John Anderson (Copenhagen), Brendan Bartley and Kasey Treadwell Shine (Dublin), Alan Middleton and Patrick Loftman (Birmingham), and Gerard Oude Engberink and Frank Miedema (Rotterdam).

We are also grateful to Neil Brenner and to Nik Theodore for their support, editorial suggestions, and patience, and to the referees for their comments and suggestions. Of course, none of them should be held accountable for the contents of this paper.

Endnotes

[1] This paper is based on a large number of research reports from the URSPIC project, written by more than twenty-five academics working on each of the thirteen cases. The paper presented here digests material that comes from all of these papers, and parts were actually written by one or another of our collaborators. References in the original research documents often come from our partners' national sources (Danish, Greek, Italian, Spanish, German, and so forth). We considered including an exhaustive transnational literature list, but this would have been unacceptably long and not all that useful for many people. Alternatively, we could have opted for inserting just a standard list of mainly Anglo-Saxon references, but this would not do justice to the wide variety of national insights on which we drew. Therefore, we chose not to have references at all, but decided instead on the following. The names of the individuals involved in the project are listed in the acknowledgments. All project reports, individual case studies, references, images, and other materials are available on the World-Wide Web

at http://www.ifresi.univ-lille1.fr; select Programmes de Recherche and then select URSPIC). In addition, five special journal issues (of which two are in English) and a forthcoming book (to be published in 2002) give detailed information on various aspects of the research for many of the case studies (see Acknowledgments section for details). In fact, all of the case studies are covered in one way or another in these publications. People interested in particular details of and further information on any of the case study projects and cities can consult either the Web site or these publications.

Erik Swyngedouw is University Reader in Economic Geography in the School of Geography and the Environment, Oxford University, and Fellow of St Peter's College. He is also an Associate Fellow of the Environmental Change Institute. His research has focused on the political-economy of the capitalist space-economy, on urban change and globalization, and on the political-ecological of water. He is coeditor of a forthcoming book on *Urbanising Globalisation* (Oxford University Press, 2002) and another on *Participatory Governance in the European Union* (Leske & Budrich, forthcoming). He has coedited (with Andy Merrifield) *The Urbanisation of Injustice* (London, Lawrence and Wishart; New York, New York University Press, 1996).

Frank Moulaert is a Professor of Economics at the University of Lille I, France. He is head of the European PhD program in Industrial and Labour Economics and Regional Development and coordinates two research projects under the EU's Framework V program. His latest book (together with A Rodriguez and others) is *Globalization and Integrated Area Development in European Cities* (Oxford University Press, 2000). His current research focuses mainly on local development and social innovation.

Arantxa Rodriguez, Associate Professor at the Faculty of Economics of the University of the Basque Country (Bilbao-Spain), focuses her research on the dynamics of socioeconomic restructuring and spatial development planning in the Basque Country. Since the mid-1980s, she has been directly involved in the production of several urban plans in that area. She has also carried out research on the articulation between physical, functional, and economic planning and local economic development strategies. She is coauthor, with Frank Moulaert, of *Globalization and Integrated Area Development in European Cities* (Oxford University Press, 2000). Her other publications include "Nuevas políticas y nuevos instrumentos para la revitalización metropolitana," in *Encuentros de Desarrollo Local y Empleo* (Coruña, 1998), and "Planning the Revitalisation of an Old Industrial City: Urban Policy Innovations in Metropolitan Bilbao," in *Local Economic Development in Europe and the Americas* (edited by C Demazière and P Wilson, Mansell, 1996).

Chapter 10
"Common-Sense" Neoliberalism: Progressive Conservative Urbanism in Toronto, Canada

Roger Keil

This paper argues that urban neoliberalism can best be understood as a contradictory re-regulation of urban everyday life. Based on an analysis of neoliberalism as a new political economy and as a new set of technologies of power, the paper argues that the urban everyday is the site and product of the neoliberal transformation. Governments and corporations play a key role in redefining the conditions of everyday life through neoliberal policies and business practices. Part of this reorientation of everydayness, however, involves new forms of resistance and opposition, which include the kernel of a possible alternative urbanism. The epochal shift from a Keynesian-Fordist-welfarist to a post-Fordist-workfarist society is reflected in a marked restructuring of everyday life. The shift changes the socioeconomic conditions in cities. It also includes a reorientation of identities, social conflicts, and ideologies towards a more explicitly culturalist differentiation. Social difference does not disappear, but actually becomes more pronounced; however, it gets articulated in or obscured by cultural terms of reference.

The paper looks specifically at Toronto, Ontario, as a case study. An analysis of the explicitly neoliberal politics of the province's Progressive Conservative (Tory) government under Mike Harris, first elected in 1995, demonstrates the pervasive re-regulation of everyday life affecting a wide variety of people in Toronto and elsewhere. Much of this process is directly attributable to provincial policies, a consequence of Canada's constitutional system, which does not give municipalities autonomy but makes them "creatures of provinces." However, the paper also argues that Toronto's elites have aided and abetted the provincial "Common-Sense" Revolution through neoliberal policies and actions on their own. The paper concludes by outlining the emergence of new instances of resistance to the politics of hegemony and catastrophe of urban neoliberalism.

The Short Life and Times of Urban Neoliberalism

On 21 September 2001, a by-election for the provincial legislature of Ontario was held in Toronto. The vote in an East Toronto riding[1] carried a New Democratic Party (NDP) politician, a former mayor of the borough of East York named Michael Prue, to a decisive victory over two high-profile contenders from the Liberal and Progressive Conservative (Tory) parties. Prue, a Social Democrat, received 50% of the popular vote; the candidate of the governing Tory party, Mac Penney, won only 10% and was even humiliated by the Liberal candidate, who garnered 36%. Prue's electoral success went almost unnoticed in the midst of the world crisis around him, yet the following day this local event triggered television talk shows to contemplate the sudden demise of neoliberalism and neoconservatism (at least in Ontario and Toronto). The neoliberal period—and the Tory Mike Harris government, which had effected massive incisions in the traditionally more welfarist Ontario state—looked as if it was nearing its end. In his acceptance speech, Prue reminded Premier Harris that he had promised to "go after" him three years earlier, when the provincial government amalgamated Prue's hometown, East York, with the new City of Toronto. This, he thought, he would now be able to accomplish in the legislature.

However, three weeks later, on 16 October 2001, Harris resigned. While he was giving a press conference to explain his decision, thousands of demonstrators assembled in downtown Toronto to protest his government's policies. Planned for months and orchestrated under the leadership of the Ontario Coalition Against Poverty (OCAP), this demonstration aimed to "shut down" the financial district of Toronto as part of a series of province-wide actions of economic disruption. While some demonstrators claimed—tongue in cheek—that it was their action that brought down the mighty premier of the province, the two events were not causally connected. What was remarkable, though—and widely commented upon by local observers—was the fact that throughout his premiership, Harris had been a symbol of neoliberal societal restructuring, which drew huge protests at every stage of his government's "Common-Sense Revolution" (CSR), so called after the election platform by the same name during the 1995 campaign. This paper traces some of the steps of this "revolution" as they pertain to the urban scale, and particularly to Toronto, Canada's largest city and the capital of Ontario.

The theoretical argument put forth in this paper is that urban neoliberalism can be read as a specific intersection of global—in the sense of both general and worldwide—shifts in the structure of capitalist economies and states with the everyday life of people in cities. As explained in more detail below, this is an extension of Lefebvre's notion of the "urban" as the level of mediation between the global (general) and the personal (lived space) (Kipfer 1998:177). As a state strategy, urban neoliberalism creates new conditions for the accumulation of capital; yet it also inevitably creates more fissures in which urban resistance and social change can take root. For the purposes of this paper, it is assumed that there are two partially contradictory but intertwined modes of explanation, which are useful to consult when it comes to the workings and effects of neoliberalism. One is the neo-Marxist political economy approach, especially its regulationist tradition; the other is a certain Foucauldian strand in social theory

which is concerned with the emergence and spread of new technologies of power, particularly in the urban context. While both of
these approaches are insightful and contain particular sorts of merits,
it will be argued here that they may be usefully complemented by an
examination of transformations of urban everyday life.

This theoretical argument is explicated using a current case study:
the neoliberalization of the urban through deliberate policy decisions
of a programmatically interventionist but substantively antistatist,
neoliberal government that has been present in Ontario since 1995.
This government's actions will be interpreted as creating a policy
context though which the everyday lives of Ontarians, and specifically
Torontonians, have been fundamentally changed in many ways.

The Political Economy of Urban Neoliberalism

The advance of neoliberalism has been an often coordinated,
politically directed, rarely self-propelled, often violent process of
change in the global architecture of capitalist production, trade,
and consumption. As many would agree, after a quarter century of
neoliberal advance, this phenomenon is now historical in at least two
ways: it refers to a more or less coherently defined *era* of recent
developments in world capitalism; and in debates among critical social
theorists and activists, it is a *keyword* with a history of its own.

In the first sense, neoliberalism denotes that period of time that
started roughly with the governments of Ronald Reagan and
Margaret Thatcher. This period "swept aside" previously held doubts
about the value and power of markets and introduced "its mantras of
private and personal responsibility and initiative, deregulation, privatization, liberalization of markets, free trade, downsizing of government, draconian cutbacks in the welfare state and its protections"
(Harvey 2000:176). The progression and success of neoliberalism as a
set of policies, ideologies, and what Larner (2000) calls "governmentalities" (see below) has been summarily associated with the
emergence of a new regime of capitalist accumulation variably called
post-Fordist, neo-Fordist, neo-Taylorist, flexible, liberal productivist,
and so on (Jessop 2001a, b; Lipietz 2001). Among political economists,
this shift has led to a general debate about the value of periodizing
(Albritton et al 2001; Candeias and Deppe 2001; Hirsch 2001) and to
a specific debate about the boundaries of periods (Amin 1994; Jessop
1993; Peck and Tickell 1994). In addition, the short history of neoliberalism has already produced internal periodizations. For example,
Peck and Tickell have introduced the useful distinction between "roll-
back neoliberalism"—the dismantling and deregulation of post-WWII
Fordist-Keynesian modes of regulation—and "roll-out neoliberalism"
—the active creation of new institutions and regulations of the state
and society (Peck and Tickell this volume).

Simultaneously, neoliberalism—together with its "cousin" globalization—has become a major reference point for social theory overall. For instance, in attempting to pinpoint the special character-istics of our current period, theorists have looked at the relationship of neoliberalism as a political project with "a new technological revo-lution (the 'information revolution'); new managerial achievements; and the new hegemony of finance" (Duménil and Lévy 2001:141; see also Castells 1997). Some debate has taken place on the renewed opening of cleavages, after Fordism, between the "moments of markctization and privatization on the one hand, and the moment of *Vergesellschaftung* [societalization] on the other" (van dcr Pijl 2001:2). As scholars have assessed the impact of neoliberalism on human societies worldwide, they have pointed to two imbricated yet counter-posed dynamics: the continued and accelerated destruction of human and natural communities and the nearly unlimited—and seemingly unopposed—potential for capitalism to unleash its disciplinary regime onto societies on the one hand (Hardt and Negri 2000; van der Pijl 2001), and the renewed capacity of subversive communities to resist the total victory of capitalism at "the end of history" (Bourdieu 1998; Hardt and Negri 2000; Harvey 2000; Klein 2000; Panitch 2001) on the other.

In all of this, debates on *space* have figured prominently in geography and urban studies in particular and the social sciences in general (among the most prominent and influential voices have been David Harvey, Ed Soja, and Neil Smith). After much neglect in the traditional nongeographic disciplines, space has now become a general point of interest in the social sciences, particularly in theories of regulation (Alnasseri et al 2001). More recently, following influential work by Lefebvre (1991), authors in the English-speaking world have moved from a widespread debate on the social production of space to a new interest in *scale* (Brenner 1999; MacLeod and Goodwin 1999a, b; Marston 2000; Smith 1992; Swyngedouw 1997). One aspect of this larger theoretical and empirical debate has been the specific interrelationships of urbanization and neoliberalization or, more specifically, globalization.

Taking Brenner and Theodore's postulations in this volume on the "urbanization of neoliberalism" as a point of departure, this paper looks at a specific case of neoliberal urbanization in Toronto, Canada. Two specific points relevant to my discussion below deserve mention-ing. First, I agree with Brenner and Theodore (and others) that neoliberalism comes in many guises, is articulatcd on multiple spatial scales, and moves through divergent historical trajectories. This means that neoliberalism—like globalization—is not a monolithic affair that impresses itself onto local, regional, or national states, civil societies, and economies. Instead, it exists through the practices and ideologies of variously scaled fragments of ruling classes, who impose their specific projects onto respective territories and spheres of influence. Second, I agree that there is no such thing as a pure form of neoliberalism that is being "applied" to various places. Rather, there is "a contextual *embeddedness* ... defined by the legacies of inherited institutional frameworks, policy regimes, regulatory practices, and political struggles" (Brenner and Theodore [paper] this volume).

The Foucauldian Critique: Explaining Urban Neoliberalism With Changing Technologies of Power

Theorists critical of traditional political-economy approaches have introduced an alternative view of its emergence as a globally visible set of new technologies of power. With explicit reference to the work of Foucault, it has been suggested that neoliberalism can be understood as policy, ideology, or governmentality (Larner 2000). Particularly important in our context is the notion of neoliberalism as *governmentality*, which refers to the many ways in which neoliberalism emerges on the basis of a restructured political subject: "Neoliberal strategies of rule ... encourage people to see themselves as individualized and active subjects responsible for enhancing their own well-being" (Larner 2000:13). In this view, citizens as active agents—or clients— operate on a governance terrain whereon previous distinctions between state, civil society, and market are largely blurred, as "marketization" rules each of those domains and the relationships among them. More than pure ideology or a set of practices thought of as imposed from outside or above, neoliberalism as governmentality becomes an over-arching frame of reference for contradictory discursive events that link the everyday life of individuals to the new world of "advanced liberalism."

Isin (1998) has looked at neoliberalism not as merely a prescription for state retreat, but rather as a complex set of *changing technologies of power*. He argues that current capitalist societies have undergone three related shifts towards such new technologies. First, new relationships between expertise and politics place more emphasis on performance, efficiency, and marketability of knowledge. Second, a shift has occurred in the technologies of power towards privatization and away from accountable public processes. Third, Isin (1998) suggests a shift towards a new specification of the subject of government, whereby citizens are redefined as clients and autonomous market participants who are responsible for their own success, health, and well-being.

This interpretation is directly relevant to my case. In Toronto, a set of practices driven by right-of-centre ideologies has created a discursive universe in which accumulation occurs in new ways, where marketization and privatization of previously public services is rampant, and where new hegemonic discourses based on and accepted by new subjects and collectives have emerged in what is clearly a post-Fordist socioterritorial compromise. Yet, as I hope to show through the discussion of everyday neoliberalism below, Larner's and Isin's views need to be complemented by a perspective that interprets the introduction of neoliberal technologies of power less as a distant state act than as a project of re-regulating the everyday lives of people through ideological/discursive, economic, and political interventions.

The Urban, the Everyday, and Neoliberalism

Urban neoliberalism refers to the *contradictory re-regulation* of everyday life in the city. This requires a brief explanation. Lefebvre thought of the everyday as "the decisive category linking the economy to individual life experiences" (Ronneberger 2002:43). Its emergence as a central category of Lefebvre's thinking is a critique of the productivist and determinist traditions of Marxism in the middle of the 20th century. In the first instance, this leads Lefebvre (1991:89) to a concern with space: "The problematic of space, which subsumes the problems of the urban sphere (the city and its extensions) and of everyday life (programmed consumption), has displaced the problematic of industrialization." Moreover, in Lefebvre's (1972a:105) view, modern societies produce a specific relationship of production and reproduction/consumption, which is reproduced through everyday practices (regulated but not entirely dominated by the state): "Everydayness is the main product of the so-called organized or steered consumer society, and of its decorum: modernity." The emergence of the category of the everyday is directly linked to the differentiation of the concept of social space and the evolution of new forms of (modern) subjectivity. As Ronneberger (2002:44) reminds us, Lefebvre's concept of everydayness "is focused not only upon the sphere of reproduction but takes into consideration the processes through which society as a whole is produced." Caught between the "economic-technological imperatives which colonize space and time" and increasingly rebellious collective social practice, the contours of the everyday are constantly shifting and can never be entirely fixed by social forces interested in the imposition of order (Ronneberger 2002:44). Lefebvre's concept of the everyday is a reflection of the Fordist "societalization" of European societies after World War II. Lefebvre captured the very technologies of power that late 20th-century capitalist states and societies had at their disposal through the channels of mass production, culture, and consumption. The recurring theme of a colonized everyday became a trope of the 1960s cultural revolutions, which have defined a rebellious urbanity since that period. Everydayness is both an imposed reality of mass society and the constantly virulent source of subversive action, never pacified, never resting (Lefebvre 1972a:105).

The upheavals of this societal constellation were urban revolts, which Lefebvre both predicted and fueled through his writing. The countercultural communes and urban alternatives that sprang up everywhere after the 1960s provided an excellent example of the powerful politics of the lived space celebrated by Lefebvre (1991). Everydayness and the politics springing from it during this period were a lively mix of adaptation (for example, the "march through the institutions") and continued radical rebellion (not incidentally, the terrorist Red Army Faction in Germany, for example, had its origins in a series of attacks on department stores, symbols of consumer society). Subsequently, both everydayness and its politics changed shape as the Fordist-Keynesian welfare state made way for the post-Fordist workfare state of our times (Jessop 1993; Peck 2001). Built on technologies of power developed in the previous era, the everyday has now become a space in which individuals (divided and collectivized by class, "race," gender, etc) are suspended in a web of control, homogenization, and controlled isolation on one side and opportunity, identity, and individual expression on the other (at least for the privileged classes, mostly in the urban north). Even though it had already been initiated under Fordist capitalism, the subjectivization and militarization of public space in cities has progressed in leaps and bounds under post-Fordism.

Insofar as they are aggressive extensions of their Fordist-Keynesian predecessors, neoliberal societies are characterized by a propensity to engulf the individual and social collectives with rules that are accepted as naturalized forms of behaviour. During the 1960s, in language that is closely reminiscent of other critical theorists of that era such as Herbert Marcuse, Lefebvre (1972a:200) described this state of affairs as follows:

> *Repression extends to the biological and physiological life, to nature, childhood, education, pedagogy, the entry into life.* It demands abstinence, ascetics, because it succeeds by way of ideology, to present sacrifice as merit and fulfillment of life. In this sense, repression also extends to the ruling classes, at least at certain moments in time. Their "values" and strategies demand discipline and constraint, which are executed into their own ranks. (emphasis in original)

As a mode of regulation, neoliberalism operates to regularize urban everyday life in ways that represent and reproduce the specific form of globalized, unrestrained capitalism that has been crystallizing since the crisis of Fordism. In contrast to the situation during the Fordist period, the workplace is no longer the unrivaled center of regulatory practices in the current era. As SpaceLab (2000:9) insists, the desires and demands of new social movements are being recast into lifestyle differences as the new "flexible" form of neoliberal capitalism evolves: "It is obvious that currently the social position of subjects does not just depend on their place in the process of work and production, but increasingly also on symbolic forms of distinction, which rest on aesthetic experiences and certain consumption patterns." In this process, the urban replaces the factory as the prevalent location in which these distinctions are produced. With apologies to Harry Braverman, it can be argued metaphorically that the mall has replaced the assembly line as the major purveyor belt of the regulatory regime. This process is part of the overall "global and total production of social space" that characterizes our period and gives global capitalism a new lease on life (Lefebvre 1972b:165). As an important part of this spatialization of industrial society, the urban plays a key role in the regulation of "contemporary" society:

> There is nothing more contradictory than "urbanness." On the one hand, it makes it possible in some degree to deflect class struggles. The city and urban reality can serve to disperse dangerous "elements," and they also facilitate the setting of relatively inoffensive "objectives," such as the improvement of transportation or of other "amenities." On the other hand, the city and its periphery tend to become the arena of kinds of action that can no longer be confined to the traditional locations of the factory or office floor. The city and the urban sphere are thus the setting of struggle; they are also, however, the stakes of that struggle. (Lefebvre 1991:386)

The intermeshing of economic and cultural hegemony on the one hand and sociopolitical control on the other has certainly intensified in the current era (see Smith this volume). However, the state's role in this process is deeply contradictory. On the one hand, it becomes an increasingly punitive rather than a caring institution in the current restructuring process. At the same time, even as issues of police brutality and the fear of crime become ever more salient in the public sphere, the state's ability to protect its citizens from attack is significantly compromised (as witnessed in recent events in the United States from Oklahoma City in 1995 to New York City in 2001) (Castells 2001; Davis 2001).

Everydayness and Urban Resistance

> [E]verything (the "whole") weighs down on the lower or "micro" level, on the local and the localizable—in short, on the sphere of everyday life. Everything (the "whole") also *depends* on this level: exploitation and domination, protection and—inseparably— repression. (Lefebvre 1991:366)

Neoliberal urbanism is grounded upon a restructuring of the political economy as well as on a changing set of technologies of power. Related to both processes are two overlapping critical discourses. On one hand, there is the traditional discourse of *social* critique (*critique sociale*), which points towards political strategies to oppose exploit-ation and inequality; on the other hand, there is a *cultural* critique (*critique artiste*), which deals with aspects of individual and collective autonomy and self-realization. Both forms of critique must be com-bined in order to decipher the politics of the neoliberal city (Boltanksi and Chiapello 2000; Ronneberger forthcoming; SpaceLab 2000). As it stands, much of urban policy oscillates between punitive local state measures and an enlightened postexclusionary discourse of social integration (Keil 2000a; Schmals 2001). To truly achieve a critical interaction of social and cultural critique, though, such policies must be superseded through an activated urban political sphere. For Lefebvre, urban politics is a dynamic and thoroughly contradictory social space: "[c]aught up in the contradictions between the macrostructures of capital and state and the microworlds of everyday life, urban politics is no mere local affair," but rather is multiscalar, potentially uni-versalist, and most importantly perhaps, transformational (Kipfer 1998:177–178). In the heyday of the 1960s, Lefebvre hailed urban society as the possible site and process of positive social change. By contrast, urban society under neoliberalism seems at first glance to have become a space for the controlled, marketized, consumerist capitalization of everydayness. Since much of the dirty work of globalization (and neoliberalization) is done in cities (Keil 2000a), the urban plays a specific role in the grounding of neoliberal modes of regulation.

Yet the reproduction of capital through the production of urban space is not a linear, capital-driven process. Urban cultures and subcultures have been subjected to and have resisted neoliberalism in its many urban guises. Cities under neoliberal rule continue to be huge nexuses of mass production and consumption, very much in the tradition of the Fordist city. In this context, traditional forms of social criticism—with their focus on power, exploitation, and inequality—remain a powerful strategic precondition for urban resistance through class struggle and collective consumption mobilizations. At the same time, however, cities have also become machines of differentiation, fueled by contradictory processes of social struggle and conflict. Typically, postmodern consumerism comes with a distinct dialectics of resistance (Morris 2001). For example, the "bible" of the anti-globalization movement, *No Logo*, by Toronto author Naomi Klein (2000), can be read as an urban manifesto in the tradition of the post-Lefebvre debate on the right to the city and the systemic lack of urbanity in our cities (Ronneberger forthcoming). Klein (2000:311) speaks of the "tension between the commodification and criminalization of street culture." She (311) goes on to argue:

It is one of the ironies of our age that now, when the street has become the hottest commodity in advertising culture, street culture itself is under siege. From New York to Vancouver to London, police crackdowns on graffiti, postering, panhandling, sidewalk art, squeegee kids, community gardening and food vendors are rapidly criminalizing everything that is truly street-level in the life of a city.[2]

In this process, the social and the cultural critique are inseparably connected to political strategies. While unionization drives among immigrant workers, citizenship struggles, environmental justice conflicts, and the like have been on the rise in the multicultural urban centres of this period, cultural events as diverse as the music of hiphop and Brit pop, films such as *Fight Club*, ad-busters, culture jamming, "Reclaim the Streets," raves, and full-fledged antiglobalization riots (which generally include diverse forms of cultural expression) provide particularly excellent venues through which the urbanization of neoliberalism and new forms of resistance can be studied (Klein 2000; Morris 2001).

In some of these events, both social and cultural forms of critique are fully developed as discourses of radical change. In others, they are exercises in cooptation and integration. In any case, the urban provides the stage for their development. The "collective daydream" or "large-scale coincidence" of a "Reclaim the Streets" event explicitly challenges the spatialization of power represented by the neoliberalized urban landscape: "Like adbusters, RTSers have transposed the language and tactics of radical ecology into the urban jungle, demanding uncommercialized space in the city as well as natural wilderness in the country or on the seas" (Klein 2000:313).

The "Common-Sense Revolution" (CSR) in Ontario

In what follows, I present a brief heuristic application of the theoretical approaches presented above to the urban impact of the CSR. I will merge the insights of the three previously discussed strands of explanation—political economy, shifts in the technologies of power, and everyday urbanism—into an interpretation of urban neoliberalism in Toronto. Implicitly, I assume the continued relevance of political-economic shifts in the construction of the neoliberal project, but I also acknowledge that, as suggested by some Foucauldian writers, the concrete implementation of new technologies of power has played a key role in these processes of neoliberalization as well. Most importantly, I propose to look at urban neoliberalism as a combination of political-economic restructuring and new technologies of power, which ultimately results in an active re-regulation of the urban everyday and in the concomitant emergence of new forms of resistance and political action by socially and culturally marginalized and attacked constituencies.

Today's Canadian neoliberalism has to be seen before the backdrop of the country's traditional "uneven spatial development" (Peck 2001:224) and its specific history of Fordism and postwelfarism (Peck 2001:213–260; see also Jenson 1989; Shields and Evans 1998; Teeple 1995). One also needs to take into account the tradition of austerity politics that has characterized the federal government, provincial governments, and municipal governments since the mid-1980s (Shields and Evans 1998). Provincial governments have been at the forefront of neoliberal restructuring in Canada; the neoliberal medicine has been prescribed across the country by New Democrat, Progressive Conservative, and Liberal governments alike (Peck 2001; Shields and Evans 1998).

In Ontario, an uncompromisingly neoliberal provincial government under Tory Premier Harris since 1995 has created a political environment reminiscent of Thatcherism and Reaganism. The Tories came to power in a rather surprising election victory on the basis of their CSR election platform. Populist in its appellations, the Tory program was a textbook case of a neoliberal policy strategy and project. It contained many internal contradictions. Despite its embrace of a rhetoric of small government, the Harris cabinet was, in effect, perhaps the most interventionist government this province/city has ever seen. The Ontario Tories preach market liberalism but practice authoritarian and classist fantasies that are bound to generate lasting effects upon Ontario society. Instead of just dismantling the state, the provincial government has inserted itself into the lives of many groups in Ontario society in a recognizable, tangible way. Teachers and school boards, universities, nurses and other health-care professionals, government workers, homeless people, welfare recipients, urban residents, and many other groups have been adversely affected through countless interventionist policies by Ontario's provincial government. Job cuts, environmental and social re-regulation, boundary redrawing of municipal government, welfare cuts, and all manner of restrictive legislation have affected the everyday life of millions of Ontarians over the past six years. In fact, amalgamation has created new and bigger local state institutions. In Toronto, for instance, the number of municipal employees has grown since amalgamation. As the government has implemented new regulatory modes—for example, in education—teaching professionals in schools and universities have reeled under the quotidian effects of changing workloads, stagnating salaries, increased class sizes, shifting curricula, altered governance, and reduced budgets.

The seductive simplicity of the CSR has led to dramatic incisions into the everyday life of many common people in Ontario and Toronto. Overall, the local neoliberal project in Toronto appears as a mix of half-hearted market reforms (including the privatization of Toronto's collective consumption, a leaner local state, and so forth) and frontal attacks on the poor, the left, labour, and so on. Among the provincial policies since 1995 that have most directly affected the urban are the following: drastic welfare cuts (starting with a 21% cut in benefits in September 1995), the "Safe Street Act" (directed against squeegee kids and panhandlers), the reduction and redesign of local government (Boudreau 2000; Keil 2000b), the amalgamation of hundreds of local governments (Sancton 2000), the reduction of the number of provincial full-time social service positions by 21,000 (Mallan 2001), the introduction of workfare (Peck 2001), the legalization of the sixty-hour work-week (based on total intransigence towards public and private-sector unions and their concerns and demands), the loosening of planning restrictions and the pursuit of an aggressive (sub)urban growth strategy (only recently reined in through a "smart growth" strategy with doubtful credentials), the elimination of all public housing programs and downloading of responsibilities to the local level (Urquhart 2001), the deregulation of the province's environmental regime (Winfield and Jenish 1998), strategic attacks on public-worker unions, the dismantling and systematic underfunding of the education system, the curtailing of school boards and their rights, and the monitoring and harassment of civil society organizations. During the roll-back phase of neoliberalization alone, the Tories rescinded the Planning Act (which had just been reformed under the NDP), killed antiscab legislation, and did away with other comparatively progressive regulations dating back to previous NDP or Liberal governments.

Certain aspects of the Tory agenda can be explained by the sociology of power. The inner circles of Mike Harris' regime, as well as their counterparts in the Toronto elites, were largely drawn from three or four distinctive groups: they tended to be composed of small, nonurban entrepreneurs (such as car salesmen and resort owners); they often displayed an antiurban bias; and they are mostly white, Anglo males. Harris and his inner circle were supported by rabidly neoliberal young right-wing intellectuals and practitioners, who were ideologically tied to ideas of market liberalism and state retrenchment. The modernizing, global appeal of their "reforms" blended in well with the more reactionary, socially conservative, nonurban or even antiurban agenda of the provincial Tory party. Yet rather than separating themselves out from the masses, these "common-sense" revolutionaries attempted to walk a fine populist line based upon a carefully guarded centrist hegemony that captured the spirit of middle Ontario (Dale 1999; see Patten 1996 for a similar analysis of the western Reform Party). Only after the public blamed the water debacle in the small town of Walkerton north of Toronto, where seven people died in 2000, on Tory budget cuts and deregulation did this

populist strategy unravel, as there was then mounting evidence that
this state was no good for the people and that this government was
associated with the notion of "death" (Salutin 2001:A13).

Urban Neoliberalism in Toronto

In what follows, urban neoliberalism is viewed through six lenses (see
Table 1). In joint work with Stefan Kipfer, I have elsewhere developed this
view in more detail for the political economy of Canadian urbanism and
have suggested that it allows a categorical glimpse into major areas of
contradiction in the country's urban system (Keil and Kipfer forthcoming).

- *Changing the space of politics*: The CSR has had severe spatial
  effects. Amalgamation has been the main venue through which
  the Harris Tories have "revolutionized" state-society relationships in Ontario. Since the province has sole constitutional
  jurisdiction over urban affairs in Canada, the shift towards
  a radical neoliberal agenda has had severe impacts on the
  province's cities, most notably Toronto. First, the provincial
  government amalgamated seven local governments in Toronto
  into one municipality. Secondly, the province downloaded
  social welfare and transit costs to the city and caused a painful
  budget crunch at the municipal level. Thirdly, the province has
  since continued to cut rather than expand the powers of local
  government to tax or otherwise raise funds in order to meet
  the growing needs of an expanding world city reality. The
  Tories gave priority to the amalgamation of mostly large urban
  regions rather than to rural or exurban municipalities, where
  their voter base was located in the 1995 and 1999 elections.
  Mostly white and relatively wealthy voters in the suburbs and
  small towns of Ontario now determine the political fate of the
  entire province and its major cities. Tax cuts, law and order,
  free-market rhetoric, and "small government" are the ingredients in a political stew that has been digested well by voters in
  the affluent "blubber belts" of Toronto and Ottawa (Dale 1999).
  It is significant to note, though, that like other neoconservative
  and neoliberal governments before them, the Harris Tories
  have made the "political splits"—resting one foot of their platform on a rhetoric of small-town conservatism while placing
  the other on a radical modernization strategy.
- *The "reluctant global city" strategy*: The same kind of political
  gymnastics have been present in the Tories' relationship to
  Toronto as an international city. While widely considered
  ignorant of urban issues and uncomfortable with, if not antagonistic towards, this metropolis's multiculturality and diversity,
  the Harris government has consistently pushed Toronto as

Table 1: Six Perspectives on Neoliberal Urbanism in Ontario

	Political Economy	Technologies of Power	Everyday Urbanism and Resistance
Changing the space of politics	Amalgamation, leaner government	Downloading, fewer politicians; Bill 46 (Public Sector Accountability) brings all public sector organizations under strict auditing controls	Suburbanization of the city, but fierce resistance to amalgamation
The "reluctant global city" strategy Bourgeois urbanism	Waterfront plan, Olympic bid, the "competitive city"; Condominium boom, high-end culture	Urban revanchism (Safe Streets Act) and entrepreneurialism; Toronto Competes and the new general plan; Gated communities; private policing; end to public housing programs; 60,000 Ontario families evicted in 2000; growth in provincial eviction rate; end of rent control (Walkom 2001)	Diversity as public relations strategy, but continued racism in institutions and on the street; new political force in immigrant politics; Priority of housing property in the public mind; renters fight back; homeless activism soars
The rescaling of the urban imaginary	The global region; the learning region; the auto region; leisure economy, sprawl, suburban subdivisions	Re-regulation of the relationship of city and countryside; no development controls; lately: "smart growth"	The reversal of the downtown-centred imaginary brings in new urban actors; struggle over development of the Oak Ridges Moraine
Ecological modernization	Development with instead of against "nature"; privatization of natural resources and services (water, sewers, etc)	De- and re-regulation of everything environmental; ecological citizenship becomes defined through markets	The Tory heartland, the "905" telephone region around Toronto, gears up for protest as their suburban exclusivity is threatened by out-of-control development
New social disparities	The new economy; continentalization; Americanization, Globalization	Cuts to welfare, workforce programs; no public housing, labour standards lowered; working time has increased; health-care for marginal groups has worsened; Bill 57 weakens workers' right to refuse unsafe work; Bill 147 introduces potential sixty-hour work-week	Redefined social norms: welfarism stigmatized, poverty made invisible; strong anti-Tory resistance throughout their mandate; days of action, antiglobalization movement localized in OCAP protests

a location for international capital accumulation. This was nowhere as visible as in the period of the (unsuccessful) bid process for the 2008 Summer Olympics.

- *Bourgeois urbanism*: Reminiscent of their counterparts in Europe, Canadian elites are increasingly presenting themselves as "urban." This is a reversal from earlier North American trends characterized by a middle-class flight to the suburbs. This new trend also goes beyond the traditional left-of-centre middle-class reformism to which Canadian cities were accustomed. Interestingly, the new urbanity of certain elite factions is quite compatible with the continued colonization of the rural countryside through wealthy urban fugitives in their pursuit for gated communities and proximity to luxury "rural" entertainment such as golf courses. The "re-embourgoisement" of the city goes hand in hand with the continued tendency in Canadian capital to reinvest its resource-based superprofits into real estate and the built environment. This tendency also corresponds well with the increased movement to sanitize, control, and suburbanize inner-city spaces so as to transform them into sites for global elite culture and spectacle. The Harris government's policies of liberalization of urban development regimes and policing of urban space have strongly supported these general trends.

- *The rescaling of the urban imaginary* (Jessop 1997): The claim for Toronto's global prominence, or at least competitiveness, is now built on the larger region, in which the old core is considered only one among many possible growth poles of economic and residential developments. Rather than being viewed as the core of a regionally or nationally constructed hinterland, Toronto now appears as an almost denationalized throughput node of a global economy, whose flows of capital, people, and information dissolve traditional spatial arrangements of the urban region. On one level, neoliberalism appears as a mode of re-regulation of the city and the countryside, town, and suburbs. This is a central feature of Ontario's neoliberal urbanism. Patches of mass-produced cheap subdivisions continue to eat up Ontario's prime farmland in the most arable areas of the most populous centres of the country. They house both the well-to-do and the newly arrived: Toronto suburbs are often now the ports of entry for new waves of non-European immigration. The Harris government has deliberately resisted any attempts to regulate development in Ontario. They rescinded extensive planning-reform measures just implemented under the previous NDP government and created the conditions for continued sprawl in the province. Only late in their second mandate did the Tories feebly voice a "smart growth agenda," which—at close inspection—was nothing more than a stepped-up and rationalized road-building program.

- *Ecological modernization*: The Harris Tories have fundamentally affected the societal relationships with nature in the province. Deregulation of the environment and cutbacks in the Ministry of the Environment have proven deadly in Walkerton. Harris has also re-regulated forests, hunting, the land-use process, and conservation, to name just a few environmentally salient policy spheres. The resulting image is again one in which government retreat, ecological modernization, and outright regulatory interventionism are recombined in favour of mostly privileged social groups (such as suburban homeowners). The exurban strategy of development—which attempts to proceed "with" rather than "against" nature—has its inner-city counterpart in diverse "green" strategies for the waterfront, urban wetlands, and a golf course next to the CN Tower in the city's downtown core. With few exceptions, these strategies are mostly apt to increase the role of the neoliberal project in the restructuring of the societal relationships with nature, particularly through marketization and privatization of land, services, and resources.
- *New social disparities*: As the social is now increasingly redefined in cultural terms, difference is also marked more or less in cultural terms (SpaceLab 2000). There is certainly a rising inequality in income distribution, debt, and wealth, accompanied by mounting rifts in labour markets between "good," well-paid, and relatively secure managerial and (selected) professional jobs and a rapidly increasing number of "bad," low-paid, nonunionized, and "casual" (part-time, temporary, or contract) jobs. These new social disparities have mostly been attributed to economic restructuring (layoffs, downsizing), neoliberal policies (tax cuts, cuts to social programs, reduced public employment, financial deregulation, high real interest rates, etc), the heightened influence of aggressive corporate interests on public policy, and the role of finance and speculative business interests in accelerating economic restructuring, prolonging economic stagnation and pushing corporate interests into neoliberal directions.

In virtually all these domains, the Harris Tories have played a decisive role in redefining the norms of poverty, welfarism, workfarism, housing, and so forth. Initial cutbacks to individual welfare payments have been followed by aggressive workfare programs (albeit with spotty implementation records). No public housing has been funded or constructed. Labour standards have been lowered. Legal working time has increased. General security has decreased. Health care for marginal groups has worsened. While the general conditions for accumulation have improved, the specific conditions of working-class and poor individuals have drastically worsened over the past few years.

Toronto Neoliberalism: Aiding and Abetting

> Anyone who says we won't save money under amalgamation is talk-ing horseshit. But we'll never save any money until we get rid of those lefties at city hall. (Mike Harris, quoted in Drainie 2000:78)

Of course, the Harris agenda could only have been successfully implemented with a high degree of collusion and complicity in society and other levels of the state. It is not plausible and not possible to reduce urban neoliberalism to the agenda of a specific provincial government. The province provides the framework and makes the rules within which local actors readjust to the neoliberal regime. Not just reactive victims (as many Torontonians like to present themselves), these local political actors merge their state strategies and projects with those at other scales of the Canadian government system. Clearly, the existence of these various neoliberal strategies and projects does not in itself mean that they will be automatically implemented. On the contrary, these policies are always contested terrains. Individual policy initiatives may be only partly successful and may be articulated with other (compatible or noncompatible) items on the neoliberal agenda (Peck 2001).

At the urban scale, metropolitan Toronto and its successor local state, the new City of Toronto, have been spearheading new pub-lic management, budget discipline for social activist and environ-mental organizations in the city's governance perimeter, and leaner service delivery as mainstays of neoliberal policies for more than a decade (Conway 2000; Kipfer 1998).

Toronto's amalgamation laid the ground for a new political regime in what is now a city of 2.5 million people. The mayoral victory of conservative suburban politician Mel Lastman in 1997 (and his subsequent re-election in late 2000), as well as a solid conservative council majority, signaled that the "exurbanization of provincial politics" found its smaller scale counterpart in the "suburbanization of urban politics" in Toronto. Lastman also represents a similar kind of mix of populism and radical neoliberalism to that encountered at the provincial scale. A former appliance salesman and reputed deal-maker, Lastman has mastered the political skill of pacifying diverse political constituencies with a law-and-order and tax-cut agenda of his own. Often involved in highly publicized political spats with Harris, Lastman postures as the defender of taxpayers and homeowners in

Toronto (alleged victims of provincial downloading and footers of the provincial tax-cutting bill), while at the same time lashing out wildly against the poor and their advocates, making racist statements, and imposing a law-and-order agenda. Lastman also plays the role of the indomitable booster of Toronto, be it for the city's failed bid to host the 2008 Olympics or for the large-scale restructuring of its waterfront.

The city of Toronto's agenda of neoliberal restructuring under Lastman's mayoralty has included the following issues: the rewriting of the City's Official Plan into a document that combines the definition of livable urbanity with the explicit goals of the competitive city; similar initiatives from the economic development office of the City (Toronto Competes, the Toronto Waterfront and Olympic Bid proposals); the restructuring of the workings of the local state administration (with a clear push towards lean government); crackdowns on marginal populations, such as squeegee kids; and so forth. This agenda may be described under the label of the "competitive city," which represents a mix of strategies to create the entrepreneurial city, the city of difference, and the revanchist city (Kipfer and Keil 2002). Other policies that have worked well in conjunction with this agenda include flexible soil clean-up policies to create new spaces for development in old industrial areas (Desfor and Keil 1999) and the privatization and marketization schemes for the city's water and sewerage system. In all cases, the understanding of what it means to be a citizen, to live everyday life in Toronto, has been shifted strongly to a novel concept of the individualized subject responsible for his or her own well-being, supported largely through the marketplace, market orientation, clientelism, consumer fees, voluntarism, and criminalization of marginal behaviours and spaces.

The neoliberal urban regime in Toronto has to some degree, been a perverse replay of previous traditions of all-partisanship: Lastman has created a new political umbrella for the continuation of previous liberal and social democratic policy traditions where needed. There is a narrative of complicity, a neoliberal storyline to which many subscribe under the hegemony of middle-class urbanism (Isin 1998; Keil 1998). The traditional Toronto liberal compromise has been eclipsed by the new times. This is personified in the decline of the political fortunes of former mayor John Sewell. In some ways, this is not surprising, as it has much to do with the changing demographics and power relations in the city: this kind of liberalism was the program of the inner-city white bourgeoisie. Meanwhile, however, the flag of Toronto's old ("red") Tory political elite—welfare-state-supporting Tories—continues to be carried by former mayor David Crombie, who is in the midst of every major political project in the city. While the trade-union movement is now entirely marginalized in the provincial regime and has little impact on the city, there is what I would call a peripheral "third-way"-type inclusion of the traditional social-democratic agenda when it is needed for stopgap measures of governance.[3]

Conclusion: From Defense to Resistance

How to be truly critical in an age of mass camp? (Klein 2000:84)

Die Öffnung? Sie hat schon einen Namen: *Das städtische Leben* (oder die städtische Gesellschaft). [The opening? It already has a name: *Urban life* (or urban society).] (Lefebvre 1972a:257)

The main argument in this paper has been that throughout this chain of restructuring and rescaling of spatialized political economies, neoliberal ideological advances, and new technologies of power, a new urban everyday is being formed which dramatically redefines the social and territorial compromise, the mode of regulation, and the lived experiences (the perceived, conceived, and lived spaces) of the city. The Tory CSR has transformed the horizon of individual and collective expectation and has altered urban subjectivity. The Premier and his ministers have repeatedly commented on what they expect to be normal, and on what they expect others—like poor people, workers, or mothers—to view as normal. Remarks on the low price of tuna fish in the face of cuts to welfare, propagating the value of a warm breakfast cooked by stay-at-home mothers in reaction to cuts to school funding, expounding the virtues of home-ownership in an age of nonexistent funding for rental or social housing—these tropes have characterized the government's tenacity in making their policy reforms stick in the minds and practices of people in Ontario. The Harris government continues to cement neoliberal hegemony over Ontarians' everyday lives.

And yet, the hegemony of the CSR is showing signs of distress. What began as the dynamic and contested spirit of the CSR's program for a new "postsocialist" everyday (after five years of social-democratic government) has ended in a politics of fatigue and even failure. For a few short years, Harris appeared—at least in the eyes of his supporters—to have the Midas touch: turning around a floundering economy, stabilizing the provincial budget, ridding the cities of bloated governments, reducing crime, displacing street people and squeegee kids, breaking trade union power in the public sector, and so forth. Now his government is haunted by a series of deadly incidents that have affected regular people in their normal everyday lives: rural citizens die of water contamination; a highly pregnant woman under house arrest for welfare fraud passes away in unbearable summer heat; and the death of a Native protester at the hands of police early in Harris's first legislative period finally seems to have been linked to knowledge in or even orders from the Premier's office.

Nonetheless, the fundamental redesign of social values under the Tory regime has led to entirely new ways of living life in Toronto. It is interesting to note that the CSR represented both "roll-back" and "roll-out" neoliberalism (Peck and Tickell this volume). The speed with which the Tories destroyed and replaced time-honoured and engrained institutions of the welfarist local state took many by surprise. The "red" Tory-Liberal social welfarism and the feeble attempts at social democracy during the second half of the 20th century have given way to a workfarist, revanchist regime; ideologies of municipal service and public government have been replaced by neoliberal governance models and market-driven development schemes. The local state has diversified into a complex web of governance functions spread out over all parts of civil society but tied to the logic and technologies of rule one finds in the market place. The willful subjection of people to ethical laws and norms that demand sacrifices (SpaceLab 2000:10) plays an important role in a regime that pretends to have all opportunities open for all people. Many observers noted the contradiction in the policies of Harris, who saw no problem with raising his own income as premier while simultaneously campaigning against welfare recipients as potentially defrauding the public, cutting back their incomes, and resisting the urging of others to increase the legal minimum wage. Ultimately, the Tory CSR has posed some fundamental democracy-theoretical questions about the meaning and future use of public citizenship. As substantive neoliberal reforms have taken shape, they have also affected the understanding of the process of politics as public and democratic: Harris has governed on the basis of what one critic, in a different context, called "the streamlined, focus-grouped responsiveness of the marketplace" (quoted in Drainie 1998:80).

The CSR occurred under constant fire of resistance, civil disobedience, and alternative developments. Attacks on the legitimacy of public protest challenged but did not break the movement to construct alternatives to "market freedom" and the punitive state. In fact, as the concomitant damages of the neoliberal shift are visited upon large parts of Toronto's and Ontario's population through the Harris regime, critical discourses of all kinds have come into sharp relief: since 1996, Toronto has become a staging ground for large-scale protests against globalization, economic injustice, the housing crisis, the welfare debacle, racism, and—lately—war. The drive and legitimacy for this new mobilization stem from the very contradictions nurtured by the Tory regime. These are the contradictions of everyday life in the city. Accordingly, these mobilizations have moved from the ideological battlefield during the early days of the CSR to the concrete life-worlds of people. One poster sponsored by the Toronto Centre for Social Justice dryly observed: "Bad water. Your tax dollars at work." This slogan ridiculed the tax-cut policies of the Harris government through the evocation of the damage they caused in the daily lives of people in Ontario.

Insofar as they go beyond the parameters of roll-*back* neoliberalism and engage with the emerging forms of roll-*out* neoliberalism, the current urban mobilizations create potentially new horizons for social change beyond both the Fordist past and the neoliberal present. This change of direction goes along with redefined polities beyond the traditional corporatist Keynesian pillars of the welfare state on the one hand and the neoliberal, asocial atomism on the other. We may see, then, the emergence of a new model of urbanity that far exceeds the mere structures of state and corporate economy and remakes the way we live our life in cities and the fundamental assumptions we make about this life. The right to the city is the right to the liberation of everyday life.

Acknowledgments

I would like to express my gratitude to Neil Brenner and Nik Theodore, the organizers of the Chicago conference on which this volume is based. Their support has been tremendous. This paper benefited greatly from the contributions to the literature produced by my fellow travelers in this conference and from their insightful comments following my presentation. Thanks also to Stefan Kipfer and Douglas Young for their ongoing collaboration on urban governance and neoliberalism in Toronto. I gratefully acknowledge financial support from the Small Grant program of the Social Sciences and Humanities Research Council, grant number 515433.

Endnotes

[1] "Riding" is the common English Canadian term for electoral districts in federal and provincial elections.

[2] "Squeegee kids" is a common Canadian reference to (mostly) youth who wipe windshields of cars for small change while the drivers of the cars wait at red traffic lights or intersections.

[3] Social-democratic councillors of the New Democratic Party play this role in various policy sectors: Jack Layton covers issues such as homelessness, housing, and the environment; Olivia Chow represents diversity; Kyle Rae stands in for the gay community; Joe Mihevic does health; and so on.

References

Albritton R, Itoh M, Westra R and Zuege A (eds) (2001) *Phases of Capitalist Development: Booms, Crises, and Globalizations*. New York: Palgrave

Alnasseri S, Brand U, Sablowski T and Winter J (2001) Space, regulation, and the periodization of capitalism. In R Albritton, M Itoh, R Westra and A Zuege (eds) *Phases of Capitalist Development: Booms, Crises, and Globalizations* (pp 163–178). New York: Palgrave

Amin A (ed) (1994) *Post-Fordism: A Reader*. Cambridge, MA: Blackwell

Boltanski L and Chiapello E (2000) Befreiung vom Kapitalismus? Befreiung durch Kapitalismus? *Blätter für deutsche und internationale Politik* 4:477–487

Boudreau J (2000) *The Mega-City Saga: Democracy and Citizenship in This Global Age.* Montreal: Black Rose Books

Bourdieu P (1998) *Acts of Resistance: Against the Tyranny of the Market.* New York: The New Press

Brenner N (1999) Globalization as reterritorialization: The rescaling of urban governance in the European Union. *Urban Studies* 36(3):431–451

Candeias M (2000) Restrukturierung der räumlichen Organisation des Staates. *Das Argument* 236(3):355–373

Candeias M and Deppe F (eds) (2001) *Ein neuer Kapitalismus?* Hamburg: VSA Verlag

Castells M (1997) *The Information Age: Economy, Society, and Culture.* Three vols. Cambridge, MA: Blackwell

Castells M (2001) Interview: Das Netz und sein Werk. *Die Zeit, Zeitliteratur* December:53–56

Conway J (2000) Knowledge, power, organization: Social justice coalitions at a crossroads. *Studies in Political Economy* 62:43–70

Dale S (1999) *Lost in the Suburbs: A Political Travelogue.* Toronto: Stoddart

Davis M (2001) The flames of New York. *New Left Review* 12 (November/ December):34–50

Desfor G and Keil R (1999) Contested and polluted terrain. *Local Environment.* 4(3):333–352

Drainie B (1998) Them against us. *Toronto Life* May:76–82

Duménil G and Lévy D (2001) Periodizing capitalism: Technology, institutions, and relations of production. In R Albritton, M Itoh, R Westra and A Zuege (eds) *Phases of Capitalist Development: Booms, Crises, and Globalizations* (pp 141–162). New York: Palgrave

Hardt M and Negri A (2000) *Empire.* Cambridge, MA: Harvard University Press

Harvey D (2000) *Spaces of Hope.* Los Angeles: University of California Press

Hirsch J (2001) Weshalb Periodisierung? In M Candeias and F Deppe (eds) *Ein neuer Kapitalismus?* (pp 41–47). Hamburg: VSA Verlag

Isin E H (1998) Governing Toronto without government: Liberalism and neoliberalism. *Studies in Political Economy* 56:169–191

Jenson J (1989) "Different" but not "exceptional": Canada's permeable Fordism. *Canad Rev Soc & Anth* 26(1):69–94

Jessop B (1993) Towards a Schumpeterian workfare state? Preliminary remarks on post-Fordist political economy. *Studies in Political Economy* 40(Spring):7–40

Jessop B (1997) A neo-Gramscian approach to the regulation of urban regimes: Accumulation strategies, hegemonic projects, and governance. In M Lauria (ed) *Reconstructing Urban Regime Theory: Regulating Urban Politics in a Global Economy* (pp 51–73). Thousand Oaks, CA: Sage Publications

Jessop B (2001a) What follows Fordism? On the periodization of capitalism and its regulation. In R Albritton, M Itoh, R Westra and A Zuege (eds) *Phases of Capitalist Development: Booms, Crises, and Globalizations* (pp 283–300). New York: Palgrave

Jessop B (2001b) Kritischer Realismus, Marxismus und Regulation: Zu den Grundlagen der Regulationstheorie. In M Candeias and F Deppe (eds) *Ein neuer Kapitalismus?* (pp 16–40). Hamburg: VSA Verlag

Keil R (1998) Toronto in the 1990s: Dissociated governance. *Studies in Political Economy* 56(Summer):151–168

Keil R (2000a) Third-way urbanism: Opportunity or dead end? *Alternatives* 25: 247–267

Keil R (2000b) Governance restructuring in Los Angeles and Toronto: Amalgamation or secession? *International Journal of Urban and Regional Research* 24(4):758–781

Keil R and Kipfer S (forthcoming) The urban experience. In W Clement and L Vosko (eds) *Changing Canada: Political Economy as Transformation.* Montreal: McGill-Queen's University Press

Kipfer S (1998) Urban politics in the 1990s: Notes on Toronto. In R Wolff, A Schneider, C Schmid, P Klaus, A Hofer and H Hitz (eds) *Possible Urban Worlds: Urban Strategies at the End of the 20th Century* (pp 172–179). Basel: Birkhaeuser

Kipfer S and Keil R (2002) Toronto Inc? Planning the competitive city in the New Toronto. *Antipode* 34(2):227–264

Klein N (2000) *No Logo: Taking Aim at the Brand Bullies.* Toronto: Knopf Canada

Larner W (2000) Neoliberalism: Policy, ideology, governmentality. *Studies in Political Economy* 63(Autumn):5–25

Lefebvre H (1972a) *Das Alltagsleben in der modernen Welt.* Frankfurt am Main: Suhrkamp Verlag

Lefebvre H (1972b) *Die Revolution der Städte.* München: List Verlag

Lefebvre H (1991). *The Production of Space.* Cambridge, MA: Blackwell

Lipietz A (2001) The fortunes and misfortunes of post-Fordism. In R Albritton, M Itoh, R Westra and A Zuege (eds) *Phases of Capitalist Development: Booms, Crises, and Globalizations* (pp 17–36). New York: Palgrave

MacLeod G and Goodwin M (1999a) Space, scale, and state strategy: Rethinking urban and regional governance. *Progress in Human Geography* 23:503–527

MacLeod G and Goodwin M (1999b) Reconstructing an urban and regional political economy: On the state, politics, scale, and explanation. *Political Geography* 18: 697–730

Mallan C (2001) Six years later. *The Toronto Star* 9 June:K1–3

Marston S A (2000) The social construction of scale. *Progress in Human Geography* 24:219–242

Morris M (2001) Contradictions of postmodern consumerism and resistance. *Studies in Political Economy* 64(Spring):7–32

Panitch L (2001) *Renewing Socialism: Democracy, Strategy, and Imagination.* Boulder: Westview

Patten S (1996) Preston Manning's populism: Constructing the common sense of the common people. *Studies in Political Economy* 50(Summer):95–132

Peck J (2001) *Workfare States.* New York: The Guilford Press

Peck J and Tickell A (1994) Searching for a new institutional fix: The after-Fordist crisis and the global-local disorder. In A Amin (ed) *Post-Fordism: A Reader* (pp 280–315). Cambridge, MA: Blackwell

Ronneberger K (2002) Contours and convolutions of everydayness: On the reception of Henri Lefebvre in the Federal Republic of Germany. *Capitalism, Nature, Socialism* 13, 2 June:42–57

Salutin R (2001) In harm's way: Death and politics in Ontario. *The Globe and Mail* 20 July:A13

Sancton A (2000) *Merger Mania: The Assault on Local Government.* Montreal: McGill-Queen's University Press

Schmals K M (2001) Eine neue Politik für die soziale Stadt. *vhw-Deutsches Wohnheimstättenwerk eV* 2(4):66–74

Shields J and Evans B M (1998) *Shrinking the State: Globalization and Public Administration "Reform."* Halifax: Fernwood Publishing

Smith N (1992) Geography, difference and the politics of scale. In J Doherty, E Graham and M Mallek (eds) *Postmodernism and the Social Sciences* (pp 57–79). London: Macmillan

SpaceLab (E Bareis, S Lanz, W Jahn and K Ronneberger) (2000) Auf der Suche nach dem Subjekt. Einleitung zum Schwerpunkt. *Widersprüche* 78:5–12

Swyngedouw E (1997) Neither global nor local: "Glocalization" and the politics of scale. In K Cox (ed) *Spaces of Globalization: Reasserting the Power of the Local* (pp 137–166). New York: Guilford Press

Teeple G (1995) *Globalization and the Decline of Social Reform.* Toronto: Garamond Press

Urquhart I (2001) "He established that things can change": Mike Harris's political style is for confrontation rather than consultation. *The Toronto Star* 9 June:K1–3

van der Pijl K (2001) International relations and capitalist discipline. In R Albritton, M Itoh, R Westra and A Zuege (eds) *Phases of Capitalist Development: Booms, Crises, and Globalizations* (pp 1–16). New York: Palgrave

Walkom T (2001) Labour gearing up for battle: Unions will put muscle into Tory protests. *The Toronto Star* 17 June:A1–A6

Winfield M S and Jenish G (1998) Ontario's environment and the "common-sense revolution." *Studies in Political Economy* 57(Autumn):129–147

Roger Keil teaches Environmental Studies at York University, Toronto. He has recently worked on urban governance as well as on urban environmental policy and politics in Toronto and Los Angeles. His latest book, *Los Angeles*, was published by John Wiley in 1998.

Chapter 11

From Urban Entrepreneurialism to a "Revanchist City"? On the Spatial Injustices of Glasgow's Renaissance

Gordon MacLeod

Recent perspectives on the American city have highlighted the extent to which the economic and sociospatial contradictions generated by two decades of "actually existing" neoliberal urbanism appear to demand an increasingly punitive or "revanchist" political response. At the same time, it is increasingly being acknowledged that, after embracing much of the entrepreneurial ethos, European cities are also confronting sharpening inequalities and entrenched social exclusion. Drawing on evidence from Glasgow, the paper assesses the dialectical relations between urban entrepreneurialism, its escalating contradictions, and the growing compulsion to meet these with a selective appropriation of the revanchist political repertoire.

Introduction

Spurred on by the unrelenting pace of globalization and the entrenched political hegemony of a neoliberal ideology, throughout the last two decades a host of urban governments in North America and Western Europe have sought to recapitalize the economic landscapes of their cities. While these "entrepreneurial" strategies might have refueled the profitability of many city spaces across the two continents, the price of such speculative endeavor has been a sharpening of socioeconomic inequalities alongside the institutional displacement and "social exclusion" of certain marginalized groups. One political response to these social geographies of "actually existing neoliberalism" (Brenner and Theodore [paper] this volume) sees the continuous renaissance of the entrepreneurial city being tightly "disciplined" through a range of architectural forms and institutional practices so that the enhancement of a city's image is not compromised by the visible presence of those very marginalized groups.

For some scholars, these tactics are further spiked with a powerful antiwelfare ideology, a criminalization of poverty, rising levels of incarceration, and a punitive or "revanchist" political response (cf Mitchell 2001; Smith 1998; Wacquant 2000). Generally, it would seem that these latter features are being imprinted more dramatically upon the urban landscapes of North, Central, and Latin America than on those of Western Europe (Caldiera 1999). Nonetheless, in an era characterized by "fast" policy transfer, and with many European cities suffering widening socioeconomic inequalities and intensified expressions of social exclusion, one key question seems to me particularly axiomatic. This concerns the extent to which a punitive, revanchist vernacular might now form part and parcel of a mandatory political response intended to discipline the deleterious social consequences and the escalating sociospatial contradictions that continue to be generated by a neoliberalizing political economic agenda. Combining theoretical discussion with a West European case study, my paper engages with this question.

I begin by illustrating the principal landscapes of a neoliberalizing urbanism, integrating the themes of entrepreneurial governance, downtown renaissance, and the active systems of surveillance that are intertwined with the advance of a revanchist city. I then highlight how the geographical contours of this emerging urban form are increasingly choreographed through the control over and purification of urban space,[1] which thereby raises important questions about the future expression of citizenship and social justice in the contemporary city. These ideas are then deployed towards an investigation of Glasgow in Scotland, a city regularly distinguished as a successful model of place-marketing and urban entrepreneurialism. I contend that Glasgow's recent experience offers some powerful evidence about the dialectical relations between urban entrepreneurialism, its internal contradictions, and the compulsion to meet these contradictions with a selective appropriation of the revanchist political repertoire (cf Atkinson forthcoming; Belina and Helms 2001). This said, the city's inherited political and institutional landscape, allied to some recent policy initiatives, reveals Glasgow's revanchism to be minor-league in comparison to the perspective's "home base" of New York. A concluding section offers some reflections about the interconnecting properties between a neoliberalizing urbanism and a revanchist political economy in choreographing the contemporary city.

Landscapes of a Neoliberalizing Urbanism
Neoliberalism and the Entrepreneurial City
Throughout the 1970s and 1980s, a number of dramatic transformations punctuated urban landscapes across North America and Western Europe. As city after city endured catastrophic deindustrialization and witnessed the suburban "flight" of high-income earners and an associated concentration of impoverished residents in their inner areas, enormous stress was placed on urban governmental administrations.

This was exacerbated by a decline in national fiscal support, itself illustrative of a general dismantling of key pillars of the Keynesian welfare state. Faced with such enormous challenges and implored to varying degrees by the rising tide of a "roll-back" neoliberal ideology (Peck and Tickell this volume),[2] many city governments moved quickly to reconsider their social bases of support, their architectures of political intervention, and their strategic priorities. A quite discernible shift in the political regulation of cities appeared underway, constitutive and reflective of new moments of "creative destruction" (Brenner and Theodore [paper] this volume).

Over the past fifteen years or so, a number of scholars have come to interpret these features as a generalized transformation from urban managerialism to urban entrepreneurialism. Guided by the axial principles of Keynesian economics and a politics of redistribution associated with postwar Fordism, the managerialist mode had been largely concerned with extending the provision of public services and decommodified components of welfare and "collective consumption" to local city populations (Saunders 1980). In sharp contrast, and in accordance with a neoliberal syllabus, the entrepreneurial regime is essentially concerned with reviving the competitive position of urban economies, especially through the "liberation" of private enterprise and an associated demunicipalization and recommodification of social and economic life (Leitner 1990).

While the literature on the entrepreneurial city has penetrated a range of academic subdisciplines, the Marxian approach developed by David Harvey has proved highly influential. Harvey (1989) views urban entrepreneurialism to be characterized by three principal features. First—and in contrast to the epoch of Fordist-managerialism, during which urban society was steered primarily by elected local government—the new urban political arena is ever more imbued with the influence of powerful business interests, especially through the much-heralded public–private partnership. Second, this business-led agenda is much less concerned with wealth redistribution and welfare than with the very "enabling" of economic enterprise, although the latter *is* viewed to generate societal benefits through the impact of "trickle-down" economics. One particularly notable feature has been the commitment to highly speculative "flagship" projects often enacted to enhance the imageability of the city. However, Harvey is quick to point out that much of the risk encountered in this place-marketing and escalating interurban competition for limited capital is often borne by publicly funded agencies, rather than "heroic" entrepreneurs. Finally, he views urban entrepreneurialism to be driven by a political economy of *place* rather than *territory*: the benefits of flagship projects like convention centers and festivals are often more readily experienced by those, like tourists and place-mobile capitalists, who live beyond the immediate locality.

The "projected spaces" (Brenner and Theodore [paper] this volume) for many of the flagship schemes so indispensable to this entrepreneurial agenda have been city downtowns, those areas that had suffered so vividly from Fordist deindustrialization. Consequently, locally mobilized public–private coalitions have taken the lead in brokering the regeneration of erstwhile derelict industrial enclaves and abandoned neighborhoods, which have been scrubbed clean and dramatically reinvented as glittering office and hotel atriums, themed leisure zones, upscale shopping centres, gentrified housing, and aesthetically enchanting cultural districts. Some of the most high-profile instances of this include Harbor Place in Baltimore, Fanueil Hall in Boston, Central Station in Chicago, the Merchant City in Glasgow, Canary Wharf and King's Cross in London, and South Street Seaport, Battery Park City, Grant Central Terminal, Times Square, and the Lower East Side in New York City (Boyer 1993; Boyle and Hughes 1994; Harvey 2000; Katz 2001; Smith 1996; Wright 1997; Zukin 1995).

Disciplining the Sociospatial Contradictions of Urban Entrepreneurialism: Marginality, Surveillance, and the Revanchist City

If the renaissance of these tenderly manicured landscapes alongside the active introduction of business improvement districts has done much to recover the exchange and sign value of many city centers, questions remain about the legitimate use-value of such spaces for a wider citizenry (Harvey 2000; Katz 2001). Not least in that the fragile maintenance of value inscribed into this recommodification of space is ever more intricately dependent on a costly system of surveillance— performed through a blend of architectural design, CCTV, private security, and a range of legal remedies—seemingly designed to inculcate "acceptable" patterns of behavior commensurate with the free flow of commerce and the new urban aesthetics. Indeed, a most lively inter-disciplinary debate continues to rage over the effects of the new urban architectures and their disciplinary technologies upon the substantive nature of public space (Bauman 2000; Coleman and Sim 2000; Flusty 2001; Fyfe forthcoming).

While I acknowledge that this public-space debate is far from conclusive,[3] I nonetheless find it hard to reason against the view that any conception of "publicness" we ascribe to the new renaissance sites is highly selective and systematically discriminating. For, as with most political-economic expressions of neoliberal hegemony, the new urban glamour zones conceal a brutalizing demarcation of winners and losers, included and excluded. Indeed, in some senses we might speculate that the lived spaces of the neoliberal city symbolize an astonishingly powerful geographical expression of the erosion of Keynesian ideals of full employment, integrated welfare entitlement, and "social citizenship"[4] (Marshall 1963)—not least in that when compared to many earlier rounds of municipal investment, which sought to engineer projects aimed at a "mass public" (Bianchini and Schwengel 1991:214), the new initiatives appear to be "reclaiming" public spaces for those groups who possess economic value as producers or consumers to the virtual exclusion of the less well-heeled (Amin and Graham 1997).

The political economies enframing such displacements and marginalities are skillfully dissected in Wacquant's (2000) theorizations on the "penal state," Mitchell's (2001) work on the "postjustice" city, and Smith's (1996, 1998) writings on the "revanchist city." This latter concept is particularly powerful and derives from the French word *revanche*, literally meaning "revenge." Smith's referent here is the right-wing "revanchist" populist movement, which throughout the last three decades of the 19th century reacted violently against the relative liberalism of the Second Empire and the socialism of the Paris Commune. Notably for Smith, as with the new urban politics of the present fin-de-siècle, the original revanchists mixed military tactics with moral discourses about public order on the streets (Smith 1998). The next section highlights what I envisage to be some of the most notable geographical contours of the early twenty-first century revanchist city.

Revanchist Urbanism: Toward a Spatialization of Exclusionary Citizenship and the Enactment of a "Postjustice" City

As noted above, while the political invocation of an entrepreneurial urban agenda offers many inner-city spaces a spectacular makeover, it also risks deepening socioeconomic polarities along social cleavages like class, ethnicity, gender, age, and occupation. And by journeying beyond the overheating downtown, we observe some additional inscriptions of this new urban geography, variously captured in debates around a "dual," "quartered," "walled," or "fortress" city (cf Davis 1990; Judd 1995; Marcuse 1993; Mollenkopf and Castells 1991). These perspectives offer compelling dramatizations about how the contemporary urban form appears to be manifesting as an intensely uneven patchwork of microspaces that are physically proximate but institutionally estranged. In fact, Soja (2000:299) ventures to argue that this splintering "postmetropolitan" landscape

... has become filled with many different kinds of protected and fortified spaces, islands of enclosure and anticipated protection against the real and imagined dangers of daily life. Borrowing from Foucault, [this] postmetropolis is represented as a collection of *carceral cities*, an archipelago of "normalized enclosures" and fortified spaces that both voluntarily and involuntarily barricade individuals and communities in visible and not-so-visible urban islands, overseen by restructured forms of public and private power and authority.

Notable examples of such "normalized enclosures" include the highly exclusive gated communities that increasingly adorn the suburban landscapes of postmetropolitan regions and the high-rent, design-intensive shopping malls and omnicenters that continually infiltrate urban downtowns (Crawford 1992; Judd 1995). Indeed, one cruel irony pertains in the way that whilst mall designers are being authorized, in architectural terms, to recreate "the street" and an organic "civic" milieu (Goss 1993), so intensifying pressures to maximize the profitability of retail space often leads to a penal exclusion of street people, political campaigners, and independent artists, all of whom might be deemed to compromise the strict ethics of "consumerist citizenship" (Christopherson 1994).

Gated communities, shopping malls, and publicly subsidized corporate plazas thereby represent living embodiments of Flusty's (2001:659) "interdictory spaces," designed to "systematically exclude those adjudged to be unsuitable and even threatening, [or] people whose class and cultural positions diverge from the builders and their target markets." Moreover, their very banality, the extent to which such interdictory spaces have become naturalized—uncritically regarded as a "mainstay" of the contemporary urban environment or, in some cases, even "quaintified" as a positive cultural presence (Flusty 2001:660)—nurtures some profound questions about citizenship and social justice in the city, particularly as these relate to the life chances of those displaced by the unforgiving social Darwinism inculcated through disciplinary neoliberalization. This arises not least in the way that such security-obsessed architectures are increasingly supplemented with authoritarian legal measures and policing tactics designed to regulate the very spatial practices of the displaced urban poor.

Indeed, Smith's (1996) revanchist thesis derives from his rousing analysis of the battle to stretch the gentrification frontier of Manhattan's Lower East Side and the brutally repressive policing practices deployed to "take back" Tompkins Square Park; deemed to have been stolen *from* gentrifiers and the wider public *by* the homeless and other victims of real-estate displacement. These vengeful state tactics intensified dramatically under Republican Mayor Rudy Giuliani (Smith 1998). Amid his growing concern about "disorder in the public spaces of the city," Giuliani identified certain groups—homeless people, panhandlers, prostitutes, squeegee cleaners, and graffiti artists—as "enemies within" and as instrumental in fostering an ecology of fear among those he considered decent, honest New Yorkers. In response, he ordered New York Police Department officers to pursue with "zero tolerance" those groups perceived to be a genuine threat to the "quality of urban life" for the moral majority (Smith 1998:3, 4).

Nonetheless, the revanchist ethos extends well beyond zero-tolerance policing (ZTP). Indeed, it relates to a whole raft of state policies wedded to a neoliberal antiwelfare ideology and—amid the heightened insecurities fostered by the new economy—a "compassion fatigue," which alleges a widespread erosion of public sympathy for the dispossessed (Mitchell 2001). Exploiting this purported fatigue, Giuliani endeavored to cut welfare further in favor of "workfare," to cease public-housing construction, to augment existing anti-immigration legislation, and to wage an ideological and financial attack on the public university system.[5] In this emergent revanchist city, then, Althusser's (1971) repressive and ideological state apparatuses are folded together in a disciplinary and, at times, penalizing and stoutly authoritarian effort. It is these senses that

> [t]he revanchist city is, to be sure, a dual and divided city of wealth and poverty ... But it is more. It is a divided city where the victors are increasingly defensive of their privilege, such as it is, and increasingly vicious defending it ... The benign neglect of "the other half," so dominant in the liberal rhetoric of the 1950s and 1960s, has been superseded by a more active viciousness that attempts to criminalize a whole range of "behavior," individually defined, and to blame the failure of post-1968 urban policy on the populations it was supposed to assist. (Smith 1996:227)

It is in these respects, too, that Smith (1998:10) defines revanchism as "in every respect the ugly cultural politics of neoliberal global-ization."[6]

Analogous themes emerge in the work of Mitchell (1995, 1997, 2001). However, Mitchell excavates a deeper cut into fundamental questions about justice, "the public," and the citizenship rights of the dispossessed.[7] In particular, he asserts that as acute poverty and homelessness intensify across urban landscapes, liberal sensibilities are thrown into confusion by the fact that, denied any permanent private retreat, homeless people are often forced to perform acts like sleeping, toileting, and washing in public space. The response by urban political regimes, preoccupied as they are with fronting an imageable city for global capital and tourists, has been to outlaw these necessary capacities from the public gaze—to "cleanse" public spaces of homeless people by banishing them to the marginal back regions (Mitchell 1995:118). This "annihilation of space" represents a profoundly brutalizing public sphere that literally destroys lives and, when backed up by a raft of antihomeless laws, reflects

> a changing conception of citizenship which, contrary to the hard-won inclusions in the public sphere that marked the civil rights, women's and other movements in past decades, now seeks to re-establish exclusionary citizenship as just and good ... The rights of homeless people do not matter (when in competition with "our" rights to order, comfort, places for relaxation, recreation, and unfettered shopping) simply because we work hard to convince ourselves that homeless people are not really citizens in the sense of free agents with sovereignty over their own actions. Antihomeless legislation helps institutionalize this conviction by assuring the homeless in public no place to be sovereign. (Mitchell 1997:320–321)

For Mitchell (2001), this punitive approach leaves the aesthetics of place to prevail over all other considerations. It also signals a notable step beyond the "malign neglect" that characterized the liberal era (Wolch and Dear 1993) toward a sadistic criminalization of urban poverty and a war against welfare. Moreover, particularly when allied to the rapid diffusion of "interdictory" privatopias and fortified cathedrals of consumption, this assault on the poorest sections of the urban population appears to be heralding the erosion of spatial justice. An immensely unsettling prospect, and with neoliberalism as its fundamental ideological backdrop, this postjustice city (Mitchell 2001) limits the performative dimensions of societal membership to those capable of confirming a financial "stakeholding" in the new economy of fast capitalism. All of this resonates with sociological work on the "precarious freedoms" associated with progressively more individualized modes of social life and of the new forms of risk absorption and subjectivities characteristic of the postwelfare age (Beck and Beck-Gernshiem 1996; Keil this volume).

The flip side of these new governmentalities leaves any talk of wealth redistribution to be judged as staggeringly outmoded and to lack political cachet amid the current fêting of globalization and the disciplinary codes inscribed through "roll-out neoliberalism" (Peck and Tickell this volume). This is the case not least in that, at all spatial scales of government, political endeavors to fully extend social citizenship[8] are continually being trumped by the perceived imperative to appease "business interests" and a related clamor to cut taxes and boast of fiscal prudence. This is a mood of which politicians like Giuliani are only too aware, and the message has been spreading (Taylor 1998). For instance, when returning from New York in 1995, then-shadow UK Home Secretary Jack Straw pledged that a Labour government would introduce ZTP and "reclaim the streets for the law-abiding citizen" from the "aggressive begging of winos, addicts and squeegee merchants" (cited in Fyfe forthcoming). And prior to the tragic events of 11 September 2001, ZTP and the "cleaning up" of the Big Apple had been "showcased" to the political elites of many European cities (Wacquant 2000)—including Glasgow.

Contriving Civic Space, Concealing "Postjustice" Revanchism? Unraveling Glasgow's Renaissance

> [In] "feeding the downtown monster" … [e]very new wave of public investment is needed to make the last wave pay off. The private-public partnership means that the public takes the risks and the private takes the profits. The citizenry wait for benefits that never materialize. (Harvey 2000:141)

From "Red Clydeside" to an Entrepreneurial Spirit: Feeding Glasgow's "Downtown Monster"

Glasgow's original wealth emerged from traditional industries like heavy engineering and shipbuilding alongside its mercantilist role as the Second City in the British empire. As the empire waned and as global demand for traditional sectors declined, the fortunes of Glasgow and its metropolitan region of Clydeside experienced steady decline (Gomez 1998). The early twentieth century saw this deterioration being met by robust political struggles, spawning an enduring image of "Red Clydeside." During the 1930s, with the city facing extreme social disadvantage, the local state began a major physical renewal of inner-city slums alongside the construction of "peripheral" housing estates designed to absorb the displaced population. From this period right through to the 1970s, the city's Labour-controlled Glasgow Corporation (later District Council) pursued a managerialist mode of social reproduction (Boyle and Hughes 1994). However, following a relentless contraction of its employment base and an externalization of its more affluent population, Glasgow declined to such an extent that by the 1970s it was officially recognized as "the most deprived locality in Britain" (Danson, Johnstone and Mooney 1997:13). Unfavorable media imagery had also rendered the city a byword for industrial dereliction, slum housing, gangland violence, religious bigotry, and hard drinking (Damer 1990).

Then, amid the rampant decline of the city's industrial base, and following a shocking 1977 defeat by the local Conservative Party, in 1980 the Glasgow Labour group returned to power with a new vision. Alongside its managerialist commitment to social reproduction, in 1981 the Glasgow District Council established an Economic Development and Employment Committee, whose remit was to generate employment and arrest economic decline (Boyle and Hughes 1994). Nonetheless, the council's intervention never quite stretched to the insurgent "restructuring for labour" initiatives that were to characterize certain English metropolitan councils during the 1980s[9] (Eisenschitz and Gough 1993). Instead, it became a quick convert to the ethos of place-marketing (Paddison 1993), as exemplified in its 1983 "Glasgow's Miles Better" campaign and in several arts and cultural projects such as the Burrell Collection. This active coaching of a postindustrial economy was augmented in 1985 following a McKinsey and Company (1994) report commissioned by the Scottish Development Agency (SDA),[10] which also urged the city's political regime to press for more active private-sector participation (Boyle and Hughes 1994). On this advice, the SDA helped institute a new business-led quango, Glasgow Action, whose aim was "to make the city more attractive to work in, to live in and to play in; to recreate Glasgow's entrepreneurial spirit; to communicate the new reality of Glasgow to its citizens and to the world" (Glasgow Action Chair Lord McFarlane, quoted in Gomez 1998:111).

Few would deny that this aggressive marketing strategy has succeeded in reinventing the landscape and imagery of Glasgow (Short 1996). Yet, in critically assessing this entrepreneurial turn, there is little doubt that when comparisons are drawn with North American cities—and even some English ones—levels of private-sector participation have disappointed (Boyle 1997). As has been the case with other British cities furiously implored to embrace the "enterprise culture," Glasgow's inherited regulatory landscape—combining radical political activism with pragmatic municipal managerialism—was to sit uncomfortably with the emerging trajectory of market-led "roll-back" neoliberalism. Instead, and in accordance with Harvey's (2000) prognosis, it has been a highly active local state that has borne the main risks in brokering a range of entrepreneurial projects that have helped to (1) establish designer retail developments like Princes Square and the Italian Centre, (2) promote gentrification and café culture within neighborhoods like the Merchant City, (3) foster a thriving hub in the arts and culture, and (4) attract "hallmark" events like the 1988 Garden Festival and designations like European City of Culture in 1990 and British City of Architecture in 1999.

Interestingly, the 1985 McKinsey Report also offered a geographical vision, designed by internationally renowned architect Gordon Cullen to reconstruct and reimagine Glasgow's downtown and to instill new mental maps for its citizens and tourists. With the main thoroughfare, Buchanan Street, as the focal point, this revisioning included a civic square, cultural venues, and shopping and leisure districts (Boyle and Hughes 1994). While such "projected spaces" rarely manifest in pure form, the fact that Cullen's vision has been implemented in piecemeal fashion has left certain erstwhile derelict zones to witness an extraordinary reaestheticization. Nowhere is this more in evidence than in

Buchanan Street's north end, which has become dominated by an ultrastylish shopping center, the Buchanan Galleries. Its architectural philosophy boasts of a "sympathetic" structure enabling a "continuation of the street ... to ensure that the transition from external to internal world would be relatively seamless" (Buchanan Galleries 2000). Paying homage to the McKinsey Report, performance spaces have been integrated into the streetscape, and the general transformation of Buchanan Street is alleged to be "making the city centre a better place for everyone [by helping to] develop and enhance [its] civic spaces" (GCC 2000:1). In achieving this—and striking remarkable chords with Goss's (1993) work on the design of postmodern retail environments—"The new-look Buchanan Street removes much of the 'clutter' and replaces it with coordinated lighting, bollards, seating, signage and street café areas, using glass, stainless steel and stone. Clipped lime trees grace the length of Buchanan Street, creating shade and mirroring the great boulevards of Europe" (GCC 2000:1).

In many respects, then, the reinvention of Buchanan Street offers a powerful illustration of Glasgow's renaissance as a postindustrial city and a key node in the intensification of consumerist citizenship. These themes are being further invested in the spectacular transformation of Glasgow's old Post Office Building in George Square, described as a "lifestyle experiment," featuring flagship penthouses at UK£500,000 each, alongside luxurious bars, restaurants, and a five-star hotel (Watt 2001). This is the reimagined, pristine, entrepreneurial Glasgow. And the procession of luxury and performance automobiles that now glide through the city streets is further testimony to the fact that a sizeable bourgeoisie has accumulated considerable wealth out of this transformation.

Interdictory Architectures and Spatial Injustices in Glasgow's Renaissance

Certain developments discussed above, alongside the continued if relatively slow gentrification of Glasgow's Merchant City neighborhood, would appear to offer some version of the "back to the city" movement so readily lauded by the UK government's Urban Task Force and subsequent urban white paper (DETR 2000). Moreover, a succession of hallmark projects and new landscapes of display are offering local citizens and thousands of tourists a fresh impression of Glasgow. A newfound confidence is being asserted around the city's role as a premier-league venue for cultural events and conferences—a confidence only heightened by the cluster of hotels currently under construction on what was previously "derelict" land in Finnieston, just west of downtown.

Nonetheless, if we search beneath the euphemistic hype and superficial glamour—if, in Cindi Katz's (2001) terms, we endeavor to "unhide" the consequences of neoliberal entrepreneurialism—we gradually unravel some distressing geographies of exclusion. For instance, as Glasgow's elites have focused sharply on "feeding a downtown monster"[11] (Harvey 2000:141), there is no hiding the fact that, with one-third of Glasgow's population reliant on state benefits, any purported renaissance is failing to "trickle down" to the wider urban conurbation (Danson, Johnstone and Mooney 1997).[12] This is most nakedly evident in Glasgow's own "badlands," the vast "peripheral" public housing estates originally established on the outskirts of the city during the postwar period (Mooney and Danson 1997). Neither is there any hiding what amounts to a major "jobs gap," since, as in many older industrial cities, the rise in service-sector jobs has failed to compensate for the dramatic fall in manufacturing employment (Turok and Edge 1999). Indeed, successive rounds of underfunded, social partnership-based strategies have failed to raise employment and income levels within large deprived areas, only succeeding as a form of "jobless regeneration" (Webster 2000:44).

In addition, Glasgow's new civic spaces appear to be concealing more active geographies of displacement and marginality—ones that might just imply the onset of a revanchist urban politics. Immediately opposite the Buchanan Galleries lies the former George Hotel. For years this building served as a cheap hostel for homeless people, particularly middle-aged men. With the opening of the Galleries, the George Hotel and its clients presumably assumed a role as part of Buchanan Street's "clutter" and were cleared from the civic gaze. Any "sympathy" inscribed into the architecture of the Buchanan Galleries was to appease the pleasures and fantasies of consumerist citizenship, and was not to be extended to those without a permanent home.

In spring 2001, the local media assumed an increasingly vengeful approach to this issue (*Evening Times* 17 April). An editorial entitled "Beggars Are Damaging City Centre" made a "call for concerted action ... involving the police" (*Evening Times* 2001:8) in response to news that Glasgow had fallen from second to fourth in the UK shopping league; and that this was viewed to be a consequence of "Beggars 'Scaring Away City Centre Shoppers'" (Nicoll 2001:4) Perhaps scenting a hint of local compassion fatigue, the director of the Glasgow City Centre Partnership (GCCP), George Sneddon, used the newspaper interview to advocate "swift action." Such dynamics underline the media's long-time role as an "auxiliary player" in growth-machine-oriented discourses (Logan and Molotch 1987) while also illustrating the extent to which an "entrepreneurial" urban politics can open up political spaces for new "primary definers," such as business leaders, "... to articulate a strategy for urban, social, and political regeneration while simultaneously identifying those who pose a danger to that regeneration. It is within these spaces that notions of the 'public interest' are being recast around discourses of crime and insecurity" (Coleman and Sim 2000:632–633).

Not that the necessary equation of a business downturn with crime was particularly new in Glasgow. Back in 1996, similar anxieties led to a blanket ban on drinking alcohol in public spaces (Fyfe and Bannister 1998). Additionally, amid a concern that high crime was leading to "business drift" from the city center, the CityWatch project introduced a necklace of CCTV cameras stretching throughout the city center, and private security now tightly patrols all malls. More recently, uniformed City Center Representatives have offered "an extra pair of eyes and ears on the street" to help channel the spatial practices of tourists (Helms 2001:91). Glasgow's elites have thus endeavored to fashion a range of interdictory architectures and technologies, and the city center now contains "a panoply of human, physical, and techno- logical methods to monitor and regulate the behaviour of its citizens" (Fyfe and Bannister 1998:254).

In Glasgow, as in Manhattan and the downtown of many other US cities (Mitchell 1997; Wright 1997), such disciplinary tactics have affected homeless people most harshly. Indeed, one study reports panhandlers being regularly moved on, arrested, or marched to the nearest charity-collection point to hand over their money (Fitzpatrick and Kennedy 2000). In addition, vending sites for selling the homeless magazine *Big Issue* have been restricted to ten locations, with the behavior of vendors now increasingly monitored, or—we might argue— purified (Atkinson forthcoming). The net effect of these microgeog- raphies is that, in addition to various communities of street people on what remain "marginal" interstices on the north bank of the River Clyde, Glasgow has its very own Skid Row. This is concentrated on one particular mini-neighborhood just to the north of the city center, a zone that, when compared to the rest of the city, is strategically policed with a deliberately light touch.

However, just as in the case of urban America, this spatial internment of intensifying inequality alongside the fundamental contradictions associated with Glasgow's renaissance will only displace rather than resolve the problem of homelessness. During 2000, at least 25 home- less people died on Glasgow's streets. Homelessness and street home- lessness have reached new heights, and city authorities openly admit that for some time now they have lacked a coherent strategy for tackling the scale of the problem and approaching its intricate association with structural forms of poverty and economic inequality (Scottish Executive 2001). A key product of this has been a chronic crisis in homeless hostels, which are considered to be poorly governed, violent, and unresponsive to the diverse needs of groups and individuals. Indeed, the extent to which certain hostels are merely "warehousing the poor" (Wright 1997) has left some to opt for the streets to be with their companions, where they might feel safer and cultivate a "sense of community" (Fitzpatrick and Kennedy 2000:39). Political concern is also mounting that plans to "sell off" the city's public housing stock might only exacerbate the crisis.[13]

In 1990, throughout its year as European City of Culture, Glasgow's political economic elite stood accused of sanitizing the past by erasing the city's proud socialist heritage (Boyle and Hughes 1994). Now, over a decade on, in the fanatical search to contrive a sanitized urban landscape (McInroy 2000), the city's elite appears to be suspending any remaining managerialist commitments to extend social citizenship and spatial justice throughout the wider populace. Indeed far from creating "civic spaces [for] everyone" (GCC 2000:1). Glasgow's city center is mutating into a plethora of interdictory landscapes contrived in the image of fictitious capital and consumerist citizenship. For unlike vacant property, which (as rent-gap theory informs us) can often be perceived as a space with a potentially higher value (Smith 1996), amid the banality of interdiction and the normalization of postjustice discourses associated with "roll-out" neoliberalism, the question of potential value appears not to extend to homeless people and other displaced groups. Here we might reflect on an argument Mitchell (2000:8) has made in a reference to the very "Culture War" that ensnared Glasgow throughout 1990:

> The city-as-landscape does not encourage the formation of community or of urbanism as a way of life; rather it encourages the maintenance of surfaces, the promotion of order at the expense of lived social relations, and the ability to look past distress, destruction, and marginalization to see only the good life (for some) and to turn a blind eye towards what that life is constructed out of.

Glasgow: In What Sense a Revanchist City?

The interdictory architectures of its renovated built environment, allied to powerful discourses about "moral order" on the streets and vengeful media portrayals of street people, would appear to indicate that, in seeking to further augment its entrepreneurial economic strategy, Glasgow bears the imprints of an emerging politics of revanchism. Moreover, following local government reorganization in 1996, Glasgow City Council has been forced to cut £180 million per year in revenue spending and raise council tax 58%. As in New York, the ensuing cuts in services have impacted most deeply upon the city's vulnerable groups (Webster 2000). It is also worth noting the escalating concerns over cancer care and after-care conditions in the city's hospitals alongside mounting anxieties about a huge drug-dependency amongst its poorer populations: for these conditions offer just the sorts of circumstances under which middle- and working-class insecurities might be further fueled and a reactionary response encouraged.

Nonetheless, in making these tentative claims, I fully acknowledge the need for caution when comparing Glasgow with a city like New York. For while Glasgow may be witnessing the routine arrest of so-called "aggressive beggars," in contrast to New York and indeed certain British cities (Fyfe forthcoming), the Strathclyde Police Force has concluded that zero tolerance offers an inappropriately "short-term" approach to crime prevention. Instead, it has introduced a Street Liaison Team, which, rather than immediately criminalizing street people and prostitutes, aims to cultivate improved relations between those "on the margins of society," the police, and the wider public (interview, Street Liaison Team, 2001). In addition, a range of inter-viewees from homeless agencies and public sector organizations were quick to point out that the views expressed by Sneddon of the GCCP (cited above) are out of step with mainstream thinking in the city. Some commitment to a "public interest" would thus appear to remain within certain sections of Glasgow's political machinery: in part, surely a legacy to its inherited institutional landscape and "constellations of sociopolitical power" (Brenner and Theodore [paper] this volume).

Moreover, whilst Giuliani boasted of demolishing the "last shantytown" in Manhattan and of withdrawing financial support for Manhattan's homeless agencies (Smith 1998), through its Rough Sleepers Initiative, the Scottish Executive (2001) has committed £16 million. It has simultaneously endeavored to establish the institutional arrangements to address the "structural" causes of the homelessness crisis.[14] Whilst such "active institution-building" may be imbued with a strong dose of compulsion and paternalistic moral authoritarianism —in this sense, it is not dissimilar to the Executive's Social Inclusion program and many other elements of Blair's "inclusive" society (Webster 2000)—it would nonetheless appear to be at odds with the repressive moments of vengeance inscribed into New York's local state strategy. Stretching this a little further, can we point to Glasgow's gentrification wars (police militia, sweeping helicopters), or its military-style sweeps on quality-of-life offenders and its vengeful political attacks on the city's universities (cf Smith 1996, 1998)? As yet, the answer to these questions remains a tentative "no"—a response that forces me to acknowledge three important caveats in concluding my discussion on Glasgow.

First, as with the Global City perspective, the revanchist-city frame-work might stand accused of being a slave to New York (cf Hamnett 1995). However, I would argue that it offers a deeply suggestive heuristic with which to reassess the changing geographical contours of a city's restless urban landscape. Deeply suggestive, not least in that, as mentioned earlier, far from offering merely a riposte to zero-tolerance policing, Smith's revanchist perspective holds within its sharply focused analytical lens a host of dynamic processes: economic restructuring, housing, welfare retrenchment, law and order, education, and counterpolitical resistance. In particular, by stressing the theme of political strategy, Smith's perspective might help us unravel key moments in the perpetual "creative destruction" of the urban political economic fabric.

Second, I fully acknowledge that in some respects my paper offers merely a snapshot of the political economy of Glasgow. In tune with the first point, then, it becomes patently evident that a fully-fledged analysis of urban revanchism would demand a deeper inquiry into the nature of urban politics, in identifying, for instance, the relative significance of a powerful mayor in shaping a local state strategy. It would also require us to analyze certain spheres of social reproduction, such as health and education, alongside changing patterns of housing, ranging from the implications of the recent sale of council housing stock to the newly formed Glasgow Housing Association to the possible emergence of common interest developments and gated communities.

A third caveat offers a partial response to the question posed in the introduction about the relationship between entrepreneurialism and revanchism. Certainly the evidence from Glasgow would appear to support the argument that, in the wake of the sociospatial selectivities inscribed into an entrepreneurial mode of governance, and amid the tight political grip of a "rolled-out" neoliberalism, the political-geographical contours of revanchism—fiscal retrenchment, interdictory architectures, and authoritarian state tactics—are being "naturalized" within the urban political arena. However, this should of course immediately force us to acknowledge that "actually existing" revanchist political economies will assume different forms in different contexts. To this end, particular studies of revanchism will require much theoretical flexibility to assess the specific structures and mechanisms that lead to certain policy transfers, calls for zero tolerance, and imperatives to "cleanse" public spaces (see Coleman and Sim 2000; Fyfe forthcoming; Lund Hansen, Andersen and Clark 2001). Without wishing to imply some "end state" urban dystopia, then, I would argue that the "fast" nature of contemporary policy transfer allied to the disciplinary fiscal environment confronting all cities should ensure that the revanchist framework offers a powerful conceptual heuristic beyond Manhattan.

Uncovering the Revanchist City

Following on from the caveats outlined above, I wish to conclude with brief reflections about how we might begin to uncover the complex choreography of urban revanchism within particular localities. One useful starting point is Harvey's historical geographical materialist method of analysis. At base, Harvey's (1989:5) approach encourages us to consider the "becoming" of cities as constitutive and reflective of "… a spatially grounded social process in which a wide range of different actors with quite different objectives and agendas interact through a particular configuration of interlocking spatial practices." Nothing is inevitable in relation to the characteristics of such actors, nor about what those agendas might be, since they will always be enacted by and inflected through an interlocking blend of agentic generalizing properties and local specificities and the meeting of inherited institutional landscapes with purportedly paradigmatic policy recipes. The Strathclyde Police Force's deliberation with but eventual rejection of zero-tolerance policing offers a useful practical example of the latter.

This unpredictability of the urban form leads on to a second important theme to consider when analyzing the revanchist city. A range of scholars have deployed the theoretical insights of Foucault, Lefebvre, and de Certeau to explore the spatializing practices and "counterspaces" of resistance and transgression that can sometimes unshackle the padlocks of "purified" urban sites and thereby challenge their official, growth-machine-dominated representations of space (Doron 2000; Keil 1999; Lees 1998; McCann 1999; Mitchell 1995; Soja 2000). Smith (1992:59), too, examines the so-called homeless vehicle as a strategy in the "subversiveness of mobility" deployed by homeless people to transcend their erstwhile limits to scale while simultaneously contesting efforts by New York's growth regime to sanction their erasure from the public spaces of the city. Such studies underscore the way in which the current erosion of the urban fabric as a series of "shared spaces" (Amin and Graham 1997:422) needs to be analyzed more earnestly at the level of dynamic social relations. In Sibley's (1995:72) words, we urgently need an "anthropology of space" that emphasizes the rituals of spatial organization: rituals so marvelously captured in Domosh's (1998) work on the "polite street politics" of nineteenth-century New York. Again, an interesting example is presented by the relatively "polite" sociospatial practices through which the Glasgow police force's Street Liaison Team monitors the geography of prostitution in the city center.

All of this illustrates how, in spite of its increased commodification, public space is "always in a process of being shaped, reshaped, and challenged by the spatial practices of various groups and individuals whose identities and actions undermine the homogeneity of contemporary cities" (McCann 1999:168). In accepting this, then, when analyzing the spaces of neoliberalism or a purported generic privatization of urban space, it might be better to conceptualize that very space as negotiated, enacted, performed, lived in and lived through, contested, representative, but also practical. The net outcome of this is that urban *public* space needs to be thought of, not as a pregiven "ideal" but as a practical moment in the process of becoming (Lees 2001). When allied to theoretically sophisticated accounts of the changing nature of urban politics, such a perspective might readily provide a more fruitful avenue through which to comprehend the processes through which the balance of power between public and private institutions become critical in the articulation of a more or less "commodified" or "municipal" public space (Boyer 1993; Judd 1995; Zukin 1995). Consider how the endeavors by the Glasgow City Centre Partnership to represent a particular image of consumerist downtown space to a range of agents—possible investors, tourists, the local media—directly conflicted with the spatial practices of homeless *Big Issue* vendors forced to earn their living in the frontal spheres of Glasgow's public spaces.

This reference to the "new" urban political arena leads me to my final point: a plea for an improved critical understanding of the state in examining the current unfolding of a revanchist or postjustice urbanism. It might be stressing the obvious that, in contrast to stand-ard neoliberal rhetoric, many of the processes analyzed in this paper—short-term legal remedies for homelessness, the planning and underwriting of renaissance sites of spectacle—are enacted through the active and sometimes brutal involvement of and penalties incurred through the local and central state. However, if contemporary work on regulation and governance might have opened up some fruitful ways of understanding the changing structures of urban politics, we are still desperately struggling to gain theoretical comprehension and cognitive mappings of the spatializing tactics and strategies of state institutions. In the emerging urban milieu, the proliferation of edge cities, interdictory leisure zones, "dead" plazas, and fortified privatopias are each generating new physical and institutional scales of enclosure, new active progenitors (Smith 1992). As the key legislator of private property, the state is certainly not absent in this. Nonetheless, discourses pertaining to "minimum government" and "private interest" do not pass without material consequences, and it seems to me that much work remains to be done in terms of exploring the nature of this postmetropolitan urban political milieu (Soja 2000). An uncovering of such spatialities might offer critical insights in the search for a progressive, geographically informed urban political praxis.

Acknowledgments

An earlier version of this paper was presented at the seminar Neoliberalism and the City, held in the Center for Urban Economic Development, University of Illinois, Chicago, September 2001. I am grateful to all the delegates for such valuable discussion and also to Mark Boyle, Neil Brenner, Nicholas Fyfe, Emma Mawdsley, Eugene

McCann, Colin McFarlane, Nik Theodore, and two anonymous referees for their very instructive written comments. Discussions with Anna Bee, Gesa Helms, Adam Holden, Kurt Iveson, Martin Jones, John Kelly, Ross Loveridge, Neil Smith, Kevin Ward, and Ian Watt also offered inspiration, as did John Kelly's informal tours around Glasgow's landscapes (especially *The Scotia*). Thanks, too, to the representatives of Glasgow's policy regime who kindly agreed to share their insights and the Leverhulme Trust for funding the research project out of which the paper emerges. The usual disclaimers apply.

Endnotes

[1] I thank Eugene McCann for prompting me on this issue.

[2] Peck and Tickell create a useful analytical distinction between "roll-back" and "roll-out" neoliberalism. The latter describes the political projects (such as Clintonism) that have sought to ameliorate the intense contradictions generated by earlier "roll-back" versions.

[3] Earlier "end of public space" perspectives (Davis 1990; Sorkin 1992) have been followed by those intimating an improved safety for a "pluralistic public" and the possibility of countercultural spaces of representation (Iveson 1998; McCann 1999; Soja 2000). This has led some commentators to talk of the "ambivalent" nature of public space in the contemporary city (Fyfe forthcoming; Lees 1998).

[4] Marshall (1963:74) defines social citizenship as "the right to a modicum of economic welfare and security [alongside] the right to share to the full in the social heritage and live the life of a civilized being according to the standards prevailing in the society." In making this claim, though, I acknowledge that Marshall's schema has been reasonably criticized for heralding "social citizenship" as the highest form, its failure to consider attacks on postwar citizenship rights, and its weakness in analyzing the gender and ethnic inequalities of postwar citizenship (Urry 2000).

[5] It is worth mentioning how this image of Giuliani as both combative and intolerant might seem at odds with the "globalized" figure who, with compassion and in fulsome praise of the city's public services, presided over a devastated Manhattan in the immediate aftermath of the terrorist atrocities of 11 September 2001. Indeed, during those traumatic times, Giuliani was the first to caution against jingoistic attacks on the city's Arab and Muslim communities (Said 2001).

[6] The extent to which the "rolled-out" version of neoliberalism is purportedly articulated through a combination of neoliberalized economic management allied to authoritarian state forms and modes of policy-making "concerned specifically with the aggressive regulation, disciplining, and containment of those marginalized or dispossessed by the neoliberalization of the 1980s" (Peck and Tickell this volume) prompts me to contend that, depending upon the particular spatial context, a revanchist political approach may well represent a key "destructive" *and* "creative" moment in the move from "roll-back" to "roll-out" neoliberalism (see Brenner and Theodore [paper] this volume:Table 2).

[7] Here it is worth noting that the concept of citizenship encounters a range of positions, one notable tension being "between the neoliberal assertion of the market and the free individual, and the civic republican tradition with its emphasis on participation in a polis fashioned by its members" (Hill 1994:4). More recent discourses have moved from such formal "political" models towards "social-cultural" approaches "wrapped up in questions about who is accepted as a worthy, valuable, and responsible member of an everyday community of living and working" (Painter and Philo 195:115). It seems to me that these latter approaches could prove most instructive in analyzing the current erosion of citizenship rights for marginalized social groups.

[8] Whilst acknowledging the various discriminations that punctuated postwar efforts to extend social citizenship (see endnote 4), it seems to me that some of the ideals of inclusive entitlement inscribed into the Keynesian and New Deal political projects offered a necessary—if hardly sufficient—condition to widen inclusive citizenship. Quoting Hill (1994:4) again: "[P]ossession of civil and political rights without social rights reduces citizenship to a façade."

[9] In explaining this more consensual mood, it is important to consider the role played by a distinctively institutionalized Scottish policy network and civil society (MacLeod 1999).

[10] The SDA was introduced in 1975 and funded by the Scottish Office (MacLeod 1999).

[11] Some 4,000 acres of land—almost 10% of the city's area—remain vacant or derelict (Webster 2000).

[12] Life expectancy in the outer housing estate of Drumchapel is ten years below the adjacent suburb of Bearsden, and people in Glasgow live ten years less than those in the South of England.

[13] While this radical move may fit neatly with a post-Thatcherite New Labour ideology, the decision to "rid this monument to municipal socialism" was taken by the Labour pragmatists running Glasgow City Chambers, albeit aided and abetted by a firm prod from the then-Communities Minister in the Scottish Parliament, Wendy Alexander (Hetherington 2000).

[14] Of course, this raises a general point about the qualitative difference the post-1999 Scottish Parliament and Executive could make to the institutional powers of Scotland's policy network. It also demonstrates how any "locally" inscribed urban political strategy is always embedded within and structured through a multiscaled ensemble of state governmentalities (MacLeod and Goodwin 1999).

References

Althusser L (1971) Ideology and ideological state apparatuses. In L Althusser (ed) *Lenin and Philosophy and Other Essays* (pp 136–170). London: New Left Books

Amin A and Graham S (1997) The ordinary city. *Transactions of the Institute of British Geographers* 22:411–429

Atkinson R (forthcoming) Domestication by cappuccino or a revenge on urban space? *Urban Studies*

Bauman Z (2000) *Liquid Modernity*. Cambridge, UK: Polity Press

Beazley H (2000) Street boys in Yogyakarta: Social and spatial exclusion in the public spaces of the city. In G Bridge and S Watson (eds) *A Companion to the City* (pp 472–487) Oxford: Blackwell

Beck U and Beck-Gernsheim E (1996) Individualization and "precarious freedoms": Perspectives and controversies of a subject-oriented sociology. In P Heelas, S Lash and P Morris (eds) *Detraditionalization* (pp 23–48). Oxford: Blackwell

Belina B and Helms G (2001) Zero tolerance for the industrial past? Policing and urban entrepreneurialism in old industrial cities in Britain and Germany. Mimeograph. Glasgow: Department of Geography, University of Glasgow

Bianchini F and Schwengel H (1991) Reimagining the city. In J Corner and S Harvey (eds) *Enterprise and Heritage* (pp 212–263). London: Routledge

Boyer C (1993) The city of illusion: New York's public spaces. In P Knox (ed) *The Restless Urban Landscape* (pp 111–126). Englewood Cliffs, NJ: Prentice Hall

Boyle M (1997) Civic boosterism in the politics of local economic development: "Institutional positions" and "strategic orientations" in the consumption of hallmark events. *Environment and Planning A* 29:1975–1997

Boyle M and Hughes G (1994) The politics of urban entrepreneurialism in Glasgow. *Geoforum* 25:453–470

Buchanan Galleries (2000) *Shopping for Glasgow's Future*. Glasgow: Buchanan Galleries

Caldeira T (1999) Fortified enclaves: The new urban segregation. In J Holston (ed) *Cities and Citizenship* (pp 114–138). Durham, NC: Duke University Press

Christopherson S (1994) The fortress city: Privatized spaces, consumer citizenship. In A Amin (ed) *Post-Fordism: A Reader* (pp 409–427). Oxford: Blackwell

Coleman R and Sim J (2000) "You'll never walk alone": CCTV surveillance, order and neoliberal rule in Liverpool city centre. *British Journal of Sociology* 51:623–639

Crawford M (1992) The world in a shopping mall. In M Sorkin (ed) *Variations on a Theme Park: The New American City and the End of Public Space* (pp 3–30). New York: Hill and Wang

Damer S (1990) *Glasgow: Going for a Song*. London: Lawrence and Wishart

Danson M, Johnstone C and Mooney G (1997) Social and economic change on Clydeside in the 1980s and 1990s. Paper presented to the European Regional Studies Conference: Regional Frontiers, Frankfurt, 20–23 September

Davis M (1990) *City of Quartz: Excavating the Future in Los Angeles*. London: Verso

Domosh M (1998) Those "gorgeous incongruities": Polite politics and public space on the streets of nineteenth-century New York City. *Annals of the Association of American Geographers* 88:209–226

Doron G (2000) The dead zone and the architecture of transgression. *City* 4(2): 247–263

Department of the Environment, Transport and the Regions (DETR) (2000) *Our Towns and Cities: The Future: Delivering an Urban Renaissance*. Cm 4911. London: Department of the Environment, Transport and the Regions

Eisenschitz A and Gough J (1993) *The Politics of Local Economic Development*. Basingstoke: Macmillan

Evening Times (2001) Editorial: Beggars are damaging city center. 17 April:8

Fitzpatrick S and Kennedy C (2000) *Getting By: Begging, Rough Sleeping and The Big Issue in Glasgow and Edinburgh*. Bristol: The Policy Press

Flusty S (2001) The banality of interdiction: Surveillance, control and the displacement of diversity. *International Journal of Urban and Regional Research* 25:658–664

Fyfe N (forthcoming) Zero tolerance, maximum surveillance? Deviance, difference and crime control in the late modern city. In L Lees (ed) *The Emancipatory City: Paradoxes and Possibilities*. London: Sage

Fyfe N and Bannister J (1998) "The eyes upon the street": Closed-circuit television surveillance and the city. In N Fyfe (ed) *Images of the Street: Planning, Identity and Control in Public Space* (pp 254–267). London: Routledge

Glasgow City Council (GCC) (2000) *Glasgow City Centre Millennium Plan*. Glasgow: Glasgow City Council

Gomez M (1998) Reflective images: The case of urban regeneration in Glasgow and Bilbao. *International Journal of Urban and Regional Research* 22:106–121

Goss J (1993) The "magic of the mall": An analysis of the form, function, and meaning in the contemporary retail built environment. *Annals of the Association of American Geographers* 83:18–47

Hamnett C (1995) Controlling space: Global cities. In J Allen and C Hamnett (eds) *A Shrinking World* (pp 103–142). Buckingham: Open University Press

Harvey D (1989) From managerialism to entrepreneurialism: The transformation of urban governance in late capitalism. *Geografiska Annaler* 71B:3–17

Harvey D (2000) *Spaces of Hope*. Edinburgh: Edinburgh University Press

Helms G (2001) *Glasgow—The Friendly City, the Safe City*. Praxis Kultur—Und Sozialgeographie 23. Potsdam: Universität Potsdam

Hetherington P (2000) Out of stock. *The Guardian* 6 September:2–3

Hill D (1994) *Citizens and Cities: Urban Policy in the 1990s*. Hemel Hempstead: Harvester Wheatsheaf

Iveson K (1998) Putting the public back into public space. *Urban Policy and Research* 16:21–33

Judd D (1995) The rise of the new walled cities. In H Liggett and D Perry (eds) *Spatial Practices: Critical Explorations in Social/Spatial Theory* (pp 144–66). London: Sage

Katz C (2001) Hiding the target: Social reproduction in the privatized urban environment. In C Minca (ed) *Postmodern Geography: Theory and Praxis* (pp 93–110). Oxford: Blackwell

Keil R (1999) *Los Angeles: Globalization, Urbanization and Social Struggles.* Chichester: Wiley

Lees L (1998) Urban renaissance and the street: Spaces of control and contestation. In N Fyfe (ed) *Images of the Street: Planning, Identity and Control in Public Space* (pp 236–253). London: Routledge

Lees L (2001) Towards a critical geography of architecture: The case of an ersatz Colosseum. *Ecumene* 8:51–86

Leitner H (1990) Cities in pursuit of economic growth: The local state as entrepreneur. *Political Geography Quarterly* (now *Political Geography*) 9:146–170

Logan J and Molotch H (1987) *Urban Fortunes: The Political Economy of Place.* Berkeley: University of California Press

Lund Hansen A, Andersen H and Clark E (2001) Creative Copenhagen: Globalization, urban governance and social change. *European Planning Studies* 9:851–869

MacLeod G (1999) Entrepreneurial spaces, hegemony and state strategy: The political shaping of privatism in Lowland Scotland. *Environment and Planning A* 31:345–375

MacLeod G and Goodwin M (1999) Reconstructing an urban and regional political economy: On the state, politics, scale, and explanation. *Political Geography* 18: 697–730

Marcuse P (1993) What's new about divided cities? *International Journal of Urban and Regional Research* 17:355–365

Marshall T H (1963) Citizenship and social class. In T H Marshall (ed) *Sociology at the Crossroads* (pp 67–127). London: Heinemann

McCann E (1999) Race, protest, and public space: Contextualizing Lefebvre in the US city. *Antipode* 31:163–184

McInroy N (2000) Urban regeneration and public space: The story of an urban park. *Space and Polity* 4:23–40

McKinsey and Company (1994) *The Potential of Glasgow City Centre.* Glasgow: Scottish Development Agency

Merrifield A (2000) The dialectics of dystopia: Disorder and zero tolerance in the city. *International Journal of Urban and Regional Research* 24:473–489

Mitchell D (1995) The end of public space? People's Park, definitions of the public, and democracy. *Annals of the Association of American Geographers* 85:108–133

Mitchell D (1997) The annihilation of space by law: The roots and implications of antihomeless laws in the United States. *Antipode* 29:303–335

Mitchell D (2000) *Cultural Geography: A Critical Introduction.* Oxford: Blackwell

Mitchell D (2001) Postmodern geographical praxis? Postmodern impulse and the war against homeless people in the "postjustice" city. In C Minca (ed) *Postmodern Geography: Theory and Praxis* (pp 57–92). Oxford: Blackwell

Mollenkopf J and Castells M (eds) (1991) *Dual City: Restructuring New York.* New York: Russell Sage Foundation

Mooney G and Danson M (1997) Beyond "culture city": Glasgow as a dual city. In N Jewson and S MacGregor (eds) *Transforming Cities: Contested Governance and New Spatial Divisions* (pp 73–86). London: Routledge

Nicoll V (2001) Beggars "scaring away city centre shoppers." *Evening Times* 17 April:4

Paddison R (1993) City marketing, image reconstruction, and urban regeneration. *Urban Studies* 30:339–350

Painter J and Philo C (1995) Spaces of citizenship: An introduction. *Political Geography* 14:107–120

Said E (2001) Islam and the West are inadequate banners. *The Observer* 16 September: 27

Saunders P (1980) *Urban Politics: A Sociological Interpretation*. Harmondsworth: Penguin

Scottish Executive (2001) Report of the Glasgow Street Homelessness Review Team. Scottish Executive Publications. http://www.scotland.gov.uk/library3/housing/grt-01.asp (last accessed 3 February 2002)

Short J R (1996) *The Urban Order: An Introduction to Cities, Culture and Power*. Oxford: Blackwell

Sibley D (1996) *Geographies of Exclusion*. London: Routledge

Smith N (1992) Contours of a spatialized politics: Homeless vehicles and the production of geographical scale. *Social Text* 33:54–81

Smith N (1996) *The New Urban Frontier: Gentrification and the Revanchist City*. London: Routledge

Smith N (1998) Giuliani time: The revanchist 1990s. *Social Text* 57:1–20

Soja E (2000) *Postmetropolis: Critical Studies of Cities and Regions*. Oxford: Blackwell

Sorkin M (1992) Introduction. In *Variations on a Theme Park: The New American City and the End of Public Space*. New York: Hill and Wang

Taylor I (1998) New York/Manchester: Zero tolerance or reclaim the streets? *City* 8:139–148

Turok I and Edge N (1999) *The Jobs Gap in Britain's Cities*. Bristol: The Policy Press

Urry J (2000) *Sociology beyond Societies: Mobilities for the Twenty-First Century*. London: Routledge

Wacquant L (2000) *The Coming of the Penal State Is Not Inevitable*. Working Papers in Local Governance and Democracy 4. Berkeley: University of California at Berkeley

Watt I (2001) From here to uncertainty: Class and interdictory spaces. Paper presented to the British Sociological Association Annual Conference, Manchester Metropolitan University, UK, 9–12 April

Webster D (2000) Scottish social inclusion policy: A critical assessment. *Scottish Affairs* 30:28–50

Wolch J and Dear M (1993) *Malign Neglect: Homelessness in an American City*. San Francisco: Jossey-Bass

Wright T (1997) *Out of Place: Homeless Mobilizations, Subcities, and Contested Landscapes*. Albany: State University of New York Press

Zukin S (1995) *The Cultures of Cities*. Oxford: Blackwell

Gordon MacLeod is Lecturer in Human Geography at the University of Durham, England. His main research interests are in urban and regional political economy and the geography of the state in a post-welfare world, themes on which he has published in a range of academic journals. His current research projects include an exploration of downtown renewal in Britain's cities and an investigation of England's "new regionalism."

Index